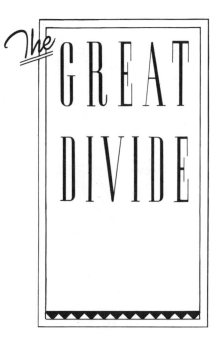

The GREAT DIVIDE

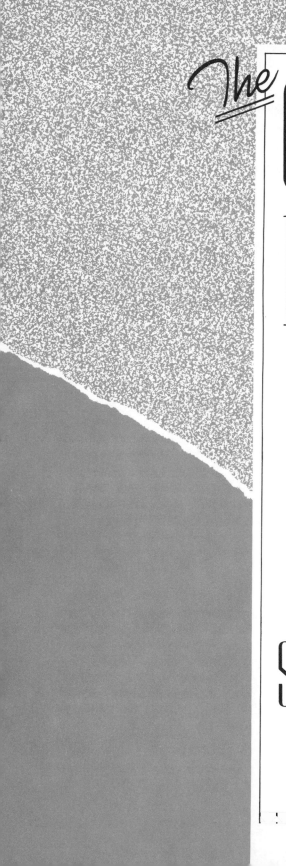

The
GREAT
DIVIDE

second thoughts
on the
american
dream

STUDS TERKEL

PANTHEON BOOKS
NEW YORK

Library of Congress Cataloging-in-Publication Data

Terkel, Studs, 1912–
The great divide.

1. United States—History—1969–
2. Interviews—United States. I. Title.
E839.T47   1988   973.927   88-42543
ISBN 0-394-57053-7

Book design by Archie Ferguson
Manufactured in the United States of America
First Edition

To Lucky Miller.

NOTE

The Great Divide is a series of mountain ranges. It crosses the North American continent and divides it into two great watersheds. The waters west of it generally flow west, and the waters east of it flow in an eastward direction. It begins near the Gulf of Mexico, extends northwesterly and ends in the small hills near the Arctic Circle.

—The World Book Encyclopedia

The Great Divide bespeaks more than the deepening chasm between the haves—and have-somewhats—and the have-nots. It is the rift of race that, at times, appears to close and then casually widens; not unrelated to having and not having. It is the split in the sphere of worship, rendering unto Caesar what may not rightfully be his and unto God what may not spiritually be His. It is the cleft that has cut us off, one from the other and, indeed, from our very selves. It is the breach that has cut off past from present.

—S.T.

Give up the feeling of responsibility, let go your hold,
resign the care of destiny to higher powers, be genuinely
indifferent as to what becomes of it all and you will find
that you gain . . . the particular goods you sincerely
thought you were renouncing.

> —William James, *The Varieties of*
> *Religious Experience: A Study in*
> *Human Nature*

We must go forward . . . but we cannot kill the past in
doing so, for the past is part of our identity and without
our identity we are nothing.

> —Carlos Fuentes

I may not always have been satisfactorily balanced; I
always tended to argue that objectivity was of less
importance than truth, and that the reporter whose
technique was informed by no opinion lacked a very
serious dimension.

> —James Cameron, *Point of Departure*

CONTENTS

CONTENTS

BOOK TWO

CONTENTS

CONTENTS

ACKNOWLEDGMENTS

I must begin with the scouts: friends, casual acquaintances, wayfaring strangers, and occasional adversaries. In a common spirit of generosity, they guided me or simply tipped me off to some of the heroes and heroines of this book: Heather Booth, Sonya Booth, Kay Boyle, Bruce Buursma, Bob Crawford, Bruce Dold, Hugh Espey, Mary Feerick, Alix Friedman, Jack Hayes, Lynn Hayes, Terri Hemmert, David Jackson, Tony Judge, Kathy Kelly, Alex Kotlowitz, Dena Kleiman, Matt Nicodemus, Kenneth Paff, Pat Reardon, Kay Richards, Ed Sadlowski.

For the sixth time around, Cathy Zmuda has revealed transcribing as an art form. In this instance, she has had the invaluable assistance of Lucy Bukowski, Tammey Kikta, Sheila von Wiese, and Amy Malina.

My colleagues at radio station WFMT have again been of generous heart in allowing me all sorts of leaves of absence: Norm Pellegrini, Ray Nordstrand, and Lois Baum. Especially solicitous, far beyond the call of duty, have been Sydney Lewis, George Drury, and Kurt Tyler.

As for my colleagues at Pantheon Books, I can only refer to them as my collaborators: André Schiffrin, my all-time editor and publisher, whose whispered suggestions have made this book and the five previous ones possible; Diane Wachtell, his assistant, whose nimble wit cannot be adequately assessed; and the nonpareil of copy editors, Jeanne Morton.

To all of them, a salute.

INTRODUCTION

In the making of this book (and even while considering it), I was burdened with doubts far more disturbing than any I had ever experienced earlier. In undertaking this self-assigned and at times perverse task, I was aware of an attribute lacking in the 1980s that had been throbbingly present in the earlier decades, even in the silent 1950s: memory.

It isn't that the gift of remembering was any richer then than it is now. I encountered in survivors of the Great Depression and World War Two egregious lapses, blockages, and forgetteries. Nonetheless, they remembered core truths about themselves and the world around them. They remembered enough of their yesterdays to tell us what it was like to live in those times. Today, amnesia is much easier to come by.

As technology has become more hyperactive, we, the people have become more laid-back; as the deposits in its memory banks have become more fat, the deposits in man's memory bank have become more lean. Like Harold Pinter's servant, the machine has assumed the responsibilities that were once the master's. The latter has become the shell of a once thoughtful, though indolent, being. It is the Law of Diminishing Enlightenment at work.

Ironically enough, Jacob Bronowski observed, the average person today knows far more facts about the world than Isaac Newton ever did, though considerably less truth. Certainly we know more facts, overwhelmingly trivial though they be, than any of our antecedents. But as for knowing the truth about ourselves and others . . .

My purpose in taking on this job—and God knows it's a presumptuous move—is *not* to seek out facts in the lives of contemporary Americans and thus determine some consensus. *Ecce* America. Frankly, that's an easy piece of work and a dull one. I suspect it can be done with a computer. Pollsters do it every day.

Rather, I was impelled by the lyrics of a gospel song I had heard

Mahalia Jackson sing some forty years ago, ''Dig a Little Deeper.''
I remember the 78 rpm record, even the scratch; the fusing of words
to music and the sudden intake of one's breath on hearing. Even
more was the astonishment on seeing her at the Greater Salem Baptist Church, moving down into the aisle as the song brought the
congregation to its feet. And the sea of waving white handkerchiefs.
It was not a celebration of what is, bleak fact, but a vision of what
still could be. What Mahalia sang about may be what the great many
in our society feel, no matter what their political persuasion, though
it is inchoate, inexpressible, buried deep; some sort of unformed
truth.

With exceptions, who appear more often in this book than in the
media (I make no pretense of ''objectivity''; there ain't no such
animal, though we play at the hunt), there emerges, to an alarming
degree, a collective Alzheimer's disease. Yesterday's headline is forgotten as a new one is emblazoned today.

A TV wunderkind explains: ''In the last ten years, we've shifted
to faster communication. We depend on these little bursts, these
little sound bites. All good politicians as well as good advertisers lay
out their programs in something that will play in ten to twelve
seconds on the nightly news.'' In an old burlesque skit, the second
banana, a Dutch comic in baggy pants, challenges the first: ''Qvick,
vat's your philosophy of life in fife seconds?'' The baldheads, pot-
bellies, and pimply faces in the audience (I was one) roar at the
randy though succinct riposte. Today's TV anchorperson asks the
same thing of the expert (fifteen seconds is the usual allotment). It
is deadly solemn in the asking, equally so in the response, and duly
acknowledged by the audience. Nobody's laughing.

Still, in my prowlings and stalkings during these past three years,
I've come across individuals, surprising in number though diffident
in demeanor (call them the gentle people, if you wish), who are
challenging the doctrine of the official idea.

Repeated often enough and authoritatively enough, on televised
Sunday mornings, by pundits of familiar face and equally familiar
cabinet members and the even more familiar elder statesman, the
Doctor (who evokes startling memories of the Dutch comic), the
announced idea becomes official. Yet something unofficial is happening ''out there.''

Consider the market research man, the up-and-coming father, the archetypal Middle American. He had been foreman of a jury that acquitted four odd birds (including a Catholic nun) who had in the spirit of Isaiah committed an act of civil disobedience. He, a fervent believer in law and order, experienced something of a small epiphany.

A caveat: What Wilfred Owen called Chance's strange arithmetic was at work in this case. It was the luck of the draw that gave these four odd birds a judge who allowed the defense of "greater necessity." Had there been another enrobed figure on the bench, the young market research man would not have heard what he heard in the courtroom; nor would he have made the leap.

"We are quiet people," he said, "quiet in our disturbance. But once confronted with facts, they're really hard to let go of. You start asking yourself, What can I begin to do?

"We see on the news today something happened. A week later, something else is presented just as important. It's got the same kind of emphasis in the speaker's voice. All of a sudden, last week is gone behind us. A year ago is even further gone. How we blow up things that aren't important and never talk about things that are important."

He is discovering where the body is buried; how we hawk things unimportant and stash things important. And people. Is it any accident that we know more than we need to know of Donna Rice, Jessica Hahn, and Fawn Hall and nothing of Jean Gump?

Jean Gump?

Mrs. Gump, a devout Catholic grandma, suburban housewife, mother of twelve, League of Women Voters' chair, sparkplug of a freeze referendum that won in her village hands down, is now #03789-045 at the Correctional Institution for Women in Alderson, West Virginia. It is known, if at all, as the women's penitentiary from which Squeaky Fromme had momentarily escaped. How Mrs. Gump became a jailbird and an enemy of the people is recounted in some of these pages.

Joe Gump, her husband of thirty-four years, a salesman in the

Teddy Roosevelt stick-to-it-ive tradition, as American as apple pie and John Wayne, decided to do what his wife did. It had something to do with a missile site. He, too, is serving time in the federal poky. It is a love story that I doubt NBC, CBS, or ABC will memorialize.* It has to do with a middle-aged couple who came to believe that Jesus Christ meant what He said. This nation, under God, can take only so much.

In dealing with time past, whether it concerns the Great Depression, its lessons apparently forgotten, or World War Two, often misremembered,† the storyteller's memory is tapped and recollections pour forth as through a ruptured floodgate.

In dealing with time present, memory is absent, stunningly so, among the young. "I am struck by the basic absence of historical memory in this year's—or any year's—college freshmen. These young students are not the children but rather the grandchildren of the atomic age, born almost a quarter of a century after Hiroshima and Nagasaki. They have never known a time when nuclear weapons did not exist. As my freshmen might ask : 'Why bother?' "‡

An elderly maverick I ran into whimsically asked a college assembly, "Why should the FBI investigate a man who had once been chairman of Young Republicans for Herbert Hoover?" There was a dead silence. When he had explained that Herbert Hoover had been president during the Depression, there was a roar of laughter.

Could Henry Ford have been right after all? "History is bunk," he declared.

Despite such bleak communiqués from the academic front, a subtle change of climate may be detected as we approach the 1990s. Courses on Vietnam and its history are among the most popular in a surprising number of colleges. A professor of Russian history and literature at a large Midwestern university tells me that his classes are standing room only. John Kenneth Galbraith maintains that his students today are the brightest he's ever had.

---

* Jean Gump did appear briefly in a *60 Minutes* sequence on the missile-site damage.
† About half of the hundred or so college graduates I encountered thought the Soviet Union was our enemy in World War Two. Several were astonished to learn that the Russians had taken any part in it at all. For the record, most had majored in business administration and engineering.
‡ Joe Patrick Dean, assistant professor of history at Concordia Lutheran College, Austin, Texas (*New York Times,* op-ed page, September 13, 1986).

Although I've come across depressingly many eighteen-year-olds who admire J. R. Ewing because "he kicks butts," a young instructor in journalism discovers that his students insist on asking about professional ethics: "This year nobody in class asked me what I make." The majority of recent graduates at a college in the Northwest accepted a pledge "to take into account the social and environmental consequences of any job opportunity I consider."

Don't bet the farm on it (if there is any farm left to bet), but there does appear to be a new kid on the block. This one is not a sixties remainder nor an eighties automaton; not as stormy as the first nor as air-conditioned as the second. He or she is more ambivalent perhaps, yet possibly more reflective.

I encountered a couple of these new ones. He's fifteen, she's nineteen. Their family backgrounds are planets apart: his, middle-class; hers, blue-collar. Each is unaware of the other's existence. He, a short Holden Caulfield, muses: "It's amazing how cynical you can get by age fifteen. Yet sometimes you really get a surge of idealism and want to go out and participate." She, born in the year of the tempest, 1968, appears tranquil in nature, yet a spirited independence manifests itself. "My parents tend to go along with things as they are. But I began to wonder why are these things happening today. You look back in history and see what caused these things . . ."

To intimate that they are the future would, unfortunately, be far off the mark. They are a baby-faced Gideon's army, considerably outnumbered by their peers who cheer on Rambo and disparage wimps. Yet the two may reflect something in the others, something unfashionable for the moment and thus hidden away, something "fearful": compassion. Or something even more to abjure: hope.

At an extension college in Little Rock, the students damned the victims of AIDS—"They deserve to die." Yet on seeing a documentary film about those they damned, they wept softly. Their teacher attributed the overt absence of generous heart to their thoughts of eventual Armageddon: "With absence of hope, I found absence of generosity. Why bother?" But why did they weep?

Of all my experiences during the past three years, it is this image that most haunts me. These young, who wept for those they damned, may offer the challenge as yet unrecognized. In a wholly different context, Tom Paine remarked on it: the nature of infidelity to oneself, professing to believe what one does not believe. Could this be "our dirty little secret"?

There was no absence of hope in those early 1920s. Certainly it was a time of great expectations. Was I eight or nine that Saturday matinee when I saw the silent film *Get Rich Quick Wallingford*? It was a forgettable movie with an unforgettable theme: making it. Fast. The market was bellowingly bullish, the goose hung higher than high, and all things on the Street looked handsome. And who was more handsome than our president, Warren Gamaliel Harding?

Fifteen years later, another eight-year-old boy, Johnny, had the curtain line of a play: "I'm not mentioning any names, pa, but something's wrong somewhere." William Saroyan's *My Heart's in the Highlands* had an unforgettable theme, too: the Great Depression.

There's no point in mentioning any names, though Herbert Hoover's was most frequently invoked. "Most people cussed him up one side and down the other," recalls an Appalachian survivor. "I'm not saying he's blameless, but I'm not saying either it was all his fault. Our system doesn't run by just one man and it doesn't fall by one man either."

I asked a Wall Street wise man, adviser to four presidents, what went wrong that black October day in '29. I, in my prepubescent innocence, had seen the silent film, and remembering it, was as curious and disturbed as Saroyan's boy. "Who knows?" the sage explained. "Everybody was stunned. The Street had general confusion. They didn't understand any more than anybody else. They thought something would be announced."

Announced by whom? I hadn't the heart to ask him.

Some fifty-eight years later, in 1987, after a new generation of Wallingfords was making it fast, came another black October day, the nineteenth. Again from the temple of wisdom came an explanation: "It's a correction."

Correction of what? I hadn't the heart to ask anybody.

Professor Galbraith wasn't quite that tender-hearted. In a speech at the Gridiron Club* on December 5, 1987, he was at his ironic tops. "Markets in our time are a totem, a symbol of our secular religion. They can do no wrong. To find flaws in their behavior is both theologically and ideologically incorrect. And we could not put our rich fellow citizens at risk by saying that they and their much appreciated tax relief contributed to the debacle. The responsibility had to be removed from Wall Street." He complimented his media

* A Washington, D.C. club of journalists and editors.

hosts on their "tact and discretion," on their "admirable restraint." I imagine the laughter that followed was admirably restrained as well.

If April is the cruelest month, October may be the most revelatory. It may provide a metaphor for the eighties and, hopefully, for this book.

> *"The poorest one-tenth of Americans will pay 20 percent more of their earnings in federal taxes next year than they did in 1977 and the richest will pay almost 20 percent less, the Congressional Budget Office said Tuesday."* *

> *"Just before the stock market crashed, Forbes magazine announced that the number of billionaires in America had doubled in the past year. Just before the stock market crashed, Shasta County, California, closed its entire library system for lack of money.*
>
> *"Is there any question that something has gone wrong in America?"* †

After half a century, eight-year-old Johnny's question still reverberates. Something is indubitably wrong somewhere. Then, a president was 'buked and scorned and sudden acres of shacks bore his name: Hoovervilles. Today, the most popular president since FDR is faulted only by odd birds. Since the Irangate scandal and Black Monday, there has been a diminishing of delight in his incumbency; yet, unlike the Great Engineer, he is not personally held responsible. Nor, despite homeless millions, is there any record of a tent city named Reaganville.

> *In a blue-collar suburb of congenital Democrats, who went overwhelmingly for Reagan, "they are almost embarrassed. They don't want to talk about it." The long-time resident*

---

* A sidebar on one of the back pages of the *Chicago Sun-Times,* November 11, 1987. The front-page headline concerned the Chicago Bears.
† Lead editorial, *Los Angeles Times,* October 25, 1987.

*recalls election night. "Watching the returns, I knew a lot
of people in the room voted for Reagan. A few whispered
it, but they wouldn't say it."*

*An Iowa farm wife says it's almost impossible to find a
neighbor who admits having voted for Reagan, yet she
knows most of them did. Her county went handily for him.*

Circumstances in much of our land are the same as in the thirties:
ghost towns, where smokestacks once belched forth; family farms
going, going, gone; and the homeless.

Two young journalists of the Sacramento Bee *hit the road
to find out for themselves.* They rode the freights; they
walked the highways; they hitchhiked; they hunkered
down in big cities and small towns; they spent nights in
missions; they saw as much of our country's underside as
Woody Guthrie bound for glory in the thirties.*

*In boxcars, old-time hoboes complained bitterly of the
greenhorns who in the last few years have taken over. Talk
about overcrowding. Fifteen years ago, there were four to a
boxcar; now there are thirty, thirty-five. A new class of
bums; an old class of Middle Americans.*

*Of the 22 million hungry reported by the Harvard
School of Public Health (an old figure by now), the sources
were churches, social agencies, soup kitchens, and sallies.†
"Half the people we met on the road don't go near those
places," said the two hard travelers. Double the Harvard
figures and you've got yourself a pretty safe bet.*

*They had studied the photographs of the thirties, of
Dorothea Lange, Walker Evans, Margaret Bourke-White.
They saw the same faces. "When people are down and out,
they always look the same."*

* Dale Maharidge and Michael Williamson, in *Journey to Nowhere: The Saga of the New
Underclass* (New York: Doubleday, 1985).
† Salvation Army missions.

The new nomads have come from the Rust Belt, the abandoned farms, the small failed businesses. Many of them had voted for Reagan because "he made us feel good." They resent being called losers, though that *is* what they are called. In the thirties (at least in retrospect), they were called victims. If there is a core difference between Then and Now, it is in language. It is more than semantics; it is attitude. Then, the words of the winners reflected discomfort in the presence of the more unlucky. Now, they reflect a mild contempt. And fear.

"It scares me sometimes thinkin' people are never goin' to learn," says the West Virginia truckdriver. "There's no trust in anybody. Used to be hitchhikin', you'd get a ride. Now they're afraid to pick you up. They're afraid they'll be robbed, but people has always been robbed all their life."

In 1934, Sherwood Anderson took a trip across much of the country. *Puzzled America,* he called his book. Yet the hitchhikers he picked up in his jalopy were less puzzled than their nomadic descendants. At least, they made a stab at unraveling it.* Anderson found "a hunger for belief, a determination to believe in one another, in the leadership we're likely to get out of democracy."

A hunger for belief is certainly no less today than it was then. It is the nature of belief that may have changed. In the time lapse, new phenomena have taken over our lives and psyches: the cold war, the sanctity of the military, union-busting beyond precedent (encouraged by the cravenness of labor's pooh-bahs), along with televised sound bites† offered with the regularity of a cuckoo clock and a press that has assiduously followed the dictum of Sam Rayburn: To get along, go along. As a result, reflective conversations concerning these matters have become suspect, or at best, the avocation of odd birds, vestigial remainders of a long-gone past.

A daughter of Appalachia may have put her finger on it. "We've gotten away from our imaginations. The reason we're image-struck is because we don't like who we are. The more we get over this fake stuff, the more chance we've got to keep our sanity and self-respect."

---

* *Sherwood Anderson,* by Kim Townsend (Boston: Houghton Mifflin, 1987).
† Some months ago, a Cincinnati TV anchorman suggested, "How about a bite?" I immediately accepted his invitation. I envisioned roast duck and red cabbage in one of the city's celebrated German restaurants. To my grievous disappointment, he had something else in mind: a sound bite in a TV studio.

Christopher Lasch, in reflecting on the thirties, said as much in a wholly different context. ''Whatever else you may say about the New Deal, there was an inventiveness. All points of view were entertained.'' In short, during the crisis, imaginations were called upon. This it was Sherwood Anderson sensed, in his hard traveling: a hope as well as resilience, despite adversity, among those he encountered. Something trickled up as well as down.

LONG LIVE IMAGINATION. It was a banner carried by the students of Paris during the tempestuous year 1968. It was an idea that crossed the waters, undoubtedly misused and abused in some quarters. Nonetheless, it was a banner of strange and exhilarating device, not unlike the one borne by Longfellow's youth: EXCELSIOR.

With all passion spent in the twenty years that followed, we've experienced 1987's best-selling work of nonfiction upbraiding the young of that epoch as a barbaric lot.* Written by an academician, it may have more closely approached in temper William Claude Dukenfield † than Alfred North Whitehead.

Another sort of banner appeared on national television in 1987. During the football players' strike, at a game played by strikebreakers, a bare-chested band of youths unfurled a flag: WE LOVE OUR SCABS. What's even worse, the game was awful.

Never in all the bitter history of labor-management battles has strikebreaking been so unashamedly espoused. Always, in the past, scabs were shadows who entered the workplace through back doors. Just as the letter A was Hester Prynne's mark of shame, so was the letter S for those who crossed the picket line. Until now.

''I'm a professional strikebreaker,'' said a genial acquaintance. I thought he was kidding until I came across his profile in the *Wall Street Journal*. He's not a club-wielding goon; he's a prep school and Ivy League alumnus. ''It's exciting.'' His pride is manifest in these pages.

Along with the expunging of memory has come the removal of shame in all spheres of behavior and thought. "When I was coming up, it was embarrassing to be considered a racist," observes a young black woman. "Now it's nothing to

---

* *The Closing of the American Mind,* by Allan Bloom (New York: Simon & Schuster, 1987).
† A.k.a. W. C. Fields.

be embarrassed about. I think people take pride in it. It's
become fashionable to be a bigot."

A young blue-collar housewife is ridiculed by her
companions, especially her husband, at the neighborhood
tavern. "They think anybody who doesn't agree with
Reagan is dumb. Anybody who gets involved is called
stupid. They laugh at me all the time." She has coined a
word: ignorance-proud.

Further evidence is offered by a teacher at a Midwestern
campus. "It's not just the ignorance that's disturbing. It's
the acceptance of ignorance. It's acceptable not *to know*
about serious things. People who are really interested are
bores, the kind you turn off, away from at parties."

With Reagan's breaking of the air controllers' strike during his
first year in office, to the thunderous applause of most Americans,
including union members, things changed. (Mystery: For all the
worried headlines of air crashes and near misses, with more than
occasional references to understaffed, overworked, and unseasoned
air controllers, hardly any mention has ever been made of the non-
persons: 11,000 blacklisted *seasoned* air controllers. It appears that
even our priorities have taken a necrophilic turn.)

The pert file clerk across the hall lets me know of her disdain for
unions. Her immediate boss, a young accountant, who describes himself as "management," nods solemnly. They put in eight hours a
day. When I ask them how their eight-hour day came to be, their
fresh faces are pure Mondrian: the absence of any detail—the fur-
rowed brow, the thoughtful squint.

It was unfair of me. After all, the Haymarket Affair took place
in 1886, a good hundred years before I asked the impertinent question. I hadn't the heart to ask them about life before the minimum
wage—and that came about a good fifty years ago. Labor unions,
along with Big Guv'ment, which my two young friends also abhor,
may have brought it forth, but that's ancient history. And we know
what Henry Ford said about history.

The old-timer understands why so many of the bright-eyed band
feel that way. "Notice something about the media? They always
refer to labor as a special interest. Unions, minorities, women. Ever
hear of corporations referred to as special interests? How many

papers have reporters that cover the labor beat? Or TV stations? What the hell, they've got whole sections on business and finance. Is it any wonder that the young are so ignorant?''

The locked-out steelworker in the country's biggest ghost town, Youngstown (although Gary could give it a run for its money), says with a newly honed sense of irony, ''My son is listed among the newly employed. He lost his $13-an-hour job and is now pumping gas at $3.50.''

At the day of this writing, the headline in the local paper reads: Jobless Rate Lowest in 8 Years. It is also the lead on the six o'clock news.

His son, an ex-marine who served time in Vietnam, says, ''This is the first time in four generations that I have it worse than my father.'' He stares at his two small boys: ''How will it be for them?''

As we pass over the Monongahela River, the defrocked Lutheran pastor points toward the dark waters. ''A twenty-three-year-old guy drowned this week, after drinking heavily. Where should he have been Tuesday morning? He should have been at work. At Christmastime, we had one weekend of fourteen suicides. All laid-off steelworkers. I guess they'll never make government statistics, will they?''

A fourth-generation Minnesota farmer, about to lose his place, tells of a stunning rise in rural suicides, alcoholism, and divorce. ''How much can a man take? There was several times that I had the gun to my head and she didn't know it. I would be drivin' and didn't know how I got there.''

Never since the Great Depression has the family farmer experienced such despair. Scores of thousands are, with a growing sullenness, sampling the grapes of wrath. If help is not forthcoming one way, they will seek another. It's a natural for the nearest con artist at hand.

The Posse Comitatus, the LaRouchies, and the Aryan Nation had antecedents in the thirties. They were hooted off the wheatlands only after the administration came through. The old South Dakota Swede wept as he remembered: ''People could at last see some daylight and hope.''

With no such deliverance from Washington today, the beleaguered farmer sees through the glass darkly. The small Minnesota beef grower swears he has the answer to this terrible riddle. "It's the big companies and the Zionist conspiracy. I know it's hard to believe, but if you're foreclosed and lose everything you sweated for all your life, as I did . . ." There may be bitter fruit ripe for the picking.

The old-timer is in a constant state of disbelief. "For the first time in the history of the country, a new generation is coming of age that will have a lower standard of living than their parents. Before, they could anticipate going beyond. What's happened to the American dream?"

The compass is broken.

In the old badman song, Duncan hollers a challenge: Brady, where is you at?* That's the question we ask one another: Where are we at? What had presumably been our God-anointed patch of green appears to be, for millions of us, a frozen tundra. We race higgledy-piggledy, first one way, and a thirty-second commercial later we're headed elsewhere: all for a piece of the afternoon sun.

In De Sica's post–World War Two Italian movie *Miracle in Milan,* there is an indelible moment. The wretched homeless of the jungle camp shove, push, elbow one another out of the way for a sliver of the sun that comes and goes. An instant later, as the North Italian cold overcomes, all is forgotten save a bruise or two, the legacy of an equally miserable peer. Nothing has been learned, other than it is good to have sharp elbows. It is the lesson we have been taught, especially during this past decade. In authoritative quarters, it has been called entrepreneurialism. Ivan Boesky had his own word for it and may have been much closer to the truth.

Yet something is happening out there, across the Divide, often in unexpected quarters; something of an old American tradition, with new twists. Grass-roots movements, with techniques learned from the sixties, have never been more flourishing. Most of their foot

---

* "Duncan and Brady" was, in time past, a favorite barroom ballad of baritones and basses.

soldiers had nothing to do with anti–Vietnam War protests, yet now challenge the Big Boys.

A bantam housewife in Chicago leads her blue-collar neighbors in a challenge to the Waste Management Corporation, a powerful multinational. She beats the outfit: there will be no toxic-waste dump in the neighborhood. A local, Bob Bagley, let Congress know about Somebody's spray trucks hauling dioxin through his forgotten town in the Ozark foothills. He won the battle. Name a place, a big-city block or a village square, and you'll find corporate dumpers with tigers by the tails. "Ordinary people, quiet in our disturbance" are the first bubbles in what has most of this decade been a tepid kettle.

The movements, remarkably disparate in issue, ranging from local grievances—utility hikes, tax inequities, developers' transgressions—to matters more encompassing—Sanctuary, Pentagon spending, threats to Social Security—have been both secular and sacred in impulse. (A young computer wizard has determined there are more than six thousand peace groups in business.) In most of these instances, the participants are unaware of the others' works. They are a movement awaiting coalescence.

It is what my two young acquaintances, the fifteen-year-old middle-class boy and the nineteen-year-old blue-collar girl, were intimating earlier in this essay. And reaching out for. It is what the newer students in that journalism class were curious about. It is what the old South Dakota Swede was awaiting in those bleak days of the Great Depression: something trickling up.

In spite of these hopeful signs, it's still clear that things can go either way. There may be a shaft of awareness sifting through. There are such signs. Or there may be a sharpening of elbows. There are such signs. There was a phrase in vogue during World War Two, shortly before the Normandy invasion: Situation Fluid. It is so now as it was then.

Nowhere has the Great Divide been as deep as in our religious conflicts today. It is in this sphere that the issues have been most dramatically joined.

Consider the case of Gary C. and his father. Both are Christian evangelicals. Both interpret Scripture literally. The son, who had done missionary work in El Salvador, reads the Bible "the same way the *campesinos* do. The Bible tells them of today, oppressors and oppressed, word for word. My father also believes in it, word for word. But he doesn't read it the same way they do. Or the way I do. He believes in this administration's Central American policy wholeheartedly. The same Book we both love is on the table we sit at, yet we're worlds apart.''

In *Division Street*, a book I had undertaken some twenty years ago, the Sacred and the Sinful were reflected primarily in hymns, spirituals, blues, and tent meetings. It was not a subject of fierce public debate.

As a radio disk jockey in the forties and fifties, my encounter with Mahalia Jackson was the closest thing to a debate, as she tried (in vain, I'm afraid) to "save" me. It was imbued with deep feeling on her part and, I hope, on mine. What I most remember is her delightful touch of humor during those frequent colloquies. Our friendship was in no way diminished, though I may have been hopelessly "lost."

In that book I observed: ''Surprisingly, God was an also-ran in their thoughts. Like a stage mother, I had to push Him forward. Once He was introduced into the conversation, He was immediately and effusively acknowledged. (And in a few cases, rebuffed.) Whether God is dead or merely sleeping or really is a has-been is for theologians to have a high old time with.''

That passage, read today, has a touch of quaintness. Not since the Great Awakening have such heated discourses on religion been so pervasive in our society.

Perhaps it is the loss of historical memory that is at work in this sphere, too. Though William Jennings Bryan may have suffered humiliation at the ''monkey trial'' in 1924, his admonition—study ''Rock of Ages,'' not the age of rocks—sways astonishing millions today, particularly the young, citified as well as rural.

A former religion editor associates this hunger for belief with the hunger for fast food. It immediately satisfies. It's bland. ''You're given answers, you're not presented with problems. The idea is not to reflect because that's disturbing.'' You may be bewitched, but you most certainly are not bothered nor bewildered. The young radio engineer abandoned Catholicism for a smiling fundamentalism because "they gave me simple answers. They were people I could relate to."

On the other side of the Divide, a company executive was profoundly challenged by another nondenominational ministry. She had, some years before, left the conservative church of her family, "but I felt the need to be religious again." Her life, which had been "respectable, comfortable, and bland," now has a new attribute: risk. She is active in the Sanctuary movement. ("I don't feel I've got all the answers, but I feel that I'm being faithful.")

She is one of the odd birds, whose flock may not be as large as Bryan's born-agains, but is out there making trouble for the Romans. They are not the olden-time street-corner Jeremiahs crying doom nor somebody leadenly reading "a specter is haunting Europe." They are a hitherto respectable suburban grandma, the fair-skinned wife of a young pastor, a plumber with the build of a pro football linebacker, a druggist out of Nowhere, U.S.A.—a wholly new cast of characters.

They cite Scriptures more often than manifestoes. Unlike the televangelists with their million-dollar Te Deums, these odd birds call on Isaiah, something about beating swords into plowshares and studying war no more. Even more often, they call upon Another, something about feeding the hungry and clothing the naked.

Nowhere is the battle joined more strikingly than in the mill-town ministries bordering Pittsburgh. Faith and paradox are at work here. The defrocked young Lutheran pastor and his colleagues live hand to mouth. Distressed by the closing down of the steel mills, the joblessness, the suicides, they challenged the conglomerates, the banks and their prestigious law firms. They took on the Big Boys.

What impelled them to jeopardize their reputations and livelihoods was a fundamental interpretation of Scripture. (They have been charged with self-righteous fundamentalism by a distinguished Lutheran pastor, who started left and made a right turn. "They have the truth. If you don't agree, you're on the side of the devil.")

They are indeed possessed by a religious fervor. "Prophetic things began to happen. It's a calling. God places things on us." The paradox is in their technique. Unlike the televangelists with their bland, fast-food, no-problem approach, they have created problems for the Big Boys. To them, the parable of the loaves and fishes has a contemporary meaning. To embarrass Pittsburgh's most powerful bank and call attention to the plight of the laid-off steelworkers (their parishioners), they deposited fishes in the safety-deposit boxes.

"It's never gonna be popular to act that strongly. It's never gonna be a mass movement. But there's always gonna be the dissenting voice that says we need justice."

They have been subjected to ridicule on TV, on radio, and in the press. More often than not, there has been a turning away by others. At the Pittsburgh airport, I caught furtive glances and embarrassed turnings away. The young pastor's face was familiar to a great many, as was his figure. He has the build of a Pittsburgh Steeler lineman. "Yet you can't walk the streets of Pittsburgh without people coming up to shake your hand. We're behind you, they say. Often, way behind (laughs). They can't bring themselves to take a public stand. It makes them vulnerable. Will they get laid off? There's fear, a lot."

A startlingly similar encounter is remembered by the imprisoned suburban grandmother. She had been rebuffed by her fellow parishioners at the church she had attended for thirty-two years. Yet while in jail awaiting sentence, she experienced something else. "The guard who handed me the tray through the slot in the door said, 'I want to thank you for what you did.' When I saw her lined up with all the other guards, she had a wholly different demeanor." Her husband, after a humiliating experience at the church, was accosted by the young hardware clerk. "She whispered to me, 'God bless your wife.' "

Could it be that the young pastor and the grandmother are on to something? It may be a more important secret than the most hushed-up eyes-only intelligence report. It is something private that still waits to be made public. What we profess to believe in this drifting decade may be something wholly different from what we really believe. Or want. Else why did those Little Rock students weep softly and privately for those they damned harshly and publicly?

#03789-045, a.k.a. Jean Gump, suburban grandma, says matter-of-factly, "This is God's world, okay? We're stewards of the earth. I think we're rather bad stewards. I want to offer my grandchild a life, that's all. We had a crack at it, and I think it's fair he should, too. Call it a legacy if you want to. What else is there?"

BOOK

1

SCHOOL DAYS

School days, school days,
Dear old Golden Rule days.
Readin' and writin' and 'rithmetic
Taught to the tune of a hickory stick.
I was your bashful barefoot beau,
You were my queen in calico.
I wrote on your slate, "I love you so,"
When we were a couple of kids.

—A turn-of-the-century popular song by Gus Edwards

SEAN KELLY

He's twenty-seven.

He comes from a middle-class suburban family.
"Somewhere between conservative and liberal, but they
voted for Reagan. I'm a lot more liberal than they are, but
I think a lot of liberals are pretty silly also."

At Bowling Green University in Ohio, he was a teaching
assistant: three composition courses.

I was twenty-four at the time, just a few years older than my students. They would call me Professor Kelly.

Their first assignment was an essay: to compare small-town and big-city life. All their examples were from television. When they're talking about small towns, they're talking about *The Waltons*. When they talked of the big city, almost all of them quoted from *Miami Vice*. What they want in life is something from *Dynasty* or *Dallas*: to be rich and good-looking. Their values come from TV commercials.

There's a six-, seven-year difference between us, yet when I mention the Rolling Stones, I could be talking about Tommy Dorsey. The gap is enormous. Even though I was only in fourth grade when my brother was in Vietnam, I was proud. It was really something to have a family member in the army. Too young to understand, yet aware of Watergate and a memory of the sixties.

They were born in '67, '68, coming of age in a blackout generation when nobody really talked about Vietnam. They have no idea who Nixon was. Most of their thoughts of Vietnam come from this surge of television interest. They've rewritten Vietnam history. In *Magnum, P.I.* and *Simon & Simon*, the protagonists are Vietnam veterans. *Matt Houston*. They use flashbacks in this wave of patriotism to show plots: go back and get the POWs. *Rambo* is a perfect example. They're refighting Vietnam as though it were World War Two.

My father was an officer in the navy in World War Two. It bothered him a lot when my brother came home from Vietnam and wouldn't wear his uniform in the street. It made him really angry. He didn't understand that this wasn't World War Two.

I've had several students tell me we won in Vietnam. They guard themselves, though. They know they're ignorant about certain things, but are not interested enough to go find out. They're amazed to see America in a confused state, that the people fighting there didn't know what they were fighting for. But they didn't really care that we were killing civilians. They've become so used to the Hollywood version, where we know exactly what we're doing and we're right. Nobody innocent ever really gets hurt and there's glory when you die.

They've been hearing Reagan's view of the world regularly. The communist takeover. They love him. Before the last election, Reagan came to the campus to speak. Five or six helicopters came down, he came in. It was carefully orchestrated. The students were very excited. Ironic, because it was just at the time he was cutting student aid.

They were furious at the few protesters, who were cordoned off and hidden behind a building. Sororities put up banners welcoming him. It wasn't that they approved of his issues. That didn't matter. He was a celebrity, somebody famous. Just the way they'd have been excited if Sylvester Stallone had come—or Bruce Springsteen.

"We had some great speakers there last semester. Dick Gregory was wonderful. He was sharp, funny, and political. It didn't matter what he said, no more than what Reagan said. Angela Davis was also there. The students knew she had been arrested and was on the FBI's ten-most-wanted list. That gave her a kind of celebrity. Who cares what she said?

"Ralph Nader was there last week. He was too low-key for them. They had no idea who he was. Noam Chomsky spoke. They listened because a lot of them thought he was the celebrity who taught a chimp how to read.

"John Stockwell drew a crowd because he was an ex-CIA

agent, glamorous. When he talked of the contras killing, dismembering women in front of their children, a couple of guys heckled him and yelled as they wallked out, 'Reagan! Reagan!' They had thought he'd be pro-CIA. I will say they offended most of the audience, who—would you believe it?—stayed all the way through.

"There is a small group of concerned students on the campus."

I had a bright class, those who had placed well in their achievement tests. There were about twenty-eight. I asked them, ''If there were war declared against, say, Nicaragua, how many of you would just pack up your bags and leave tomorrow?'' All but two said they'd go. I followed up: Who were we fighting for? What side would we support? Did we support the government of Nicaragua? The two knew. The other twenty-six didn't know.

They've become so conditioned to follow trends, not make waves, even though they might get killed for something they didn't understand. Or kill the wrong people.

They're assailed by all these armed services commercials. They're shown working computer boards or walking the streets of Rome (laughs). They don't show them getting mowed down.

In one of the chapters of the textbook some of us use, there's a chapter on obedience to authority. I usually tie it in with the trial of Lieutenant Calley, whom none of them have heard of.* Many of them get bored. Some of them are fatalistic. ''It's just out of our hands. The government's gonna blow us up anyway.'' Or else, the government's in control and they'll take care of it. Most of them are in business administration or engineering. They're very conscious about how much money they're going to make and what they're going to own. They can't understand somebody who would like teaching.

It's not just the ignorance that's disturbing. It's the acceptance of ignorance. It's acceptable *not* to know about serious things. People who are really interested are bores to them, the kind you turn

---

* Lieutenant William Calley was the defendant in the celebrated trial concerning the My Lai massacre in Vietnam.

off, away from at parties. I think it's been fostered by the media: it's okay to be ignorant. If the important thing is to have a nice car and be well-dressed, who wants to listen to somebody talk about Central America?

A colleague of mine was urging his students: "You have to *think* about things, to care." One of the students came out, kind of sore: "Why should we have to think?" After all, everything's laid out for you to be successful.

They're not ashamed to come in late to class. About ten students would walk in regularly fifteen minutes late. I'd say, "Hey, what's goin' on?" They said, "We had to wait till *All My Children* was over." They looked at me as though I were rude for asking.

I had a conference with a girl who couldn't write a sentence. She was leaving as another student came in. She said, "I hope you know I'm missing *Days of Our Lives*." She was serious. She had made this sacrifice for this conference. This other guy said, "Yeah, I know. *All My Children* is starting now and I'm gonna miss the first twenty minutes of it." There was no irony—they weren't joking. I've overheard conversations in school cafeterias: "Oh, my God, you know what happened to Ryan yesterday? He was caught in bed with Melissa." And I'll be thinking they're talking about real people.

Twice a semester, students fill out a midterm evaluation of the teacher. Several students wrote about me: "He's a real good teacher, we like him, but he really should get a haircut." My hair wasn't that long. One student in the creative writing class was outraged: "I can't believe that the university lets someone like this stand in front of a class and have him as our image." These are popularity polls and, since you have no tenure, may affect your getting a job. I find myself holding on to these evaluations until I've had a good class. After I turned back a bunch of awful essays that I was angry about, I was tempted to hold back the forms.

With obedience to authority, you want your father figure to be clean-cut and presentable.

I brought up the My Lai massacre and Calley, who had been obedient to authority all his life. I gave them material on both sides, so they could make up their own minds. You could be shot for disobeying orders in combat. On the other hand, any reasonable man should know you don't kill hundreds of innocent, unarmed people. I tried to spark a debate: "How many of you think he should be found guilty?" A couple raised their hands, then a few more. Pretty soon all did. Guilty. I took the other side for a few minutes. "Now what do you think? How many of you think he's not guilty?" They all raised their hands.

I got angry and argued the first side once more. I again persuaded them: guilty. I tried to engage them in debate. I changed their opinions four or five times. I was exasperated. They wanted to know what the teacher thought. I was the person in control and should know. I was the authority and should be obeyed. I was actually worried I was humiliating them too much. It never got through.

I tried another test on obedience and authority. I asked the nicest girl in class, the kindest, to step out of the room. I said to the others: "Your assignment is to write the nastiest things you can about her. You'll be graded on how scathing and insulting you are, how you can destroy her character. The people who pass this class are the ones who maintain a B or above. You also know the worst two will be read to her. Aloud. How many of you would go ahead and do it?" Just about all of them said they would. Without question.

I asked them why. They said, "We want to get a good grade and we don't have to take this class again." Not one of them said, "Hey, screw you, you can't do this." Their morals were never engaged. Not one thought, It would make the girl feel humiliated, my grade isn't worth that. It was simply, Okay, this is authority telling me.

Last semester, I had a girl who wrote a term paper saying that Adolf Hitler was really a peace-loving man who really wanted to be left alone to work out the problems of Germany and really wasn't aggressive. These are her actual quotes. I thought, My God, this girl is a neo-Nazi, eighteen years old. I was more horrified to find out that she didn't really care that much. It was just another assignment. It didn't really matter.

I give people a chance to ask questions before the class ends. If there are none, they leave early. This ROTC girl was always asking questions—the rest of the class hated her. They would glance at her, look up at the ceiling, and roll their eyes: Oh, God, not her again. She was always challenging me. It wasn't that they disagreed with her views. It wouldn't have mattered if it were a liberal student against a conservative teacher. They just wanted to go back to their dorms.

Every now and then, something happens that gives me a slight hope. It was the class on the My Lai massacre. It was really quiet, except for these two ROTC guys, who were glorifying the military. "Calley was doing what he had to do. These people were probably

Viet Cong anyway.'' I wasn't challenging them. I was hoping some-body else would.

This meek, self-conscious girl, who never said a word the whole semester, suddenly stood up in the middle of the class and yelled, ''You don't know what the fuck you're talking about!'' She yelled at these guys (laughs). The whole class was completely quiet. I started laughing, and then she and everybody else burst out laugh-ing. She turned red. She didn't believe she had done this. I said, ''Make sure you read this article so you'll know what the fuck you're talking about.'' That broke 'em up. It was all right—the authority laughed.

She explained her views later on. The last thing I remember she was breaking out of something comfortable: being meek and quiet. I hope.

QUINN BRISBEN

He is huge, bearded, and usually wrapped in a poncho. He has the appearance of a man-mountain. "I'm compared to Santa Claus or Colonel Sanders. I often show the kids which finger to lick."

He teaches American history and world geography at a black high school in the Far South Side of Chicago.

Our school used to be half working-class black and half underclass. Lately, the scale has tipped. We had postal workers, firemen, people who had small businesses, and some professionals. They no longer send their children to our school. We have what's left. Some of my best students have come from what's left, some of the most interest-ing. Nonetheless, without these middle-class kids to help me teach, I'm finding it more difficult all the time.

We have a lot of people who are on welfare sometimes. But they will work when they can get jobs. Some of the trouble is, parents are working two jobs apiece and don't have time to spend with the kids. These are people who are just barely making it. If one of those jobs poops out, they're in real trouble making the payment on the house the next month. Or even providing sufficient food for the family.

There are lots of things we used to do in our school that we can't do any more. In the old days, I'd make a homework assignment for twenty-five students. Perhaps eight or nine would come the next day with the assignment done. Okay, I can ask these students questions, I can chew out the rest. We can establish an ambience: do your homework in class. They would do it. Now, I assign homework and two or three will do it.

The eight or nine were people who were going on to college. This had been expected of them since they were small children. Their parents had not had much education but had high expectations for their children.

It becomes much more difficult to bring the bulk of the class along when I don't have students to help me teach. Mostly, students don't learn from teachers: they learn from each other.

No one sets the tone any more. It's not a big deal to get on the honor roll any more. It's not fashionable to study. They're turned off by the whole bit of being in school.

I used to be able to get kids, creatively, by making outrageous statements. They'd get angry and respond. They'd jump up and yell ''Bullshit!'' ''In my day, we said Point of Order. Now what is your objection?'' We would get some very good discussion. Suppose we were talking about the Boston Massacre. I would say, ''There's very little proof that Crispus Attucks was black.'' I'd get angry resentment right away.

One of the great things that's happened in the last twenty years or so is that they've come to know of fifty or sixty eminent black Americans. If I'd find some kid interested in photography, I'd say, ''You're gonna do a report on Gordon Parks.'' The kid would do that. Now, they're not really that interested in much of anything. Whether black people have succeeded in that field or not, they don't believe that they can succeed in anything.

Eight, nine years ago, when I'd say, ''Suppose Crispus Attucks was a Native American instead of black. Why do you need him to be black? Why do you want to be part of this?'' A kid would jump up and say, ''We've been here for all these hundred years and we contributed just as much as anybody else.'' Once in a while, I still get it.

I tried it a few months ago, doing the American Revolution. I just got dead silence. First of all, they weren't paying close attention. Second of all, being part of the myth of American history, they feel, has nothing to do with them. They didn't feel that because Crispus Attucks was a leader of a revolutionary mob which turned out to be historically important, they would have a chance to lead a protest demonstration that would ever mean much of anything. They don't think they're going anywhere.

Sports figures are fine, especially if they make big money. Even these heroes don't seem to give them much hope now. Who wants to be like that poor kid who got a magnificent offer at the University of Maryland and then OD'd on drugs? Who wants to be a thirty-five-year-old ex-athlete who can't read?

After they leave school, they'll maybe go into the army for a few years. The army can give you something to do when you get up in the morning. They'll even say, "I hope it straightens me out. I hope it gives me a chance to get my act together." Oh, they're very aware that something is wrong. They're cynical about it, they resist the teachers and all that, but they have a very good sense of what's wrong.

They are not really satisfied with their picture of themselves. Like all adolescents since time began, they've been trying on one role model after another. Prince walks into the room five or six times a day. You'll find a kid with a curl of hair down the middle of his forehead who will move like Prince. Then he'll turn around and look at us, see to what extent we believe it. The Fridge* has been very nice for the big, heavy kids. I used to model my smoking style on Edward R. Murrow until he died of lung cancer. The sad part is ten or a dozen years ago, I'd have kids imitating Gordon Parks.

I like to work against the book. Our book sets up some marvelously foolish things. We get into World War One. They'll come up to me: "It says here we got into this war to protect our right to be neutral." I say, "Doesn't it seems a little funny to you that we would fight a war and kill thousands and thousands of Americans just to protect our right to be neutral? Let's think of some better reasons." They say, "That's not in the book." Well, I mean, the book's not Jesus.

We don't get these discussions as often as before, but we did get some good ones a few weeks ago. Why did the United States feel it

* William "Refrigerator" Perry, celebrated linebacker of the Chicago Bears.

necessary to take Florida? The book had a beautiful sentence: "Planters near the border were worried about the loss of property." Now, class, what kind of property was it that would move across a border all by itself? (Laughs.) Of course, it was runaway slaves, was what they were worried about. We'd get a bit of back-and-forth on it. Much more in the old days.

They can't read very well. They can learn to read stuff they're interested in, at least the words. Years ago, I stopped using the Mickey Mouse eighth-grade books. I put a book in front of them now: If you want to learn how to read this stuff, you can learn how to read it. You're no dumber than anybody else. Now get busy and work. Sometimes it works, sometimes it doesn't.

Their situation is so hopeless that a bunch of 'em one day are just going to strike out in blind fury. Like Bigger Thomas in *Native Son.* I live among these kids, I love these kids, but sometimes, by God, they frighten me the way Bigger frightened Richard Wright.

It just can't help but explode. Remember Langston Hughes's poem "Raisin in the Sun"? "Does it sag like a heavy load? Or does it explode?" You can't predict the day, you can't predict the hour, but a dream deferred is inevitably going to explode sometime.

If you want to raise my kids' reading levels about two years, get a job for their parents, a good job. Fix things so that these job-training programs actually lead to jobs. Get something where it can lead up and out.

We had a new fast-food operation open in the neighborhood and they were gonna hire about twenty kids. We had four hundred show up for the interviews. This is common. They don't want to work for nothing. They don't want to work in a job that pays below minimum wage and never get up and out of it. But they are as hard-working people as you'd ever find anywhere. I'm talking about full employment.

I'm from Oklahoma and my whole subclass of culture of poverty happened to disappear with World War Two. All of a sudden us dumb Okies were not dumb Okies any more. We were capable of working in defense plants at two dollars an hour. I know a hell of a lot of people that felt guilty that it took a war to do it.

Looking at all this construction, how nice it would be if my kids could get some of those jobs. But . . .

There haven't been any victories for a long time for people like my students. My freshmen next year will have been born in 1973. King died five years before they were born. Vietnam is something they hear about from their dads. It's just been a long, long time since anything happened.

Most of the lives of these children have been in the time of Reagan, whom they understand extremely well. This is where the black community has an advantage over the white. When a politician makes a speech, they don't listen to the words very carefully. They catch little clues about the attitude: What is this person really saying about me? They get the feeling that Reagan is more than willing to exploit racism in order to get votes. The kids in my class easily see this. I said they had difficulty reading. I didn't say they were dumb.

I live in the neighborhood. I walk back and forth to school. I stand out at a distance. I do it on purpose. They've been seeing me, many of 'em, all their lives. Many of them have big brothers and sisters who were my students. Some of 'em, God help 'em, have had fathers and mothers who were my students. The system is not set up to encourage teachers. A lot who are quite decent get burnt out pretty badly.

People flip out. We've got one bangs his head against the garbage can in the men teachers' lounge. We've even got alcoholics there. We've got all kinds of people close to burnouts. You bang your head up against a blank wall just too many times, you've got to have some kind of outlet. I gotta take off some pounds. I eat too much.

What gets you is these kids have so much potential. Except for the fact that white kids have more pimples, there's not a hell of a lot of difference. Most of the difference is the difference in what's happened to you. These kids, of course, do have a very rich oral tradition. The sermons, the songs, the speeches. Most talk better than they write. They're used to it.

Sometimes we can do some beautiful things. In my class, in addition to two term papers and a book report, if you want to pass, you have to come up with thirty minutes of a taped interview with an older person, your grandmother, usually someone over sixty. The Board of Education gave me a three-hundred-dollar grant four years ago and I bought three tape recorders. Only one of 'em's disappeared so far. That's not bad at all.

I get a different order of excellence when I have these kids do these tapes. Much better than I do with the written lessons. They're more attuned to an oral culture. I'd say, Talk to some old person, find out how their experiences were different from yours, what life was like without television.

This one girl brought back this tape. She interviewed her grand-mother.

> *He turns on the tape recorder. We listen to an old woman's voice:*
>
> *"The radio was our biggest for entertainment. Fletcher Henderson would come on, my goodness, you could hear it all up and down the streets." (She imitates the introductory music and laughs.) "And then there was the fights. Joe Louis. Boy, that was the high time of our life. We just looked forward to that, just like we're looking forward to a black mayor. We looked forward to having Joe Louis win this fight, because he was our idol then.*
>
> *"People have been prejudiced all of their life. I found out about that. There was a restaurant I used to pass on my way to high school. I often said, 'When I grow up to be a woman, I'm gonna go into a restaurant just like that.' But you never heard of a black person going into a restaurant just like that, in the days I was coming up. Martin Luther King changed all that."*

The girl who brought the tape was a C student, sixteen. Some tests she'd study for, some she wouldn't. She didn't seem to care very much. And then she did this. I had just started the project and these were the first really good ones I got. Oh, she improved quite a bit. I showed her off, I played these excerpts for all the classes, so the students could get a better idea how to do this. I got her permission.

Last I heard, she was at Illinois Normal Teachers' College and doing quite well.

ART SPIEGELMAN

*An illustrator and writer, he is best known for his book of
unique cartoon strips,* Maus : *the subject, Auschwitz.*
   *He is teaching the history of the comic strip at the
School of Visual Arts in New York.*

These students just don't have a
sense of history and they're not
literate. It's very frightening to be teaching a generation of cartoonists that can't write. That's what comics are all about, being able to
think and tell stories coherently, with pictures, of course.

What shocked me was my students knew nothing about the sixties.
They had never heard of underground comics. Nobody in the class
had ever heard of Robert Crumb. This is not the general public
we're talking about. These people are aspiring to be cartoonists and
he was one of the most important seminal artists of our generation.

I had to go back and *explain* how people were protesting against
the Vietnam War, and that there was a drug culture, that there was
a movement toward sexual liberation. I was talking as if I were
from another planet. It made me feel very old, and there was only
an eleven-year gap between me and the students. They range in age
from nineteen to twenty-two : mostly white, middle-class male.

I talked to the administration about their appalling level of literacy, and they blamed it on the open-admissions policy, allowing
Third World and ghetto people into the school. Now that the policy
has been withdrawn, I would say, if anything, it's gotten worse.

When I was a kid, I wanted to be a beatnik. It meant reading
poetry, getting my life experience, and finding obscure little crev-
ices in the culture. Students today, the beatniks of now, don't watch
prime-time television. They watch weird old reruns, so the kids
who are hip in my class are the ones who talk about *The Three
Stooges* and *The Honeymooners*. Shows like these are part of their
obscure culture. They feel superior to the others. They are the
avant-garde.

I found I could not talk to my students about George Grosz,

Daumier, Picasso. Anything that happened before Andy Warhol was news to them. He was a television celebrity and TV is their culture. All they had read were the comic strips when they were growing up. They're aware of *Peanuts* and *Garfield* and *Spider-Man*. They were unaware of the history of comic strips and that there were greater achievements in the past.

They were given a questionnaire at the beginning of the semester: Who are your favorite authors? A number of students left that question blank, as if it hadn't been there. Their favorite, by far, was Stephen King. When other authors were mentioned, it would be a student trying to appear bright. He would name Nathaniel Hawthorne. He had him in high school, so he knew Hawthorne was an author.

What they wanted to do was learn how to get a job in the commercial art racket. I kept telling them that my class was not going to help them do that because it would make them less equipped for survival in an eighties American environment. It was necessary for them to learn how to think and look in order to be good cartoonists. These are the people who should be learning how to be social commentators of the next generation.

FRANK WILKINSON

He is seventy, director emeritus of the National Committee Against Repressive Legislation. His FBI file made the Guinness Book of Records: 132,000 pages. "My lawyers estimated that the FBI spent $17 million of taxpayers' money, following me around for forty years."

In a test case before the House Un-American Activities Committee (HUAC), he refused to cooperate. He was subsequently found guilty of contempt, the U.S. Supreme Court upholding the decision 5 to 4. He spent a year in the federal penitentiary.

While a student at UCLA in the early 1930s, he was president of Young Republicans for Herbert Hoover.

*He frequently lectures on college campuses, most often
at law schools.*

I find no apathy on the campuses.
Once the students are there, you
don't lose one. What I do find is a lack of a sense of past, no sense of
history.

At Utah State in Logan, where the students are overwhelmingly
Mormon, the response was enthusiastic. I was telling these young
people that HUAC, which we abolished in 1975, has come back as
the new Committee on Terrorism. I told them about my case in
detail.

I told them how the FBI had a working relationship with the law-
school boards from 1936 until 1976, concerning every student taking
the bar. There was private clearance. The students asked, jokingly,
"If I give you my name and address, I'll get on the list, won't I?"
I answered, "Because we fought back and filed a lawsuit eight years
ago, we're one of the few organizations you can write to and not get
on the list." That got a laugh and much applause. At the University
of Georgia Law School, I was introduced on the twenty-fifth anniversary of my being subpoenaed by HUAC. This may be the most
yuppie law school in the country. Even the first-year students wear
three-piece suits. The MC threw in something I'd been trying to
forget for fifty years: I was the leader of the Sigma Alpha Epsilon
fraternity at UCLA back in the thirties.

Here I am talking about a new HUAC coming back, a girl runs
up front and cries out, "I'm youah little sistah. Let me give you the
grip. Now put youah cheek against mine." Now she whispers, "Let's
say the secret code." I thought I had all the students won over till
that moment.

In Anchorage, I jokingly asked, "Why would the FBI go after
me, who was head of Youth for Herbert Hoover?" Nobody laughed.
They didn't know who Hoover was. I said, "He was president back
in the Depression." Then they laughed.

The editor of the student paper came up afterwards. "You mentioned two different Hoovers and I don't understand who they
were." I said one was J. Edgar. She asks, "How do you spell it?"
She obviously had no idea who he was. Then she said, "The other
one, I think you said, was the president. I've got it clear now, that's

all I needed.'' The next morning, the student paper has a banner headline: MAN WHO FOUGHT HERBERT HOOVER FOR 35 YEARS SPEAKS ON CAMPUS.

They're ignorant because no one's ever told them. If you use the acronym HUAC, they know nothing. If you use the full words, they still don't know. Think about it. The average student I'm talking to is about twenty-two. J. Edgar died in '72; the twenty-two-year-old student was seven. When HUAC was abolished, he was ten. Our schools absolutely do not teach these young people about history.

Once they are informed, they definitely want to do something. I've seen this during the past several years in all parts of the country. I have never felt as positive about the future for civil liberties —provided these young are not cheated out of their history.

BRUCE DOLD

He is thirty-one, a journalist. "I was eight when Kennedy died. I turned eighteen when the Vietnam War ended.

"I remember being up on my sixteenth birthday because I realized I'd be drafted in two years, despite Kissinger's 'peace is at hand.' I was still young, but old enough to be cynical. I couldn't see myself going over, and I don't know what my conservative parents would have done if I'd said I was going to Canada.

"I remember really arguing with my parents about Watergate. They defended Nixon. I knew right off the bat that you didn't have to believe everything the government was telling you. It made me think you didn't have to believe what anybody tells you. Including your parents. You can love your parents, but you don't have to believe what they tell you.

"By the time I went to college, the activism was really over. Here I was, where'd it go? The only demonstration was to get the Grateful Dead on campus."

In 1980, he taught classes at the Northwestern School of Journalism. "The kids were worried about money. In every class, it seemed, the first question they'd ask is 'How much do you make?'"

This year, nobody in the class asked me what I make. They asked me questions about ethics: could they follow their own impulses if they worked on a newspaper? I told 'em, on my job I'd just pick up on things that I thought people should know about. I can't be an advocate working on a paper like the *Chicago Tribune,* but I can cover anti-apartheid protests on campuses and at least give them coverage.

I sensed for the first time that kids were really interested in that stuff. About six, seven years ago, it was always money. I think it's changing.

I think part of it is Ronald Reagan. A lot of the kids went to the right because Reagan looked successful. Sure, a lot of people voted for Reagan, but that doesn't mean they're conservative. I think they just went with the success idea. The same thing with Iacocca, I guess. He looks like he made a financial success of himself. If you could find somebody who was liberal and *successful,* and sell him as well as you can sell a Reagan, he'd be in, too.

My sister, nine years younger than me, was attending Notre Dame in '84. She told me she was going to vote for Reagan. A year later, she's out there demonstrating against apartheid. She had been ready to get involved. With me, it was Watergate. With her it was apartheid.

I have no complaint with kids on the right. The ones I've talked to are thinking about issues, at least. However, I think they're a pretty small group. Last year, 125 kids stood up enough to get arrested at Northwestern on apartheid demonstrations. Twenty kids were putting out a conservative review. When the press gives such great play to the *Dartmouth Review,* we almost create something out of nothing. 'Cause they tore down the shanty, right? I'm sure the majority of kids aren't involved one way or the other. That was the case in the sixties, too. I think they're looking for something, ready to get upset.

There was a lot of quiet protest over draft registration. Kids refused to fill out the cards because they're opposed to it. Even though no one was telling them they'd be called up at any particular time, there's something out there that could really swell up if we were suddenly to send kids to, say, Nicaragua.

I think a lot of people, even in their twenties and thirties, have an innate sense of fairness that they've put under wraps for a little while.

MATT NICODEMUS

"I pledge to thoroughly investigate and take into account the social and environmental consequences of any job opportunity I consider."

—16th day of May, 1987

It is a graduation pledge first offered during a commencement ceremony at Humboldt State University, Arcata, California. He is co-author of what he calls "the pledge of environmental and social responsibility." He is twenty-seven years old.

He teaches a course at Humboldt State "on military funding of research at universities." It is his third time around with this subject. He had first taught it at Stanford. His students "range from freshmen to a retired missile designer-engineer."

The draft-resistance movement which began in 1979 is still alive all over the country. It is now over a million. In this respect, there hasn't been much change on college campuses. More importantly, between 7 and 9 million, though registered, fail to send in their new addresses when they move. This is one of the main reasons we don't have a draft right now.

I don't think political activism on the campuses has ever receded. What has happened since the sixties is that it has become more variegated. There are many more issues. The students are not in such close touch with each other as they used to be, so it's hard to get the media to cover it. There is more of a personal focus on economic security right now. It is hard for a society which is so focused on immediate results to talk about the need to be slow and steady, to think long-term, to plan. I think it will have to happen. That's our real challenge right now. Apathy among student has so much to do with their not believing they can make a difference. When they discover they can, they get active.

Back in the early eighties when the draft-resistance movement began, many of us who were resisters first appeared in public. We debated representatives of Selective Service. Frankly, we'd usually make them look pretty silly. By 1982, Selective Service changed their policy. They refused to appear in public with known nonregistrants. They had become so afraid that young people, knowing they had a choice, would choose not to register, even though it was against the law. They had become afraid of us because we were powerful. It's that simple.

With over a million people that haven't registered, they have indicted only twenty. They found that when they indict people, the publicity causes more people not to register. It doesn't scare them, it inspires them to resist. It lets them know they can only put a minuscule part of us in prison. Selective Service, out of fear, will not release statistics.

One of the main reasons they have the draft-registration program is not military preparedness. It's to convince the American public that its youth supports current policies. When many of the youth don't support it, that defeats the purpose.

When I refused to register, I wrote to the president, the secretary of defense, the head of Selective Service, the media. I said under no circumstances will I register and I am prepared to go to prison. You know what happened? Nothing. I did lose five thousand dollars in student aid, but I had expected that.

In the last five years, there's been much more discussion of ethics on the campuses. Remember, many of the young people of the sixties are the professors of today and they haven't changed their basic beliefs.

I discovered from my early days in college there was a whole web of forces to produce students and faculty members who'd participate in military policies, one way or another. Often they deny reality. They say, "My research is pure, basic. It has no application." It's perfectly obvious that the military depends on that basic research for its long-range development. Now, with Star Wars, they're pushing for quicker turnover. They're spending close to $1.6 billion on campuses.

My sister, who's twenty, took part in a survey at Berkeley. They questioned students in the physics department. These are usually labeled the most self-serving, out to get the high-paying science jobs, the engineering jobs. They'd work in the military industry and anywhere else. She found out that many of them are very concerned. They'd rather not work for the military, but they just don't see alternatives. How to create those alternatives is the challenge.

There was a top student, all set to work at Bechtel. When she read the pledge at Humboldt State, she decided to take another job. When people feel they have support from their peers and from the faculty, it's okay to make a decision of conscience. We brought this pledge to a vote, to have it included in the graduation ceremony. Fifty-eight percent voted for the pledge. We discovered that most who voted against it thought it was mandatory. I wouldn't vote for a forced pledge. It was voluntary, of course.

We decided to give the students an opportunity to sign it during graduation. If the university would not officially allow us to be part of the ceremony, we planned to be outside the building with a table. We contacted the media at once. The faculty senate unanimously supported us. The Arcata City Council unanimously supported us. The university started getting these calls from the *San Francisco Chronicle* and the *Examiner*. So they agreed.

During the ceremony, when the names of the graduates were called, they received the diploma from the provost, shook the hand of the president, and descended the stairs. In full view of everybody, one of us was standing there, offering the pledge to each graduate. Out of 893, 750 accepted it.

We don't know how many signed. Next year, we'll ask the university to allow students to sign it right in front of everyone. It would be more dramatic. We handed out leaflets to all the parents and guests, so everyone knew what was going on.

During the past five years, I traveled to dozens of campuses and small towns. In almost every one, there's some sort of peace group. A friend of mine maintains a computer data base on peace groups around the country. Three, four years ago, he had about two thousand, three thousand names. Now he has six thousand peace organizations in his computer. I'm talking about conservative places. You saw the ranchers of Wyoming come out strongly against MX missiles on their land. With increasing militarization, more and more people are seeing how it affects them personally. Students are seeing clearly how under the Reagan administration, particularly, military spending equals cuts in student aid and grants. It's a simple equation.

That's the challenge: to make these issues personal. It's fine to talk about the suffering peasants in El Salvador, but let's not neglect issues closer to home. There are lots of local issues. There are tenure fights. You have popular professors, who are excellent scholars, being denied tenure because they hold the wrong views. These teachers are starting to fight back, with support from students and often from the community.

It's more than just going to rallies. We must have community support in these hard times that I think will get harder. Unless we can offer alternatives, something people can feel good being part of, we're not gonna make it.

ROBERT FRANKE

For the past several years, he has been teaching an honors course at the University of Arkansas–Little Rock: Science and Society.

Most of his students are from Arkansas, urban as well as rural. Almost all come from fundamentalist families; politically conservative and middle-class.

They have learned how to take college tests. They score high, especially in math. They are quite verbal. They give the impression of being bright. Encouraged by their families, they come with the conviction that education is something they want, something they need.

But their definition of education is something else. To them, education is not treated as an opportunity to explore new ideas, to sort out what other people think. For most of these young people, to be educated is to better articulate what they stand for, why they're right.

Early in the course, we talked about the nature of science. We look at it as a process, as a way of discovering ways of looking at our world and universe. They look at facts as something you memorize and tell your kids about, and that's what science is. We're telling them it's a voyage during which we sometimes take a wrong turn, and new findings help us get back on course. Trial and error. They work from a preconceived set of ideas.

They've been taught that the university is a dangerous though necessary place. It's something you need if you want to live comfortably. It's good to be educated, but it's a necessary evil.

You don't challenge any doubts you may have. There are some truths in the world and you know what those truths are, because you've already been taught in church and by parents.

First and foremost, there are religious truths. The assumption is that everyone does or should hold these truths. Almost a hundred percent of my students do not believe in evolution. I ask, ''What is your source of information about evolution?'' Two-thirds say, Home. The other third says, Church. They are assigned reading and they're very conscientious about it. They come to class prepared, their chores done. As though girded for battle. The enemy is any part of society out there that isn't quite what they are. The enemy is anybody who is not a fundamentalist. The enemy is anybody who is not a Reagan Republican. They would never say, I don't like you. They are attractive young people who even like their enemies. They come to school to find out more about those others, to learn how to cope with them. A student told me: ''I'm glad to hear you talk about evolution. I really know what it's all about, but I haven't changed my views. I can answer you better.''

Surprisingly, with these young people, communism is a bit dated as an enemy. They know it was something to worry about in the fifties. Today, it's sort of vague and historical. They have no conception of anything historical. It is only now that counts. We exist for ourselves. The past has nothing to do with us. There's a puzzlement about Russia. They sort of respect Russia because it's developing in technology. They, the Russians, are trying to make it, like everybody else. There's almost a kinship.

We frequently go to the original works. They've read *The Origin of Species*. They become torn because Charles Darwin is so logical. He is also very gentle and persuasive. As you get into his work, how do you respond to a kindly old man writing something interesting? It's very hard to get mad at him. That's what makes this book so diabolic. They're thrown into a turmoil and become very uptight, very angry.

I don't lay this on them very hard at all. I try to be gentle. I tell them I don't expect them to change their point of view, but I do expect them to be receptive to another's so they may be able to contrast the two.

For them, it's a new way of looking at things. I represent a peculiar sort of openness. They're not used to it. They're disturbed. I think they appreciate my respectfulness toward them, but they suspect me as they do anybody who deals with science. I tell them that we need to look at ideas for their own sake and see how they fit into the way they look at the world. It doesn't mean we dislike each other because we have different ideas.

A student, early in the course, will tell me, "Charles Darwin didn't go over too well at home." What probably happened is he took this idea home, took a point of view similar to mine, and threw his parents into an absolute dither. He tried it out just to see how it would go. So when he said, "You won't believe how upset my father got," I realized he was taking the course seriously.

Amazingly enough, the parents are very respectful toward us teachers. We represent authority and knowledge. Their children have been taught that we have some of it and they should get it. Knowledge is something you buy, you own, and then pass on to your children. A piece of property.

I have a hunch, because of their native intelligence, some of these students will do pretty well. They'll probably be managers, directors of laboratories, or work their way up in computer firms. Believe it or not, I have a feeling we may get a couple of writers and possibly a poet. Though these few haven't wholly abandoned the teaching of their parents and church, they're taking into account other ideas, and one day these will fall into place with their earlier views. Perhaps when they're in their thirties, they'll make a radical breakthrough.

Remember, in most cases, they've never been out of Arkansas. Church and family is all they have. It's out of this milieu came their values of what is right and wrong. They believe in Authority. Authority is knowledge. Authority is government. Authority is parent. Authority is church. You do not question Authority.

Robert Franke taught at Iowa State during most of the sixties. "They had their Bible Belt, too. The students were not that much different in upbringing."

Before the Reagan era, they were more willing to grapple with what was right and wrong. They were willing to assume responsibilities of moral choice. I know it's been referred to as a decadent era. I found it just the opposite. There was a search. The great unrest among my students came out of a dissatisfaction with some of the presidents, with what was happening in our society, with wars. I saw it as a time of the young searching, examining alternative ways of doing things, better ways. Always questioning.

The students in my class today are very reluctant to assume responsibility for their own moral choices. If I were to tell them persuasively something patently false, they'd probably go along. It doesn't really matter to them.

In the sixties, there was beneath all the turmoil a hopefulness, a genuine hopefulness that the world would be better. That gave spirit to the time. It is false to describe the young then as lost souls.

I took a poll in my class recently: How many of you feel there will be a nuclear war? Seventy-five percent of the class raised their hands. I was appalled, thinking of their absolute hopelessness. Assuming the Vietnam War were still going on, I have a terrible hunch these students would have said there's nothing to be done about altering the government's stand. What's the point if nuclear war is inevitable? When they all saw *On the Beach* on TV—the world destroyed by the Bomb—I tried to make it personal. They'd have none of it.

With absence of hope, I find an absence of generosity. We had a course on disease. We contrasted today with the time of the bubonic plague: how medicine developed, how attitudes changed, how superstition was challenged. Inevitably we came to a discussion of AIDS, of its devastating effects, of our fears. The prevailing attitude in class threw me for a loop: people with AIDS deserve to die. Others would say, I want nothing to do with them. There was hardly any show of compassion. They were so cold. Of course, if you're going to be blown up, you have to be dispassionate and not worry about people with disease. I don't think that was true in the sixties.

Yet when I showed them a film on AIDS and the dying, they were disturbed. Some in the class cried openly.

PERSONAL NOTES

Girard, Pennsylvania, 1982. It is an industrial town, thirty miles out of Erie. Its people, mostly blue-collar, are experiencing hard times. Since then, things have become much worse.

A controversy had arisen concerning the use of the book Working *in a high school class. A teacher, Kay Nichols, had made it mandatory reading, in conjunction with a course on American labor. The parents of two students objected: they had discovered some four-letter words in the book. It had been an assignment since 1978. Until now, there had been no objections.*

I was invited to the school by the Girard Board of Education. There was to be a public discussion in the auditorium that evening.

I am visiting a classroom in the afternoon. The students range in age from fifteen to eighteen.

HELENE: Our neighbor has the book. My mom looked at it and said some of the words are unnecessary.

How did she discover the words?

HELENE: She was glancing through, I guess.

Have you any idea what effort it would take to find those words in a six-hundred-page book?

BOY: I found one. (General laughter.)

ANGIE: I could see the Christians' point of view. They don't think that language should be used. But we're not lookin' in it for smut words. We're readin' the book as a book.

JIM: A good book moves me. When I read one, it makes me think I should read more instead of just throwin' it back on the shelf.

PEGGY: I don't see why they're objectin' to it. They read worse every day. They speak the same language that's in the book. They're no better than what people say in there.

Do you know anybody who's read the book?

DON: Maybe some of those words could be changed and get the same meanin' across.

JIM: If he would have used any other words, it would have had a totally different meaning. Like Clark Gable in *Gone with the Wind*, when he said, ''Frankly, I don't give a ——.''

BETSY: Some people aren't used to that kind of language. All my friends use it all the time, but should it be in a book?

Jim hesitated in using the word "damn."

BETSY: If they use a word like ''damn'' all the time on TV, movies, people get used to it. Like this movie, Clark Gable said, ''Well, I don't give a damn,'' that was really shocking back then. And then people got to thinking if they said it on TV screens and on the radio, you got used to it. So they started using more offensive words.

What does "damn" mean to you?

BETSY: It's damning to hell. Think of the meaning behind that word. If somebody didn't look through that book, aha, they got away with it.

You interpret the word literally, not as a piece of slang. The Bible, too?

BETSY : Of course.

You don't believe in evolution?

BETSY : Of course not. Hardly anyone here believes in that.

Does anyone in this class believe in evolution?

(Silence. No one raises his or her hand. There are about fifty students.)

GIRL : (Calls out from the rear of the room) I know a girl believes in evolution. Everybody knows her. (Several laugh in recognition.) She says all kind of goofy things. I guess she says it to shock us.

STACY : I personally don't believe in evolution, but we've got it in social studies.

JIM : If you don't read, you always keep that same opinion.

BETSY : I'm not saying it's wrong for you, it's wrong for me.

JIM : Try to keep an open mind about things, not right away shuttin' it out.

BETSY : I know people read this book before and they don't want to read it again because they didn't enjoy it. They should have this choice.

Did you read this book?

BETSY : No, but I seen parts where the so-called words are.

Why did you read the parts where the so-called words were?

BETSY : I wanted to see how bad it was.

STEVE : I read the part in the book about the garbage man. I thought it was good. I wasn't lookin' for dirty words.

TERRY : Do you have HBO on your TV at home?

BETSY : Yes.

TERRY : Do you see PGR movies? Did you see *Endless Love?*

BETSY: If he wants to have these words in the book, fine. But the child should have the right to decide whether he wants to read it or not. Shouldn't be failed if they don't want to.

TERRY: They're not required to read the whole book. They can skip the parts with the smut words.

BETSY: But if there's something I didn't believe in, I wouldn't want to read it.

STACY: Do you always believe in everything you read, evolution and all that? I think it's good to sometimes read something you don't believe in because you see other people's views and it helps you form your own.

That evening the school auditorium was standing room only, overflowing with parents and students. It had something of a carnival spirit rather than a girding for battle; not too dissimilar from the feel of a crowd at a high school basketball game.

There was a touch of tension when the objecting parents entered, with twenty or so of their supporters, in tight formation. Yet there was something else, something poignant, It was not a Roman phalanx so much as a *laager*. They were in encircled covered wagons, surrounded by hostile forces about to overwhelm them. They were moms and pops who had worked hard all their lives so their children could grow up as decent, hard-working, God-fearing Christians in a world of woe. And Sin.

The image of Mrs. R. is still with me. A tough little sparrow, resembling the Irish actress Una O'Connor, she really let me have it. Constantly shushing her boy, Tom, who was wildly erupting with scriptural citations, she was eloquent in her wrath, her hurt, her terrors of something dark out there.

It wasn't the language so much to which she objected. It was the spirit of discontent she found in the book. As, once more, she pushed her boy aside—he was now Jimmy Swaggart sailing into me with Colossians or Corinthians—she spoke of a hard life, heavy laden enough without still more sorrows burdening the young pilgrims at school. Why not show the happy side of people's lives, the cleansing and godly side? Isn't there enough trouble in the world?

All the folks in Tennessee are as faithful as can be
And they know the Bible teaches what is right.
They believe in God above and his great undying love
And they know they are protected by his might.

Then to Dayton came a man with his new ideas so grand
And he said we came from monkeys long ago.
But in teaching his belief Mr. Scopes found only grief
For they would not let their old religion go.

—Fragment from a song by Vernon Dalhart, 1925

1960. John T. Scopes, middle-aged, is listening to the recording. We are seated in a Chicago radio studio. Dalhart's voice comes through bell-clear, despite the record's scratch. I tell my guest it sold a half-million copies in '25. "I didn't know I was that popular," he says.

John T. Scopes, a young teacher in a Dayton, Tennessee high school, a young teacher of biology, had been tried for having violated a state statute: no theory of the origin of man could be taught that contradicted the Book of Genesis. The trial lasted eleven hot July days in 1925. The contest between Clarence Darrow, attorney for the defense, and William Jennings Bryan, prime witness for the prosecution, is celebrated in folklore as well as history. The devastating effect on Bryan's life is also common knowledge.

Toward the end of our studio conversation, another recording by Vernon Dalhart is heard. He had written it as a tribute to Mr. Bryan, who died five days after the trial ended.

There he fought for what was righteous and the battle it
*   was won.*
Then the Lord called him to heaven for his work on earth
*   was done.*
If you want to go to heaven and your work on earth is
*   through,*
You must believe as Mr. Bryan, you will fail unless you do.

"Yes," says Scopes, "I think the tragedy is more man's than Bryan's. Because we haven't advanced too much."

JEAN PRICE

"I'm a mother, a grandmother, a WASP, a principal of a large elementary school." She headed a school in Churchill, Tennessee, a rural community along the North Carolina–Virginia border.

"I was reared in the Baptist Church. My mother and father were very religious and I was taught that everybody is good. When I was dating, I wasn't allowed to go to movies and certainly no drinking."

I'm a believer in God and each morning I would say my devotions. There was a saying: I could do everything through Christ which strengthens me. Norman Vincent Peale had it in one of his books: Say this ten times each morning and it'll help you. I did.

When I was classified as a secular humanist, I was deeply offended. I'm not sure I understand what it is. I was not trained to deal with the issues that have confronted me in the last few years.

I took a mother's complaint as a serious thing. She was trying to help her child, I thought. I trusted her. We spent several times together discussing certain textbooks. She didn't want her child, a second-grader, to be taught from these books. She shared the Gabler Report with me.* Some of the things she complained about was the role reversal of men and women. The mother should be in the home. Jim was cooking in one of the books. She said this was offensive because men should not cook. Neither should boys. That was a woman's role. My husband wouldn't have been eating if men couldn't cook (laughs).

When she talked about the story of the Three Bears, I knew I had a real problem. Why wasn't Goldilocks punished for breaking into

---

* Mr. and Mrs. Gabler of Longview, Texas, put together a 76-page report on the Holt, Rinehart and Winston children's series "and why they should not be taught in public schools." It has been sent to school boards throughout the country. "They've been in this business for several years."

the Bears' house? In the same primer, there were the Three Little
Pigs. They were dancing gleefully and had happy smiles on their
faces, and that wasn't right. I don't know what she wanted. I imagine maybe a sad face.

They formed an organization, COBS. It was the acronym for
Citizens Organize for Better Schools. I was shocked: what do these
people want? She wanted to take her child out of the classroom to
the library or cafeteria and teach her reading. I said that was not
permissible. I went to the board and let them know I could not honor
her request. The school board backed us.

For many weeks, I had no idea how the community was feeling.
Our PTA had a forum to show how our books were selected. Over a
thousand people showed up. We asked them to decide if they want a
democratic process in book selection or a small minority telling them
what textbooks their children would use. When the community ral-
lied behind us, I felt much better.

When I asked this mother to leave the school, she refused. She
herself called the police. She was challenging me to have her arrested. Of course, I had no intention of having a mother arrested.
She had been to City Hall that morning and told the ladies to pray
for her, that she might be arrested. She called the police from my
school. The policeman came after her call, and arrested her. A year
later, I was sued for a million dollars for false arrest.

The charge was that we had violated the mother's civil rights.
Aside from myself, the defendants were the police chief, the arrest-
ing officer, the school board, and the city. We were found not guilty,
except for the school board. The court gave her $70,000. It's on
appeal. The plaintiffs are asking for a complete new trial to bring
us all back in.

The community is a conservative one, but very supportive of me.
When they'd see me on the street or in the grocery store, they'd pat
my arm and say they were thinking about me. They were getting
tired of reading it in the papers. Occasionally we'd get a phone call
from somebody: Why are you doing this? One time I was concerned
that something might happen was when the Ku Klux Klan said they
were coming to town to represent this mother. I thought, Oh, no,
they might burn a cross in my front yard. They came, but there
wasn't enough support for a parade. It was frightening because my
daughter and I were living there alone while my husband was in
Texas.

I'm afraid this has deeply affected teachers. It's caused them to censor what they're teaching. At Hallowe'en, a teacher asked me, "Can I put up witches and ghosts?" I said, "Haven't you always done it?" She said, "Yes." I said, "Why wouldn't you go ahead now?" She said, "The COBS wouldn't like it." I think it's made us question everything we do. Hopefully, it's not harmful to the children, but I'm afraid of what the long-run effect will be.

I always put up bulletin boards during the holidays. During Christmas, as I was putting Santa Claus on the board, I suddenly thought, Do I put Santa Claus up? One of my teachers came by and said, "Santa Claus on the bulletin board? You know the COBS won't like it." I grinned at her and said, "Oh, okay, we've always done it."

At a nearby town, Bristol, a group went to the school board and asked that Santa Claus, Easter bunny, witches, and ghosts be removed. They didn't want their chidren seeing this in school. I guess they feel this doesn't go along with the traditional Christian belief.

I'm afraid of the chilling effect. Every time we get a new parent, my school secretary worries: Is this a true parent or someone brought in to cause trouble? She's had to go through our trial, too, as a witness and the fear has rubbed off on her.

It has affected my entire family, my entire life. Everything I've done has, I think, been affected. When I join my husband, who has a new job in Dallas, I'll probably go back to teaching. But there's this nagging thought that tells me no. I'm suspicious of everybody. I used to be very trusting of everyone. I was very open. I would have said whatever I wanted to say in public. Not any more. It might be used in a court case someday.

She had been addressing a civil liberties group in New York. "Even here, I was suspicious. When the guy got up and asked what I thought of tuition for religious schools, I didn't feel I could answer him. I thought, Are you planted here for a certain purpose, to get me to say things?

I think this fear spread out into the whole community during our court cases. People were afraid to say things, afraid they'd be subpoenaed.

It's changed my attitude, I guess, toward people who are so-called religious. I think it's even affected my going to church. I still go to church regularly, but I don't take everything the preacher says as one hundred percent true. I had always been taught that preachers were right. I've learned through the years that they're not always right, that they're human, too. It's made me question the purposes of some ministers. I never questioned before.

I've always been very positive. I always got up in the morning knowing everything was fine. Now, when I leave home—what's going to happen today?

I'm worried about public schools. I think children need to be taught how to think. So when they get into society, they could make decisions of their own.

My two daughters are teachers. I'm sure they're more cautious now. One of my daughters is talking about getting out of teaching. She said she wasn't sure she wanted to stay in if this is what she might go through. They had to take the telephone calls at home when I wasn't there.

I'm sure our school librarian is very conscious of the situation. I imagine if somebody came in and complained about a book, it would upset her very much. She might just put it in her desk drawer. That would be censorship. I'm sure that would be the easy way out.* We're more aware of the First Amendment and censorship itself. I feel my life has been censored since 1983. I now know what censorship is about, my family knows what it's about. In the lawsuit, my telephone bills were subpoenaed. I thought your home telephone bills and conversations were supposed to be private. But they're not. If I were calling you or any person, I'd think twice.

I definitely worry about the country. We must be aware of attempts being made—in every state, probably. I think public education is at risk.

I hope this episode will not embitter me toward religion, toward school systems, or toward people who have opposing ideas. I hope that I will be able to look at things and know that I have the First Amendment right of free speech.

---

* Judy Descher, director of libraries, Shelby County, Tennessee (including Memphis), tells of a new technique among censors. A book is withdrawn by a subscriber, presumably lost, and paid for. Will the librarian reorder it? If there was controversy surrounding the book—often one that is feminist in theme—she'll think twice. Forgetting about it will be less trouble.

FAMILY CIRCLE

Love, oh love, oh loveless love
Has set our hearts on goalless goals,
From milkless milk and silkless silk,
We're growing used to soulless souls.

—A blues by W. C. Handy

CAROL ROYCE

I'm very happy with my life. It's not the life I would have expected to have twenty years ago. I've got three kids who I'm proud of. Not perfect by any means. Have a house in the 'burbs. I have a job at a place I love. I find life better and better as I get older.

She works as an administrator at a classical-music radio station in Chicago. Invariably, a well-thumbed paperback is on her desk: often, a contemporary novel or a classic. Most frequently, the author is a woman.

Her sons are nineteen and eighteen; her daughter is sixteen. She lives in Lake Zurich, thirty-eight miles outside Chicago. "In the course of eleven years, when we came out here after my divorce, there was one small grocery store that closed at six. Now there are three major shopping centers. But the population has doubled in the past ten years.

"One of the things that's attracted people is the base price of the houses. They are maybe $20,000 less than, say, Rolling Meadows or Schaumburg. There are still lots available with old trees. The subdivision we live in is all four-room houses built for returning Korean vets. These are all little starter homes.*

"We bought the house in '80 at a horrendous interest rate, which is still less than some people are paying. It has a glorious huge yard and big old trees. Now you pay $120,000 for a house that's on a postage stamp.

---

* Chicago middle-class suburbs. Schaumburg has one of the largest shopping malls in the country.

"There's a lot of small industry, artfully concealed. The Mexican population, quite large, is the labor force for the factories. There is a goodly number of very expensive houses hidden away."

My family has gone from middle-class to blue-collar.

I'm forty-four, born two weeks after Pearl Harbor. There was never any doubt I would go to college. When I got married, I expected my children would go to college. The possibility for that was lost in the divorce. There isn't the money. There's only so much you can do as a single parent. And you're gone from the household during the day. None of my three kids has gone to college.

I think Ernie, my oldest, wouldn't have made it at college anyway. He's neither real swift nor interested in pursuing things academic. But even the chance was taken away. Mike would have. He's bright, with a lot of smarts, but he's losing out. When they were little, they saw us reading books all the time. Now, my oldest son and his wife sit there, glued to the TV. Picking up a book is unlikely. They have a four-months-old child.

Ernie is working as a window washer. At least, he has the possibility of making a relatively good wage. But it's something with no security, no pension plans. His wife waitresses sometimes, if he can watch the baby. There's no thought of child care, 'cause they couldn't afford it.

His vision of the world is very small. Hers is smaller. She's young and she's had a hard life. Ernie assumes there will be a nuclear war, that some idiot like Qaddafi or Reagan will start a war. He feels powerless. I say, Get out there, register to vote, for heaven's sake. If you believe in this strongly enough, join a committee, go do something. But this is not his way.

Mike's the one who can really profit from college. I don't see college as a be-all and end-all in itself. I just see it as a way to widen your horizons. He's growing up in a small town. There's a time when you have to leave.

Right now, he's working the night shift at a twenty-four-hour service station, with ten or twelve pumps. He pumps the cash register. His goals are very short-term, to get through the day. Right now, it's to get through the court business and get the fines paid off, and not get his can thrown in jail. He got busted for pot and DUI: Driving Under the Influence. The whole point is he thinks he's smarter than the average cop and obviously he's not (laughs). He plays bass guitar, he's interested in rock music. He's intent and alert in watching the news. He really expected to get drafted and shipped out to the Middle East over this last hoo-ha with Libya.

My daughter, Sarah, is apolitical. She couldn't be bothered to watch a news program. She works in a pizza place and her goal is the restaurant business. She's taking courses in a vocational school. She's single-minded about this.

Ernie hasn't a whole lot of choices. He's got to go out and work at something to feed his family. He's honest, he'll work his full time and not try to cheat you, he'll give you value for your money. But he has no marketable skills.

Sarah has learned a lot from both of them. She thinks getting in trouble is stupid. Happily, she also thinks getting pregnant is stupid. She has better things to do with her time (laughs).

There's really nothing organized to do in this town. There's no YMCA. There's nothing for kids to *do,* except hang out. And there's this constant need to be entertained. Every kid has his little Walkman radio, playing tapes; just as black kids swagger down the streets with ghetto blasters, see how many people they can annoy. There's this constant need to be distracted. I think this is a rejection of thought.

I'd like to get to the bottom of the psychology behind wallpaper music: the stuff you get in dentists' offices, elevators, Muzak. It's meant to get in your ear without being attended to. It teaches people to tune things out.*

I'm worried most about what's gonna happen to my grandson. My worries are small and local. Otherwise I do what I can. For causes in which I believe, if I'm not willing to give my time, I'll give my money.

Sarah says she wants to marry a rich man, so she can have a Porsche. My rejoinder is always: Go out and get rich yourself, so you can buy your own. I think that sunk in. But Ernie I really worry about. He loves his wife, he loves his son, but he's a passive individual, who sees himself as powerless in the world. Mike will get

---

* My first awareness of wallpaper music occurred about twenty years ago. Ten of us entered a restaurant late at night. We were the only patrons. Music, sweet and loud, was being piped in. Conversation was impossible. The hostess, on being asked to turn it off, was indignant. No one had ever complained before.

himself straightened out. He can't be as dumb as he has been (laughs).

How can I compare my experience with theirs? My life was secure and stable, theirs isn't. I don't know one of their friends, in this conservative, middle-class town, who has a mother and father married—to each other. When I was growing up, I didn't know anybody whose parents were divorced.

MIKE ROYCE

Carol's second son. He's eighteen. "My parents were divorced in 1975. I first moved in with my father in Minneapolis. When he decided to go to California, my brother, sister, and I moved in with my mother in Lake Zurich."

I just finished high school and am undecided. Playin' it by ear. I get new ideas here and there about makin' money. I figure once I get money, I don't need anything else. I don't think money's too important, it's just you gotta have it in order to live.

Workin' at a gas station is relatively easy. Doesn't require any major training or anything to run a cash register at a self-service station. The hours are flexible. My boss, he just asks me, Do you want to work today? I say yeah. He goes: When do you want to come in? I'm makin' $4.50 an hour, which for me is good enough. Used to work at K-Mart, and I was only gettin' $3.50. It's okay until somethin' better comes along. A job I would enjoy. I just don't know what it is, unless it came along.

My father was a counselor at college. I think he has a degree in psychology. There's no real pressure that you have to follow in your father's footsteps. In Lake Zurich, there's a lot of rich people, who think they're high and mighty. Those kids'll be pressured, 'cause their father has high status. Their fathers have great expectations for them. They feel obligated to follow in his shoes.

I play bass guitar. Go to hard-rock concerts whenever I scrape up my pennies to buy a ticket. I try not to play other people's music. I like makin' my own music. In a couple a years I'll be doin' my own thing. I'm not setting it as a career, like I'm gonna make it, be a superstar.

I see a lot of my friends at work, so work isn't always work. We talk about what's goin' on, what we're gonna do the next night or I just got a ten-speed about three days ago. I just keep livin' my own life. If somethin' happens, I guess I just have to go along with it.

I read the papers, I watch a lotta news. I let people know what I'm thinkin' when I'm upset. Like a while back, Reagan used Libya as a diversion while he's tryin' to get a hundred million dollars sent to these contras to go fight their own government. Some of my friends are just like: Right on, Ron. Nuke Libya. They're all John Wayne. They loved *Rambo*.

I start a little debate with my friends who sit around an' say, Nuke 'em, get rid of 'em. I tell 'em what I think and if they don't like it, they can just go jump in the lake. I get it out of my system an' feel a lot better. When I turn on TV, I wanna see if Ron has nuked anybody today (laughs).

If you were president, what would you do?

I'd resign. I would not want to be president right now. We're not gonna make it. If I make it to seventy, I'll probably be in pretty bad shape. Just 'cause the way I'm livin' now—fast! Right now, I'm takin' it easy, 'cause this earth is not gonna last much longer. You think two hundred years ago, this land was all trees and all green and animals and everything. In two hundred years, we managed to screw up and put concrete and asphalt on just about every square inch of it. And we have the power to just wipe it out.

A farm I used to work at three years ago, they took three-quarters of all the farmland and built model houses, a waste in itself, because they're not gonna sell those homes to anybody for—what?—three, four, five years. Nobody's got respect for nature any more. Like with real estate. You see all these shows on TV, sayin' how to be an instant millionaire with no money down in real estate. And everybody's getting' into that.

I see Vietnam vets all the time. People come into Mobil, you could tell they been in the war, 'cause they're missin' a couple knuckles on the fingers or the rest of the arm or they come in a wheelchair. We went into a country that we didn't know nothin' about and we got creamed. And these poor guys . . .

I think we had enough wars.

I know the Russians realize that if one nuclear bomb is detonated, that's gonna be it. I think they're smart now. They made that offer in cuttin' down on the arms, I don't see why we don't take 'em up on it. I think it's time. People wanna get married, have families.

I don't want to get married till I'm twenty-five an' have a financial base. Anyway, the virtue of American women is not the high standard it used to be. You can't find decent women any more. Once they turn fifteen, they already know what everything's about. They just start goin' out an' doin' it. By the time they're eighteen, twenty . . .

The wife I'd like has to be a very complicated individual, 'cause she'd have to understand me real good. I'm a nonconformist. The girl we met last night, she's gonna be a mechanic. She's goin' her own way.

I don't think woman's place is in the kitchen. If she stays in the kitchen a lot, she's gonna get fat that way, and who wants a fat wife? Nobody (laughs). If she's out bein' a mechanic, she's smarter than most of the average guys you meet.

WILMA GREEN

She lives in an apartment on Chicago's Near Northwest Side with her two daughters, aged ten and six. "It is a multiculture community. You have your young urban professional. You have your poor single parent living on welfare. You have your newly immigrated Iranian. You have your older people, who've been here from birth up and have seen the community change. And you have your illegal alien."

This evening, the older daughter is at a neighborhood theater seeing Lorraine Hansberry's To Be Young, Gifted and Black.

There are all sorts of books, mostly paperbacks, and record albums scattered about the living room: The Color Purple, Autobiography of Malcolm X, Native Son, *as well as Holly Near and Sweet Honey in the Rock. She works in the office of the ward's alderman, seeing through, at the moment, a tenants' bill of rights. She is twenty-seven. Her energy and ebullience are immediately perceived.*

Myself? The first word I'd use is independence. Pretty, pretty independent. And versatile in my life-style. I think I have a sense of humor, too, that's helped see me through.

I was born and raised in the Robert Taylor Homes.* We moved out when I was fourteen. I'm the youngest in a family of ten children. My father died when I was in seventh grade. My mother raised us herself. I've always seen her as a working person. She set an example for me. This is expected of you: you work. She was an assembly-line worker in electronics. When she was laid off, she worked as a cleaning woman at Malcolm X College.

She said, Don't be, quote, the public aid family. Don't be, quote, the public housing family. Don't be what people expect you to be. Be more than that. If you came home without homework, she would say, You have homework? You'd say no. She'd say, You know everything? You'd say no. She'd say, Well, you have homework (laughs).

In those days, there were strict requirements in the Robert Taylor Homes. You didn't just move in. There was respect which came along with living there. It wasn't a thing of being poor. I never considered myself poor or that it was bad to live in the projects until we moved out. That was thirteen years ago.

We all went to school together. It was family-oriented. There was respect. You didn't walk on the grass or you were fined five dollars. My family won the family-of-the-year award three times in a row. A lot of people cared about where they lived. If your parents

* Chicago's largest public housing project.

weren't around, someone else's parent was gonna set you straight. And you knew it.

We left the projects because of the lack of management and control. Some of the fears were beginning to be coming in at the time. But while we lived there, I sensed a lot of hope.

Why is it that people in the projects feel so hopeless today? You walk out your door and you see the deteriorating atmosphere. I don't mean just the buildings, but the people deteriorating. You never get away from that. You never understand there's a way to get away. It becomes accepted: it's hopeless.

When you go to public aid offices, you sit there all day long. Why don't they have bulletin boards: employment opportunities, skill development, odd jobs? Why aren't they available, where they're gonna be sitting there for a while? I love the city and I get around a lot. I get to see so many different things. Public aid recipients should get bus passes, it would be nice. Why aren't there books for their children?

They feel hopeless because the system imbeds it in these people. Why doesn't somebody tell them there's something out there? We used to have social workers, right? Now we have *case* workers. We used to have workers who understood why people are like they are. And *personally* followed the case. They weren't numbers. Today, a caseworker is someone who deals with paper. There's no history involved. What they do is keep a record and fill out forms.

I remember how they treated me. They didn't even look at my face. Get your number, you sit there and wait. You get your picture. They ask you questions: Who's the father of your kids? Do you know who he is? Can you prove where you live? Can you prove these are your kids?

They wanted social security numbers for my children. Wait a minute, I thought. People got social security numbers when they started working. What's the connection here? My oldest daughter was three and my youngest, three-and-a-half months. I decided not to supply social security numbers for my children. Whenever somebody'd punch up this little child's card, it would indicate she's on welfare. What's the point? That's the only reason they'd need it.

She told me I couldn't get around it. I called the state. I appealed. I didn't have to supply my children's social security numbers. But now everybody has to do it.

I was also going to school at the time. I was involved in welfare rights. And I went to college for two years to Wiley in Marshall,

Texas. A black Methodist school. I came back to Chicago because I was pregnant with my second daughter. I had my first when I was fifteen, while in high school. At the same time, I was part-time cook at a day-care center. While there, I met this guy, a white Catholic organizer. He explained organizing to me. I said, "You mean people get paid for this?" I been doin' it on my own all the time (laughs). Never once entered my mind that people organized around these very things. I was twenty-one at the time.

I started goin' to welfare rights meetings with this guy. One day, I had my youngest daughter on my back, I had on blue jeans and I was looking real scrubby. Well, they put me on a bus and I'm off to Kankakee. I had never really been to southern Illinois.

There must've been two hundred, three hundred people at this meeting. Everybody was dressed except me. It was the annual convention of the Illinois Public Action Council. I'm sitting there, amazed. These people standing up, talking about rights, passing resolutions. I had my little baby with me, so I had to keep goin' in and out because she was cryin'. I went over to the organizer and said, "You guys got me here with my baby. Take her out in the hall and play with her for a while. This meeting's interesting." (Laughs.) I wanted to be part of this meeting.

I saw this real radical group of senior citizens. I could not believe it. Radical seniors! "I was a nursing-home administrator." Wow, this is really incredible. I was standing there in total amazement. Maybe, somehow, there was a role for me.

The woman who was playing with my baby says, "You can be a VISTA volunteer." VISTA, what's that? They explained that it's on-the-job training and would not affect my public aid.

I became educated in organizing and how to get people geared up about an issue. My writing skills were enhanced. I got to know a lot of people. A lot of things I would not have gotten on any other job. Now, I work for the alderman on tenants' grievances.

When I became pregnant at fifteen, a lotta people in the community telling their daughters not to talk to me. Look at her, her life is ruined. I knew in my heart I wasn't a bad girl. I was gonna prove it to people. My mother and my sisters encouraged me to go to Harriet Tubman, a school for pregnant girls. My sisters would say to me: We don't want to see you with your head down. Be proud. Who's to say that because you're pregnant, you're bad.

Nobody mentioned abortion. Nobody mentioned adoption. Nobody even mentioned marriage. You're pregnant, you had a baby, that's it. In black culture, it's something imbedded in you as a Christian. To be honest, I wasn't even dating the guy. It was just one of those things. That's how my family supported me: Hey, this is it, deal with it.

One of the saddest things about Robert Taylor right now is that it's not family-oriented. It's kinda like the waiting room of a public aid office. People are just sitting there. I don't even know if waiting is the word. It's just—we're here. No hope.

There is incredible racism in this world, in this city. When I was comin' up, it was embarrassing to be considered a racist or a bigot. Now it's nothin' to be embarrassed about. I think people take pride in it. Every racist issue they can bring up, they'll bring up. If you can get a case where you can prove affirmative action is discriminating against you as a white person, boy, that's really great. If you can prove that black people movin' into your community really bring down property values, then you really got a case goin' there. If you can prove that havin' a black mayor can really ruin a city, then that's really wonderful. I think it's become an accepted thing.

I think Reagan made it very accepted to be a white bigot. It's the most fashionable thing. Now they say: America is white. America isn't single women on welfare. Why should us taxpayers support these people who ride on our backs and bring this country down? I'm afraid of what's gonna happen to blacks in this country. There are a fortunate few who will get over. But for the many, no way.

What do I see for my two girls? (Sighs deeply.) I feel hopeful about them. They've gotten an education few black children get. They've seen a lot I've gone through. They've seen us grow, they've seen our situation improve. They understand things have improved because of what we've done together.

The discrimination against a woman with children, especially if she's black, becomes part of your working world. When you go apply for a job, they treat you different. They may want to give you the job, but you have two children. Where's the father? That's an unasked question. The curiosity is there. I remember for a while I didn't even mention that I had kids. When they found out: I didn't know you had kids! I look at them: Do you feel I'm a different person now? My children know that because we don't have a man in the house, people short-change us and that you have to watch out. But I don't feel fearful about them.

You can't blind yourself to the real world and what's out there. The younger generation? That's a tough one. I think a lot of white teenagers have found something in music. Bruce Springsteen.

I see a lot of fear when I think about black kids. I always think about the black *boys*—how they lack, quote, positive male role models, unquote. I don't see a lot of black men teachers in schools. Not that they're not out there. I just don't see them in the community where black children happen to hang out.

Because the black men they see are part of the underclass, success is measured by how you dress and the car you drive. In the white community, you hear people sayin', This is your uncle Joe, the doctor. Not in the black community I'm talking about.

Today, the army commercials are wooing black kids especially. I hear people say all the time to their black children: When you graduate from high school, you need to go to the army, to the service. You need the discipline anyway. You can learn a trade.

The dividing line is becomin' clear and the bitterness is growing. You can't help but wonder why. Look at the West Side of Chicago. The major plants have left the community. Why is it? Why is it our streets are not taken care of?

I'm not saying it has to be a city program. It could be church-oriented. It could be grass-roots. Whatever the path is, if people were educated to the different options, they would use 'em. I really do believe that. Look at me.

I still see my mother. She said, "Leave it to Wilma. She figured out a way to make money. Makin' trouble and gettin' paid for it." (Laughs.)

RAY AND SANDY SCHOLL

Lancashire is "your classic bedroom community," says a resident. It is more an enclave of subcommunities, one being wholly alien to another. Though they are all within the radius of a couple of square miles, they are planets apart. There is no downtown. Now are there through

streets. There are several modest-sized shopping malls.
Each of these is the heart of the subcommunity.

Finding this suburb is easy; finding the street you seek is
something else. The names they bear are without exception
Indian: Blackhawk, Seneca, Tomahawk, Sundance, Pueblo,
Ottawa, Iroquois. Despite tell-tale markers—Century 21,
McDonald's, Osco, K-Mart—you are lost. You have gone
round and round: no sign of the street you seek, let alone
the house. Did Parsifal have it this tough?

Four natives, stopped along the way, were courteous,
earnest, brow-furrowed, and of no help whatsoever to the
weary pilgrim. They had never heard of the street. At last,
by accident, you find it. It is within 100 yards of wherever
you had been.

RAY: This is a gray-collar area. You have everything from your welfare Section 8 to some rather affluent people. You can't call it blue-collar, you can't call it white-collar. I guess gray is a good color.

SANDY: The middle class seems to be disappearing here. You have your working poor and your elite. No matter how well you do, you're never quite able to stay ahead. It's harder and harder for the average person to attain the average American dream.

RAY: If you're able to stay even, with those values you had when you were growing up, you're doing well. But your heart of America seems to be eaten up. The average person can't keep up mentally to what's goin' on.

A person today to make a decent livin's gotta make twelve, fourteen dollars an hour. If you want your little house, to get a new car every four years, after you get through payin' it off and maybe go up to Wisconsin fishin' one week with your kids, there better be a second income.

I'm an insurance broker. A small independent. I'm not at a point where I can be your typical insurance agent and spend three days a week at the golf course (laughs). My family when I was young was in the tavern business in Bridgeport.* When I was ten years old, I had a paper route. My dream was to reach the comfort zone. I haven't hit it yet

I was in Vietnam from '68 to '70. We got married right after I came back. We got a sixteen-year-old daughter who goes to parochial school.

SANDY: I started working when I was fourteen, selling Avon. Then my mother and I worked like a team in the basement of a department store, selling.

RAY: I don't think we shoulda been in Vietnam the way we were. But if we were gonna be there, we coulda owned it within a year. They didn't do it right. They lost a lotta people because of stupidity. I can't see doin' somethin' half-assed. This country, if we don't have a war every twenty years, the economy goes raunchy. We need war. It's the only quick fix around. We haven't had a war since 1945. Unfortunately, we haven't progressed to the point we can do without it.

Wasn't Vietnam a war?

RAY: No, it was a conflict.

SANDY: It was a police action.

RAY: No. Korea was a police action. Vietnam was an advisory action. I taught a bunch of dinks to jump out of planes. I taught 'em how to pull a patrol. I got into more firefights because of the Vietnamese. They were so damn stupid. But that's beside the point.

Some of these demonstrators had a sincere belief that Vietnam was wrong. They did what they could to make their point. I guess we ought to build a wall for them, too. All right? That's what's nice about this country, you can have an opposing view. If you can afford the lawyers and take the heat, you can make your view felt.

I couldn't take the heat and say No, I'm not gonna go. Not from my background. I went. I ended up being a Ranger and went a little crazy. I was eighteen. I didn't know which way was up. I didn't even know where Vietnam was on the map. All I knew is a bunch of hillbillies was teachin' me how to kill people. I didn't know what

---

* An old working-class neighborhood in Chicago. Mayor Daley lived there all his life.

the hell right or wrong was. All I know is pretty soon people were shootin' at me.

SANDY: (Cries.) It hurts to think that the men who went, died, weren't even looked on as being patriotic. That was such a disgrace for our country. They came back, not even a thank-you, I'm sorry. You gave your life—for what? So someone could call you a baby-killer?

I'm not saying it was right to go there. But this country was made by people who believed in what our government said. The whole ideal of the American dream was destroyed totally. From that time on, our way of life has changed. It's like another world moved into our system.

RAY: I went there as a little young street punk. I was in gangs on the south side. My twentieth birthday, my presents were fire-fights. I came back a survivor. I gotta do whatever I gotta do to survive. I know what bein' poor is. I lived in the jungle and a couple times I hadda shoot monkeys to eat. Okay, that's poor.

No matter how bad I have it in the United States, I can never be that poor. United States, if a person has any amount of intelligence or ambition, there should be no such thing as adjunct poverty. If he has any intestinal fortitude, the guile, the drive, he can be comfortable. We got more millionaires today than we had in the history of the country. It's because a little maverick came up with an idea, found a couple of marketing people, and hit it. They shot the dice and they won.

All I wanna do is be comfortable. I feel that dream is very attainable in the near future. All right? I have certain associations now, opening doors for me, where the dream is attainable.

I'm not talkin' extravagant. I mean bein' able to get my new car every eighteen months, being able to pay for it on time. Possibly a little vacation place, a camper. Able to take a two weeks' vacation. Put my daughter through college. Go out on a Saturday night, a couple times a month, for dinner on the Gold Coast and not have to sweat about it.

SANDY: I own my own business. A commercial cleaning service.

RAY: We couldn't survive without it right now. We got a hard time survivin' on the two incomes that we do have. I wouldn't want to be my daughter. With what I'm goin' through now, what's it gonna be like fifteen years from now? Things are so fast today. Where's it gonna stop? How high is up?

If you're able to keep up economically, socially, educationally, this has to be one of the brightest times in the history of mankind. But if you're not gonna reach the comfort level, you're gonna have a problem. The average Joe American is gonna give up only so much before he starts gettin' teed off. I got a feeling he's beginning to get upset. He's livin' from paycheck to paycheck.

SANDY: I think the American dream for most people today is just survival. When people came here from the old country, it was for a better life, not just survival. I see that people that come over today seem to prosper faster than the ones who were born here. Maybe it's because they know what it is to do without. They scrimp and save and live meagerly, where the American person, no matter what color, is spoiled. They're more docile, where the new people seem to stick together and help one another. But the average American is just out to help himself, to survive.

RAY: I think Ronald Reagan has done a lot of good things. Mistakes, sure. The last perfect man died on the cross. I don't know anybody who can walk on water. But he's been okay.

The economic situation has improved. There was rampant mass unemployment. For me? It's a bit harder than before he came in. But it was my choice to shoot dice. Most people don't take the risk I took, going on my own. It's not Reagan's fault.

I run a real laid-back insurance business. I got clients you would consider affluent and I got some on welfare. Everybody's cryin' about the same stuff. How society's becoming so cold.

SANDY: Deteriorating. Their morals have deteriorated.

RAY: I'm not much on the moral aspect. I tend to stay away from religion and politics. It's safer that way. But there are certain groups of people, they're able to stick together for a common cause. They've been able to make great strides in a very short time. There seems to be too much of a silent majority today.

I'm used to working with diverse racial groups through the years. Okay, I grew up in a neighborhood where there were derogatory phrases for certain types of people. Black, Hispanic, okay.

We have a situation in this area. It's about a 70–30 mix out here. Everything from people on welfare to all the way up. They keep their grass cut, get along. You got a couple of Archie Bunkers, you got 'em all over. Everybody seems peaceful.

What I'm saying is, certain socioeconomic groups are able to get their story across because they stick together. Black, Hispanic, Asian, they form a cohesive, maybe a bargaining unit. They say, Hey, we've been getting stepped on all these years, and the government pays attention.

But the average American person that's workin' forty, fifty hours a week, they're not puttin' their heads together. Until we do and start sayin' we're payin' too much in taxes, there's too much waste in government, you're spendin' money in wrong ways—until we get that point across as clearly as minorities do, we, the middle class, got a problem.

All right, we, as American, God-fearing people, have an inalienable right to help people that are incapacitated. But since the days of the WPA, there seems to be an underclass of healthy people and all they do is go to an office a couple of times a month and cry. And they get a check. Most people there probably deserve it. I'm sayin' it's not being administered fair. I've gone and written people up insurance, all right? They got a job at the post office, they're workin' for the CTA, and they're givin' me a down payment with a welfare check.

I'm not workin' the ghetto any more. I used to work the Promised Land. That's what the gang-bangers down there call it. In and out of Robert Taylor Homes, in and out of Ida B. Wells. I've worked with people on the dole, all right? I sat there and ate chitlins and greens at the table with 'em. Eighty percent of those people deserve what they're gettin'. There's something wrong with 'em. God bless us that we live in a society that we can help people like that. But you got about twenty percent of them that are pullin' the wool over the government's eyes.

That's a lot of money. That could go into education, into job programs, so you could get people off their rear ends. I don't mean working for $3.50 an hour at Mickey D's. I mean a job that takes some sort of skill.

American people have no pride any more in their work. They want more money, more benefits, and yet we're in worse shape today than we were in World War Two. Why has education dropped? Why do teachers not care? Why do they always go on strike? When I was in school, I don't remember a grammar school teacher goin' on strike, because they were dedicated. You could go into a hardware store and they'd be more than happy to spend time with you. Today you've got a seventeen-year-old kid who doesn't know how to use a saw.

The reason I know some people around here is because I'm active in the community. I do building maintenance, I do landscaping. If I were just an average homeowner I wouldn't know anybody on this block. There's no coffee klatches here, no block parties.

SANDY: I'd say three-quarters of the women work. They have to. Even though our generation has more dollars and more things than our parents', we really have less. We have no pride in our work. We're not as patriotic. No sense of family. A lot of women would like to stay home and make cookies the way my mother did, but they can't afford to.

RAY: I'm shootin' dice right now. I took a big cut to do it, because I couldn't put up with the hypocrisy and innuendoes and the petty bourgeoisie attitudes. I'm not a butt-kisser. It causes me problems. I see a lot of heavy hitters, but they don't bother me. Status is up here in the head.

I see a light at the end of the tunnel. I know what's there. If I'm still here in five years, and God willing I'm healthy, it's gonna be good.

(A long pause.) How do things look to you?

MARY GONZALES

She is associate director of UNO, United Neighborhood Organization, which she helped found. "What is missing in our neighborhoods is a sense of community, a sense of tradition. How do you build it in a society that is losing it?"

The moment you enter the kitchen of her frame house on a street of such houses in this predominantly Mexican community, coffee and cake are served.

Obviously, the name by which this neighborhood has

long been known—Pilsen—signifies non-Latino beginnings.
It has been one of Chicago's early Bohemian settlements.
"It was about ten percent Mexican when we moved in. It's
now about ninety-five percent."

I grew up in Hyde Park, got displaced through urban renewal, went to public housing, moved to Pilsen.

When I first came here, I was shocked. I had never seen so many little frame houses off the street. And they didn't like us, the Bohemian people. They just didn't like Mexicans, they made it real clear. You'd show up at a bake sale, and no one would talk to you. They would speak about you in their language, they would get mad if you used the kitchen: You're not supposed to be in here.

I had come out of this neighborhood where I hadn't felt it. I had spent one year in a black community, where I did feel it, especially young blacks. But here, it was just—slap—like this, it was hard. Pow. Immediately, the first day I was threatened, I got angry.

I was thinking in my mind much like a gang-banger does. A sense of needing to survive. I was less able to deal with it than I could in the projects, because it was more subtle. It wasn't young people accusing me, it was older women and men. Mother was tremendous at building bridges with these women. I used to say, Forget 'em.

There were eleven children. I was the oldest. My father was the only person working, a laborer at Wisconsin Steel. It was hard. My mother was always out in the neighborhood, trying to figure out what she could bring to the family.

I was in a different place than my parents were when I was growing up. My aspiration was to learn to type, get a job as a secretary, have a desk, a telephone, and make a good living.

As more Hispanics were moving in, the Bohemians were much more accepting. I'd made friends, getting involved with the local school, and suddenly it wasn't that bad a place. They changed, knowing us. So did we. I got my neighbors together and said, Let's buy our food together at the South Water Market. A buying club. Once a week, we would shop for everybody. Like potatoes for three cents a pound. It was great. We used to close the streets and have parties for the kids once a week during the summer. Everybody would show up.

In the sixties, values were changing. People were beginning to live with one another versus being married. Okay? Now abortion gets introduced. In the forties and fifties, when I grew up, the rules were very clear. Now, what does it mean to be a Catholic? It depends on what church you go to.

People are now shopping for churches. In the old days, you went to the church where your parents and grandparents went. And you expected your chidren to go. There were expectations of a community. You never thought of living with your boyfriend, because what would the community think? They expected you would marry in their presence in the church. Those expectations are gone because the community's gone. The community is based on shared values.

My father died a year before retirement. He prided himself as being the only person who never missed a day's work in thirty-five years at Wisconsin Steel. My mother gets forty dollars a month pension from the state.

Goin' through your life, these experiences are burnin'. My mother was more aggressive than I was. I remember as a child being worried, thinking, Gee, my mom's taking a risk getting involved with the landlord. It could get us in trouble. I remember her standing at the door—there were nine children, my mother, my father, my grandfather—screaming at the landlord at the top of her lungs, because there was no heat and she had a new baby. We had the oven on to keep the baby warm.

In Pilsen, she volunteered for a lot of things. The first project we pulled off was for my brother Bobby. He's severely retarded, used to get grand mal seizures. He'd break windows, attack people, throw things.

One day, a crazy man came to our door, a professor. He was interested in handicapped children. Would we help him get public funds for a school for kids like Bobby? People warned us that this guy's weird and might pass things on to Bobby. I felt if Bobby can learn anything from him, it's a plus. So we began Esperanza School for Retarded Children. Esperanza—Hope. We did everything to get the state to put up the money. And Bobby went to school for the first time in his life and made friends and looked forward to every day.

Some of the same crazy people we were warned against now said, Let's get a program started for adults. The state said there's no documentation of a need for a sheltered workshop in this area. So we knocked on every door in the neighborhood, looking for people physically or mentally handicapped.

We came to the state with seventy-eight names. They said there's no money. We were so frustrated. We went to the people of Esperanza School, it was now established, and said, We're going to the bank and would like you to guarantee a loan for us. We got $10,000, went to a local priest and said, Can we use your empty school? We hired someone at a minimal wage and opened shop with twelve people. We didn't know what we were doin', but we were doin' it. Within a week, the state was crawlin' all over us: You're not allowed. We said, We did it and we're not closin'. So they sat down, negotiated, and gave us $20,000. That was 1972. Today, this workshop has four residential centers and a baby center. And is $1.7 million. This all started because we had to get something for Bobby.

We had trust in each other, no matter how scared we were, and made the vision possible. That's what's missing in our society today. That's why we have such a low electorate: people saying I can't make the difference. You get a group of people together and you can do any damn thing you want. This whole drive to individualism. People don't know one another on the street. Afraid to get to know. They don't know people that go to mass. Remember the old days of the local grocery store? People would see each other. They're gone. They've been replaced by Jewel Foods, by Osco, by nameless shoestores. This neighborhood still has a lot of the old and we're trying to preserve it.

There's another isolation: within ourselves. We feel incompetent. I lost my job at Wisconsin because I'm worthless. If I had more skills . . . Instead of saying, It's Chase Manhattan that created Wisconsin Steel's closure, it's not you. So we turn to alcohol, drugs, and television. So we live in the world of *Dallas,* of daytime soaps, in a world of fantasy. So we don't have to deal with the real world.

In the sixties and early seventies. I viewed myself as a person who had to change something. I had to get the garbage picked up regularly or get rid of some principal or get a new school constructed. Now, evolution has brought me to saying: I have to change how people view themselves in the world. I have to get people to believe that they can in fact make the difference. If I can create the transition in the human being, the garbage and the school will get taken care of. We view ourselves more as people trained to develop people. Issues are only tools.

Think about the guy who works in a factory. He's on the assembly line. He's a nobody. He doesn't do the kind of work that's ever gonna get him recognition. Take that same person and he's a key leader in the parish or in a union. Suddenly that same man, who from Monday to Friday stands on the assembly line at General Motors and is nobody, is somebody over here. People look to him. He makes a difference and he knows it. He counts.

GRACE AND JULIE MERRILL

Grace, sixty-six, the mother, is Spring Byington in appearance, placid in nature, sweet of face, girlish in voice. She works as a cashier at the Ariadne, a teenage juice bar. It is night work.

Her husband had been a physicist at the University of Chicago, invited by Fermi. He dropped out, became interested in Scientology, went on to other work, and "just kind of got lost."

Julie, the daughter, is twenty-four. Her granny glasses and pioneer dress offer the image of the hippie of two decades past. She attends classes at the Chicago Art Institute.

GRACE: Oh, boy (laughs). I'm a seeker of all good things. Just an observer of life. I really dig living and the variety of people and places.

I had my daughter late, when I was forty-two. I was one of those good-time people, not much different than the generation today. I was daring. I was drinking and dancing and whooping it up. Not really thinking too much about the future. I had a baby girl in 1962. I was in with the hippies. I wasn't a pot smoker, but I enjoyed the people as they came along. We had a lotta hippies in our house.

The kids today seem to like incongruity. They're daring, they're hopeful, yet sometimes they're lost. I never hear them talking politics. It's more the New Wave type I see at my work. You do your own thing. You play music. You dance just as you feel it.

When I'm taking their money, oh gosh, I wish I were a talent scout. They're so sweet and dressed so nicely. Others have the weird hairdos, where they spray their hair and pull it out in points. Spiked. Punk rockers. On Saturday night, it's so jam-packed you can hardly move.

They've got their tape recorders. They're playin' that music, dancin', carryin' on. Ariadne's asked them not to go to Dunkin' Donuts because the police are after them, say they're rowdy. Some of the music they play I like. Some of it is just intolerable. I can't make out the lyrics very well. The music is very loud, awful.

Sometimes the guys look like girls. There have been occasions when I've smelled pot. We have to stop it immediately. And no drinking. We have no license. The neighbors blame any kind of theft or car-breaking on these kids. Our security doesn't allow gang members in. They turn away undesirable people.

The Ariadne kids are tougher than the flower children, yet they're tender, too. Back in the sixties people started using all the four-letter words. Everything was fuck this, fuck you, fuck. Some of the older people, like myself, understand and don't rebel against it. But other people: Oh, it's just terrible! Most people's attitude is, Well, fuck you. Isn't that so? That's just about the size of it.

These punk rockers want to belong in a group, yet they want to be individual. That's why they dance by themselves even when they're together.

The middle-class kids are the only ones who have the money to buy the records and buy the fashion the lower-class kids started. The underground is expensive. It's primarily a middle-class thing.* They're upset about they've been brought into the world, like they're mad at just the fact that they're here.

JULIE: The music has a thrashing sound. Techno-pop. Thrash music is very fast: a pulsating guitar and a lot of screaming. A lot of slam dancing.

Doom and gloom has kind of died out. I can't figure out what's replaced it. A lot of hard-core punks don't want any of this political

---

* A familiar sight along the posh, expensive Lakeshore: the doorman, half bowing toward the bizarrely clad young gypsies. They are the children of the sleekly groomed condominium owners.

shit. They're not interested in politics at all. They don't register to vote. A lot of them feel there's no future. We're not gonna survive this lifetime, so we might as well have a good time. The poorer kids find piddly jobs to do. A Xerox boy downtown in an office. A messenger, waitress. Ariadne is blue-collar as well as upper.

Ariadne started out as a gay place. Gayism has a lot of infiltration into this young new movement. It's easier to come out of the closet. To a large extent, though, it's heterosexual. They like to drag, to crisscross. It's androgynous. Mom gets pissed off when I dress like a guy.

GRACE: Sometimes she gets in slacks and this, that, and the other. I mean, she's not lesbian, but I don't like that. I mean, she should dress to attract a man.

It's astonishing the number of girls I've talked to and they'll say, Yes, my brother's gay. It is absolutely rampant. It bothers me.

JULIE: It bothers me, too, because every guy I meet seems to be gay. Or they're not sure. They can't make up their minds. I was involved with a guy in high school and he turned around and said he was interested in another guy. I've even had gay feelings myself —(hesitates, then softly) I'm sorry, mom. She can't— But it's disturbing when half the people you know seem to be gay. Maybe it's because I worked at Ariadne. I worked in a gay restaurant. And I go to art school. It does attract . . .

GRACE: She's living it. I'm just observing it.

JULIE: Mom's been through it all. She went to Europe right after the war and lived in Jean-Paul Sartre's house. Was involved with all those poets in Europe at the height of the beats and the Dadaist movement.

A lot of people have dropped out of the scene. People I used to hang out with, after high school, they've gotten jobs. One guy I ran into on the street, he said, ''Do you remember me?'' He's doing computers and he's gonna get married.

I went through the same scene myself. I wasn't gonna go to school. I didn't read. I didn't do anything except listen to rock music and dance and drink and carry on. I did a lotta drugs. It fell apart and one day I flipped out.

Who can you trust any more in this constant making of arms? The world is a little bit too heavy for itself.

It works in cycles. Like with my parents. My mom and dad were very liberal. Kinda whacky in a sense. I don't mean this in a bad way.

GRACE: Isn't the whole world nothing but creation? How can it be any different? It's all scrambled eggs. I think it's in one grand, glorious mess all over the world (laughs). But I'm optimistic.

FAMILY FARMER

Oh, the farmer is the man,
The farmer is the man,
Lives on credit till the fall.
With interest rates so high,
It's a wonder he don't die,
For the mortgage man's the one who gets it all.

—A Populist song, 1890

LOU ANNE KLING

*We're heading out of Minneapolis toward Granite Falls,
130 miles to the southwest.*

 *She is state coordinator for the farm advocate program
of the Minnesota Department of Agriculture. It is in the
nature of ombudsman work, advising distressed farmers of
ways and means of survival. "There are twenty-five of us, a
drop in the bucket." It is the first such program in the
country.*

 *We pass through too many small towns with too many
deserted Main Streets that evoke too many images of too
many rural hamlets of the Great Depression: Bird Island,
Sacred Heart, Ghent, Montevideo, Renville.*

 *It is 11:54 A.M. as we pass through Bird Island. The
restaurant—is it closed or open?—is empty of customers.
There is a lone figure shuffling along the street. His
baseball cap, blue and red, offers the only color aside from
the overwhelming dusty gray. The appliance store is
empty. The Legion Club is closed. There's Bob's Country
Market, but where are the patrons? In one store window is
the sign HAPPY MOTHER'S DAY.*

 *There is a pervasive silence in all these towns. She says,
"Both a silence of protest and a silence of acceptance."
"Look at the new bank," she says, as we pass through into
Sacred Heart. Immediately, here, we see boarded-up stores,
one, two, three in a row; the Vets' Club, three flags out,
closed; the funeral home, closed; the beauty shop, closed;
Red Owl Hardware, closed; 232—a speed wash—closed;
the pharmacy, closed; an Archer general store, closed.
"A new bank has opened," she says.*

In Olivia, capital of the county, we stop off at a restaurant frequented by the local farmers. Three young people pass by our table without a nod, without any acknowledgment. "Of course, they know me. They're loan officers of the Farm Home Administration. I've dealt with them many, many times. I guess they're not very fond of me.

"As advocates, we find out what the rights of small farmers are, the rules and regulations. They're on a different course, so we often butt heads. One of them told me he's sick and tired of serving these poor farmers. They are frightened more than usual at this moment because I have a stranger with me. They think you might be a lawyer. These are a new breed of farm children."

I was born on a family farm. My great-grandfather homesteaded it. It is known as "the Long-View Farm." It is of great concern to me that the farm stay in the family for future generations.

Today none of the younger generation even has the slightest hint of its distinct name. Here all my great-aunts and uncles were born. The young don't know it and don't care to know. They've been schooled that history is not important. It just doesn't make any difference. They've been taught the belief that production, book-keeping, and expansion is important. The land and its conservation has no meaning. Self-centeredness and selfishness has become the farmer's way of life out here, instead of neighborliness, conservation, and families.

My father would tell about the Great Depression only as a sermon: "You always pay cash. You don't buy things you don't need. You don't run up bills. Or you're gonna lose it all." The Depression was never a big topic of conversation. It's the same with most farm families.

My husband, Wayne, and I have become involved in the farm movement and we talk of the Depression. The farmers don't seem to understand what we're talking about. It's scary that people don't look back on history.

With the farm crisis, there's tension between fathers and sons. The father is trying to hold the reins on things because he can remember the Depression, but he hasn't told his son about it. So the son, on his way to town, sees a couple of neighbors have got some new machinery. He goes to the implement dealer. He starts kickin' the tires of the new machinery. The dealer comes out: "Do you need something new?" "Yeah, but I can't afford it." "Ah, anybody can afford this. No interest till fall, no down payment. Why, we'll deliver it this afternoon for ya." "Okay, I gotta have it."

He comes home and tells dad, "I bought a new tractor today." The dad says, "You shouldn't have done it. We can't afford it." The son says, "You old duffer, you don't know what you're talkin' about. My God, So-and-So bought one."

The kid gets mad and huffs outside. And dad sits in a chair and says, If I'd have been a better farmer, we'd have had more money and would have been able to buy that new tractor. I'm gonna cash in my life insurance policy and pay that bill so my son don't know that we're in tough shape. He'll hide it from his son as long as he can and let him continue to think it's okay. The majority of farmers still feel that they're failures. They didn't produce right, they didn't farm right. They've been farming forty years and they don't think they've done anything right. They blame themselves.

> *"Of course, he blames labor, too. High wages are the reason why the tractors cost so much.*
>
> *"During the P-9 strike at Hormel up in Austin, a number of us farmers drove our tractors up there, in support of the strikers. A lot of the other farmers couldn't understand why the labor people wouldn't go to work. They themselves were in such financial difficulties. So they became scabs, union-busters."*

I don't hear a solitary farmer say, If we had organized and fought those responsible, we wouldn't be in trouble today. They say, If I would have farmed a little bit better . . .

Farmer Brown had just about lost his farm during the Depression, but some of the Holiday guys* went with him to the insurance

* The Farm Holiday Association was a militant farmers' group in the 1930s.

company and helped him renegotiate a new loan and that's how he saved his farm. But there's no way he'd ever admit it and he surely never told his kids about it.

I just had a minister down here. I was talking about one of his parishioners: "Your farmer is in serious trouble. I feel he's close to suicide. He needs you to come see him." He couldn't understand why his minister hadn't been there. He felt he was a failure, and this was further proof. I said, "You got to go out there." The minister said, "But it is his fault." I'm flabbergasted. The minister's wife chimes in: "Do you know when those people had graduation, they had to have fresh-cut flowers?" I said, "Is that a sin?" "No, but they were extravagant."

There are a lot of suicides out here, but it's kept very quiet. Families are ashamed of it and don't talk about it. Teenage suicide among farm kids is alarming.

I couldn't figure out why these two little kids wouldn't come home on the school bus any more. One afternoon, they came home on the bus and they saw the machinery being hauled away. On another afternoon, they saw the livestock hauled away. The kids said, if they rode that bus again, they'd be hauling mom and dad away. So they would not get on the bus. They were about eight.

I knew this sixteen-year-old boy. I was at his farm, working something out with his parents. They kept shushing him out of the room. He asked if he could have a ride to town with me. As soon as we got in the car, he screamed at me, "What's goin' on in my house? Is my father dying? Is my mother dying? What are you doing there all the time?" I just told him his parents were losing their farm. That boy just cried and cried and cried.

It's just tumbling down the generations. They're not sharing history. They're not doing it as a family. When a farm foreclosure is printed in the paper, the kid's in school the next day and the other kids talk about it. They heard their parents at home: "Oh well, they did it wrong, that's why they're losing their farm." The other kids may mock him, while their own families may be just weeks away from having it printed about themselves.

There's a meanness in the land that wasn't here in the thirties. We're losing a feeling as a people.

When we moved to our farm in 1970, there were ninety-six farms in our township. We counted a year ago, there were only thirty-six. People just don't realize how fast the decline is happening. The farmer who has retired is still living in the house, but he's not farming the land. It is being rented out. There are fewer and fewer family farmers, while some neighbor may be getting bigger and bigger landholdings. There's not much excitement because the old-timers are still there in their building sites. "They're only renting that land out to a neighbor boy."

The average age of the Minnesota farmer is fifty-five to fifty-eight. In the next ten to fifteen years, that land will be under some new ownership. There are some corporate buyouts, but Minnesota has a tight corporate law. So our communities are not too upset. They see the local boy making good. That local boy has been taught to get self-respect in the community, you gotta be big and successful. Stomp your neighbor, if you have to. He's come through the seventies educated at the university in farm management. He knows nothing of history, of Farm Holiday, of the New Deal. I'll bet he wouldn't know who Franklin Roosevelt was. But he does know being big is being successful.

The kids have given up farming. They move to the city or join the military. They see it as a schooling and a way out. Our second son is in the marines. I don't think our oldest son ever wants to come back and farm. He's just seen it as a place of work, work, work and no money. Our two youngest boys are different. They grew up with us protesting and involved. They say they're gonna be farmers.

I see megafarms coming in with young land barons managing them. All around us we have these new father-son teams really expanding. Wayne says, "I feel like a pimple. They're squeezing all around. How many years am I going to be able to hold out before they pop me out?" He comes from a four-generation farming family.

The ones that stay no longer own their land. Major lenders out here say, Deed the land to us and we'll rent it back to you. They're hiring farmers who have lost their farms. Tenant farmers in Minnesota! Yes, it could be like feudal times.

Take the farmer with three thousand acres of land. His hired men are his two neighbors who have lost their farms. There are no jobs here in the countryside. They have to make a living. The broke farmer can live on his own building site for nothing and work his own land for someone else.

Our job is really to go door to door educating farmers on their rights. What I run into is a shrug of the shoulders: No problems. In 1982, when the crisis was already here and they're paying twenty percent interest, I'd ask, Don't you have an issue? No, not really. You have to bang your head against the wall.

But I do see, at last, more farmers getting militant. He's the one who says, "This is *no* fault of mine." I had a farmer in the office the other day who'd been at it forty years. The FHA tried to break him down, so he'd believe it was his own fault. He finally exploded: "It's not my fault. It's the government's fault. It's the fault of nobody giving a damn." So, he's fighting.

A couple of years ago, in Minnesota, we had 17,000 farmers on the Capitol steps. On a cold January day. It was a new organization called Groundswell. We got one of the best farm bills passed in years. But so far, there's been no real follow-through. When we had that tractor parade to Washington in '78, I thought to myself: Boy, this is it. Old Milo Reno and the Farm Holiday reborn. No. All this stuff was short-lived. The farmers grab one little parcel and run home.

Wayne, later on, in the kitchen of his parents' farmhouse, recounts an action of Groundswell:

"Two years ago, in '85, we were backing up this small implement dealer. He wasn't selling enough machinery to make his payments. Tenneco, which owns J. I. Case, the farm implements manufacturer, decided to foreclose on him.

"We guarded his machinery for several weeks, twenty-four hours a day. They were gonna haul it away, repossess. This small dealer was a symbol of what the family farmer meant to us.

"About seven one morning, a bunch of truckers came. We got the word out. We had barricades across the gate. They were tearing 'em down. We asked them, 'Are you with the farmers or the company?' Several others lay down in front of the semis. We were arrested for obstructing the legal process. I asked for a jury trial and was released.

"My neighbors don't talk about it. They'll discuss weather or fertilizer or bugs, but not the farm problem. If they don't talk about it, it doesn't exist."

There are far less implement dealers. We're losing all our country elevators. They're merging, merging, merging, becoming bigger, bigger, bigger. We had three co-op elevators in in our area that were swallowed up. Harvester States bought 'em up. We've got Cargill buying up local elevators. We have one implement dealer in our town. He lost his Case dealership because he didn't have the thousands of dollars to put up.

> *She points toward a barren field that appears endless.*
> *There are vast spaces that offer the incongruous*
> *appearance of baldheaded crowds. The color—the pallor—*
> *is a sickly sandy gray.*

All those acres, not a tree, not a blade of grass. Nothing to stop the wind from blowin' across. When you lose the farm, they bulldoze the grove down.

Our land is very vulnerable. There used to be a lot of pasture land. That's all been broken up. It's now dry and wide open to Mother Nature to do with as she pleases. The grasslands are gone, because the farmer can't afford conservation any more. Production is what it's all about today. He's got to farm every inch to make a living, to stay alive.

There's no topsoil left. It's been worked and fertilized and washed away. There's six inches left. It used to be six feet. Multiply this—these white-tops—by hundreds of thousands of acres, all of a sudden, with a dry spell and drought and a wind, you've got a dust storm. Will it happen again? People are beginning to talk about it.

> *We're at the Rural Education and Resource Center in*
> *Granite City. It's her office; two of her colleagues are at*
> *work.*
> *Near the entrance, against the wall, is a shelf laden with*
> *canned goods. There is a hand-painted sign: FARMERS,*
> *YOU'RE WELCOME TO THIS FOOD ANY TIME. Underlined are*
> *the words SERVE YOURSELF.*

A lot of farmers are coming in and getting food. We get their paperwork straightened out and send 'em home with food. They're real hesitant to take food off the shelf. You have to practically push it on them. It's a big help to them. We've served at least ten farmers during this past week.

Many of them are no longer coming in as farmers, but as the hired man.

PETER RYAN

"Social and religious movements linking the troubles of farmers to an international money system have emerged periodically in the Middle West and the Great Plains since the late 19th century.... These movements took on a strongly anti-Semitic tone in the Depression when Father Coughlin of Royal Oak, Michigan, and the Reverend Gerald B. Winrod of Wichita, Kansas, attracted hundreds of thousands of believers by preaching religious fundamentalism and anti-Semitic economic theories.... Meetings are occurring in this season when snowdrifts and sharp winds bring idleness and despair to much of the Middle West."

—New York Times, *December 7, 1987*

His voice is soft, gentle, friendly, yet the tone of despair is unconcealable. During the conversation, a rising feverishness sets in.

His Minnesota beef farm is ten miles from the South Dakota border. He is forty-nine, has three children, none of whom plan to farm. "No man in his right mind would want his son or daughter to be a farmer today. They'd starve."

He had for a time been football and basketball coach at a rural high school. He lost his job because of declining enrollment. "In 1975, when I started, the graduating class was 132. We had 46 teachers. This year, there are 51 kids graduating and 15 teachers."

It's worse than the thirties. There are no young farmers out here. They go to the Twin Cities to find work. There is no work. They become street people. Instead of raising food, they end up in soup lines.

Just the other day, the grandson of a neighbor shot himself to death. His ma and pa had been kicked off their farm. It was too much for him. He was twenty-four.

Last Friday, the bank foreclosed another neighbor. They hauled off his equipment. His son went to where they stored it and drove the tractor home. He needed it to farm. They now have him on a felony. He can get up to twenty years. For stealing his own tractor.

In 1982, when the bank foreclosed on me, I was able to hide some cattle. I saved nine heifers.

The government bails out Wall Street banks in New York but not family farmers. I went to Washington in 1977 to testify against the Federal Reserve System. Two days after I came home, I was shot at from a car waiting in the driveway. I think there's a connection. They were trying to scare me. They brought charges against me for filing a false police report. They say it never happened. I was put on bail for a year and a half, so I couldn't leave the state. I sent my wife and kids on that tractorcade to Washington.

We are the birthplace of the American Ag Movement.* There were six of us who started the tractorcade ten years ago. There was fight in us then, but it's gone for most of us.

Who's responsible? It's the five big grain companies. Most of them have summer homes in the Ukraine, Russia. They're all communists.

A small group of farmers agree with me. I think there are a lot more, but they're afraid, have given up, have lost the will to fight. Not Larry Humphreys. He travels across the country and still has lots of fight in him.

---

* The American Agricultural Movement is a moderately militant farmers' group with a small staff in Washington, D.C.

These companies have all the power. They killed Franklin Roosevelt. Poisoned him to make it seem like a heart attack. The Pugwash Conference had something to do with it. Averell Harriman, the Rockefellers. They wanted a balance of power in the world, so they decided to give all Eastern Europe to Russia. Elliott Roosevelt told me—though he'll deny it—that his father said, ''Over my dead body.'' It was over his dead body.

I went to the Legion hall to tell them about these things. They didn't care. They said, ''We don't want any more wars.''

Lyndon LaRouche is the last game in town. I like Lyn. The first time I met him, he seemed too far-out for me. I now see he was right on target. Most farmers are scared of him because he tells the truth. He and I differ on a few things, so I'm not a member of his group, though I've been accused of being. He doesn't believe in the Zionist theory as I do. I wish you could be a Christian so I could explain it better to you.

I began to get these feelings after more and more small farmers, myself included, were being pushed against the wall. My teacher was Arnold Paulson. He wrote a book on it. They killed him. I can guess who.

Most farmers can't handle the conspiracy theory. They tune you out. I believe in it. It goes back to Adam and Eve, good against evil. Christ in Matthew 6:24 identifies it. You can serve two masters: God or money. If you're a Christian, you can serve only one.

I know it's hard for you to believe. But if you're foreclosed and get beaten up a few times as I did when I ran for Congress, and get shot at, you begin to see the truth.

They say the Jews are the Chosen People. There are Jewish people who are lovable and I'd give up my life for them. I believe they will eventually come to Christ. But Revelation 2:9 says be careful of those others who say they are Jews. They're not. They're the synagogue of the devil. The Zionists. The international bankers are not Jewish, they're Zionists. I believe they want to set up a messianic kingdom, with them as masters and the rest of us as slaves.

Think of what the farmer faces today. You have no idea how desperate he is and how hopeless things are. I personally think the enemy has won. We're beaten.

I liked Reagan until recently. He was a good man until Casper Weinberger left him, when he sold out. It's the forces behind him. The merchants of grain and David Rockefeller and Armand Hammer. He's the biggest scoundrel in the world. When the fourteen-member Politburo swore in Gorbachev, the third man to his left was Armand Hammer. Reagan is taking the missiles out of Europe, so Russia can take over. Just as they'll take over South America. Our Constitution will be rewritten so the Bill of Rights will be erased and trial by jury. You realize a foreclosed farmer can't have a jury trial now. If he commits a felony, he can.

Larry Humphreys still has some fight in him and he gets farmers to listen. But I feel most are so beat-down that the family farmer is destined for collapse. They're going to make him a peasant. Once they have all the farmland, we'll be serfs on our own ground. The farmer can only go down on his hands and knees and pray. I don't know what else he can do.

We need a revolution. We need a dynamic new leader, a George Washington.

LYNN HAYES

She is thirty-one, a staff lawyer of the Farmers' Legal Action Group (FLAG), St. Paul, Minnesota. She is active in defending the interests of the small, beleaguered farmers, often against heavy odds. Most frequently, they are class-action suits.

She majored in the humanities at Coe College, Iowa, and subsequently attended Catholic University Law School, Washington, D.C.

The reason I went to law school—I thought there were underprivileged classes in the country who did not get a fair deal. They either couldn't afford big-time attorneys or they simply weren't recognized. I entered school with the intention of practicing public-interest law, working for the underdog. At school, there was a definite push to put the people at the top of the class into big corporate law firms. I had to wake up in the morning and remind myself why I was there.

I'm not the kind of person who fights outside the established order of things. There's a procedure in the United States that should be helping the underprivileged: the judicial system. My older brother, who is more of an activist than I am, thought it was crazy: by going to law school, I was buying into the whole establishment.

My parents did a wonderful job of raising independent-minded children. My mother had always been active in helping the migrant workers near our town.* My father had always been sympathetic. They always allowed us to make our own decisions.

I did fairly well in law school. A lot of the professors were pushing me to be on the *Law Review*. To me, this stood for a very establishment-minded way of thinking. People go on the *Law Review* because it looks good on their resumés. I avoided it. Friends with whom I graduated walked out of law school with $50,000-a-year jobs. I walked out without a job. I landed one with Mid-Minnesota Legal Assistance. It was partially government-funded, helping low-income people.

I'm all excited, I call my parents up. The first thing my dad does is give me a lecture for twenty minutes on the phone how I'm not even going to be able to pay my bills with that salary—and I had lied about my salary (laughs). I told him $13,000. It was like $12,500 or something. He was happy that I had a job, but he thought I was crazy. It was about a fifth of what my classmates were making. I assured him it would be tight but I'd make it. My mother was thrilled. A couple of days later, the nicest letter I'd ever gotten from father said how proud he was of me. So I'm sure it was after my mother talked to him (laughs).

There were about 165 in my graduating class. The school had a very good reputation for social-minded legal work. To tell you the truth, a nun who went into a legal service program was the only other person in class.

I worked in a small Minnesota town of about 7,500 people. It happened to be an all-women office—three attorneys, a paralegal, and two secretaries. I got involved with farm work because our paralegal had lost her farm to the FHA.† They were foreclosing on people without giving them their due process rights. Congress, in

* Rochelle, Illinois, eighty miles west of Chicago.
† Farmers' Home Administration.

'78, had given FHA authority to grant farmers deferrals: more time to make their payments when they fell behind. FHA refused to use the program at all. We were getting hundreds of calls from farmers all over the country. We couldn't represent all these people, so we published a guide to FHA: farmers' rights.

In 1985, we started the Farmers' Legal Action Group, funded mostly by the farm aid concert of Willie Nelson. I feel safe with this group, because the Reagan administration is putting lots of restrictions on government-funded legal services. I can't take individual cases, there are too many. More than fifty percent of the family farmers are in deep trouble. We have a class-action suit right now representing 230,000 farmers across the nation.

I've been to about seventeen states, usually staying with the farmers and ranchers. I see the same things you saw during the Depression: thousands upon thousands losing their farms. I see ranchers in central Wyoming, whose families have been there for 150 years, threatened with foreclosures. I see a dairy farm family in Minnesota about to be kicked out. A devout Catholic family, twelve children; along with portraits of the Pope and the Blessed Virgin, they showed me the deed, signed by the president, when their great-great-great-grandfather homesteaded.

We have Reagan telling us how important the American family is and yet his administration is destroying the most stable family structure there is: the farm family, working the land, staying together. There never have been so many rural divorces. Last week, a farmer's wife told me her husband is divorcing her, not because he doesn't love her, but because of the crisis. They're having what they never had before: violence in schools, child abuse, drugs and alcohol. We're talking about the heart of America.

Many have already gone. I don't know where they are. A rancher in Wyoming lost his land. I talked to his wife a few months later. He's skinning rattlesnakes for a living. Many are hiding out with relatives, as the FHA is sending out a collection agency. Many are on welfare. The irony is that the farmers who are raising food for the nation are on food stamps. I remember some of these very same clients saying to me welfare people are deadbeats, who refuse to work. This was four years ago. They were very conservative people and to some extent still are.

They're certainly more questioning. Even today, they think they can handle themselves individually. Once they decide it's not their personal fault, they'll start talking to others.

I've seen demonstrations. I've seen them stop a few foreclosure sales—a few. You really can't go in and bid two dollars an acre, buy the farm, and give it back to the original owner. That would have happened during the thirties, but not now. Lenders come in and bid at least the debt amount. So they're the ones buying it.

American land is falling into fewer and fewer and fewer hands: people who are in it purely for profit. They don't care about conserving it. They don't care about the pigs. A farm woman put it to me: Who is going to stay up with the corporate sow? On a family farm, the parents and children are out in the hog barn all night long during farrowing. Or during the calving and lambing season. The whole family. They're not going to let anything happen to those animals. What's going to happen when you have corporate farming?

Black farmers in the Deep South, who are still living on the sharecropped land they got after slavery, thirty-, forty-acre tracts, are being threatened. Where they'll go from there, God only knows.

There's definitely anger, confusion, and frustration. There are right-wing anti-Semitic organizations feasting upon this despair. Their militant line is: Don't pay taxes, use arms, international Jew bankers. Lots of farmers are going to these people out of total desperation.

> *"Kearney, Nebraska.—Huddled under blankets last weekend in a cold, dark grain-storage shed, 200 men and women from around the Midwest listened intently to a tall man in a dark business suit pledge to take up arms in defense of dispossessed farmers. . . . 'It's pretty much common knowledge that most of the international banks are Jewish. . . .'*
>
> *"In the course of two months, Larry Humphreys has become a figure of national significance in the mythic world of heartland politics. . . ."* *

The farmers are so desperate, they will do anything to save their land, to save their family. They go to lawyers, who don't have solutions. They come to us. We can't say, we'll save your farm. It's a government policy problem. They go to the right-wing groups, who give them bad legal advice and tell them not to trust lawyers because they're part of the Jewish banking conspiracy.

---

* James Ridgeway, *Village Voice*, February 4, 1986.

There is an alliance beginning between the farmers and labor. In the case we're handling, *Gamradt versus Block,* it's happening. The Gamradts were unable to get their hay in one season because they didn't have the money or the equipment. Workers from the factories, members of labor unions, came out and baled the hay for them. These are the first outward signs of an alliance. Farmers are asking for the same things that labor is asking: fair prices for their products.

You hear people say the crisis was caused by the farmer's greediness to expand, to buy these huge tractors. That isn't true. During the Carter administration we were told: We're going to feed the world. We're going to have this huge agricultural market. Land values shot up. The lenders, especially the FHA, were going to farmers, offering them money, wining and dining them like they were big businessmen. I have one client who went to FHA for a $50,000 loan. They said, We'll give you $150,000 if you'll build a new dairy barn.

What happens? Land values shoot down, there is no equity, and farm prices are lower now than they were during the Depression. A farmer says to me, "I took a load of corn in the other day and I got 98 cents a bushel. I can't buy one box of corn flakes for what I get for a bushel of corn." In one week, three farmers called. They took their corn to the elevator and were told they have to *pay* six cents a bushel. It was worth negative six cents.

I'm dealing with people who are in serious despair, but I love my job, because I'm doing something about something I really care about. That's why I didn't take that $50,000-a-year job. I try to maintain optimism, but sometimes it is very difficult. I feel there is a change in the air . . .

CARROLL NEARMYER

A farm in Iowa, twenty-four miles southeast of Des Moines. Instantly, you sense hard times. It isn't that the place is neglected; it's precisely the other way around: the farm's well-kept appearance evokes the image of the proud working poor, tatteredly neat and clean. It is the old house itself that gives away what is now an open secret: the desperate circumstances of the farmer.

It is an especially soft and easy twilight in May. His wife Carolyn is preparing a meal: not a farm supper of tradition and legend, but a bit of this, a dab of that, and more of something else. Thanks to her skill and care, it turns out to be wholly satisfying and filling—hunger, of course, being the best sauce. It will be ready by the time their son Chris gets home from his factory job in Des Moines. Eight-year-old Cary, a good talker, is ready any time.

This kitchen is part of the old house. My great-grandparents bought the place around 1895 or somewhere in there. I'm fourth-generation. Chris is not about to be the fifth. Just like all kids that lived on the farm, he followed me around quite a bit and was driving a tractor at, oh gosh, what age? Eight or nine, just old enough to touch the brakes and the clutch. The reason he's not working at that, I could not help him get started in farming.

It does look like the beginning of the end. I can go up and down the road and point you out the neighbors that is in the same predicament that their sons won't farm and that means the end of the family farm.

Dad was always telling me about it, and I didn't listen to him. The older I get now, the smarter my dad gets, even after he has passed away. "Don't trust a bank." He says they'll do anything when things are going good, but the minute it turns around and starts going bad, they'll jerk the rug from out under you.

The particular bank I dealt with was in Newton, Iowa. The Prairie City Bank, right by here, closed just eleven months ago. It went belly-up. I believe about three hundred here in the state of Iowa that has went down.

Oh, the bigger banks are getting bigger. You want to go in there and borrow $50,000, they won't talk to you. But if you wanted to borrow 2 or 3 million, then they'll talk to you.

When problems started coming up, I went to talk to my banker. I knew him personally and he knew me. But he had pressure from up above and so he was putting the pressure on me. He was trying to convince me I was a bad manager and for me to come home and write up a sale bill, list everything, and sell out. If I did that, I could pay them off and they, therefore, would not have had the pressure from up above. Being's as I'm a fourth-generation farmer, I wasn't about to just come home and sell out.

They come at us with, You gotta have a cash flow, you gotta do a better job on your bookkeeping, a better job on your farming. But still when you sell that bushel of corn for less money than you produce it, you can only cut so far. Our taxes kept going up, interests kept going up on us. At one time, I was paying eighteen percent interest on my farm notes. I came up more short on payments. If I don't make a go of it now, the Newton National Bank will take it. They'll turn around and sell it to someone else. It will probably be a corporation. We call 'em vultures.

I've been involved in farm activism for three years. There is less people now than there were then, involved. They just gradually fall by the way. It's just like a cancer. Pretty soon one goes, then there's another one gone. I would say in three years' time, we lost somewhere around forty percent of them. Some of them don't have the money to come. It takes gas to go somewhere. If it comes to the choice of feeding your family and buying gas, you're going to feed the family.

> *Jerry Streit, a farmer from West Bend, Iowa: "We had a son playing baseball. We quit going to his away games because we didn't have gas for the car. I told him it wasn't because I didn't want to see him play. I loved it, but we just couldn't afford the gas."*

When I was really down and out, I couldn't find a job. You talk about prime of life, I'm forty-six years old. That went against me. I was already too old. If we're forced off the farms, we'll have to take jobs like ridin' on the outside of the garbage truck. Carrying garbage for a minimum wage. What we'll really become is white slaves and just barely livin'. When they're coming down here after ya, you really feel what happens to a person on the inside. When you realize you're losing everything and be forced out of your home, you get mad. Damn mad.

I kept the whole problem to myself. She didn't know and the kids didn't know that I was having problems. There was times that I got suicidal. I would be driving and didn't know how I got there. There was several times that I had the gun to my head and she didn't know that. And then I got damn mad. I got to thinkin' about it and I got madder. These people don't have the right to do this to me! I have worked, I have sweated, and I have bled. I have tried out there to keep this place goin'. And then they tried to take it away from me! I worked out there to keep food on the table for the people over this whole nation. Nobody has the right to keep me from doin' that! I got so damn mad that I would have picked up arms to protect myself and the family. I would have shot somebody.

Then I got involved with this farm group, and there is people just like me. They get tagged as radicals right away. 'Cause we're supposed to be civilized now. It's all right for some S.O.B. in a white shirt and tie to come along and take our farms away from us on paper. But it's not all right for us to try to keep him from doin' that. The minute we say we're not gonna let him do that, we become radicals.

We have went to farm sales and helped farmers that was being sold out, to keep their machinery and stop the sale. Again we get tagged as radicals. I've helped organize farm sales to stop the sheriff's sale. Most of the time it's in winter. He stands out in the cold, the farmer being sold out. Sheriff comes. If you shout him down he still knocks off the farm to the bank. The farmer's sold out and they they try to put the guilt on you.

My banker even suggested, ''You don't want to let your neighbors know that you're having financial trouble, 'cause you're the only one that's having trouble.'' I know several other farmers he's told that to. There's a neighbor down here two miles, we was meetin' each other on the road, we'd wave at each other but we wouldn't stop to talk to each other. He thought I was doin' all right and he was wonderin' how come, and I was wonderin' the same thing about him.

There is a neighbor across the road. He's a lot bigger than I am, but last summer when the Prairie City Bank foreclosed, they took his son down, too. The only thing his son saved was his wife and his kids. But they won't come and speak out. I don't know why they don't.

The next neighbor down the road is just a young guy. Him and his wife both work in town. He farms evenings, after he gets home. Just to survive.

There's another neighbor down the road, he was borrowing money from FHA. They turned him every which way but loose and he still hasn't said anything. There's one here last winter, wasn't able to put any food on the table, and he still hasn't ever said anything.

I've had some farmers argue with you that they have the right to go broke. When our administration is ruling out what we can get for our product, then we don't have that right. There ain't one farmer in the state of Iowa that says he voted for Reagan. They just won't admit it!

FHA was supposed to loan you money and stretch it out to ten or fifteen years or however long it took. When people started having trouble, first thing we heard from FHA was that they were running out of funds. They accelerated some notes on farmers, even if they was keeping up on their payments. Demanded payment in full. They would call it high-risk, so they would raise the interest two percent each time.

There's a big bunch of money the Pentagon has, unspent, unobligated. All they'd have to do is transfer just a very small percentage of it to FHA, and it would save thousands of small farmers.

I've got a reputation of talking. I'm trying to get them to understand. They will listen a little better than they did six months ago. I have been called crazy: "You don't know what the hell you're talking about." I've even been told if I get to talking about Reagan or the Federal Reserve, I am not an American any more. Yes, I'm a troublemaker.

A year ago last winter the governor of Iowa was to give his state speech. We wasn't allowed to go in there and listen to him, but we could be in the rotunda. We decided to do a demonstration there, 250 of us farmers. As he come off the legislative floor, I stopped him. I asked him to listen to us and we would tell him the real state of the state. He refused, of course.

Slowly, real slowly, we got the American Ag Movement started in Iowa. You will get people that will say, "I'm supportin' what you're doing, but I can't afford to join." It costs one hundred dollars a year to be a member. To a lot of people, it is a difference between putting food on the table and spending money for something like that.

I can see support coming faster and faster. Knowing what the administration has planned for us, we're going to see more people finally stand up and say, Enough is enough. Let's change this thing.

How much can a man take? I've seen it cause a lot of divorces. I can name you family after family that have split up. It has caused problems between me and my wife. Sometimes I take off and travel from one state to the other and she accuses me, and rightly so, of putting this ahead of the family. I've got an older daughter—is she twenty?—that no longer lives with us. She couldn't stand the stress. As soon as she was out of school, she moved to Des Moines. Me and my son have at times exchanged words. I know fathers and sons where the son has took off on account of the stress. You bet it affects families.

Our youngest, who is eight—when they had the sheriff looking for me to give me a repossession notice on the machinery—she stood out there on the deck as a lookout. He come down on me after dark, we started moving and hiding the machinery. Anytime she saw car lights, she told us and we scattered. We caught her one time hiding her tricycle. She said she didn't want the sheriff to find it. That's the kind of stuff families go through.

Take this situation here in Iowa, with a banker shot by a farmer. I knew this man. This particular farmer had two days before deposited money into his checking account. His wife told me that day they didn't have groceries in the house. He was going to write a check at the bank for sixty dollars so they could have food on the table. You understand, if a guy is going to bounce a check, he doesn't go into the bank to write a check. He handed the check to the teller and she told him she couldn't cash it. There wasn't any money in the account. He said he just deposited two days ago. She told him it had been seized by the banker—the guy that he shot— put on the note that "you owed here at the bank." That was the straw that broke the camel's back. That story has not been told publicly. How come?

If we don't stand up as citizens and as farmers, we're going to become second-class citizens. We're going to be fighting over jobs. At the same time, prices in the grocery store are going to skyrocket as soon as the corporations take over. Even the people that's got good jobs now are going to be struggling just to keep food on the table. It's not only what's gonna happen to us farmers, it's gonna happen to us as a nation and a world.

I see labor coming together with the farmers. For a long time they kept us separated. Whenever a farmer complained about a high-priced tractor, they say the labor man is the cause of all that. We come to find out, you take a $100,000 combine, the labor man got eleven percent of that. That includes his benefits, even his parking-lot cost. So it wasn't him that was causing it. They was trying to keep us split, but we have got ourselves educated. We're coming more and more together.

I went to the line a lot of times on different things. We was picketing the Board of Trade in Chicago. They are the ones that control our prices. They can sell one bushel of beans that we grow fifteen times on paper. We was trying to get them to change that policy.

We had a tractorcade to Omaha, Nebraska, last September. That's about 130 miles. It took four days to get there. We tractorcaded from four different directions. There was some four hundred tractors when we all got there. My tractor and our bunch barricaded the main street downtown to keep the traffic out. We was kickin' off the Harkin-Gephardt bill to give us parity. During the 130 miles, we got horns and waves supportin' us and some was givin' us the finger. Those was thirty-year-old people.

The young guy that lives on his mother-in-law's farm over there doesn't speak out. But he privately supports us. He donated fifteen dollars for diesel oil for the tractorcade. The older guy right by here won't publicly back us. But I've talked to him in his shed. He got so mad, he was takin' the wrench and beatin' it on the corn picker. He was almost in tears as he was doin' this. His son just went through a foreclosure. When we protested the Board of Trade in Chicago, he said we should have drove a loaded gas tanker through the front door.

It takes a lot of time and a lot of studying to get insight into what is going on. And that's another thing. Time. A farmer is just like a bird. When it comes spring, a bird flies north, and a farmer is the same way. When it comes spring, he's gonna go out and plant his corn. He don't care if he's gonna lose money. It's born in him, it's a natural instinct.

When it comes time to go to the field, I throw away whatever I'm reading to educate myself, and go out there. Even at times when I should be someplace screaming and hollering, I'll still be in the field. Every one of us is like that.

CAROLYN NEARMYER

She is Carroll Nearmyer's wife.

"My grandparents were farmers on both sides of the family. My dad always told the story: In the Depression, whenever they cooked bacon, they would have to put grease in the skillet because it was so lean. It didn't have any fat on it. Times were really hard for them."

I tend to live in a lot of fear. Every time my husband goes out, supporting other farmers, stopping a foreclosure sale, or something like that, I am so scared that he's going to make too many waves and someone is going to take a shot at him. Every time he's gone, I can't sleep. I stay up until he gets home.

My eight-year-old senses this, too. A lot of times, she cannot sleep and she'll come downstairs and want to know if daddy is home. Then it reflects in my mind: what if he doesn't come home?

This was a house that my in-laws lived in and their folks. They always took so much pride in it. Today this house needs painting really bad. The ceilings and everything else needs repair.

Whenever you have to feed your hogs or buy chicken feed, that's gotta come first. You just don't have any money for leisure stuff. We used to go out and eat every once in a while when times were better, like in the seventies. We'd go to the harness races, which we enjoy. Now we buy all our clothes at garage sales, and I mean *all*. Hand-me-down clothes.

This is my husband's terrain, it sure is. My blood, sweat, and tears have only been here for twenty-three years, where his is double that, because he was born here. I've seen him get up before daylight —like when he was planting just this spring—and he wouldn't get home until nine at night. He doesn't mind the hard work, to him, it's a pleasure. What is so heartbreaking about the whole thing is that he doesn't get any reward for it.

(Cary peeks through the door.)

She plays a very important role because she has to. It's not just something she hears about and goes on with a normal, eight-year-old's life. It is something she lives day to day. When we were going through our foreclosure, I was really concerned about her because she couldn't sleep at night, just nervous, really flighty all the time.

You bet she was aware of it. She saw her father when they came to repossess our grain truck. As soon as the wrecker was pulling it out of the driveway, she was standing out there watching her dad cry. He couldn't stop 'em and there was nothing she could do to stop 'em. That's hard on kids. They shouldn't have to go through that at that age. She was watching for us, to make sure the cops didn't come. If the lights were coming down the road, she'd run in the house and tell us. She brought her tricycle on the porch 'cause she was afraid the sheriff would take it, too. I reassured her that it was paid for and after you have something paid for it's yours. She didn't understand that.

Whenever the deputy came out to take our stuff away from us, I asked him, "How can you go home and face your family?" I happen to know he has an eight-year-old girl too. I said, "How can you sleep tonight, knowing that someday this could be you?" You don't have to be a farmer. This is not just a farm crisis.

He said, "If I didn't do it, somebody else would be here. To me, it's just a job." Auctioneers at foreclosures say that, too: "If we don't sell 'em out, someone else'll get the profits. I just as well do it." To me, that's heartless people. I wouldn't do that to somebody just because I needed the money. Money to me is just not that important. If we can pay the light bill and the phone bill and have food on the table, that's it. We know in our hearts that we're doing a good job raising our kids, teaching them decency and right from wrong. We've always taught them to respect the flag and respect authorities and obey the law. I still make sure Cary stands up to the flag and pays honor. But if the sheriff comes out here and takes your stuff away—I mean, how are these kids supposed to say, Okay, you're the sheriff, go ahead and take it? It does hurt me, it really does.

The women I know are apt to talk to other farm wives about the problems, rather than sit down with their husbands. In our instance, if I would come up with a suggestion, he'd get very upset. It was not that I did not know as much as he did. It was just he was keeping it inside himself. Really, I thought it was some kind of problem between him and I. I could definitely sense his attitude was completely different.

I think maybe we can make it, since we've refinanced with the bank, if we watch our p's and q's and don't eat too much (laughs).

When things went bad, we saw the need for food pantries. I went to the town of Monroe and met with all the ministers and helped them get it started. When I went to partake of it, for ourselves—we were a farm family in need—I was turned down. They told me I was in the wrong school district and they had to follow guidelines. I helped set up this food pantry. I felt bitter: Never again will I get anything like that started. I don't feel that way now, because there is a need.

We applied for food stamps once and we got 'em. Some paper came out and did a story on us. They took some pictures. In the background, there was a whole lot of pigs. Human Services saw the picture and said, You don't qualify. If you're hungry, all you have to do is sell them hogs. We tried to tell them there was a note against the hogs, they was not free and clear. They turned down the biggest end of farmers because they don't know how to deal with farm income.

When we went to Chicago, protesting the Board of Trade, I was one of 'em that went through the barrier. I got to look around and found several other ladies that was willing to do it with us. It was the coldest day I had ever seen in my life. At a certain time, we kinda knocked down a few policemen and went right into the building (laughs). We were arrested and taken to jail in a paddy wagon. It was mostly staged for the media purpose. I think it's off my record (laughs).

When we went to Washington on that parity march, we walked around all over. There was so many signs of what our forefathers had did. Freedom and justice and liberty and every man is created equal. When we were refused entrance into the USDA* building, I felt real heartbroken that a farmer would be turned away from his own building. They have guards there saying you have no right to go in there. I felt if anybody has a right to go into that building, it would be the farmers. I wasn't impressed with our government at all. I'm afraid it's big business who owns this country.

* United States Department of Agriculture.

CHRIS NEARMYER

*He is the son of Carroll and Carolyn Nearmyer. "I'm
twenty-one now, I'll be twenty-two next Saturday."*

I work at a storm-door factory in
Des Moines. I drive a forklift and
load semis. It started out when I was in high school. No, that wasn't
the work I wanted to do. I wanted to farm. But the way things are
with the economy, that's what I've gotta do.

Whenever I was little, I rode a lot on the tractor when dad was in
the field. Practically every day in the summer, I was out helping
him. The first time I drove that tractor by myself, I thought I was
pretty high and mighty. I was doin' somethin' on my own. I was
eight.

A couple of months before I graduated high school, there was a
farm over here for sale that I wanted to buy. I went to a Federal
Land Bank and tried to borrow the money. They laughed me out of
the office. They thought it was real funny, a high school kid trying
to buy a farm. At the time, I didn't know this crisis was going to
happen. Now that I look back, I'm glad that they told me to come
back in ten years.

None of my friends are in farming, either. There's one that's in
the marines. He grew up on the farm. They was one of the first
families to really start going downhill. I've got another friend that's
driving a truck now. He wanted to go into farming. The same thing
happened to his dad. He's selling feed down here in Monroe because
he can't farm.

There's another friend I had that I don't know exactly what he's
doing. They were dairy people. They went broke. I was in the FFA*
and he was too, and he acted like he wanted to farm. If he ever had
the chance, he probably would have. There were about seven or eight
of us in the Vo Ag† class in high school. None of them are farming.
All were sons of farmers, sure.

* Future Farmers of America.
† Vocational Agricultural.

Probably what's going to happen is the big corporations are gonna end up taking them all over and we're gonna end up working for them. 'Cause we're gonna need a job and being's as we're here, we're handy. They'll put us to work for whatever they want. Being's the farmers aren't banded together, there won't be no union, and they'll be able to make us do whatever they want.

Me and my friends always talk about this. We start talking about we need money for this or that or about what we're workin' at. One kid right out here last summer standin' in the driveway told me he wanted to farm so bad he could taste it, But there was nowhere he could get any money to farm with. It's in the back of everybody's mind, but a lot of people just don't talk about it. They live from week to week.

I've got another friend that his mom and dad are farming. They're just like us. He isn't out of high school yet, but he still has to do a lot of the work because his dad's driving a truck. He is having trouble understanding why there's no money comin' in. He does bulldozer work when he isn't farming. He's even running a cat,* a high school kid running a cat.

They talk a lot about troubles in the families. A lot of times they don't get along with their parents. Everyone is kind of tense.

(We look out the window.)

My dad, he's doin' one last chore, feeding the hogs and the cow. I don't know how many there is. I used to know every one of them out there.

* Caterpillar tractor.

A VIEW FROM THE FLOOR

REX WINSHIP

*He deals in futures. In fact, he deals in just about
anything: grains, metals, livestock, bonds, bills, currencies,
interest rates. "Anything you can buy, we can trade."*

*His offices run to two floors in a skyscraper near the New
York Stock Exchange. There is a plenitude of art work,
courtesy of his personal collection. He is one of the Forbes
400 richest Americans. His estimated net worth is more
than $400,000,000.*

*Adjacent to his private office, the size of a small gym, is
an enormous trading room, where forty young commodities
brokers are single-mindedly studying the quote machines,
one on each desk. They are among his 470 employees in this
city. His payroll, in cities throughout the world, runs to
1,500.*

*Imagine Robert Duvall, to whom he bears a remarkable
resemblance, in shirtsleeves, handling a continuous flow of
messages, the phone constantly ringing. His feet are, of
course, on the desk. He is, it is plain to see, a take-charge
guy. One of his young traders said it all: "When he says
jump, you ask, How high?"*

*In his private dining room, a chef-attendant serves
lunch. "This is all macrobiotic, no fast food." The talk,
though, is a fast flow, free-associative.*

I'm just a poor old country boy, a
fella who likes to work. Some peo-
ple enjoy tennis, I enjoy work. I only put in about sixty, seventy
hours a week. I enjoy being a leader. I enjoy being the guy every-

body looks to. I like the responsibility of having thousands of people working for me.

I started out as a runner twenty years ago. Eighty-two bucks a week. When I got out of the army in '66. In 1968, I bought a membership; 1969, my uncle and I started the company. In '74, I bought him out. A whole bunch of people from the grain industry came with me. In those years, I was probably the largest commodities trader in the world. I had a vision I was in the right place at the right time. I also have a high energy level.

It was a robber-baron period for the commodity business. LBJ. Guns and butter. The Shah of Iran. Decontrolling of railroads, of airplanes. Gold-market window closed. Floating foreign-exchange rates. All taking place at the same time, okay? As that happened, we expanded the money supply.

We had every fruitcake as president, but they made you make money. We had oil at three dollars a barrel. We had interest rates at five percent maximum yield. We had everything pushed down. When they released it all, the budget doubled, inflation took off.

I was dealing in cattle, grains, gold, everything. You had a tax roll, so you could defer your taxes. If any dummy cannot make success out of that— The robber barons made a lot of money. They didn't have to pay any tax. The rules of the game in 1975 were very loose. The robber barons had everything going for them. We did, too. We were coming out of control prices, out of control exchange rates, out of control currencies. All of a sudden they were let go. I was in the business where you could trade it. I knew it was a unique period in history and it wouldn't go on forever.

If you were in real estate in Houston, up until five years ago, you were considered a business genius, right? If in the same twenty years, you were in some real estate business in Sioux City, you were considered a schmuck. You're in the wrong place, okay?

In '66, what if I had gone into the stock business instead of futures? The only thing I knew that was smart was being able to sell short. Having the flexibility of being short easily was a big advantage.

What if General Motors could hedge their auto production for a year out? What if every pension fund could hedge? What if U.S. Steel could sell futures forward and lock up their margins? I saw the concept of futures as a winner.

Now in our world of money, money management has become the sexiest topic there is. We're risk managers.

I'm sure we're close to another change. I don't know if it'll come next week or ten years from now. I'm not sure if we're going to have inflation or deflation. Deflation takes money out of the country into the city. New York's a gold mine. Inflation moves it away from cities back to the country. So all you have to do in life is figure which way the money flow is gonna go.

Nothing is forever. You always have to stay flexible, so you can change. That means education. Five years ago, we were in the commodity business. You bought and sold. The customer was a farmer in Iowa. Today he is a major New York bank. That kid who talked to the farmer can't talk to a New York City bank. The kid isn't educated enough. Either I fire him and hire one of those guys at $500,000 a year. Or I have to re-educate him. I re-educate him.

There's a business we should go into: training people to be in the service business. Give them basic skills: math, speaking, diction. Right now, we give diction courses here. I take 'em. You can't be in the business world and not be able to communicate. It wasn't as important when you had a screwdriver in your hand. Now there's satellite communications all over the place. The globalization of the communication market is going to be dramatic. You're going to be able to sit in your office in Chicago, look up at the wall. The conversation will be about interest rates and taxation.

It'll mean you'll have longer days. It'll be a young man's game, which it is already. Back in the fifties, when you went in for a job, the guy said, How old are you? Twenty-six. Married? You bet. Boy, that's good. What a guy, you're married. Stabilizing force, right? Today, you don't want the kid married.

You want to be able to move. You want to be able to send him to Singapore for two years, Sydney, Australia, for a year, and then back to Chicago. Two, he's gotta go to school nights. He's gotta learn math, statistics, he's gotta learn Fed policy. When he goes to school from seven o'clock till nine three days a week, and he's newly married, and he gets to work at six, gets out at six, has to be at school at seven, gets home at nine-thirty, what's his new wife gonna say to him?

How can you compete when the Japanese come over here, without their wives? They get to work at eight o'clock in the morning, get home ten o'clock at night. The average work week of the American executive is fifty-four hours. It's probably sixty-some hours in Japan. It's a question of time before the guy who works sixty hours will have all the marbles. Everybody must adjust to the market-place.

What happens to that most solid of citizens and family men, the American farmer?

Why is he a solid citizen? That's a myth. The myth is that land is good, right? Farmers work hard, right? That's also a myth. The guy that runs the local dry-cleaner store works longer hours, right? He's in a fixed location. He can't move. He's got his plant and equipment tied up in his building, right? Except no one sends him a check and says, You're entitled to 3¼ for your corn. What business in the world says you gotta make money? Why should you make a profit? Without loss, no one can win. Unless you have losers, you cannot have winners.

Just because, forty years ago, half the population lived on the farm, and people thought, Wasn't that a great life? Today nobody lives on the farm. The American government ruined the American farmer. Three embargoes: '73, '76, and 1980. There probably aren't as many Third World countries that have defaulted as much as we have. An embargo's defaulting tells you that your contract's no good, rip it up. That's why we have to spend 35 billion a year to support the farmers. Australia, Canada, Argentina, Brazil expanded. We made them all rich.

Cargill takes half their money outside the United States. When you go spend a billion in Brazil to build railroads and trucks and terminals, it doesn't come back very easy here. Harley-Davidson never got it back from Honda, did it?

Ten years from now, there will be less farmers. We don't need them. We've imported food. We import more meat than any other country in the world: more chicken, more beef, more pork. When the government gets out, the people that are left will produce what we want. Some farms will collapse, some won't.

And unions. As you change society, unions are not set up for the change. They're designed to keep people out. They're designed to lock prices. Isn't that how you raise prices? They're built for inflexibility. They have to go the way of the fixed exchange rate. Why should the most talented electrician make the same as the biggest dummy? The union is unfair to its own people.

Why aren't there any more craftsmen today? What happened to all those ethnic craftsmen? I believe kids work harder today than ever before. Maybe they don't want to go into these crafts because the pay wasn't right. Maybe the greatest carpenter didn't make enough money because the guy at the low end made as much as he did. Unions.

They stop the top guy from becoming great. Why shouldn't the greatest carpenter become a multimillionaire? The greatest basketball player does. Why shouldn't the greatest stonecutter? Why? Why? Because the union says, You gotta stay here because we gotta pull this other guy up.

Unions are less and less important. The trend's already in place. It's gonna keep goin'. The market will take care of it.

We need accountability. You can't fire the union guy, so the boss has an unaccountable work force. What if the girl types up your manuscript backwards? I couldn't fire her because she's gonna go to the grievance committee. No accountability, you have no business. Another obstacle to free progress: government regulations. The government caused the Depression in the first place. The Federal Reserve didn't know what it was doing. It kept tightening the money supply. Today, if our Fed was not expanding our money supply, we'd have a depression, too. To say controls took us out of the Depression, that's another myth. Like the farmer's good, and the land's good. Myths.

We have social security, right? Japan doesn't have it. You got to save your money to protect yourself in old age. Does anyone ever think maybe there's a correlation between social security and non-saving? The Japanese weren't born savers and we weren't born spenders. My uncles and aunts and grandma and grandpa saved string and butter wrappers and everything else. They were savers. Now, with social security, why save? Everybody consumes.

Reagan had a chance to change the social security laws and didn't have the guts to do it. So that will be a tremendous debt in the future. Reagan is a good president and could have done something. He could have gotten rid of the COLAs, cost of living adjustments. He could have changed America forever.

Jimmy Carter's administration was a trader's dream. Made more money with him than either Nixon or Reagan. Because he made distortions. Wage and price controls, no wage and price controls. Credit controls, no credit controls. Embargo, no embargo. Wonderful for me.

It's very hard to make a profit in a free market. Look at the airlines decontrolled. It's hard to make a profit since Jimmy Carter. With controls, you're simply smarter than the controllers. You just outsmart the regulators. Knowing how to get in and get out, you make a profit. It's easy. Christ, if you can't outsmart one little government staff, you shouldn't get to work in the morning.

If you're called a freebooter—

A free what?

A pirate, a robber baron. Is that a putdown?

It's a compliment. Absolutely. I wish I had their money. Who developed America? The regulator? The president? Or was it Mellon, Rockefeller? I mean, *tell* me what they did bad? Seriously, what did they do bad?

Rockefeller shot down some workers in the copper fields. Some say he exploited them ...

Absolutely. And who's benefitted? There's still Standard Oil, isn't there? Mellon's bank's still around. Chase Manhattan's still around. Listen, how many charities were started by these people? How many national parks were preserved by these robber barons? We look at them, we say they didn't play fair. Absolutely not.

Kid Pharaoh, a minor syndicate tiger in Chicago, caught in a reflective moment:
"I might have been a success at the turn of the century. If I was born fifty years ago, I believe I would have been a multimillionaire. I shoot the same shot that Rockefeller shot while somebody was tapping an oil well that was competitive to him. He put guys in trick bags. Got 'em in jail. There's a history written about these guys. John Jacob Astor, with his trapping, with his furs. Hitting guys. This is the way the system works. What else is there? These new laws are holding them back, destroying incentive.

> *"These were the giants who built the cities. These are the guys who built our country. They elect presidents. All these guys came up the hard way ... shoeshine guys and bust-out crapshooters ... shoot a shot against blackjack. These are the guys we need in our country. Who needs educated mooches?"* *

The robber barons made it because the marketplace wasn't fluid enough. The Rothschilds had carrier pigeons. H. L. Hunt had the guy drunk in the room and had his friend out on the pay phone. Today this could never happen. You'd have nine hundred reporters there. And it's all on the news the same night. Instant communications. Our robber-baron period lasted from '73 to '80. What killed it was (slaps hands) instant communications. Now it's shifted to securities. The market'll take care of it.

The rules of the New York Stock Exchange on insider trading make more profits for the rich arbitrager. If they had no laws against insider trading, these risk-arbitrage guys couldn't make any money, 'cause the market's broader and they don't have the edge. The law makes it easier for them because they outwit the regulators. I'm saying the marketplace knows more than the regulators.

Here's another kind of flow: mergers and acquisitions. Everybody's merging, right? Big conglomerate, right? What's the next thing's gonna happen? They're gonna take 'em all apart.

Small, independent companies? Good, right?

Wrong. Terrible. Very, very scary to me. A lotta competition. I can move quicker against the big inflexible ones.

The only way you can keep everybody upwardly mobile is to have the GNP get bigger and grow. If it grows, you don't have to have have-nots. If it doesn't grow, you have to have have-nots.

Like the frontier was. Space mining, space technology, space health. How far can we grow? Forever. We're only limited by our imaginations.

In the trading room, where his scores of young brokers are intently studying their quote machines, his public relations

---

* *Division Street: America* (New York: Pantheon Books, 1967).

*person, in the manner of a gracious hostess, guides me. "We
are young and energetic. It's fast, intense. But it offers a
lot of money. At a certain age, that's what you're interested
in, making money.*

*"The turnover is tremendous. Two to five years with one
firm and then out. The business just changes so fast. Lots of
stress, so if you make a lot of money, you get out early
(laughs).*

*"We affectionately call it the war room. You feel like
you're going to battle (laughs). Yeah."*

POSTSCRIPT: *Another visit, another macrobiotic lunch. It
is precisely one month after Black Monday, October 19,
1987.*

A five-year bull market had a correction. As long as there is
greed, you'll have days like October 19. Interest rates and lack of
leadership were the cause. It will probably take two years for us to
get back in shape again— '89 and '90 will be bad.

It will not be like 1929. The bear market can be over in a day.
Isn't it better to have a down in one day than for four years? Bonds
went up twelve points in twenty-four hours. In my business, futures,
it was pretty good. I picked up a few bucks.

If the stock market went back to 1,200 tomorrow, it will be all
right. It's high-volatile. There's a scare and a correction. People
will take less risks in the future, which is what they should have
done in the first place. It probably won't happen again in the next
ten years.

In 1929, you didn't have world trade in cash, futures, and options. If Germany makes a decision, it affects America, because of
telecommunications, the computer. You have a decision to make
quickly. But no matter what policies are made, the market is gonna
adjust to it. So it's a much safer world. The reason for the thirties
Depression was the government not allowing the free market economy to work its way out. The Depression wouldn't have lasted that
long.

In contrast to 1929, there is far less playing the stock market. The
big traders are now in pension funds. They have made so much
money that in the long run, they'll be okay.

October 19 has changed our policy. Now we are addressing our budget deficit. The market will discipline the politicians. People will tighten their belts in some spending. They'll buy less VCRs, less Sonys, less Mercedes. But they won't be stinting on U.S. clothing, U.S. food, services.

If we lowered the taxes and cut down on government spending, the business sector will explode. The first thing I'd cut would be the military spending. Blowing up bombs in practice doesn't help the economy.

I wouldn't cut welfare payments. When you give money to somebody on welfare, she spends it to buy food and clothing. Jobs are created. I would change the way the government gives them the money. I wouldn't spend a buck and a half to give her a buck. I would just mail her the check. I would always give poor people money because they spend it.

I see a couple of years sideways and then we'll adjust. We'll pull out better than 1929.

THE GOLDEN CALF

The golden calf still stands upright!
Its might is extolled
from one end of the world to the other....
King and commoner dance together
to the murky chink of money,
dance a mad round about its pedestal....
The golden calf has vanquished the gods.

—Mephistopheles' aria, Faust, *act 2*

JACK MAURER

At the Board of Trade Building, Chicago. Outside
Maurer's office, a man in a blue jacket with badge attached
—it appears to be the uniform of the commodities world—
is in a whimsical mood. "I am a broker. Yes. Yes, I am. Yes.
Our bottom line is a game of need and greed. We fill orders
for the entrepreneurs who buy and sell and hope.

"It's a young man's game now. And young woman's, too,
don't you forget it. People in their twenties, early thirties.
In my forties, I'm an old man today. Let's say I'm more
older than I am younger. Have you heard the one about the
mother whose son graduated from medical school? She was
disappointed because she so hoped he'd go on the Board of
Trade. Not my son, the doctor—no, no, no, my son, the
commodities broker. Why mess around?"

Jack Maurer's appearance is more that of a Talmudic
scholar than a commodities broker. He runs a clearing firm
as well. "I'm just tryin' to make a living trading, running a
good firm, one step at a time, one day at a time."

I'm gettin' old, I'm thirty-eight.
You have bad days, bad months.
The risk is enormous. You can lose hundreds of thousands of dollars
in one day because somebody went crazy. That's the world I'm in—
risk.

I was brought up in a socialist household. The biggest thrill of
my life was hearing Norman Thomas. I think it was '64, '65. I
was in high school, involved in the civil rights and antiwar movement.

I ran the SDS* at the Circle, University of Illinois. I was editor of the school newspaper, the *Chicago Illini*. I still own it. The university didn't want me to be editor because of my left politics. They removed the subsidies to the tune of $80,000 a year. I said, Screw 'em, and we borrowed some money, we incorporated, ran the paper, and it's still there.

I have a degree in philosophy. I had no interest in the business world at all. In fact, I abhorred it. A former philosophy professor of mine did some research at the Board of Trade. When I graduated, he said, "Come work for me." I had no interest. I finally said to this guy, "I'll take the job with you on the Board of Trade, but it's only till I get into graduate school." I wanted to teach philosophy. It was my goal in life. I loved thinking about things, the interchange. Not the business world, I said.

So I went to work for him and I *liked* it. I liked the challenge of solving puzzles. A year later, I became director of research and had five people working under me. That's when I decided business was fun, that you could find freedom here. You didn't have to have a boss, you didn't have to deal with any bureaucracy. You could buy the freedom to do what you wanted to do for the rest of your life. In 1973, I became a trader on the floor and was successful enough to become independent. It's won me freedom.

To me, this is not the business world. You're down there trying to outthink the market. You're trying to be right one more time than you're wrong. And you're just trying to make some money. You're all by yourself and you sink or swim on what you can do. It's like a puzzle game. You've got to understand what's motivating the hundred others and how they're gonna react to different circumstances. If you're playing chess, you're counting victories. We just happen to count in money. The money's incidental to the feeling of figuring it out.

You stand in the pit with the same people, day in and day out, months, years, whatever. You see how they behave in the marketplace. Different commodities have different relationships to different things. Each has a life of its own. It begins to breathe and ebb and flow. If everybody's selling soybeans because they think it's going down, but they don't seem to break it, I say to myself, These guys are wrong. I start buying. You use logic. If I'm trading soybeans, I'm interested in what corn is doing, what wheat is doing,

* Students for a Democratic Society

what the currencies are doing. My eyes looking up at all the boards, watching other people. It's exciting.

My philosophy training plays a role in the long run. You can learn about the commodities business in three months. It's not such a mystery. The key is being in touch with your own makeup, with what kind of human being you are. How you react to profit, to loss, to pressure. It's philosophy in the sense of becoming aware of how you respond to certain situations. The reward and punishment in this business is immediate. When you're right, you feel like the smartest guy in the world. When you're wrong, you feel like a dummy. I've been here since 1970 and I've got more money than I ever thought of.

When I got my first job, all my friends were still in the radical movement. I just had a difficult time explaining myself to people. And explaining myself to myself. At first, I'd say it's just a place to earn some money until I enter graduate school. But as I started enjoying it, it became more difficult. It became obvious the only reason I was invited to parties was so everybody could jump on me.

You realize as you raise a family, start a career, begin to pay rent, this, that, and the other, you view the world in a more complex way. You realize compromises are sometimes necessary. Your beliefs don't have to dictate entirely what you do for a living.

There's no contradiction in earning a good living and believing in political ideas that might end the business you're in. This business afforded me an independence. Coming out of SDS, we really believed in individualism, the association of free peoples. The real world gives you a chance at financial independence. Otherwise, you're on the fringe. Youth in college is a wonderful time. You have so few responsibilities. That doesn't go on forever.

As we get on in life, most of us worry less about the big issues. It's the small ones that concern them. Where's my career going? Can I buy a new house? Can I buy a new car? Our lives are circumscribed more and more in narrow ways: family, children, maybe some close friends. There's nothing wrong with that.

I've changed a lot of my ideas. I still believe in democracy, but I'm convinced socialism is not the answer. I think the answer is the freedom to make choices. That requires an economy that allows for a good deal of social mobility. If you're not happy in one place, you should have the opportunity to be happy someplace else.

It's an economy that has an entrepreneurial spirit, so it's easy to enter into a solo business, high-tech, low-tech, or no tech whatever.

It's a society not constricted by bureaucracy or government in terms of the workplace.

My father's generation felt that labor unions were *the* essential from the 1880s to the 1940s. We see them now as constricting society, smothering it. I think labor unions missed the boat. If they'd been truly interested in helping the workingman, they'd have bought the damn companies they worked for instead of investing in billion-dollar pension funds and playing the stock market along with Ivan Boesky. They've become little different than the world they were struggling against.

They fell into a very easy alliance with business in the fifties, sixties, and seventies. Each year they'd go to the fountain and say we want X percent more. Business would say that's reasonable, and the price of the product went up, up, up. And the world passed them by.

I used to argue with my dad. I never remember a time when we didn't argue politics. I felt it very early on: the labor movement as a pro–Vietnam War force, dumping on Martin Luther King when he marched against the war, AFL-CIO gung-ho all the way.

I see a lot of changes since the 1960s. How many black faces did you see on LaSalle Street in the sixties? When I became a member, how many Jews were there on the Board of Trade, let alone women? There's an enormous amount of opportunity for people. Back in the sixties, civil rights was a novel idea. Now it's the norm.

I think my ideals have remained intact. My political philosophy has altered in terms of affecting those ideals. The original ideals I was exposed to as a youth and in SDS are still with me. I think antitrust laws ought to be strengthened so that large conglomerates cannot put the damper on new ideas in industry. I see little difference between the federal government as run by Ronald Reagan, United States Steel, the Teamsters' Union, or the University of Illinois.

That's why I've always enjoyed the anarchists. In our business, we have no built-in organizations either. I've always thought that if everyone had a little bit of anarchy in him, life would be a little better. Here, it's every man for himself, but everybody has an opportunity. It's a tough business.

I'll tell you right off the bat, I voted for Ronald Reagan. I felt inflation was the most serious threat to a democracy. It could ruin the society by destroying those people who make democracy work: the middle class. Before I entered this business, I would never have dreamed I'd vote for Reagan. I don't know how I would have felt if I were a professor.

I think the arms race is insane and the military budget should be cut in half. They're throwing big money at Big Business. Yet I voted for Reagan in 1984 as well as '80. I viewed Mondale as somebody owned by labor unions. I also hoped Reagan would make a deal with Gorbachev. Maybe I was kidding myself.

I haven't signed a petition in the last eight years. Antinuke or anything. I believe a solution to the arms race comes in negotiations with the Russians, not unilateral disarmament. I absolutely believe in demonstrations. I have no problem with people chaining themselves to the fence of MX missile sites. I wouldn't sign the petitions, but I think they're wonderful.

I'm very much an egalitarian about race, obviously. I believe education and jobs are the only thing in the long run that will solve this problem. But blacks themselves are not addressing it. It's not the obligation of the government to provide something that people aren't striving to get. If a person is unable, that's fine. You certainly have to care for the needy and the elderly, but when people are reasonably able-bodied . . .

I grew up in an environment where my parents sacrificed their lives for their children. They came here as immigrants, circumscribed in opportunity, to a country that allowed freedom. Whether I became a carpenter like my father or a professor was irrelevant as long as I strove and availed myself of what this country offered. It's difficult for me to see groups of people who don't have this ethic.

Most of my old SDS friends are in the business world. Some have gone into teaching. I think all have changed.

I constantly struggle with being a person who owns a house in Wilmette, who owns a seat that's worth $300,000 on the Board of Trade, who never had a nickel when he was in college, who had to work to put himself through school, who believed in socialism. It's the clash of ideals and reality. What amount of guilt does it involve me in? Betrayal? I think about it, I talk about it.

Any human being who's been lucky in life ought to have a touch of guilt. There's nothing unhealthy about a touch of guilt. Luck had a lot to do with where I'm at, more than talents.

My father, the socialist, is very proud of me. He doesn't understand what I do for a living. When I first started trading, he'd ask me every day, "How'd you do?" I'd say, "I lost five hundred dollars today.'' Oh, my God, two weeks' work. Or I'd say, ''I made a thousand dollars.'' Oh, my God. All the money in the world. One day, I told him I'd lost ten thousand dollars. He almost had a heart attack. I've never told him since.

As the market got more volatile in the eighties, fluctuations, movement, young people started coming in. Because it's a merciless business. Eighty percent fail. It burns you out. I've seen dear friends of mine destroyed. They either went bankrupt or they just couldn't take it any longer. I'm gettin' to be one of the older guys around here.

If you're wrong a bunch of days in a row, you're gone. It's as simple as that. Knock on wood, I'm holding up pretty well. I'm very pleased with how my life has come out.

I still have a yearning to teach. I still love philosophy.

> POSTSCRIPT: *A revisit. It is a month after Black Monday,*
> *October 19, 1987.*

That Monday, I was at the Chicago Board of Trade, in the soybean pit. We were standing, watching the Dow go down, down, down. Nobody could believe it. The confusion, the fear was infectious. The depth of the break astounded everybody.

To us, 1929 is a legend. I'm thirty-nine. Most of us are between twenty-five and forty-five. We're all reasonably well educated and know about the '29 crash and the Depression. The magnitude of this break brought all those anxieties really home. There was a fear that this might cause a financial panic, banks to close down, exchanges to close. People were just looking at each other. It was so thick, the feeling, you could cut it with a knife.

Before, there was a euphoria about the market. The correction was gonna come, but it was something you could handle, no big deal. There was a general sense of well-being: life is good, America is good, the marketplace is good. We were doing well. A feeling of invulnerability. Now it was gone.

For about two weeks, the anxiety level was unbelievably high. Stories were coming about firms losing huge amounts of money and were gonna close down. There were rumors about Merrill Lynch and E. F. Hutton going bankrupt. This, that big outfit going bust. Ninety percent of the stories were unfounded, but the fact that the rumors were making the rounds told us that something like this could really happen.

In the next two days, Tuesday and Wednesday, over a hundred

seats were sold at the Board of Trade. Unprecedented. Your seat is your tool that allows you to trade. Seats that had gone steadily upward to $500,000 for full membership went down to $300,000. In two days! Special memberships that allow you to trade in the stock-index market went from $75,000 to $30,000. Nobody in his night-mares thought anything like this could happen.

I was down on the floor during the Hunt silver market days and the big breaks. I was there when the Franklin National Bank went bust, when Continental was taken over. There was never *this* kind of anxiety. If the Fed had not stepped in and eased the money supply as quickly as it did, you could have had a replay of the panic of 1929.

After a month, much of the anxiety is gone, but there's a real nervousness. A feeling: Hey, wait a second, a lot of strange things can happen. What's it gonna lead to? Lunchtime conversations have changed. They wonder about a cyclical depression. They wonder about their life-styles. There's a lesson, important to all of us: it *can* happen. It means being born in the forties and fifties doesn't mean being born in an amusement park, where things are always wonder-ful. Generally, this is the way these white middle-class kids feel. In that one day, they've discovered the world is a serious, potentially disruptive place. Nobody owes them a living. Nobody owes them luxury and good times.

We hear on TV that things are going well and we shrug our shoulders. So it's a few hundred billion dollars more for defense. Little difference between 100 billion and 150 billion. It's unreal. We've been anesthetized. The Reagan administration has cut civil-ian programs and has kept building the military budget. It is crazy. I voted for the jerk and have for the past three years rued the day. I deal with a lot of young traders, the yuppies. Their fantasy land has been invaded by something disruptive. They are beginning to realize the all-day joyride may be over. Till now, they were brash. It was all up, up, up, go, go, go. That's gone. Guys whose fantasies were in making huge amounts of money are now happy they can grind it out.

This could be positive. It may make them less self-satisfied and more human. Before, if someone went bust or had a horrible day, they'd shrug their shoulders: it can't happen to me. They'd assume that person did something wrong. Now, they are beginning to see that even if they do what they're supposed to be doing, the world can do something to them. That's a new emotion and that's good. It can happen to *me*.

The feeling of invincibility is gone. Hopefully, it'll stay gone.

MICHELLE MILLER

She is one of the young commodities brokers in the trading room of Rex Winship's company. She is in her mid-thirties.

I'm a very bottom-line person. I'll tell you my opinion, whether you like it or not. That's how I am in business and trading. I do not beat around the bush.

When I was fifteen, I was a volunteer candy-striper in an Evanston hospital. I went to one of the best public high schools in the country, but was never really a big student. Went to a junior college and became a medical lab technician in the hospital.

They put me in a burn unit and in an elderly section. I couldn't stomach it. I really hated it. I mean, you walk into somebody's room and their body is ninety-eight percent burnt. I couldn't stand it. The other was for very old people. It's very depressing. Why do you have to see it? It's like watchin' a horror movie. Come on.

A neighbor who was in the Chicago Mercantile Exchange said, "Why don't you come down here?" That was some fifteen years ago. I was about twenty. I had a job on the floor, working the cattle pit. Recording trades. They just call 'em a pit clerk. I didn't understand what was going on down on the floor at that point in time. I don't even know if I cared to find out. After six months, I got into marketing, took a couple of classes in futures, and started to get to know the business. I didn't want to spend the rest of my life working for the Exchange. If you really want to make some money, you've got to get with a brokerage firm. That's where all the action is. It's fierce competition.

I took courses at night, offered through the Exchange. Options, trading, speculation, almost anything you could think of. I got to handle actual clients. The way I got most of my accounts is smile and dial (laughs lightly). Basically, it's making cold calls, okay? I'm not really calling you cold. Let's say you answered an ad and said you were interested in futures information. I'm not tryin' to talk you into anything, I just want to give the prospect what he wants, okay? I am not trying to talk anybody into anything. I never have and never will.

The type of business I'm going after is not Joe Blow who wants to trade corn or cotton. I'll tell you somethin': most people that trade commodities lose, okay? Not because it's hard to make money. It isn't hard. There's too much ego, too much greed (laughs).

And fear sets in. A guy says, Okay, I'm gonna make a killing and I'll trade once or twice in pork bellies. He loses, say, two thousand dollars on his first trade, he says I'll trade silver. They'll make two or three plays and then they'll forget it. It's just entertainment for them. The odds are probably ninety percent against them. For the individual who wants to take it seriously, do technical analysis, the odds go down to fifty percent.

I'm not interested in Mr. Joe Blow. It's just as easy to find companies and institutions and banks, and they're gonna do a lot more trading. And there's less risk for me.

When you're right in the market, it's the best high you can imagine. It's a high without any alcohol. When you're wrong, it's the lowest low you can imagine, okay? Although I'll tell ya, tradin' your own money is different from tradin' someone else's money. I could be a lot more objective with other people's money (laughs). It's a lot easier to say, Okay, get out, you're wrong.

My battin' average is pretty darn good. People on the floor call me and ask me what I think. I'm confident. The hardest thing is to pull the trigger and put the trade on, but get out when you're wrong and get out fast. The hardest thing to do is to admit you're wrong. I'm able to do that. My sister who's in sales always says, "I don't know how you do it. I couldn't sleep, I couldn't stomach it." It's a lot of risk.

As far as this business goes, it's a positive and a negative. They don't give a woman any credibility, especially the bankers. Prejudice? Oh, absolutely. Some people won't even talk to me. That's okay, no problem. Just tell me and good-bye. Other people, once you prove yourself, which in my business is very easy, they don't give a damn who you are. Or what you are. Or what you look like.

The other problem is the usual sexual advances. I would say every single one of my customers has come on to me in one way or another (laughs). I've had some bad experiences, too. You always have to have your guard up. I almost always expect it, okay? You just learn how to deal with it.

> *During the conversation with Rex Winship, one of the frequent interruptions was a telephone call from a colleague. There was some light banter, as Winship laughed: "If you don't watch out, they'll sue you for sexual harassment."*

There's still a lot of chauvinism in the business. There's a woman's been on the floor ten years and you get a new twenty-three-year-old kid, he thinks he can sit there and boss her around. That's all over the place.

My social life is feast or famine (laughs). I have three dates a weekend and no dates. Generally, if business is real good, my social life is lousy. If business is kinda slow, my social life picks up. We usually talk about business.

Sports I'm very interested in. Football most of all, the Bears. I'm not really a big bar person. I'm more of a let's have a nice dinner, let's go to a show. I like to have a good Scotch.

Politics? Not really. Oh, if we get really down drunk or somethin' like that, you could solve all the world problems, you know (laughs). I don't think the world will ever blow up, or if it does, what are we gonna do about it?

I think Ronnie's done okay. I think he's been fairly honest. He's a good speaker. Oh, I'd like to see more out of this tax reform. About the Russians, I haven't lost any sleep. Have you?

I don't think most brokers think like I do at all. They think of one thing, their paychecks and their commissions first. Sure, I want to make money, but I really try to think of the customer first. I'm conscientious and I'm honest. I don't think a lot of brokers are, I just don't. They overtrade the account. They just keep trading for no reason. That generates a commission. They just trade, get in, get out. It's motion.

You can't trust a lotta people. It upsets me. I don't care how well you think you know somebody, you can't trust them. I know, I've found that out twice already. Two people have stuck me. I have to be on my guard all the time. Even with some friends, too. Aside from my family and one or two girlfriends, I don't trust anybody else. No point getting stabbed again. I just think that's the way life is. There are a lot of dishonest people in the world.

BRUCE BENDINGER

He was a wunderkind in the world of advertising during the 1970s. He had been creative director for Gerald Ford in 1976, during his campaign for the Republican nomination for the presidency.

He is forty-three.

I'm a hired gun for a couple of companies fighting the warfare of the marketplace. I'm a 1980s version of Paladin. The battlefield is corporate America. I'm still fast on the draw, and I'm quick to pick up trends. One of the things is called pattern recognition. It's the ability to pick up a couple of quick little bits, out there in the environment, and come to the right answer ahead of the rest of the pack. They pay me enough to do it that I can't afford to take time off and tend my garden. In the last ten years, we've shifted to much faster communication. We depend on these little bursts, these little sound bites. All good politicians as well as all good advertisers lay out their program in something that will play in ten to twelve seconds on the nightly news.

If you look at films or TV commercials or even news programs, the visual information is coming at you faster and faster and faster. Whether it's Sesame Street going A-B-C-D-E-F-G or MTV or the nightly news. You look at some old television, like Ernie Kovacs, and you're struck by how slo-o-o-w everything was. Even a guy like Ernie Kovacs, who was very bright and hip, seems to be doing it all in slow motion compared to what we're currently used to.

The marketplace has changed in another way. We have major

class shifts in America. The middle class, as traditionally known, is disappearing—being split. You have a growing upper class. Two middle-class incomes together add up to a lot of cash. Young couples, guys who have hit it big with their investment brokers. Those going up the line have disposable incomes of fifty, sixty to over one hundred thousand dollars a year when they get into their peak. If you look at commercials, most of them talk to NYPNS: neat young people in neat situations. Simultaneously, a lot of that old middle class are working to get by on twenty grand or less.

You've got what we used to call working-class: people trapped in dead-end jobs, service economy. They're clerks, they're fast-food, they're whatever. They know they're not goin' anyplace.

You have the knee-driven underclass, which we continue to market sugar and salt and alcohol and nicotine to. We make a good amount of money off of them. You'll find black America still drinkin', still smokin' a lot of cigarettes, still spending a high percentage of their cash on this. You can understand this in terms of what their options are. Much more concerned with short-term gratification, for reasons that are sad but obvious. Marketing things like potato chips, salty snacks, may seem innocent. If you're black, chances are you will retain a greater percentage of salt and be more prone to high blood pressure. Take a look at the mortality rates in black America, you'll find one of the side effects of these consumption patterns. They are fueled by the Michael Jackson type of marketing, which contributes to—I don't think you live as long.

Yet children of the working class have a bit of new cash. A forty-year-old guy workin' in a gas station isn't makin' a lot of money. But a fifteen-, sixteen-year-old kid makin' that kind of money has somethin' in his pocket. He's spending it on fast food, on records, on boom-boxes, on levis, on movies. He's got a higher percentage of disposable income than somebody twenty years older.

There's a new kind of poverty in America. It's *time*. All the people makin' all this cash, you know what they don't got? And I'm one of 'em. They don't got *time*. The time-poor. Both of 'em are workin'. They're workin' hard, makin' all this money, fifty, sixty hours a week. Mom isn't home makin' the tuna casserole. They both come home beat from their jobs. They're gonna go out, they're gonna order pizza. They don't have time to make dinner, to do a lot of things. It's really changed the way a lot of America lives. My lawyer says every couple in business together needs a wife, because there's no one who's cookin' the dinner, who's cleanin' the house.

Another way that's reshaping America is the move from parenting to child management. You don't have mom raising the kids. She gets 'em till it's time for Montessori, then she's back in the work force to make the money to pay for Montessori and the designer kids' clothes. And the tube in that age group has an incredible dominance in kids' lives. They're watching this thing three, four hours a day.

People are concerned with marginal tax rates and whether their mortgage interest is going to be a write-off. So many other values have diminished: patriotism, religion, family. All that is really left is money. It is the way you keep score. It's one of the few values that still survives.

The teacher or the minister, who didn't make a lot of money but was respected in the community, is less and less a factor. Now everybody's getting their M.B.A. because that's the game these days.

The only value is common currency. A woman who is a good mother at a cocktail party, with all the other people doing all these other things, is almost embarrassed. There are a lot of people doing a good job taking care of kids, but in terms of what's hip, it's Bill Cosby's wife, the lawyer. Not Bill Cosby's wife who stays home and is a mother. That's where the action is, where the media buzz is.

Who are the real forces behind this electronic thing everybody's gettin' fed? You're finding greater and greater merging. The number-crunchers have taken over business in such a way that they're able on paper to create all these entities.

Investment bankers can make incredible amounts of money. I'm talking about multi, multi, multi multiples of millions, by leveraging these deals: leveraged buy-outs, spin-offs, venture-this, all that stuff. You're watchin' TV and you're not aware that some company just bought one of the networks and has cut back forty percent of the staff. If I can make more money running *Wheel of Fortune* than a community service show, guess what's gonna run on the air?

There is no evil cabal of capitalists with dollar signs on their bulging vests making these decisions. There's a bunch of hardworking number-crunchers who look at the numbers on the rules that have been set up, and they're making decisions. If you see seven boats sailing in the same direction, it ain't because it's a conspiracy, it's because that's the way the wind's blowing.

Another trend that bothers me is that somebody makes a living in advertising as soon as something becomes bad for you. It turns into big business. There's an ad in *Advertising Age* that just came out today: ''Liquor use drops. Liquor consumption fell five percent in 1986. It was the greatest annual decrease in more than thirty years.'' Now that's good news.

It's good news for the health of America. It's also good news for advertising. Advertising budgets will probably go up by 10 percent. They're going up because these people in the marketplace fight harder and harder to get their share of the shrinking market pie.

A friend of mine is working on a very big piece of business now: the Beef Council. Ten years ago, beef was not a $20-million-a-year advertising account. People are trying to get America to eat more beef because America's concerned with cholesterol. Suddenly they say, We've got all these cows sittin' around, we gotta market them. For every cow slaughtered, you put a little money in the pot for the Beef Council.

Guess how much is spent selling cheese in America? Twenty-two million dollars. All the nice little dairy farmers from my home state, Wisconsin, are trying to get you to eat more cheese because you're not eating enough 'cause it's got cholesterol. So we're gonna spend 22 million.

If you don't have any ethical problem, you can make an unconscionable amount of money advertising cigarettes.

I'm optimistic about the near future, but I see a downloading in the nineties and then into the year 2000, I see other things happening. You'll see some sort of upper-class enclave trying to protect ourselves from the unwhite, unrich, unhappy hordes, who just want a decent life, not too much to ask for. I think you'll see some real tough times coming up. We may be in decline. Some old historian once said, ''In declining cultures everybody eats well.'' In the cowboy captain, we may be seeing the end of something.

ISABELLE KUPRIN

She's twenty-eight, restless, voluble; her talk is free, easy, sassy, as though the stranger were a familiar. In the manner of a hip comic, she casually throws away her lines; intimations of more where that came from.

I'm a copywriter for an ad agency. It involves being a total asshole. I do it for the money, it's easy and horrible. I do nothing good for society. I mean, I help people sell cheese. The talent is being able to sit in meetings and listen to people talk about an adjective for four hours. There's nothing redeeming about that, but I can wear what I want to work. I'm doin' okay, better than maybe some of my friends.

My parents live outside Detroit. Middle-class, definitely. I can't believe that people like that ever got together. They were very mismatched and got married because it was the thing to do in the fifties.

I was raised to be this independent woman, yet caught between the two. I'm half Janis Joplin and half June Cleaver sometimes—she played in *Leave It to Beaver,* the mother.

My brother's a year older than me. He had a job in computers and quit that. Right now he's not doin' anything. He's not sure what's he's gonna do. He's a very angry person, also totally frightened of the world. He's a complete loner, by himself all the time.

I always thought he was unique, but the more I meet people, the more I find a lot of 'em alienated, frightened, crazy. They seem to be kids my age, from my generation. They were raised with these expectations that we would do much better. You get out there and you realize—man, you're lucky to be makin' $15,000 a year and you're gonna live in a dump and not really have a great life.

I look where my parents live right now and I could never imagine having a place like that. They have a house on four acres, two cars. And they sent us to college. The sick thing is my father makes maybe $10,000 a year more than I do. I'm one person and he's raised a family of four.

At Ann Arbor, I first wanted to be Jacques Cousteau. But I had to have a Ph.D. and I didn't like school that much. So I just took biology and English and got out and realized I could analyze urine for three dollars an hour or wait tables. I was good in math and people I knew who had Ph.D.'s in math are delivering pizza.

I think we were really spoiled. I grew up expecting I would get out of college and make $40,000 a year. I grew up expecting that when I was sixteen years old, somebody was gonna deliver a Mercedes-Benz at the door. I don't know where I got that idea. It was quite a rude awakening (laughs).

I got out of school in 1980 and waited tables for a year. Did a lotta drugs. I decided I needed a real job, so I moved to my parents' house, thinking that would force me to find one. I laid around the house in a robe for eight months, watching reruns of *The Love Boat*. I answered ads in the paper, went to interviews, and just ended up in dumpy hotels with acne-faced twenty-year-olds tellin' me there was a future sellin' life insurance to college students.

Even had an offer to sell velvet paintings to ghetto families in Detroit. They'd advertise: Art gallery manager wanted. You'd go down to this sleazy hellhole somewhere in Detroit and some really sleazy guy would be like—hey, yeah, go out and hustle these cheesy paintings to these people that can't afford 'em. So I went into advertising because I figured it was easy and I could at least do that.

When I waited tables, I had a lotta cash and started hangin' out with all the people I waited tables with. You do that for eight hours, you need to go out to the bar for a while. A couple I went with worked at a publishing house for $8,000 a year. I just thought, fuck that! Some went like into Xerox and IBM, and I didn't want to do that. I had some image of myself doing something meaningful, writing, biology. Not much of a market for either. I was on the brink of becoming a yuppie, settling for IBM, nice house, that kind of thing.

Then there are other people. Like my mother. Influences you had as a kid play a role. She was into demonstrations, that kind of thing. I remember 1968, feeling it was very exciting and really wishing I was old enough to take part. I remember going down to demonstrations in Detroit when I was eleven. By myself. I wanted to be Janis Joplin. I wanted to be Angela Davis. They sort of fit my personality that wanted to rebel about something.

People I work with feel they're creative and living a wild, cool life. I think it's a lot of bullshit. It's a business. Other friends I have don't feel that way. One's trying to be a musician, another is trying to be a fine artist. They're living on $4,000 a year, a hard life. I'm the one working for a big corporation, makin' money. I'm the yuppie of my set. We meet at somebody's house, sit around, have dinner, and talk about what's goin' on. Art, music, movies, books. I read a lot. We hit political things, too: South Africa. Reagan. They're not highly political, but they're aware, bright.

I've been shocked by people at the agency. I'd say the majority's my age. They were sitting around the table and every single one of them voted for Reagan. I couldn't believe it. I used to be very righteous: if you vote for him, you're as evil as he is. But most of these people are very nice. They mean well. It becomes harder and harder to put judgments on people once you know who they are. It scares me, because it confuses me. It's like you can't even hate them (laughs).

I give money to causes, I know what's goin' on, but I'm not that left-wing. I mean, I'm not out there with signs, marching.

I went back to Ann Arbor three years after I got out. I just couldn't believe it. I thought it was gonna be more radical than 1980. I was shocked. There were people walking around in mono-grammed Shetland sweaters, drinking Stroh's. That's not what I had in mind.

You see people walkin' the streets, havin' a hard time livin', and others treat 'em like they have a disease. They just bow their heads and walk the other way. I think the society is a lot worse off than everyone makes it out to be. It's not just that easy of a place.

One day I bought a sixty-dollar sweater at Marshall Field's. On the L train going home, there were a million women and men with Marshall Field bags. There was this empty seat that people kept walking over to and not sitting down in. Next to it was a man who was dying, a bum. This guy is like starving to death. A conductor finally came by to see if he was breathing. Then people just started laughing. Nobody did anything.

There's people around my house that sleep on the streets. I realize it's not easy to take care of 'em either. I tried to fight a guy on the street one night. It was real cold and I woke him and said, ''You're gonna freeze to death, can I take you somewhere?'' The guy ended up tryin' to pick me up, tryin' to kiss me, then he threw up on me. I mean it's hard tryin' to help these people.

I remember my first real dealings with black people. I was in a dorm on a floor that were mostly black women. None of them would talk to me. I would go in there like—Hi! I love you all. They would just like—Fuck you! One day I confronted them. This woman said, "Look, you're ninety percent of the population and we're ten percent. And fuck you."

I went through a period of major prejudice thinking, Oh, well, all black people are horrible. I started to understand what prejudice was. You get over it and you're friends. You realize there are good ones and bad ones. I have quite a few black friends now. I went out and found them.

I don't feel hopeless about the world. There are people out there who want to move and change things. I'm glad the peace marchers and the antinuke demonstrators are there. I don't think they have an easy task these days.

It's hard to get the energy to care. You have to get the facts, in order to fight something. It's too hard to live your life, get to the bank, and talk to the dry cleaners and then sit down and learn what a nuclear plant is all about and how you can help. That takes time, it takes knowledge, it takes some work. It's taking time out of your life. Even though it's to your benefit, it's easy to go—Well, someone else will take care of it.

I think I'd like to contribute to society in some way. I don't know what that might be. Right now, I just sort of give bums money on the street. I mean, that's about it. 'Cause I don't trust organizations. I think they're full of shit. I don't know where the money goes. I would rather give them twenty bucks and let 'em go drink on it if that makes 'em happy. I'd rather see that happen than give it to the United Way and have them put it into an advertising campaign.

The issue is, what do I do? Little things. I have more money than most of my friends, so I give money away. I don't know.

SAMANTHA HARRISON

A scattering of magazines on the coffee table in her
Manhattan apartment: Architectural Digest, The New
Yorker, Publishers Weekly, Atlantic; *no business journals.*
After ten years in the world of book publishing, she is

working toward her M.B.A. at the Columbia University
School of Business.

She is thirty-two, of an old American family
distinguished in the fields of academia, law, and
architecture. "I have had a wonderful life up to now. It's
just that things change all the time."

Our class is almost fifty-fifty men and women. The average age is twenty-five. Most have undergraduate degrees in economics, engineering, and business. You really don't talk about your undergraduate degree any more.

A friend of mine, who is forty, had been a stock analyst on Wall Street fifteen years. She married, had babies, raised her children, and now wanted to go back. They said, It doesn't matter what you did before. So what, you went to Smith? So you worked on Wall Street for five years? You don't know anything. The only way you're going to get a job is with an M.B.A. They feel the stuff being taught in business school grooms you better for the quick fix.

More and more young women are abandoning teaching, social work, nursing, for business. That's where the money is. Getting there is not as hard as studying law. It's eighteen months rather than three years. I think a lot of people look at it as insurance for the future. It's a piece of paper that doesn't mean diddly-squat, but it gives you something that is transferable. You can make sixty, seventy, eighty thousand your first year out of business school.

The younger students are very easy to place. I heard of a student last semester who was offered a job for one of the major investment firms at $125,000. She was twenty-four years old. Twenty-four years old! What can you do with that? (Laughs.)

The people I hang out with are all over thirty. With liberal arts backgrounds. We talk about what we're gonna do when we grow up, when we get out of business school. It's a change of life in a way, being here. We've formed a Renaissance Club, yakkin' about Shakespeare, theater, books, politics. We don't want to become these little number-crunching automatons.

I don't know many of the younger ones who will join up with us. They're very one-track-minded: I'm gonna be at the top of the class and then I'm gonna go and run Wall Street. They're a more aggressive crowd. I mean, there are a lot of little fascists running around up there.

The girls are as aggressive as the guys. They want to run Wall Street also. They are equally determined to ace the finals. And are equally upset when they don't. Interestingly, the place is quite sexist. In a class called Managerial Behavior, we were studying stereotypes : successful and attractive men are thought to be successful by virtue of their ability ; successful and attractive women are thought to be successful by virtue of being attractive or something else. Not their ability. What was unusual was the reaction of the class. The little male chauvinist piglets that came out of the woodwork were unbelievable (laughs). I couldn't believe what I was hearing! They were agreeing with the study : of course it's true. Women are simply —you know. Most of the women in class were quiet. I was not.

We have a course in business ethics. It dealt with plant closings. They're in favor of closings because of cost benefits. A friend of mine argued with me about unions. Get rid of them all, she said. I said, You have to remember why they got there, the history, their purpose. I don't care, da-da-da. She was twenty-three.

It's the same way in law school, where the students are even younger. A friend of mine was in this class. They were talking about the Dow Chemical plant. The professor mentioned napalm. They didn't know what napalm was. They hadn't a clue about Vietnam or Watergate. It wasn't that long ago and they weren't that young. They're illiterate, too.

Most of the talk you hear in the hall is, Did you do your finance homework? Can you believe what a jerk this professor is? That's about it.

They're married, a good number of them, quite young. They don't have children yet. It's a two-career match. In the sixties, there was a feeling of finding yourself before you attach yourself to somebody else. People born after that period are much more conservative, much more traditional home-and-hearth. They back Reagan, of course.

And the last two taxi drivers I had were PH.D.'s in liberal arts.

LARRY MORAN

*He appeared out of the blue; bothered, somewhat
bewildered, and not at all bewitched by the current state of
affairs, i.e., his job. He is twenty-two.*

I was a bright guy who was educated by the Jesuits for the last eight years (laughs). Brainwashed. I come from average roots in Chicago, a regular city neighborhood. Economically, we've always been bad off. That's what motivates me to work for the Board of Trade. It's not a natural thing.

When you study philosophy or the liberal arts for eight years, all those wonderful ideas, and you come back to the real world (laughs), you have to make a living. But when you just come out of college with a philosophy degree, it's disheartening. I don't know what to do with it.

I'm a mere runner on the agricultural floor, where they trade corn, soybeans, wheat contracts, futures. You're not actually buying the commodity, you're buying a promise to deliver it. My work is meaningless. You bring an order from a person that takes the order over the phone to a person that executes an order in the pit. I don't see the value. When you choose a career, it has to mesh with your values. There are a lotta people down there who make a good deal of money. That's something I can use (laughs). But if you don't have a natural interest in financial things, it's tough.

I do want to make money. Most people do. I thought if I went there and took some classes quickly—financial futures, interest-rate markets—and worked really hard, I'd make enough money to eventually do whatever I wanted to do. 'Cause money in our society is power, freedom. But you really have to have some belief in that to go through all that work.

I don't mean to sound moralistic, but it's just not for me. I should be doing something more intelligent. All you're doing is figuring out which way prices are gonna go. Making money is proof that they beat out the other guy. That's their way of keeping score. That's their culture. What would I like to do? I don't know. That's my problem.

It's weird. I feel like I'm on the fringe and just trying to cultivate a philosophy or political conviction that is good or upright or whatever. It's weird to be on the fringe, trying to have a basic conviction that a few years ago people were taking for granted. You know?

When I first went to college, there was this guy in the dorm who had a poster on the wall: a rich man standing in front of a Rolls Royce and on the bottom, Poverty Sucks. I was appalled. Such insensitivity to people who struggle.

It was always a struggle for my family. Our educational level doesn't match up with our financial. My father, who died a few years ago, was a commercial artist. My mother's a free-lance writer. My oldest sister is a Chicago cop. It's neat to tell people that—it frightens them. The other's in graduate school, married, has a kid and problems. It's made me appreciate more the people who have to struggle.

At the same time, I can imagine myself making money, slowly moving my way up to be an executive and forgetting about all the struggles and losing my care for those people.

I'm not that worried whether I make a hundred thousand this year. It's not that important when you're twenty-two. At the same time, you see your family struggling and you see a city full of such people. You see them on trains all the time. You got to balance your own security and your wanting to help other people. That's what I'm struggling with. It's almost that I want to do something that can't be done.

I don't worry about the arms race. I don't ignore it, but it's so much out of my control. A lot of good people are trying to deal with it. I don't think everyone has to have a personal involvement in that. Everyone should care about the issue, but I don't think everyone has the obligation to be an activist.

I can't say for sure I support peace marchers. It's too complex an issue. Marches are very nice, compassionate things but they're too simplistic. I've had lectures on the morality of nuclear deterrence. It's so hard to make judgments. The reason I find all this too complex is I see people devoting their lives to disagreeing. Two truths can seem opposite and yet you know they're both true. Does that make sense?

Is that part of Jesuitical training?

Yeah, it's confusing. I'm definitely very religious. Sanctuary? I don't know. It's not just a religious question, it's political. Breaking the law is not something you take lightly. At the same time, people really need help. I guess I'm passively neutral again (laughs). I could talk to you all day about how confused I am. I know a girl who went down to Nicaragua, an activist Christian. She makes everything seem so simple. If you have any faith in the U.S. government, it can't be that simple.

It's troublesome, because I feel I don't have any backbone. Sooner or later, I know I will have to stand up for something. At the same time, I deliberately get conservative and liberal publications to try to understand things from different points of view. It doesn't do any good. I'm a confused person.

I just handed in my notice. Next week's my last week. I couldn't tell them why. I merely said I didn't enjoy it any more. I wasn't that interested any more. They said, Well, it's not everyone's cup of tea. (A long pause.) That's why I came to you. Give me an idea (laughs).

PAUL W. BOYD

> *He is forty-three. He attended a Jesuit seminary in the 1960s, "during a tumultuous time in the church. We were on the cutting edge of change. I left about three months after I got ordained once I confronted the real world."*
>
> *His father had been editor of the* Cincinnati Enquirer; *his mother, a social worker involved with public housing.*
>
> *He is now a real estate broker in Chicago.*

How does someone who had my idealism get into real estate? I find what I'm doing now is consistent with the same urgings that led me to the Jesuit seminary.

I didn't last in the seminary, the celibacy thing didn't mean too much to me. Anyway, it's one thing to study liberation theology and then go to a parish and someone wants you to give a sermon on the rosary. The reality of what the public church wanted and what we were trained to be didn't fit. So I left.

I got into housing programs for the city of Chicago. I was giving grants to rehab groups in the inner-city neighborhoods. I was sort of grant manager and planner. I wanted a further expression of my idealism. And making a living. I worked there for about six years and it was a frustrating experience. There was a real core of thinkers, who designed good programs. We all left in disillusionment. It all turned out to be so wasteful and so extraordinarily expensive for the cost benefit, we said, What good is all this? It doesn't work. Everything we did, the most creative programs, when you got down to cost analysis, helped nobody but the people who got the grants. Those for whom they were designed didn't take advantage of them. I just came to a brick wall.

During that time, to help me understand the programs, I took real estate courses. My degree in theology taught me how to think, so I did quite well. I got a broker's license.

One day, I was browsing in a bookstore and saw the jacket of Adam Smith's *Wealth of Nations*. I saw this quote, I'll paraphrase: When you seek to help the poor or bring about the common good, you usually don't achieve it; but when you seek your own self-interest, as if by an invisible hand, the common good is served. People benefit indirectly through your pursuit of legitimate self-interest. Boy, it just struck me as so true to my experience. So I got out of planning and just one day walked into a real estate office and said, Hey, can I sell real estate? I'm gonna forget all this other stuff. It just doesn't make sense. Maybe I can buy a building, fix it up, make a living, and see if somehow my idealism can live through this.

For the last eight or ten years I've been doing that and making a good living. I have the leisure to work with community groups. We have four thousand housing units, mostly for modest- and low-income people, in use out of ten thousand abandoned buildings. It's revivified the neighborhood. What a contrast to the public approach! When you seek to help the poor directly, it doesn't work. When you instigate the private market, it works.

Our community council got $50,000 to hire an organizer and a staff. For the public program I was in, it took $2 million to produce eight units. So I've come to a full circle in realizing what works. I'm convinced public projects can only work if they instigate, leverage the private market to do things.

I sell to legitimate people who pursue their self-interest and who fix up buildings and improve the neighborhood. The net result is a community where the poor have better opportunities for jobs, better housing, where the working class is happier, and where the crime rate is dropping. The economy is flourishing in a modest way, and the middle class is moving in and enjoying it.

I grew up thinking that making money was not noble. My parents were always involved in social causes and I followed in their steps. But I found out by following my present bent, it's satisfying, fun, and I end up helping more people than trying to figure out how I can help them. I'm forty-three years old and I'm in gear now. I figured out how to satisfy my original urge.

As much as I can't stand Reagan as a person, I voted for him. The liberal approach didn't work: Model Cities, the Johnson poverty program, down the drain. I came to feel in voting for Reagan —as much as he is such a jerk—we needed that direction toward the economy.

Public do-gooders were trying to exorcise their guilt by casting off responsibilities to government to solve our problems. I realize now that private, voluntary effort is more pure, direct, and to the point. It's like a paradigm for the problems of the world. You don't bother with public money, tempting as it is to use it.

My mother and a group of women went to work in a public housing project in Cincinnati, just as volunteers. They were teaching these poor Appalachians and Southern blacks how to cook and sew. They formed a teaching center. Over the years, it just grew and grew, filled with volunteers and private donations. It was held up as a model. It was all private, all volunteer.

The state of Ohio came in. We'd like to fund this and make it part of the state welfare system. My mother was drowned in reports. People backed away. Within six months it closed.

Did they have a tenants' council?

Tenants' council?

In the late 1930s, Elizabeth Wood was head of the Chicago Housing Authority. She remembers:

"In 1937, the United States Housing Act was passed. . . .
We built quite beautiful projects throughout the country.
But it never occurred to anybody that the people might
make their own decisions about playgrounds, housing
design or management policies. . . . Sometimes these people
have awfully good ideas, better than ours. . . .

"There were lots of unsystematized, uninstitutional,
good native works. After two babies died of whooping
cough, a group of women in the project volunteered to find
out about preventives. They knocked on all the doors, so all
youngsters under six got whooping cough inoculations.
They had so many creative ideas.

"In a little three-room apartment, this mother made the
house work its full magic. When the sixteen-year-old
started to date, there was a front parlor for her to sit in.
There was a plant. There was a sofa. I had kept this room
bare. She filled it. The mother had the girl buy a pink
electric light bulb, so it looked pretty when she had a date.
She was one of the best social workers I ever knew.

"We had a perfectly good staff, nothing wrong with
them. We simply had no idea of the independence, the
creativity of these people. They had tenants' councils that
always came up with fresh ideas. . . ." *

I've made a profit on something, but I've provided good. There's enough cash flow to keep the building fixed up, and it's growing in value. The prior owner took everything he could from the building. He didn't make life any better for the people living there. The property declined in value. He abused the bottom line. Slum landlords make money. But you could make a lot more money running a building humanely and reinvesting money into the building.

As for public housing, I've never seen it work. In the near future, we're going to see terribly exciting experiments of private-sector involvement in public housing. I'm hopeful that the right teams of

* *Hard Times* (New York: Pantheon Books, 1970).

managers and developers will finish the scattered-site program. It's a wonderful opportunity. You can't delegate it to a public body.

I don't think the privatization of housing policy has had a long enough time to really work. If by the year 2000 the problem is worsening, then we'll realize something is wrong. I believe the trickle-down theory will work. I see townhouses being built all over the community. I see people moving out of upper-end condos into these townhouses. I see people moving out of lower-end condos to the upper-end condos. I see people moving into rental buildings that were upgraded from poor buildings. I see a dynamism in the real estate economy.

The trickle-down approach is imperfect but working better than anything I've ever seen. People who are in $300,000 situations are moving into $500,000 townhouses. People who were in $100,000 situations are moving into those vacated, and people in $50,000 situations are moving into the $100,000's. I don't think the rich figure on the dynamism, when they buy a $500,000 townhouse, that somewhere down the line some poor person is gonna move into better digs. They don't care, but it's true.

Frankly, I don't see a massive upsurge in homelessness in the past twenty years. I'm a salesperson, so I'm an optimist. I think things can work better if you push hard enough. A salesperson can create a new reality. I sell anything I get involved with. If it's a dog, if it's ugly, I create its good values and everyone says it's a pretty dog. It becomes pretty.

DR. NEIL SHULKIN

He has been practicing dentistry for twenty-three years.
He is forty-six.

I'm a dentist entrepreneur. I enjoy the business aspect of my profession as well as the practice. In a nutshell, that's who Neil Shulkin is.

The professions today are becoming more businesslike. They must. I've been franchising dental centers. The biggest part of our practice right now is cosmetic dentistry: capping, orthodontics, things like that.

The traditional dentist is slowly phasing out of the picture. What's really changed over the past ten years is the marketing concept. Since the Supreme Court decision allowing professions to advertise, it is necessary to market in some fashion. We were one of the first to advertise. It's called the Dental Store.

The only way marketing could be buried in the budget was to market for a large group of people. We had two practices at the time. We opened three more. Five different locations, basically storefronts, but very professional.

I have nine dentists in my own private practice, including all the specialties. It's probably one of the most modern facilities in the country. We also, because of our size, have tested products for companies. We were one of the first to get this Karidex 100. Drilling with the chemical.

To be honest with you, I just cannot sit still. It's just one of those things. I'm involved in my own company called Dental Development Service. I'm involved in a franchising company called General Health Systems, Incorporated. I'm vice-president of Strategic Health Care Management Systems. We administrate for other insurance carriers. I'm involved with a new company that's just on the stock market, that's called Systems for Health Care.

I started when I was about ten years of age. My father owned one of the largest dental laboratories in the city. I got involved with teeth. I knew nothing else. The natural thing was to go to dental school. I loved it. I finished early. I was the second youngest to ever graduate. I was responsible for the University of Illinois sending work out instead of having the students do it. Send it out to a professional laboratory, which was my father (laughs). I got him the account while I was in dental school.

I've been on television, I can't count the number of radio stations throughout the country. I've won awards for my advertising. I've been on CBS national news.

Basically, we're talking about the future of dentistry. The profession is just sitting there, waiting for somebody else to dictate what's gonna happen to it. I'm out there hustling. I'm looking for business.

I was taught traditional private-practice dentistry. But you really learn your profession, like you learn your business, out in the world. When I entered dental school, I didn't expect to be involved in business. Because I started from scratch twenty-three years ago, I had time on my hands. Rather than sit there and wait for the first patient to walk in the door, I had to do something to get the business. I had to be competitive.

It cost me a fortune to learn business. I mean, a fortune. That's one thing they didn't teach you at dental school. I tried to get the university to add those marketing courses. I was willing to provide it at no cost, just so these students come out with some realization of what's happening out in the real world. It was a very costly experience. The dental schools are ten years behind in business.

My day is very busy. I get up at four in the morning. I'm in the office between six and seven. I'm constantly going. It's my life-style. I enjoy it. I cannot sit for ten minutes. I watch television all day long. I mean, it's on but I don't know what the hell's on it (laughs). I read the paper maybe once a week. That's how much time I sit down.

I practice about twenty-five hours a week. Because I have such a large practice, I probably produce as much as the average guy who works forty hours a week.

I keep my mouth shut with a patient when it comes to politics. I once said something about a senator. I thought it was normal conversation. The patient was for the most part in love with this particular senator. I never saw that patient again. This is when I was young in practice. No more politics.

I voted for Reagan, but I don't even remember who I voted against. I voted for him because he was popular, and the country needed an uplift. I don't know if I'd vote for him now. Some of the things that sounded terrific are not turning out that way. However, he did cut down on regulations: laws restricting advertising and so on. I feel he did the right thing. The marketplace should determine what's happening.

I have four children. One of my sons is in dental school. Another is graduating in business and finance. My daughter's going into fashion merchandising. And then, I have a thirteen-year-old.

My wife is an entrepreneur also. After my kids went off to college, she got bored at home. We went on a cruise and met somebody who was in business herself. Ladies' fashions and accessories. My wife opened up—and then went into another business with a bag full of jewelry. From that, we came up with the name The Bag Lady. She's opening Saturday on Michigan Avenue, across from

Water Tower. She's been in the *North Shore* magazine, the local papers, and the *Tribune's* coming out on Friday.

I have one hobby : I collect spittoons. I thought it was appropriate. I like archaeology and things like that, but I hate antiquing. To me, it's all old junk. But one thing I felt I could relate to my business : spittoons. I've been written up in several publications regarding it.

We also have a thing that got us in every newspaper in the country, as well as some of the rest of the world. I was on every radio station. Our kids and my wife and myself have license plates that say TEETH, TOOTH, INCISOR, MOLAR, and CUSPID. Mine is TOOTH. My wife's is TEETH. My children are INCISOR, MOLAR, and CUSPID. We each have our own car. Everybody smiles when they drive by.

DR. QUENTIN YOUNG

He was medical director of Cook County Hospital from 1972 to 1981. He is currently director of the Health and Medicine Policy Research Group. "We believe health and medicine are not synonyms. Frequently the medical system works against health. Our concern is access to care, quality of care, and empowerment of communities."

The advent of corporate medicine is the darkest development in a very troubled health-care system. Gigantic penetration of the market : these are their words. It's venture capital seeking to make profits out of the health-care system. The AMA had all sorts of laws—they still exist—against corporate medicine being practiced, yet these laws have been ignored. Large conglomerates came in.

Some of the old AMA homilies were true. The doctor was a single person working in a community. He went to the same church, had to meet the same people every day. If someone was down on his luck, he'd put the bill on the tab. He was certainly one of the most pres-

tigious people in the community. Today, under the high-tech alien-
ation quality of the health-care system, doctors are way down on the
list.

The perception is that they're overrich, venal, and greedy. They
do things to people to make money. They don't talk to people, they
don't care. The malpractice explosion is a real issue. I don't think
doctors are less skilled. Nor do I think venal lawyers are giving
doctors a hard time. They're around if the patients want to sue.
Why do patients want to sue so much? It's been said, If the patient
really believes you care, you can cut off the wrong toe and he won't
sue. But if he thinks you're greedy and look at him as a fee to be
paid, he'll be dissatisfied even with good results.

Before World War Two, eighty percent of the doctors thought of
themselves as general practitioners. Today, eighty percent become
specialists. They do what they've been trained to do. They never
treat the whole patient. They are expert in eyes, heart, or rectum
and they do a superb job of fixing whatever is wrong with eyes,
heart, or rectum. But they don't do a very good job about understanding the patient and his life, his fight with his wife, his loss of a
child, his job. It's all so ironic. Until World War Two, there was
very little doctors could do. There were no antibiotics. The germ
theory is just a hundred years old. The first lung was removed in
1935. The doctor was very much the comforter. His most important
skill was at predicting when the patient would die. Technology has
expanded the power to intervene, to heal, and to make him more
distant. That's the central paradox.

How do you bring these two wholes together without sacrificing
what is valuable in technology?

The absolute symbol of the degradation in corporate intrusion is
Humana's offer of a hundred free heart-lung machines à la Schroe-
der. Remember the first heart-transplant patient? The biggest
wrong was not the naked venality—it was giving the American
people the wrong message about heart disease. We have illusions
that machines like this will solve our problem with heart disease.

There was no real corporate medicine until the middle of the
sixties. It glommed on nursing homes very quickly, moved into the
hospital business where they boomed. Now, there's the beginning of
the backlash. Public hospitals, which were improving until about
ten, fifteen years ago, have become the absolute dumping pit for all
these contradictions. The system always dumped on the public sector

everything that had no profits in it. Today, it has become the specific uncivilized behavior called prudent management.

The concrete act is taking a patient in an emergency room, who needs hospitalization, and moving him by any means possible to the public hospital. Go there to get your care. This is not our responsibility. We don't take these people, because they don't have resources, and we're a business. Sisters of Mercy could hardly say these words, but even so, they've been forced by this vampire effect to do the same thing. They must emulate to survive: getting rid of losers. What's a loser? It's a sick person without resources. They send 'em off to the County.

A prudent manager who has his M.B.A. has a patient who appears to have had a heart attack in the emergency room. He has to have systems in place—all systems go—meaning, he has to train his doctors and nurses to think in this way. If they can move that person in safety—though sometimes the transfer is hurtful, even life-threatening—he has just saved his hospital ten thousand to twenty thousand dollars. That's as good as getting a gift from a wealthy donor. Increasingly, this is the way the private sector is looking at the unsponsored patient.

In recent years, more and more Americans are no longer sponsored by Medicare and Medicaid—incomplete supports, to say the least. The move from industrial to service work has created an enormous group of people who have no protection against serious illness. It may be as much as one out of three Americans.

Until five years ago, there were free clinics, teaching hospitals. People felt they were taking charity and their pride was hurt, but dammit, they could go and get some care. Now that's gone. Outpatient facilities are drying up in all the big cities.

If a person has appendicitis and goes to Cook County emergency room, no problem. But if he comes in and says he's been coughing for six weeks or has seen some blood in his stool or a swelling in the neck he can't explain, he gets an appointment for nine months hence. A nonappointment. It's a unit that sees 450,000 visits a year. Some of the clinics have a four-month wait. It's the end of an option.

Charitable behavior by private doctors has ended. The rationalization is Medicaid. It has been so butchered by the private system, most doctors will not take the knocked-down fees. In some states, not more than ten percent of doctors will accept Medicaid. Some use this low pay as a basis for churning them out and sending them to their friends, doing tests that are not necessary. By and large, the Medicaid system is terrible.

We are the only country in the industrialized world—with the exception of the Union of South Africa—that does not have a national health program. In Canada, two states, Saskatchewan and British Columbia, introduced a statewide system of entitlements. It was so popular that in five years it was federalized. In the last fifteen years, we've had no national health policy that was not based on cost control.

Ever hear of DRGs? Diagnostic Related Groups. It's got doctors biting their fingernails. If So-and-So comes in with this diagnosis, you get X dollars. If you get 'im out in one day, you've made a profit. If he stays in twice the length of time, you've lost. Go to it, tiger. Any child with one-and-one economics knows what will happen. The hospitals started getting people out, misleading people by saying DRGs limited how long they'd stay. It's this administration's technique to control costs of Medicare. It allows so much money for a particular diagnosis. It's just one more deadly cost-control strategy. It's two years old now, and the harvest is bitter. Elderly people are being dumped out of hospitals prematurely. There's been some serious suffering and death.

It's a government that is driven by a marketplace strategy. Applied to health, it's a form of social Darwinism. In effect, it will eliminate the "inferior"—defined as the disaabled, the sick, the elderly without money. That's a very big river to cross. How different is it from the Nazi decision to eliminate the unfit?

Unlike the half-generation ahead of them, young doctors coming out today have a dark vision. They come out fifty thousand dollars in debt. They are pushing thirty, maybe have a kid or two. They're deeply in hock, indentured. They can't go out, have a few lean years and build up a practice. They have to immediately become available to these corporations at a salary. They don't have the luxury of being socially concerned.

We're rapidly getting to the point where the doctor is essentially a highly paid technician. We've been told there's a doctor glut. That hundred thousand coming down the pike will be used, as labor forces have been used from time immemorial.

Imaginary conversation at a corporate HMO: Doctor X, we love you here, but you're seeing only 4.2 patients an hour. We'd like you to see 7.2. I can't do that, my standards will fall, I'll miss things. It wouldn't be fair to the patient. Well, hate to tell you, we got a guy out there who's willing to do it.

Patients are worried and they're organizing. The elderly are forced to organize. Their numbers swell. Doctors have made sure we're going to have ever more elderly people. The Medicare system lies there, tantalizing, failing. With the elderly in the vanguard, more people are organizing for their health needs.

I envision—it's really my epiphany—a new kind of union between physicians and the objects of all their training, the patients. Something beyond Father Knows Best.

The alternative vision is really frightening. An industrialized system, controlled by five or six monopolies, care allocated, exclusion of the unworthy or unfit, as we move toward a euthanasic society.

AYN RAND AND THE TRUCKER

BARBARA BRANDON

During the past twenty years, in visiting college campuses
across the country, there has been one constant; two or
three—often more—students in attendance, bright-eyed
and self-assured, have asked rhetorically: "Have you read
Atlas Shrugged? Or, The Fountainhead?"*

Barbara Brandon had been a disciple of Ayn Rand for
many years. She wrote her biography.

Our culture has changed since the
forties, in significant part by the
works of Ayn Rand. Her ideas have spread and made a difference.
Ayn Rand defined two ways of facing life, two types of men: antag-
onists. The man of self-sufficient ego, of independent mind, and the
parasite, who is directed by others. The man who lives for his own
sake and the collectivist, who places others above self.

She was passionately against placing others above self. It was
dangerous and bad in a man's soul. It made him a robot, pushed and
pulled by others. You didn't just decide: If being cruel to people
makes me happy, I'll do it. No, you had to rationally justify your
actions.

Originally, her influence was underground. One didn't see it pub-
licly. Today it is no longer so. Everywhere I look, I find prominent
people accepting her ideas, in government as well as colleges. Alan
Greenspan has been very influenced by her.* The head of J. P.
Stevens was an actual student of Ayn Rand.† When I went to the
UCLA, I was the campus pariah, because I was arguing pro–free

---

* Chairman of the Federal Reserve Board.
† The Southern textile company whose employees had been on a bitter strike that lasted
years.

enterprise. People were not talking to me. This was considered next door to an obscenity in those days. Today, it's quite acceptable.

When Ayn wrote *Atlas Shrugged,* students in college were being taught that the industrialist is the symbol of evil. Ayn recognized this brilliantly. In the book, a young man called Wet Nurse, who had been taught to hate people like Hank Reardon, the book's hero, comes to admire and love him. He ultimately acts on that, against all his supposed principles. Since then, many young people have become Wet Nurses.

She taught us how to recognize communist propaganda in movies. For a period of time, you couldn't see a movie with a businessman who was anything but a villain. She warned us: notice that, watch. Profit making was presented as sinful. Giving away everything was good.

The Best Years of Our Lives was one of them.* She didn't say it was subversive or anyone should go to jail. She thought the public should recognize it for what it was. As I remember, the banker decides to give loans to the poor without collateral. That was considered virtuous. That it breaks banks, that was ignored. Virtue was to give away other people's money.

She was certainly not opposed to generosity. If there's someone one wants to help, that was perfectly fine. What she objected to was involuntary help. The New Deal was anathema to her. She had come from communist Russia and she did not want to see the first steps of that here. It's not that she thought all New Dealers were communists. She didn't. The individual was sacred. The most important thing in the world was the single, lone individual. Not a collective. The unchosen, the forced, is what she objected to.

She certainly disapproved of the Civil Rights Act. It was government-related morality. She was violently opposed to racism, but you don't force people against their will. Many in the Free Market Foundation of South Africa were interested in her ideas. Leave us alone, they were saying. Leave the blacks alone and the coloreds alone. Leave everybody alone (laughs).

Her philosophy, Objectivism, is easily explained. It is not only okay to pursue your happiness, but it's a moral good to do so. It's an ode to self-interest, yes. She also called it selfishness on the premise that if this be treason, make the most of it.

She shared a view which is held by some women of great achieve-

---

* Academy Award Winner, 1946.

ment: I did it myself, nobody helped me. Any woman can do it if she has the ambition and the brains. She liked the idea of man as superior to woman in drive, in force, in intellect.

Even as a small girl, she had contempt for people who were less bright than she, who didn't understand what seemed clear to her. She had a truly great mind herself. Such a mind is starved for minds to admire. Her desire was to be a hero-worshipper, to find a man she could look up to. I suppose a lot of feminists wouldn't like it.

The reason her influence is so great today is that the young students who read *Atlas Shrugged* and *The Fountainhead* are in positions to make things happen. There are new generations coming out, making their own way.

SAM TALBERT

He is a member of Teamsters for a Democratic Union (TDU). It is a maverick group of truckdrivers, who are challenging the administration of Jackie Presser and the Teamsters hierarchy.

He lives in Charleston, West Virginia. He is fifty-five, divorced. "I raised my own two children": a son, thirty-one, and a daughter, twenty-eight. He lives by himself.

I drove a truck all my life, ever since I was fifteen. What little education I have isn't formal. It's all from behind the barn. For years, I didn't know much about labor, but here and there, I've picked up a few things.

I know more about farmers than anything else. My dad and mom lived on a farm all their lives.

Most people around here voted for Reagan. I visualized him as being something like American apple pie. He just said things that I had always, since I was a kid, thought was right. Now I feel I've learned a little.

Some people are advancing and others is backtracking. It's just like in our unions, I think we're going backwards. Everybody's just tending to their own business, meantimes the ones that are gettin' the profits from all this is banding together and controlling the majority. You have young people that come on the job, started out with decent wages, that takes it for granted. They think the company is giving this to them out of the goodness of their hearts. They don't know that down the line somebody had to fight to get this.

I've seen these young fellows as soon as they get there jump in and buy 'em a new house. They get married, they have two or three kids. Well, the company come along and ask for concessions. These fellows that thought this company was giving this money to start with, say, Okay, I'll do it, because I've got to meet these payments. They just give to the company and give and now the company has a hold on everybody. The younger people is the majority that hadn't had to fight for what the older people had to do.

They're tryin' to get the right-to-work law passed in this state. People thinks if they get this law passed, some of the companies moved out of the valley, shut down, will come back. They seem to think the high cost of labor is what's makin' all these people move out. So they've a tendency to lean against the unions, ordinary working people. They get it from what they read in the papers and what their bosses tell 'em.

I learnt that things I dreamed of when I was a kid just wasn't there, because we live in a land of plenty and there just isn't plenty for everybody. Just like the poor old farmer, for instance. I'd see him feedin' the country and just havin' nothin'. I used to wonder about these things. I'd think, well, what in the heck. They talk about workin' hard all your life and the American dream. Here's old Sanford down the road. He's worked hard all his life and the poor old fellow can't make it. Things just didn't fit together.

They give me the Silver Star in Korea. Yes sir. But I'll tell you what, if I had to do it all over, I don't think I could do the same things that I done then. We had no business there, because some fellow wanted to make war materials, is the way I see it. They brainwashed me into believin' those people were my enemy and they wasn't.

Those people didn't want to fight and I didn't want to fight. Just for instance, they promoted me to staff sergeant. I wouldn't sew my chevrons on. They said, "You won't get this extra pay if you don't put 'em on." I put 'em on because I was poor and I'd send my money home to my mom.

They said, "Well, what do you think of this war over here?" I said, "I oughta be home and the fellows that start it, come over here and let them fight it. 'Cause I don't want to be here, I don't want to wade this mud, I don't want to be here in this heat in the summer. I want to go home, I don't care about your war."

This instance, it sticks with me, inside of me, and I think of it quite often. This ROK* soldier, he was a good friend of mine. He was attached to our unit. We were sitting eating one day, we was backing up this hill so we could go in to attack, and they brought us up some hot food. Boy by the name of Sneed from Alabama said, "Yong, if it wasn't for us over here, you wouldn't be eatin' this food." So Yong, he looked at us and said, "You're all my friends and I don't wanna hurt your feelin's. I like your good food. But those people over there's my people. I just wish all of you would go home." (Deep sigh) It sticketh in my heart like I don't know what.

I didn't pay much attention to Vietnam. I was like a lot of people in our tribe. It didn't affect me directly. I was working, I was getting a paycheck, business was good, was hauling plenty of chemicals out. I was getting overtime. I didn't really pay much attention.

I really started paying attention when these younger fellows starting runnin' to Canada. At first I thought, those terrible people. But after a while, I thought, well, now, if I had to go back, what would I do, knowing what I know? I started puttin' those two things together. Now those fellows that went was educated people. They knew what was happenin'. I knew what was happenin', too, because of my experience. I thought, well, hell, I'd go to Canada, too, before I'd go back.

Mostly people worry about what's gonna happen tomorrow. If you belong to a union for twenty years, you never asked for nothin' and you file a card against your company that's right, they subject to tell you that you're a troublemaker, you're liable to put this company out of business.

First time it happened to me, I thought what the heck is this thing? Then the TDU started fillin' me full of knowledge of my

* Republic of Korea.

rights, and what's wrong and what's right. And they mentioned some books to read.

Things out here is gettin' tougher. The Volkswagen plant just moved out, it went to Mexico. True Temper Corporation, they just sold out, operating someplace else under another name. Another plant sold out to a Swedish company. People who worked in those plants are in service places, like hamburger joints. They get far, far less money. Poverty wages, I guess you'd call it.

My daughter and my son are both workin' for Carbide. They're doin' okay. I try to talk to them, it's like tryin' to talk religion to some people. They don't want to hear it. They're livin' high on the hog. They work long hours and it's rarely we discuss anything. They're both very generous. They're people that would help their neighbors. They'd loan you their automobile or money or buy food for you or anything—but they're just not involved in anything.

They've asked me a few times why I'm doin' it. Passin' out literature, writin' letters to the papers. I get some write-ups. They read about me. I had one in the paper today about Jackie Presser. I called him a dirty dog. Every advantage I get to put out word on him, I do it.

I have had threats. I was goin' to have my windows knocked out. I better stay in the house at night. I had a threat from the local president that I'd lose everything I'd worked for, that I'd lose my pension.

Oh, they tried to intimidate me. But they don't know, the more they try, that just gives me the juices to keep goin'. That makes me not want to quit.

I don't hunt, I don't fish. I wouldn't catch a little fish and tear its mouth up, or I wouldn't shoot a deer. On the other hand, I'd like to go up there and shoot some of those union officials.

I get tired, I get aggravated, I quit sometimes, for two or three days, but, then, I can't quit. I feel there's a principle, they's morals involved, they's human lives involved. I feel like I'm doin' a little somethin' that's contributin' to the cause of the workin' class of people.

One time, I wasn't gettin' enough contributions to keep our newsletter goin'. I said, Hell, I'm tired of fightin', I'm gonna quit. The word got around.

One Saturday mornin', I heard a knock on the door. This big redheaded fellow said, "Sam, we wanna talk to you. There's five fellows with me.'' They had three hundred dollars among them. said, ''We want to give you this. We heard the rumor that you were disgusted and wanted to quit. We come out to ask you not to quit. You keep on doin' what you're doin'.''

It's been my dream to find a young fellow interested. Now we have a lot of educated people in our union, as truckdrivers. We have people that are good talkers and I'd love to get one of them that can talk, can talk with compassion, to where he can lay his feelings out, to work with me. And let me work with him and try to build him up to be the leader in our local.

I'm one of those fellows that can get a whole lot inside of me. I can have this feeling, that I don't know how to get it out into words how I feel.

I think things is going to continue to be bad until the majority of the people gets pushed down to where they're all equal. Am I making any sense? It'll have to be like when I was a kid. We was all poor and we had to stick together and look out for each other.

Everybody's afraid, everybody's holding on tight to what little they have, but when you're pushed down to where you don't have nothing you don't have any choice but to band together.

It scares me sometimes thinkin' people are never goin' to learn. I sometimes get to thinkin' people's gettin' too hard-hearted. There's no trust in anybody. Used to be hitchhiking, you'd get a ride. Now they're afraid they'll be robbed, but people has always been robbed all their life. So it's hard for me to pass up a hitchhiker.

One day last week, I was in the grocery store. This fellow come in, he's pretty well dressed, nice, tall, handsomelike fellow. He said, ''I was told from the register to come back here, that you-all might cash a check for me. I'm hungry, I don't have a nickel in my pocket and I'd like to get a five-dollar check cashed.'' She said, ''No, there's no way we can do that.''

I said, ''I'm goin' to give you five dollars.'' He said, ''You gotta be kiddin'.'' He wrote me a five-dollar check and said it's good. He asked me, ''Why did you do that? Here they won't cash my check and you, an individual, you will.'' I said, ''Buddy, I've hitchhiked, I've come from a poor family, I've been all over the country, and I have been fed by people. I have not had a penny in the pocket and people say here's fifty cents.'' He said, ''I hope I can repay you, this generosity.'' I said, ''Don't give it back to me. Give it to somebody else along the road.''

HIRED HANDS

Hold the fort for we are coming,
Union men be strong,
Side by side we battle onward,
Victory will come.

—Knights of Labor song, 1880s

VICTOR REUTHER

*He and his brother, Walter, were founding members of the
United Auto Workers (UAW)–CIO. Subsequently, Walter
served as president of the UAW until he died in a plane
crash.*

*In his Washington, D.C. apartment, where he is
convalescing from surgery, there are multitudinous
plaques, certificates, and objets d'art, mementoes of long-
ago labor battles, triumphs, and ordeals.*

For the first time in the history of
our country, a new generation is
coming of age that will have a lower standard of living than their
parents. Before, they could anticipate going beyond. What's happened to the American dream?

Do you realize the disillusionment that can set in? It can tempt
people to look for the man on the white horse. And a scapegoat, too.
The labor movement can be it: "We've priced ourselves out of the
world market." The blame for the decline in the American way of
life can be placed on the victims. Then there will be a real threat of
American fascism, with flags waving and bugles blaring.

There is a new kind of labor leader who doesn't understand the
source of his power, the membership. It's somewhat painful to suddenly be cast in the role of dissident.

If the trade union movement had still been as relevant to working
people as it was in the thirties and forties, they wouldn't have been
sucked in by corporate sweet-talk. As institutions grow older, they
tend to become more bureaucratic. The heads become administrators
instead of real leaders in day-to-day struggles. So if you don't have
that impulse from bottom up—the membership—you go to the bargaining table as an easy sucker for corporate strategy.

How many struggles has Lane Kirkland led? How many battles

on the picket line? George Meany used to boast that he never walked a picket line. I thought he was a strange kind of labor leader coming out of the CIO. Lane Kirkland is even more remote. He sounds much more like corporate America.

The Big Boys' emphasis is now on wage competitiveness. Even in the depths of the Depression of the thirties, we never set wages on the basis of what was paid in Mexico or Taiwan or Japan. We based it on what the companies could pay or what we could force them to pay, when we knew their earnings permitted them to do so. What we paid in Mexico and Formosa was totally irrelevant. And it is irrelevant today, despite the worldwide nature of corporations.

The character of corporate America has undergone a change. There were old-line entrepreneurs, who were really interested in running the business and making things the market needed. Now, the money manipulators have taken over. They don't give a damn what they make. If they close the goddamn thing down and buy another oil well, that's okay with them. No amount of wage concessions is going to interest those people.

They don't feel any sense of responsibility to the workers in those valleys in Pennsylvania and Ohio where the steel mills are being shut down. Or to the people in Austin, Minnesota, where the Hormel strikers, the P-9 local, are battling overwhelming odds.

Doesn't today's trade union leadership understand that you have no power to counter management unless you mobilize your members and build allies in the community? Hell, the labor movement has kept its mouth shut when consumers have been robbed. They say, Oh hell, to protect our own interests, maybe we ought to get in bed with the boss. This is not the first time it's happened in American labor history.

Back in the twenties, there were some old AFL types who were sucked in to join what was called New Capitalism. They were invited to dinners and wore black ties and white shirts and were privileged to break bread with corporate America. This is the beginning of a new age, they said. We have a new partnership.

They're not talking to the workers, for God's sake. Those poor guys are not looking at this as the wave of the future. They think they're having their brains beat out. And they're right. Everything about this new partnership is concessions, concessions, concessions. The workers are pitted against each other. They're constantly told, Ah, you're not competitive with Mexico or Korea. We may have to go across the border with this job.

Corporations in America are riding high, wide, and handsome today. They've got labor on the run. It reflects itself in the media. How many newspapers have reporters that cover the labor beat? Or TV stations? Who owns them? What the hell, they got whole sections on business and finance. It's rare that you find a labor column. Forget about a labor page. Is it any wonder that young people are so ignorant about unions?

Notice something about the media? They always refer to labor as a special interest. When you fight for the needs of ninety percent of the population, you're a special interest. Damn right. Unions, minorities, women are special interest groups. Of course, corporations are not special interests.

A lot of it is the fault of labor itself. If it retreats behind closed doors in secrecy and signs giveaway agreements, it is not carrying its message to the community. It can lead the fight for a shorter work week. A forty-hour week is enough for anyone. You don't have to have both spouses working in order to survive. If you can't make it on forty hours work, your wages ought to be raised.

Can you imagine any single thing that would have this appeal to the disenfranchised and idle one-third of us, who have been sloughed off, the young with no seniority, the blacks with no job at all?

The peculiar thing is, labor has more resources today than it ever had in the thirties. The white-collar anti-union stereotype is over. Schoolteachers, nurses, flight attendants—all organizing. All labor leadership needs now is strategy, imagination, and guts.

CLIFF (COWBOY) MAZO

East Chicago: a blue-collar suburb, thirty miles or so south of the big city. It is—was—the archetype of Steel Town, U.S.A. Most of its breadwinners worked in the mills: Youngstown, Inland, U.S. Steel.

On this rainy afternoon, the journey on the IC train offers a bleak landscape, as other industrial suburbs are whizzed by. Smokeless chimneys. No orange flashes in the sky. Empty parking lots. Not a Ford nor a Chevy to be seen near the deserted plants. An occasional abandoned jalopy, evoking an image of the thirties. A stray dog, no humans. A fleeting glimpse of the business end of the towns; enough to see boarded-up stores and empty Main Streets.

A mind-flash of Willard Van Dyke's 1938 documentary, Valley Town. It was Lancaster, Pennsylvania, a steel city of the Great Depression, stone-cold dead. It is a moment of déjà vu in reverse.

The front lawn of every other bungalow in East Chicago, it seems, has the sign: FOR SALE.

There's a decal on his door: an American flag as background to "My son is a U.S. Marine." He is retired, trim, astonishingly young-looking.

My family furnished cannon fodder for about fourteen generations. My maternal grandfather was in the Civil War, my grandson is in the army.

My wife and I came out of the same briarpatch, Franklin County, right next to bloody Williamson. I grew up on the story about how the UMW of A guys, in southern Illinois, turned back the strikebreakers. They stopped a caravan from up North, shot 'em up, and turned them all back. Great victory.

I never got the other side of the story till years later, when I was selling insurance. That caravan was absolutely unarmed. They were of the Progressive Mine Workers faction. They said, Look, there's a bigger issue here than wages and hours. We want better schools and government. The UMW of A guys were deputized. I should have known something was wrong.

It's always that way, isn't it? Workingmen fighting workingmen. The last time we were threatened with a strike in the steel industry, I said, "I don't have the stomach to stand out there and hit my fellow worker over the head, because he's tryin' to come in and feed his kids." We got to find another way to keep that plant down. Blowin' up a blast furnace or destroyin' some stuff. I'd rather take that approach.

My grandfather and my father were all in the United Mine Workers. When I grew up, it was more a religion than a union. There were certain things you did not do. That was to cross a picket line or take another man's job. You couldn't do that and hold your head up and live in the community. If a paper boy just quit for conditions, you didn't say, I'll take the job, deliver the papers. Your dad would tan your butt.

My uncle was a Progressive. He was out, he wouldn't work. My grandfather was working in this mine. My uncle, or course, was calling him a scab. We used to take grandpa's wages and buy groceries and take over to my uncle's. They didn't have nothin' to eat there. They were on rolled oats and powdered milk.

You had a whole society who was caring about their fellow man, about someone goin' hungry. You had guys in Congress sayin', The measure of our society is how we treat our old people, our sick people, and those who can't take care of themselves. Not how many countries we can blow up. That don't make us great.

Back in those days, unions knew who the enemy was. Today, you got guys who go in for what they call labor-management participation. You set down and figure out how to do your fellow worker out of a job or rat on him. You can sit down and bargain and come to an agreement, but you just don't capitulate. Militancy is all eroding away. You have workers disciplinin' each other, rattin' on each other, and voting for Ronald Reagan. If you ask him, Do you agree with his position on this? No. You agree with his position on that? No. You gonna vote for him? Yeah. Why? Aw, he just turns me on. Twenty-three years ago, this was a boom town. Money all over the place. This city produced more steel than anyplace in the world.

There's two halves to the town. This is the Irish and the Polish end. Closer to the mills is where you had all the hotels and where they recruited Mexicans and Puerto Ricans and blacks from the South. They imported the Mexicans with one thought: to weaken the union. Actually, they became our staunchest union people.

This was never a garden spot to live in. You had mills and refineries spilling dirt and God knows what. You got a chemical plant down here, DuPont. All this and noxious vapors. So without the boom in the industry, people perceive property values will go down and they're probably right.

There are more and more without jobs. People are on welfare. I never know how to classify these guys who go up and down these alleys, picking up cans and rummaging. I don't know if that's another guy who used to be employed. I saw none, then I saw one, then two, three. Now they fight. It's a regular race to see who can get there first. We're gettin' a better class of garbage pickers.

It would be much worse than the Depression I knew as a kid if it wasn't for the social benefits. That's all that's keepin' us from much, much worse than the thirties.

They keep talkin' about these service industries, where there's more employment. Anybody with an ounce of brains knows we can't all sell hamburgers to each other. Caring for lawns or whatever service you're in does not produce anything. A man sweats, he should be producing something, making something. We ain't producin'.

You can't do it with computer chips, with buffalo chips. Know what buffalo chips are? BULLSHIT. We used to pick 'em up and burn 'em when they dried. You've got to have steel, you've got to have iron, coal. We've got to rebuild the cities. A bridge just went down with people on it. We know most bridges in this country are ready to collapse, at least past the point of safety. And we don't replace 'em. Instead, we build some gigantic goddamn thing and stick it in the ground in Montana. I worked on that, so I know. There's so much difference in the social makeup today. This is where the breakdown occurred in East Chicago. Most of the workers in the mill, they walked to work together, they drank at the bar together, they went to church together on Sunday.

What happens? You get a few bucks in your pocket. The union gets you three, four raises in a row. You say, I want to get away from these blacks or Mexicans or Polacks. So you move out to Munster or Schererville. Technological advances come along. You get your big color TV set. You don't visit your neighbors no more. You don't go over and talk.

Now you don't talk to anybody, 'cause you got your head stuck in that TV. You put a little plastic swimming pool out in the back yard, so your kids don't associate with the neighborhood kids. Everybody is tryin' to become middle-class. I can take care of myself, my family.

That guy pickin' up cans in the alley, you tell him there are three classes in the country: lower class, middle class, upper class. What class are you? He'll say middle-class. Ask a brain surgeon, he'll say middle-class. Horseshit. Such a job has been done that everybody is middle-class.

He places a fifth of Seagram's V.O. on the table, glass with ice cubes. Memories of old-time workingmen's taverns are evoked: the bottle, the glass, and the dice is yours.

You're not born a labor person. They're made, not born. There's a lot of father-and-son-on-down awareness, but that ain't gonna do it. These kids are gonna have to be tapped on the head by some of the times, see their kids go hungry a few times, and then you're gonna have some militant, hard-nosed union guys who know where it's at. It's kinda like a phoenix, I guess. It's gotta die and be reborn. Maybe it gets better each time it's reborn, I don't know. I ain't been here that long (laughs).

IKE MAZO

Cliff's son. He is thirty-six. With his wife and three sons, fifteen, thirteen, and twelve, he lives in an archetypal Chicago neighborhood: bungalow, blue-collar.

The mailbox reads: Mazo-Dudak: a new phenomenon in this community.

This is the first time in four generations that I have it worse than my father. My father had steady employment when he wanted it.

You had a thirty-, forty-year period where a guy could come in off the street and get a job. And go on. There were always strikes and layoffs, but you always came back. You could plan your life financially. You could say, I'll take X amount of income and I'll buy a house. I can put away X amount of income, so I could send at least one of my kids to college.

That's changed for me. My wife has went to work. Incomewise, we're the same. Standard of living, we're not. My father had hospital benefits. He was paid something while he was off sick. We pay our own hospitalization, what little we have. If I break my leg right now, we're gonna lose this house.

I went into the Marine Corps at seventeen, I came out at nineteen. I volunteered, of course. Came out of that, all screwed up mentally. It wasn't what I expected. A seventeen-year-old kid had been exposed to combat films and glory and stuff such as that: everything you had been brought up with. I swallowed all of it: George Washington, cherry tree, and everything. You come out and it's all gone.

You always felt that this country could do no wrong. We were always the good guys, whoever we take on are the bad guys. I was pro-Vietnam, I was one hundred percent. It was really funny, because I came home and my father was involved in anti-Vietnam demonstrations (laughs). My twin brother, Mike, was the same way. I called him a hippie. He was workin' in the mills, but he was goin' to college at night. I wanted to sweep through there and kick ass, get it over with, get out. We had some good discussions (laughs).

I started readin' and readin' in depth. I started readin' the news more than the sporting page. You gradually start to change. Plus there was a great deal of influence around.

I got out at nineteen, when most people were bein' drafted. Prior to Vietman, I wanted to go to college. For two or three years after I came back, I got jobs here and there, and made a conscious decision to be a worker.

I was walkin' by Southworks, U.S. Steel, and saw the sign: HELP WANTED. This is 1972. You could literally walk across the street and get a job. So I got an apprenticeship as a boilermaker. That's what I am now, a journeyman boilermaker. The main reason I stayed at Southworks was the satisfaction in bein' a griever. You know, the one people come to when they have grievances. That was the greatest experience in the world. Up until this time, you're a worker and they're the boss. They have no problem pointin' that out to you damn near every day. I would sit in there as a high school dropout and I'm up against this college-educated superintendent, and you're on one-and-one and you're as good as him.

My father didn't want me in the mills. He cussed me and my brother both. Said he fought for twenty years to stay out of the mills, and me and my brother were lookin' at it simply as a job. You had to have a job.

I would want my chidren to go to college. But I never shared that idea that you strive and work and struggle so your children can rise above your class, which is working-class. If they choose that, so be it. I don't know if my father wanted me to be a doctor, lawyer, but —I wouldn't want my kids in the mill.

What do I see for my kids? I really don't know. It's kind of frightening, scary. It's not only for my kids. It's that whole young group. You get enough of 'em out of work and those are the ones that'll trip across the picket line. If they've never worked, they don't have that tradition. They've never worked with that old guy next to 'em.

I had a very close friend who went across the *Tribune* picket line. What do I do? I go shun this guy? Don't have nothin' to do with him? My father said, Yeah, cut him off.

I don't think this guy will ever do it again. When we bought this house, I had a little get-together. He didn't wanna come. He was ashamed. I remember him tellin' me, ''You're treatin' me like a piece of shit.'' I said, ''What do you expect? If they break that strike and you're gonna be permanent there, they'll want your head right. They don't care about you.''

When you come back from Vietnam, you're angry, chip on your shoulder. You go to work and you start gettin' treated a certain way. You don't wanna be a suck-ass, you don't wanna take that shit. So you try different things. I was gonna be so good at my job that no boss was ever gonna mess with me. Then you realize that's not the answer. Look what happened at Southworks. The logical answer is havin' unions, all around you. These young kids figure the time for a union has come and went. They figure they can make it on their own. Individualism and makin' it on your own is an admirable trait. But it don't work that way. They never had the one older guy tellin' the next guy come along what it's all about.

Why did Southworks close? U.S. Steel bought Marathon Oil. And they was gettin' millions of dollars every time they shut down a facility. They had until April to shut us down to get the writeoff for the previous year.

This was one of the most modern facilities around. They got caster there, they got electric furnace, they got the oxygen process. And thousands of guys were laid off. So how's the individual gonna make it on his own? When the mill closed down in '82, I was out of work for a year and a half. That's when my wife went to work. The kids are old enough, she likes her job. Even if I make considerably less at my new job—just got it five days ago—it's gonna be two incomes.

This new job is a real pain. I'm hopin' they lay me off in thirty days.

I'm a journeyman with fourteen years experience. They're treatin' me like a dog. The reason I became a craftsman was for a certain amount of dignity. They don't want craftsmen at this place, they want animals. How they're gonna treat these kids that are goin' out there, I don't know.

I've heard it many a time: Them people don't wanna work. There's jobs out there for six dollars an hour and they won't take 'em. When I was in high school, they told you: Go out, work hard, make something of your life. Now they're tellin' you you're not a good citizen if you're not willing to accept less. The whole country's supposed to accept less. It's steadily comin' down. It's an attack on the living standard of workers, since Reagan. And the best way is to hit the unions.

I'm workin' harder, makin' less money, got less of a future. I was put outa work in the steel mills at the ideal age. With ten years in the work force, still in my thirties, that's the guy they wanna hire. But now I'm pushin' forty. I know the law says they're supposed to do it, but they just don't hire you. This guy I know is gonna be forty-five, great skills and work history—just went back at a plant —maintenance. My wife is working. Friends of mine have problems with it. That guy that crossed the picket line. He didn't have to do it, he wasn't that hard up. He was right there with me in the union. He didn't take no shit from anybody. But I know he felt low being at home. He felt it was a reflection on him. He's Mexican. His pride, his macho.

There's somethin' in my life that I always wanted to do. I'd like to be a cabinetmaker. I'm makin' a table there. Before I die, I would like to make somethin' and stick it in the window and say, "I made this. If I sell it, I sell it. If I don't, I don't. But what I've made has never been made before."

SUSAN DUDAK

Ike's wife. They had grown up together in the old neighborhood and "knew each other from grade school." Her father was his high school baseball coach.

My life-style's changed quite a bit. I'm not the little housewife I was when I was twenty-one, twenty-two (laughs). I loved it at the time, when I had little babies and was the nice little homemaker. But you have to wake up.

I was never what they called in the sixties an activist (laughs). I was more of a sideline. I remember about eight, nine years ago, a friend of mine got married and did not change her name. It stirred up quite an upset in the family. Eight years ago, you didn't hear of women doing that.

Out of high school, I went to a beauty salon. I was a licensed beautician. I worked part-time while the boys were babies. When the steel industry started going bad, I had to stop and think twice. The boys were getting older, they were starting school. Okay, now what do I do?

I decided I needed more of a training. I joined a program in word processing, secretarial. Since then, I've landed a real decent job as a paralegal. I work with a lot of immigrants who are having a hard time.

Being away from home so much, the boys had to adjust. I think in the long run it's been good for them. They learned how to wash their own clothes and do all kinds of goodie things. That's the only way we've been able to make it through this whole mill shutdown, is by me going to work.

I worry about their future every day. Will we be able to put them through college, if that's what they want? Will they be out in the work force working for four dollars an hour? What kind of home can you buy on four dollars an hour? Ike's nephew, he's married, twenty-one, and working for four-fifty an hour.

Is that the next generation coming along after us? Will it be that way for our children in five, ten years? I don't have the answers for them. I don't know.

JAMIE WALD, JR.

He is a member of a respected mercantile family in the Midwest. "I've had a fine education at private schools, prep schools, and the Ivy League college bit."

During his thirty years with the family business, he was active in philanthropic and civic work. "All this changed startlingly in the early eighties, when our company got bought out by another. I found myself out on the street without a job."

He set up his own company and has been at it for the past four years. Its success has given him "considerable gratification." His ebullience is apparent.

For lack of a better term, you could say I'm a professional strike-breaker. I provide special services to management whose plants are on strike: where people are locked in the plant, if you will, while the pickets are outside. In most cases, it's management bringing in non-union people from other parts of the country. In order not to aggravate the emotions of the strikers, they will want the people to live in the plant.

In effect, I'm setting up a hotel in premises that weren't designed for the purpose. These are anxiety-provoking circumstances, because you not only provide top-flight food but facilities for these people cut off from their families.

Before this, I had been doing off-premise catering: a wedding, a debut, or a back-yard party. Very upscale. What I'm doing now is much more exciting. I had gotten into this work strictly as a sideline. Some corporate executives who were our clients for social affairs would occasionally have a problem at the plant and call me up.

We had done a very elegant party for the head of a major chemical company. He said, ''You did such a beautiful job in my back yard. I've got a problem at our plant in Hanging Rock, Ohio. A hundred people are living in the plant because we're having a strike. We've been feeding these guys TV chicken dinners for two weeks and they're really getting upset. You've got to send one of your chefs down there with some really good food.'' So we loaded a truck and sent our people down there. That was the beginning. It was quite successful. Then, word-of-mouth.

In ninety-five percent of my work, no strike really takes place. They hire me to plan all the facets of service and equipment, while they're negotiating with the union. They go right down to the wire.

Last May 1, I was at a motel in Pocatello, Idaho, with five trailerloads full of food, kitchen equipment, beds, laundry and recreational equipment, cooks, drivers. We were waiting. The contract was expiring at midnight. At nine o'clock, we got a call: We just settled. Send everything back. This is typical. In one case, I got a hundred Gs. That was a four-day wait. It's like buying an insurance policy. Management knows it doesn't have the expertise or the time to pull this stuff together.

Does seeing all that lovely stuff have an effect on the pickets?

Sometimes. Often, my clients want me to have a high profile. They want the union to know they're serious. Other times, they want a low profile because negotiations are at a delicate point.

I just got through doing the LTV Steel thing that went on for like a week. They called me at nine in the morning: Can you have enough food and personnel to serve five hundred people by five this afternoon? That was very short notice.

Five hundred scabs?

Five hundred management and supervisory personnel.

You're not dealing with quiche-eaters or alfalfa-sprout specialists here. This is a more meat-and-potatoes situation. We get top steaks and lobster tails. The guys on the picket line probably know about this. 'Cause lots of time, when the weather's good, we'll barbecue outside. Often, it's within the sight of the picket line. The smell comes wafting off—we're not there to aggravate emotions. It's our primary concern that the people in the plant are taken care of and happy.

Is there a name for this new vocation?

The *Wall Street Journal* called me a mercenary caterer (laughs). Somewhat tongue-in-cheek. Kinda cute, I thought. You can't hate a guy who describes you as a middle-aged adventurer living life on the edge (laughs).

I was involved in a terribly violent coal-mine strike for six months. The Massey coal-mine situation in West Virginia. It was so fascinating from a sociological point of view. I was a history major. These were fourth-generation coal miners, who come from that Appalachian culture, which has its own peculiarities.

Here were these guys who regard their union as the Iranians regard the Ayatollah. It's not only a religion, they're fanatic about it. I don't say this in a critical way. I mean, I'm a paid-up Teamster myself. I'm a union member, of course. Here we were with all this stuff on our shoulders right in the heart of the old coal wars of the twenties and the fights with the Pinkertons in the 1890s.

In most strikes, pickets are not hassling people crossing the lines. There's frustration, there's anger, of course. Guys my age—I'm fifty-eight—went into the labor force in the late forties. Every three years, they'd get an eight or ten percent raise, fringe benefits, and life went on. All of a sudden, in the late seventies, early eighties, the Germans and Japanese had our markets.

I got into this business at a good time. Management is saying, Fellas, we not only can't give your normal increase, we may have to take some back. With those original contracts expiring, management is tougher than it ever was. And it's got an ally in the White House.

Massey has tried what's never been tried before: make a union mine non-union. I think they succeeded. We were down at one particular mine for six months. We were feeding guards brought in to defend the premises. The mine had been closed for several months when we were brought in, along with seventy or eighty guards. The company was about to bring people in to mine the coal.

It was fascinating. There were five hundred documented incidents of physical violence. And a thousand cases of violence to property. One of the purposes of the guard unit was to obtain intelligence in detail as to what the strikers were doing.

I'm not anti-union. Unions are a necessary thing. God knows, somebody has to protect workers' rights. Ninety-eight percent of the problems are management dereliction. But in West Virginia, a pro-union state, we had state policemen walking along with union officials, as a striker with an axe handle would smash our car window. The trooper would smile at the official and walk away.

We couldn't get in the ground. They were shooting at us. For six weeks, we used helicopters. A couple of weeks ago, we used barges to get into East Chicago, 'cause the steelworkers were a little perturbed.

Of course I have sympathy for the unions. Listen, those guys aren't much different from me. After all . . .

It's a service I provide. I have a number of highly qualified chefs. They're available when I have one of these situations. They get good pay, about six, seven hundred a week. Living in a plant, working seven days a week, cut off from their families, it's no bed of roses.

I enjoy the work a lot. I'm a city boy of a privileged background. I'm getting out into parts of the country I never in my life would have gone into. You can't understand America unless you understand where these people are coming from.

When a strike gets intense as with Massey, I got combat pay for my cooks. I said to management, "My people are risking life and limb out there. I've gotta make it worthwhile." I got those guys a nice healthy raise.

At one of the mines, our convoy was attacked by strikers. My car was smashed up. A guy hit my windshield with a crowbar. We were shot at. There were bullet holes in my catering truck. We were even issued arms one wintry West Virginia night to defend the building in which we were lodged. We were warned the miners might try to blow it up. All we were were a bunch of guys who came to cook some dinners (laughs).

No, they don't have any qualms about this. One of 'em said, "I gotta feed my wife and kids." I don't have trouble finding applicants. My friends are usually management people who think it's a great idea.

Here I am in blue jeans. I haven't worn a tie more than twice in the last five years and I used to be a real buttoned-down kind of guy, you know? I'm really reveling in this situation. It's so stimulating.

Politically, I'm a liberal Democrat, okay? I was involved in the civil rights movement of the sixties and seventies. I think my own children, who were in college in the seventies, are more conservative that I am.

I've become a little disillusioned with the sixties. But, there's an old Latin expression my father has quoted to me for fifty years: Forsan et haec olim meminisse iuvabit—Someday we will look back at these pains with pleasure. I look at the sixties wistfully. I see a lot of the things we thought would work didn't work. The guys who said it wouldn't work were the guys I didn't respect.

I think Ronald Reagan is a straw man. He's not real. He's an image. I voted for him, but I'm not really pro-Reagan. I didn't really make up my mind until I walked in the booth. I had worked with Jesse Jackson early in his career. I still have admiration for him. But I couldn't bring myself to pull the lever for him. I felt the country was in better shape in '84 than it was in '80. And maybe a simplistic guy like Reagan is what was needed at this particular time.

I don't criticize his attitude toward labor. You don't have to be a Reaganite to recognize we have to get our labor costs in line. You've got guys in Korea earning a dollar an hour and our guys are making twenty-five an hour.

My job's a dirty one, but someone's gotta do it. It's not really that. I enjoy the work. I don't really look at in ethical or moral terms. You can certainly find plenty to criticize about unions, too.

Listen, maybe by helping management arrive at a contract that's livable, I'm saving the guy's job, even though he doesn't know it (laughs).

My father's very pleased that I'm enjoying what I'm doing and doing well at it. That's what parents generally get the most kick out of. What parent doesn't want his children happy?

RON RAPOPORT

He has been a sports columnist for eighteen years. After putting in ten years at the Chicago Sun-Times, *he is now covering the beat for the* Los Angeles Daily News.

he football players' strike of 1987 was one of the most depressing stories I've ever covered. Not because the owners were so intransigent. You expected that of them, though their arrogance in this case was unconscionable. What really disturbed me was the attitude of the fans. How easily they were manipulated into support—not of the players, whom they come to see and love to watch—but of the owners, who never played a game in their lives.

I think it has something to do with the attitude toward unions generally in the last decade or so.

During the three weeks of scab ball, it was a sad spectacle to see fans watch players they never heard of play an inferior brand of ball and curse out their own players. After the strike, there were some who were booed by their own fans.

In a non-union town like Dallas, the scabs became heroes; the ones who said, "This is my one chance to play. I'm in it for me, nobody else." We've heard the hackneyed phrase many times: Sports is a metaphor for life. Yet it never had a greater meaning for me than during the strike.

My mail was overwhelmingly anti-player: "They make so much money." The average career is four years, so it's not such a big deal. And when is it against the law in America to make money for possessing a special skill? Sylvester Stallone signs for $12 million a movie, no problem. Elizabeth Taylor, Joan Collins sign for millions, no one says boo. They don't possess a fingernail's worth of talent compared to professional ballplayers. It was amazing to hear million-dollar sportscasters criticize half-million-dollar ballplayers: "They make too much money."*

---

* Chicago's most popular baseball broadcaster makes $2 million a year. Yet hardly a day passed during the 1987 baseball season when he did not comment on the "outrageous salaries" of the players.

The owners of the football clubs are some of the richest men in America. A dozen of them are on the Forbes 400 list. They, who are making incredible millions in football, have succeeded in doing a remarkable thing. These twenty-six had the working people of this country in their corner and turned them against 1,600 athletes who are tops in their profession.

It has something to do with the fact that we played these games as kids. How often have you heard: "I'd play for nothing"? It's a privilege to be allowed to realize your sandlot dreams. There's something about the purity of love for a sport that a child has. Going on strike for more money brings it into the real world and sullies our memory of it.

For young children, sports is their first sense of self, away from the family. They're in a larger world from the very beginning. Playing until dark, until your mother called you for supper. Not even keeping score sometimes.

We may bemoan so much time spent on something not particularly serious, but it's better if we try to understand it.

On Mondays, during the football season, the Bears are on the front pages of the *Chicago Sun-Times*. If World War Three were to break out that weekend, you'd have to turn twenty-four pages to find out about it. The publisher told me that it was worth a million dollars to the paper when the Bears were in the Superbowl. Sports takes over in everything.

Look at football. Everything that happens in the greater world takes place in this capsule corner. It's all there: the racism, the labor troubles, drugs, the compelling ambition to make money, money, and more money. All that's happened in the greater American society is here overwhelmingly.

The growth of the mass media, especially television, has changed sports in ways we're just beginning to understand. We spend as much time talking about broadcasters who tell us about the games as we do about the players who actually play the games. In some cities, baseball announcers are better known than the mayor.

Night baseball started in the thirties, ostensibly to let the American workingman watch it at his leisure. Television came along and found a way to infuse tremendous amounts of money into the game. They forced a change in the nature of the sport. There was a World Series a few years ago where none of the games ended before midnight.

Baseball was something the young could share with the old. It was generational. I'm a Cub fan because my father was a Cub fan and his father before him. This was one of its charms. It was completely lost to the money men.

In the last World Series, a game couldn't start till after the *Bill Cosby Show*. The game had to conform to the TV's idea of prime time. With a pregame show, the actual game didn't start till nine o'clock. The kids were long in bed before the game was over. It has become a show rather than a game. It's television programming, computer software, just something to fill up the hours instead of *Dynasty* or *Dallas*. The World Series now goes on until the week before Hallowe'en, when it's cold. It simply doesn't matter. To solve the weather problem, they build these terrible dome stadiums. Baseball wasn't meant to be played inside.

The new wrinkle is the ultimate expense for the ultimate expense-account guy: the sky box. You pay not just $20 or $50 for a fancy seat, you pay $50,000 for a long-term lease to sit way up high, with the windows down so you can't hear the crowd. In these boxes, you have gourmet food and drink and TV sets, so you can watch instant replay. They're wonderful for people who don't want to watch the game. It's a status symbol, a perfect place to bring your clients. Instead of peanuts and beer, you're served caviar and champagne. These have become very popular in the eighties.

Ball clubs will desert cities that have older parks and can't afford to put up stadiums that will meet the sky-box demands. They will move to Sun Belt towns that have no big-league tradition, but will bid because it's good business. In the old days, the basic income came from ticket sales. Now it comes from TV and sky boxes. There's now a third group: club-box holders. Your seats are a little higher, a little wider, and you get a free parking pass. You're sitting in the same area as the regular fans, but you're paying ten times as much: $120 a ticket and you have to buy it all year long. You don't even have to go to the ball park at all. You have access to a fancy restaurant and can watch it from there.

As for the athlete himself, in any professional sport, he is very insecure. He is always looking over his shoulder, wondering whether this season will be his last one. His career, especially the football player's, is very short. When he comes to training camp, he sees half-a-dozen lockers cleared out of his team mates from the year before. Their places have been taken by half-a-dozen bright, young dewy-eyed kids from college. He knows that any play can result in a career-ending injury. He can be cut or traded at any moment. The sense of playfulness disappears from all but a few.

The football players' strike was a watershed for me. It made me think how interdependent we all are: the players need one another, the fans need the players, the players need the fans, and the owners need both. It's all part of one community. The same ills—fights over money, racism, drugs—that beset society beset this enclosed world. When these problems impinge on the games we grew up playing and loving, our first window to the world, it comes as a terrible shock.

In the immediate future, I see as little chance for a sense of community in sports as I do for the larger world. But the game is still marvelous to watch. After eighteen years, I'm still excited about being a sports writer. The athletes are as good as they've ever been, probably better.

FRANK LUMPKIN

He had worked at Wisconsin Steel for thirty years, until the gates were shut on March 28, 1980. He's black.

They locked the gates at three-thirty with no notice, no nothin'. The company had just borrowed $80 million from the government to modernize the plant. A week before they locked the gate, they put in $300,000 worth of new equipment. New blast furnace, water treatment, continuous casting.

We figured we'd be out of work for a couple months. That was seven years ago. Chase Manhattan, who was financing the checks, put a lock on the gate: 3,600 guys knocked out without notice. Republic is down to 800 from 13,000. USX, that's U.S. Steel, had about 16,000. Now about 800. About 40,000 unemployed in this area alone.* Some of the guys still got hope. We're suin' for our back

* The numbers have altered for worse since then

pay, for our pensions, vacation pay. They didn't pay nothin'. Just closed.

I think the federal government should take it over, nationalize it, like they did in the thirties, with the dams. The government takes over Amtrack, it becomes prosperous, and then they dump it. And it goes private. You see all this infrastructure in our country rusted out. Bridges all over the country fallin' down. We could use hundreds of thousands of tons of steel. They import steel from South Africa, from Venezuela. While the American steelworker is standin' in line for surplus food.

I started this Save Our Jobs Committee. I'm puttin' in full time, six days a week, sometimes more (laughs). We started in with this surplus food. We'd pass it out once or twice a month to workers and their families. We give out five pounds of cheese and some butter. We get some rice and honey and make them a bag and these steel-workers come around and pick it up for their families. Five hundred bags run out, just like that.

Somebody from the state was here this mornin'. "Do these people bring ID cards?" "Nah," I say. "We start givin' food at nine-thirty and I'm tellin' you honestly, it may be five below and these people will be here at five o'clock in the morning." I said, "Mister, lemme tell you somethin'. If anybody's standin' in that line five o'clock in the morning to ten o'clock, they either gotta be hungry or they gotta be outa their mind! If you gotta present an ID, it's gonna take a lotta time." The state people are down here now, checkin' my food out. They gotta be outa this world! Some get partial pension, don't amount to a hill of beans. Some work in the underground economy. You contract out. I come to your house, say I fix your roof, and you pay me $150. I put that in the pocket and let it go at that. Because if I put down that $150 that you give me, they cut off my ADC (laughs).

A lot of the families are on welfare. What they do is pick up a little here, a little there, enough for medicine. They can't put down they got it, it's illegal. A lot of guys meet their family in the park on Sunday because if they live with their family, they cut 'em off welfare.

A TV woman's comin' from New England next week. She wants to do a story on Wisconsin Steel workers and their plight. She'd like to talk to somebody who knows somebody who committed suicide. I told her that's ticklish, because if I commit suicide, then my family don't get anything. Everything goes out the window. Pension, too.

With Save Our Jobs, I sit down and talk to men and wives and try to hold their families together. What happened in 1980, when the plant went down, people went to Houston, to New Orleans, to California, wherever there was mills. Those jobs closed down and they come back tryin' to save their home.

I had a reporter about a month ago come over, she said, "I'd like to start a discussion about the homeless people." (Laughs.) Sometimes you wonder where they're comin' from. I said, "Lady, I don't mean no hard feelings, but if you walk down State Street in the cold, you can find twenty people layin' on the grates, so you don't have to come out here to look." See that smoke comin' up from the underpass, that's homeless people down there. All over the city, all over the country. To make news, you gotta have somebody jump off the bridge and commit suicide. Otherwise they don't see you. Today, if a plant goes down with 20,000, that's not news any more (laughs).

I'm invited to a conference to discuss abandoned homes. They're not abandoned, they're evicted! We've been fightin' like the devil for people to try to save homes. They put these people out. They throw their bags out, lock, stock, and bond. They board their homes up and run around hollerin': Abandoned! Who the hell abandoned them? They was put out, man!

Somethin's bound to happen. They talk about the soup lines in the thirties. What they're not talkin' about is the marches. The old soldiers. People were marchin' all over the country in the thousands, in the millions. They said what happened to people, but didn't say what people were *doing*. Roosevelt didn't just do what he did out of the goodness of his heart. This world was in turmoil. It could have been a revolution then.

If Reagan thinks he's gonna roll the country back to the old days, he better think again. I see the spirit among the peoples. What has got to be developed is the leadership.

I been doin' this thing for seven years. We've been able to carry marches to Springfield, marches to City Hall, marches to Washington. Three, four years ago, we marched to Springfield all the way from City Hall. On the highway, all the trucks'd blow their horns, wave at us. Peoples in town, they'd know we was comin' through. An old, old senior citizen would meet us down the way and give us cool water to drink. We had about twenty thousand people in Springfield. We started out with twenty. It's there, I tell ya! It's just gotta be organized, you know what I mean?

It was so *good*, you know? When you walk into town and find hundreds of people to meet you, to come out and say your fight is our fight. Great sympathy. You've got to scratch the match that's going to spark it.

There's no way the people is gonna be taken back to where they were before. You can't do it. The president can do it for a while, but I do believe the pot is going to really boil.

I been on lots of strikes. I remember the night before. The workers are tellin' me, Ah, man, I need the money, my family need this, I just bought a car. I sit down and say to myself, I really don't know whether these guys are gonna walk out or not. The next day, the bell rings like a fight in the ring, they jump at attention, and every single guy walks outa that plant. I see the same spirit risin', I ain't foolin'.

I don't think race is that serious a factor. It can be used by this administration, but we can prevent it. Remember Trumbull Park?* It was right next door to Wisconsin Steel. We had to drive in, and these people were throwing rocks at the cars. The workers in the plant was white, black, and Latino. We'd sit down and all talk about this thing. There was a black worker got off the bus with his lunch bag in his hand, he started comin' to the mill, and a mob got in behind him. He was runnin' and the white guys in the plant saw this and they says, "We gotta stop this." And we did, never mind the politicians. The guys who work together know each other. That's what it's all about.

I'm glad I'm living in this kind of time (laughs). It don't come easy. It's beginning to start, because people begin asking Why? They begin to ask, "Why am I being treated this way?" When they lay blacks off, they lay whites off. The whole thing is going on together. Fighting me is not solving the problem. I'm telling you, I'm over here at the office handing out those surplus-food bags, and it's as many whites as blacks standing in line.

I had the pleasure of going to that high school over there. They asked for a trade union leader. I told those kids I got a son who's a doctor. He was able to borrow $50,000 from the government to go to school in order to be a doctor. How do you think this happened? It's because we in the trade unions fought for all these grants. We fought for all the gravy, all the good things that students got.

Those high school kids asked why we'd strike every two or three

* A racial incident in Chicago during the 1950s. It was touched off when a black family's home was stoned, after their arrival in a white neighborhood.

years. I said workers don't strike to get ahead, they strike to catch up. Already the price of everything is going up and up and they're telling us we have to live like the people of Mexico, but we can't!

Let's see the beginning of the end of this business where if you're born poor, you gotta die in the slums. All these kids can do is sell hubcaps and tires to the junkman. And steal. The answer to crime is full employment. We gotta start figurin' a way to get it. It's no mystery.

TOM COSTELLO

He is thirty-seven, a graduate of Harvard Law School, '75.
Among his clients are Frank Lumpkin, the retired
steelworker, and the Save Our Jobs Committee.

I am what used to be called a public-interest lawyer. I cringe when I hear that term. I do a general practice: labor, civil rights, pensions, the causes of rank-and-file people. I take on cases mainstream lawyers avoid. That's why I became a lawyer.

When I was fourteen years old, I went to Washington, D.C., with an old friend of my father's, who worked for Robert Kennedy in the Justice Department. I saw these guys in their shirtsleeves late at night, ordering federal troops into the South during those civil rights days. It was still the Warren Court era, though Burger had just joined.

The *Harvard Law Review* in '72 had a discussion of the Fourteenth Amendment. Did the equal protection clause prohibit discrimination based on wealth as well as race? It was hot stuff. You felt we were on the edge of something: possibilities of reconstructing our society.

Never mind that Burger was on the Court. There was still an enthusiasm then. The odd thing is it was a more activist period from '68 to '72 with Nixon in the White House than it was under Carter in '76 to '80. There weren't ideological litmus tests then.

There has been a radical change in judges. Under Reagan, the federal judiciary has become a political battleground. Back then, you had more autonomy as a judge. There was a lot struggling with issues. They had open minds. I don't mean to romanticize. Of course, there were the others. The judiciary has always been a conservative body, but there were many still feeling their way. There wasn't a party line. Today, the moderate ones have stepped into line with the conservatives on the courts of appeal. I certainly sense a fear of being overruled and their reputations being tarnished.

In my work, I'm particularly vulnerable to these changes. These aren't personal-injury cases, where you do a number and you occasionally hit a few and collect. I'm in an area where you're trying to make a new law: union democracy, pension class-action suits. These are political decisions, where the temperament of the judge often decides the outcome.

Often in court, I have the feeling the case is over the minute the judge is assigned. You pop down the complaint, they pick a name off the wheel, Judge Blank and you think: Oh, God, the case is over. Unfortunately, you're too often right.

It may be a case where you represent two hundred guys whose pensions have been cut in half. It's over before it begins because Judge Blank always defers to the establishment. The litmus test is paying off. During my second year at law school, I got involved with Miners for Democracy. When Arnold Miller, following the murder of Yablonsky, beat Tony Boyle,* I joined the legal department of the United Mine Workers.

When I entered the world of labor law, it was a period of great excitement. There was a fair amount of unrest in the unions. There were an awful lot of wildcat strikes. There were an awful lot of guys my age affected by the Vietnam War. There was an older generation still there with memories of the Depression. It was a coming together of two generations. It was really a hot time.

It was hard to sustain, the intensity of that period. You run out of energy after a while. Maybe people like me didn't do a good enough job (sighs). In some cases, union elections that were stolen shouldn't have been stolen. Maybe we relied on a Labor Department to enforce the laws and, of course, it didn't. Maybe we didn't realize

---

* It was a successful rank-and-file challenge to the corrupt leadership of the union. Boyle subsequently went to prison.

that you can't beat machines the first time out. We became dispirited.

It was a time when the unions were very militant, certainly at the bargaining table. There *were* some terrific unions where that unrest *was* expressed by the leadership. A militancy that now appears gone. Maybe what happened in the sixties, with the antiwar and civil rights movements, not enough attention was paid to labor. It's curious. In the thirties, when the nation's industry was in a shambles, the labor movement came alive. The unions were powerful because a labor bureaucracy had not yet been established. Unions are powerful only to the extent that they aren't bureaucratic. That's what the fight for union democracy is about. The more people feel they have something at stake, the more they attend union meetings, the stronger the union is. The more the political controversy, the more the members are interested. The more bureaucratic the union, the more the membership is kept at a distance, the weaker it is.

I didn't go the corporate law-firm route. I think there is a great deal of naiveté in believing you can do important pro bono work with a big outfit representing the big boys. You can't lead two lives. You can't spend ninety-five percent of your time representing Acme Foods, helping them dilute FDA regulatory standards, and then leave at the end of the day and say, Gee, I wanna do good, I wanna change the world, isn't it awful what these corporations are doing? You're living a life that is out of joint and something snaps at some point. You become schizoid.

We saw the Kennedy justice people as our models. The generation just ahead of us. These were the best and the brightest. The pro bono people. It looked a lot more glamorous than it really was. They were really mandarins. They were the elite, redesigning a social order. In fact, that's not what it's about. The Kennedy justice days are over.

The idea is not to change the world in your spare time. The real models should have been people like Joe Rauh and Len Despres.* They practiced law when the Judiciary was just a fleabag institution of political hacks. They were the tribunes for ordinary people, fighting for justice at the margins. It wasn't glamorous. They were there, year in and year out.

---

* Two labor lawyers whose careers extend back to the New Deal days. He works in Despres's office.

I remember a guy telling me that to protect his political purity, he was going to work for a big corporate law firm. So if he ever faced something like the Vietnam War, he could resign in a minute and go out and make $100,000 a year. Talk about a schizoid way of doing things. In some of those outfits, the bright kids start at $80,000 a year. Imagine them as Joe Rauh or Len Despres.

Everything you do changes you. You work on municipal bond offerings ninety-five percent of your time, you're gonna be a different person in two years than one who spends ninety-five percent of his time helping out black schoolchildren or unemployed steelworkers. These two people may start out with the same political philosophies, but—the first becomes active, the second becomes passive. I mean, as citizens.

Kids in their twenties looking at people my age see what? Nothing. I tend to hear from the ones who are idealistic and active, who go into Legal Aid work, but they are a pitiful minority.

My contemporaries haven't changed nominally. They're still looking for their former selves in the students they interview. They complain, These kids are dead. They don't express any interest outside of how much money there is. My friends, who are making these big salaries, are scandalized by these kids behind them who want the same amount of money. Where are their ideals? they cry. They don't look at themselves. They're responsible for a lot of this.

Some know what's happened to themselves. There was a meeting at a big law firm in Washington in the late seventies. A friend of mine, who was an associate in the firm, said, "If we really want to do something pro bono, we'd all stay home from work for just one day."

On top of everything else, corporate law is pretty boring. Put that together with political disenchantment and what have you got? $80,000 a year to start, sure. If that's the only reason you became a lawyer, fine.

I've lost some of the starry-eyed attitude I had when I came into it in the early seventies. Thank God. It's not reordering, changing the world. It's not the heroism of being a radical social engineer. It's picking up causes that the system isn't taking care of. Most people who have a need to be in Federal Court can't get there because there's no lawyer to represent them. The job is to help real people with real problems. It doesn't change the world, but it's awfully important to these people.

I've been sobered in a lot of ways. I still think what I'm doing is important. It may be more important now, even if you're hitting your head against a stone wall. I don't know how much longer I can keep doing that. I don't recommend it as a way of life indefinitely for everybody. But it's important to make the record. I still think it's up to my generation. I'm not completely throwing in the towel yet.

> POSTSCRIPT: *One year after the conversations with Frank Lumpkin and Tom Costello, the laid-off steelworkers of Wisconsin Steel, represented by the Save Our Jobs Committee, settled a lawsuit against Harvester* for $14.8 million. It was eight years after the plant's closing. Six hundred of its workers had died since. Several law firms had turned down the case because Harvester at first considered the suit frivolous. "Well," Costello said, "Harvester learned otherwise."*
>
> *"I'm just so proud we can get $15 million out of Harvester's pocket, because they kicked us out of the mill," Lumpkin said. "I don't think anyone's entirely happy. It's like I guess winning a war. A lot of people have lost their homes."*
>
> *Joe Harris, a laid-off steelworker, told Lumpkin, "If it wasn't for you, we wouldn't have got nothing." He offered to buy Lumpkin a cup of coffee "sometime."*
>
> *It was a front-page story in both Chicago newspapers.*

BRIAN DEVLIN

> *He is twenty-two. He lives with his mother and two sisters in a conservative blue-collar suburb of Chicago.*
> *"I'm a laborer, Laborers' Union, Local 4. We do*

---

* Harvester had taken over Wisconsin Steel as the result of a complicated merger. The gates were shut shortly thereafter.

remodelin', wreckin', maintenance. Everything it takes to
run a building. It's a house crew, is what it's called. So I'm
pretty lucky."

Guys I still hang around with all live right on the block. Most of 'em are in construction. None of 'em went to school or anything. I went to college for a year after high school, Illinois Benedictine. I really didn't know what I wanted to do, so I just started workin' construction. I figure I'll do it for the rest of my life.

We usually run into each other, my friends, on a Friday or somethin' at the local tavern on the corner. We talk about everything: girls, what's goin' on, all sorts of garbage. Once in a while, we'll talk about stuff you read in the paper. Politics.

It wouldn't bother me if some little country down in South America becomes communist. I think we should be pals with 'em, trade with 'em, make some money off 'em. Why go down there and fight with 'em?

My mom's a heavy-duty liberal, you know (laughs). Some stuff I don't believe in with her, other things I do. We always get in big fights about ERA, 'cause I think women belong in the kitchen still. I guess I must be an awful chauvinist.

I'd like to get in the trades more instead of bein' a laborer, somethin' like electrician. I'm on lists, but there's a lot of trouble gettin' in because they lost court cases. They gotta bring in minorities into the trades, so I'm sittin' on the bench waitin'.

I think I'm gettin' discriminated against, myself. My father came to this country and worked hard all his life and never collected a day's unemployment. These guys, they're second-generation welfare and they're gettin' into the trades. While here I sit, my dad's worked and paid taxes all his life. I don't like that deal.

Maybe they did get ripped off for a long time. Maybe they have somethin' comin' to 'em because how they were treated, but they shouldn't take that out on people now. I've been on that list two years and I haven't been called.

I got friends that can't get a union job, 'cause the contractor has to have minorities. My friends are killin' themselves at scab labor for six bucks an hour.

I got nothin' against blacks. My labor foreman's a black guy.

194

Best boss I ever had. There's other black guys I hate. I don't like those guys with an attitude: Hey, I'm black, you owe me somethin'. I was a slave two hundred years ago. Those people you can have.

Lot of people where I live, most of 'em came from neighborhoods where they moved out 'cause the blacks were movin' in. They're heavy bigots. They hate blacks just to look at 'em. Them I have no time for. I take people one by one. If a black family moved in Oak Lawn, it wouldn't bother me as long as they were all right. My boss could move next door to me, I'd be glad. But it'd cause an uproar in that town (laughs).

Most of my friends hate blacks. One of 'em comes in the tavern— they got a carry-out in the front—they might say, Get that nigger outa here. They always say nigger this, nigger that. But they also work with some guys they like. They'll say, He's all right for a nigger.

There's some guys don't like unions. They're nuts. If it wasn't for the union, I wouldn't be makin' what I'm makin'. Reason I hate Reagan's guts, he's a union-buster. A lotta union people voted for him 'cause they're stupid.

Vietnam was before me, so I don't know too much about it. None of my friends went there. But it's still in the news with all these vets, 'cause they got treated bad. They probably did get a raw deal. It didn't make no sense to go all the way over there to the other side of the world to fight—like what they're about to do in South America. A lotta people got killed for nothin'. I wouldn't wanna go walkin' in some parade. I'm kinda sick hearin' about it myself. All these movies, *Rambo,* doesn't interest me at all.

People nowadays who were never there all of a sudden are real gung-ho about Vietnam bein' so great. I got one buddy who thinks he's a soldier of fortune. He thinks it would be fun to go to a war. He wouldn't be sayin' that if he was there. It seems like the movies and everything today are tryin' to get people geared up to be stupid enough to go back to some other war.

I think the contras are a bunch of murderers. The majority of the people down there seem to be on the Sandinista side. We're backin' the wrong side, we're backin' dictators, just like we done every other place we ever go. We don't care about all the masses of people who are starvin' to death. But I wouldn't want to live in a communist country. The way we have it is all right.

If I was drafted to fight in Nicaragua, that'd be a hard choice to make. I'd probably end up goin'. But you never know what's gonna happen when you come right down to it. I'd like to say deep down inside, I'd leave and not do somethin' I thought was wrong. But I don't think I'd have the nerve to go up and hide out in some country the rest of my life and never see anybody again. And also be hated by a lot of people. You'd be thought a traitor, you know? I wouldn't like it, but I'd go. I'd just try to stay alive until I came home (laughs). I wouldn't get gung-ho about it.

If somethin' was really buggin' me and I thought there was a chance of changin' it by protest, I wouldn't go like these idiots and have a march of thirty people. It's not gonna do anything. If there was a chance to get a million people somewhere to show you meant business, I'd join along. The thing that scares me is that someday the work will run out. I feel sorry for these guys who've worked twenty years for a company and all of a sudden they get the axe. That's the worst that can happen in a country. And farmers gettin' a raw deal. That's the kinda stuff we could do with the money instead of throwin' it into defense.

That doesn't always make sense to me why some guy has five million, ten million, a hundred million dollars and other people are broke. It seems like my class of people, my neighborhood, are the ones payin' for those people that aren't workin'. And the people makin' millions are loopholin' here and there and not givin' a thing back. They say they're puttin' money back by buildin' plants. The trickle-down theory, that garbage.

Workin' in a building like this, I come into some guy's office and I look around. The guy's worth millions, president of such and such company. Why's a guy like this got all that cash? I drive home down Dan Ryan, drive through Bridgeport, and you see these people strugglin' to get by. I never realized till I worked downtown how much money there is in this country. I just grew up in a neighborhood where everyone had the same thing. I thought everyone lived that way. You go down to the parking garage and all you see is Porsches and Mercedes. You read about these loopholes they get in taxes. And here I am killin' myself workin' and I pay a ton of money in taxes. And I don't believe in them others either, people sittin' back and takin' welfare and not doin' anything.

Everyone I ever talk to, older guys, say, I don't want my kids in trades, because the unions are gonna be dead ten years from now anyway. That's another reason why sometimes I kick myself in the head for not goin' to school. It seems like technology is takin' over, where you're not gonna have your normal guy takin' over.

Older guys, twenty-five, thirty years ago, they got outa high school, they could just pick a job. Do I want to be an electrician, a plumber? They had a choice on what they were gonna do with their life. Nowadays you don't have a choice. You get out and scrape for whatever you can get. In back of your head's the feeling that some-day it could even get worse. I don't know what I'd do if fifteen years from now, after I get a family started, I suddenly get my pay cut in half because the unions go.

You're used to livin' at a certain standard and all of a sudden you're chopped. You know most people are livin' on borrowed money anyway (laughs). That's my biggest worry in life. Jobs are gonna be taken over by technology.

I think the workin' class is goin' down. There's not gonna be any middle class too long. You're either makin' big bucks or little bucks. There's nothin' in between. That's what I always wanted with my life. Have my family, take it light, and maybe have the enjoyment of a little cottage in Wisconsin. No mansion anywhere. I never ex-pected to be rich. But I expected to have what a workin' man has.

It scares me that fifteen years from now it's not gonna be like that. You're gonna be menial labor for peanuts. Even my buddies think about that. Why can't I be like my old man? It was so easy for them and so hard for us.

Every generation was always better. My kid will have it better than me and his kid will have it better than him. Now it's the reverse. You're not gonna have it as good as your old man. Maybe if you go to school, you have a chance, but if you don't . . .

Unless somethin' changes. It wasn't easy gettin' unions started, maybe when they start really bustin' unions, maybe we'll have to go after management again (laughs). I'll fight for a decent wage. That's one thing I'd protest for. Maybe where we only have the poor and only have the rich, all these little people are gonna get sick and tired of people givin' 'em shit and they're gonna go after the big guy. Maybe that's a hundred years from now and I won't be around when it happens. I just might get the bad part of it, a depression.

My old man worked hard to get where he's at. I don't want to come along and in fifteen years I end up bein' a lower-class broke person. You'd feel like a bum. It's the fear about maybe takin' a step down in society. Everyone's got that fear.

BILL AND YVETTE GARDINER

Bill is a pilot of Trans World Airlines (TWA).
    Yvette is a flight attendant for TWA.
    The flight attendants of TWA were on strike.
    The pilots of TWA did not support the strike.
    The flight attendants walked the picket line. Yvette was
one of them.
    The pilots crossed the picket line. Bill was one of them.
    Bill and Yvette are husband and wife.

BILL : *"I came from an upper-middle-class family in
Kansas. Went in the navy, served in Vietnam for a couple
of years, flew fighter bombers over aircraft carriers, got out
in '66, went to TWA in '68, and have been flying there
since.*

    *"My father was a staunch Republican. When he went to
New York, he asked to be taken to Idlewild. The taxi driver
would say, 'You mean Kennedy?' He'd say, 'No, I mean
Idlewild.' My dad would have rolled over in his grave if he
knew I belonged to a union.*

    *"That's the way I was brought up and I've maintained
that political belief."*

YVETTE : *"I grew up in the Panama Canal Zone. My
stepfather worked as a civilian for the Army Department.*

    *"My first introduction to unions was when I first started
flying with TWA. I was chagrined that I had to pay union
dues. Why would I need a union? I'm a good kid. I don't
need someone to take care of me. Well, I found out how
much you do need a union. The scab flight attendants are
now discovering it. They're trying to form their own union.
The courts have already ruled that IFFA* is the*

---

* Independent Federation of Flight Attendants.

*recognized bargaining labor union. The scabs have to pay
union dues."*

YVETTE : When I said I was going on strike, Bill seemed to accept
it very well. He said the most important thing is that we have each
other, somehow we will get through this together. The decision to go
on strike was very difficult. We had only been in St. Louis for a
couple of years. We purchased our house, based upon our two incomes. There was a real possibility we would lose our house.

As time progressed, Bill's patience ran out. He felt that eventually I would see the light and as more of my friends crossed the
picket line, I would follow. That didn't happen. I've stood firm.

I thought about crossing, a number of times—to save our marriage, when I realized how strongly Bill felt. But I realized I
couldn't do that because I'd be unhappy, untrue to myself.

*Bill has worked for TWA for nineteen years. Yvette has
been with the airline for fifteen years.*

BILL : Every day we went to work we crossed the picket line. I
used to be a blind follower of the union doctrine. I'm not any
more.

Their strike was very ill-timed. In this day and age, it is time
when unions, in an effort to save the company, might allow the
company to have a strong foundation: to build and go forward in a
highly competitive market.

(There are interruptions.) Now, are we riding home together?
(General laughter.)

YVETTE : At one point, you were very pro-union. Bill walked the
picket line with Continental pilots. That's a real contrast to the
person I see before me now.

BILL : At that time, I was a union representative for TWA and I
believed we were doing the right thing in supporting them. Looking
back on that decision, I think it was terribly incorrect.

There are different ways to fight a battle. In this day and age, I
don't think a strike is the right way. The other labor groups on
TWA property see that, especially the pilots. When management

came to us in '82 and '83 and asked us to lead the way in concessions, our union had long discussions.

One of our wise old pilots made an analogy: "You're on a boat that is leaking quite badly. The captain says, 'Now, people, I'll give you a bucket, and if we all bail, we might make it. If you don't bail, we might all go down.' Do you dare sit there and just say, 'I'm not gonna help'?"

The strike of the TWA flight attendants was ill-timed and unjustified. The other two labor groups on the property had made wage and working-conditions concessions. The pilots were giving thirty and forty percent. The mechanics didn't give that much. The flight attendants were being asked to give an amount commensurate with the mechanics. The pilots were not sympathetic to their strike at all.

YVETTE: No, you can't say "at all." You can't speak for all of them. A number of TWA pilots were very sympathetic to us. United pilots did so much to help us. Bill, you haven't answered the question: What caused your change of heart?

BILL: I just didn't think it was wise. Having a wife and son committing occupational suicide was very painful to me. I have a son, Jeff,* twenty-four, who had worked as a TWA flight attendant for nearly a year when the strike occurred.

He walked the picket line also. Nothing I said could convince him that he was sacrificing his job. I pointed out to him, "The only way you're going to keep your job is to cross the picket line, distasteful as it would be to you." It was suicidal for him.

YVETTE: I know you think things like dignity and principles and values are hollow words. They don't make our mortgage payments. Yet you must have taught him *something*. My loss of $35,000 plus a year has been, for all of us, a very hard loss to accept. Nonetheless, I still feel I did the right thing.

What you've done is just wrong. I'm all for giving and helping my company along, but what they were asking was unconscionable. I just couldn't do it and there are quite a few—to the tune of five thousand others—that couldn't do it either.

Did you ever cross the picket line when Yvette and Jeff were on it?

---

* His son by a previous marriage.

BILL: No, I never had to. I would have, though. Gladly. Their career profile had been all the way up: a very, very spoiled group of people. At the first sign of having to step backwards, it was very distasteful. I don't think anybody likes the idea of stepping backwards.

YVETTE: At the risk of upsetting Bill—when he went to work during the strike, he was met headlong by a number of macho-like pilots, who said, "Hey, Gardiner, haven't you gotten your wife in line yet?" That really bothered this guy, who's for the most part a leader. There's something in all of us that wants to be like the other guys. Peer pressure. He hasn't been able to "get his wife in line" because I can think for myself.

This has been the most painful issue in our entire marriage. We don't have the friends we used to have. We used to socialize a lot. We gathered very often with other pilot–flight attendant couples. Those flight attendants who crossed the picket lines I don't want to have in my house any more. These are the same girls—the same women—that walked the picket line with me and said, "I'm never gonna cross the picket line."

I guess they needed to pay to have their swimming pools cleaned or their maids come in. Most of them are very well-to-do. They didn't cross because they needed the job. We have single mothers with one or two children that didn't cross the picket line. Our black flight attendants, especially, have been wonderful. They had some scruples. When the others crossed the picket line, it weakened my fight. I don't care to be friends with them any longer.

This has made it hard for Bill. There are people we do not invite to our home any longer. One time when he complained, I made a crude analogy: We've got this pile of dog-do in the middle of our carpet and we're supposed to walk around it and pretend it's not there? Ignore it? Can we try to make polite conversation, when this horrible thing is right in our midst? I can't do that. I'm not that kind of person.

It has forced us to cultivate friendships with our neighbors. We have met a lot of new people, non-airline people, with whom I'm comfortable.

BILL: We agreed before the strike started that we would not talk about this. We had a horrible struggle over it at dinner. I did not abide by the agreement because it was like watching someone you cared about very much cutting their wrists. You're supposed to stand there and watch them bleed to death? I couldn't do it.

The financial picture was a large item in my thinking. We are now married to a house we bought, based on two incomes. It has created a heck of a strain on us.

Every time I saw a bit of weakness in her—she would make a remark one day, "I'd like to go back to work. I miss my job"—I thought, maybe she's thinking about crossing the picket line. I thought that was great. You can go be based somewhere else. You don't have to face your friends in St. Louis or Chicago. We'll send you to Kansas City, which TWA was doing at that time, so that friends did not have to face the peer pressure.

YVETTE: That's interesting. I thought they sent flight attendants to another base because they needed them there. Are you saying they had something to hide? They had something to be ashamed of?

BILL: It's an avoidance. A great factor in people not going to work, not crossing the picket line, was because they'd have to face all those people saying, "Where are you going?"

People inquired about Yvette whenever I would go to work: "Has she come back yet?" She was probably one of the best flight attendants TWA ever had. She's charming. She's good with people when they're in nasty moods. She did an outstanding job. People knew that and that's why they asked, "Has she come back yet?" I'd say, "No, she's one of the stubborn ones, she's gonna stay out." They would just shake their heads.

YVETTE: Come back to what?

BILL: Come back to the job as it was offered you at that point and build from that.

YVETTE: But it is not the same job. There was really nothing to go back to. I'm leaving a nine-year-old at home to be taken care of for many more days than I would be there. By the time I finish a sitter, I wouldn't have any money left over. I'm much better off staying home, taking care of him. Than being disgusted with myself. These people have made whores of themselves. That's what scabs are. They're saying, "If this is all you want to pay me, fine. This is the little that I'm worth to myself." I could not do that.

BILL: You thought you were irreplaceable. In fact, you've been replaced by a work force of younger, not as talented, not as charming. . . .

YVETTE: Far less professional.

BILL: They're getting there. They'll get trained. The fact remains that you have been replaced for about one-third or one-half of what it was costing the company. Kids out of high school. In a matter of three weeks they were put on the line and they gain the experience that you gained in fifteen years. They are making between $15,000 and $20,000 a year. That's not bad for a kid out of high school.

YVETTE: Instead of being upset about this, Bill is very pleased. His wife and his son, two people closest to him, are being hurt—

BILL: You're saying that I'm gloating.

YVETTE: I'm saying that you're gloating. You don't look at me as your wife when we're on TWA property or when you put on that uniform. Somehow, to me, you become a different person.

There is a lot of good in that man. But if he can't look at me and be sympathetic when I hurt—instead, he's entirely on the other side. The most important thing here is for our marriage to continue. I've learned to turn a deaf ear to Bill's talk, to his attitude.

If I found another job that paid me the same amount of money, I don't think Bill would care. What has hurt us most is the loss of my income. I think that's what it all boils down to.

BILL: There is no question about that. Prior to our marriage, I was a very conservative spender because I have been laid off twice by TWA. Rather than a career with a continual upslope in earnings and benefits, my past has not been that way. I'm better at taking the knocks and downslides than Yvette is.

When we got married, I was convinced by Yvette that it was time to start living. Are you going to save that money forever? We went out and bought this house. It is huge, with a huge price tag. The turn of events has been very painful.

It was apparent the strike was being busted, the union was being broken. The mechanics of TWA were forced to go back to work. They may or may not have supported them. The pilots unquestionably did not support them. Even the most staunch union advocate would say, You guys better go back to work and fight another day.

YVETTE: We didn't have support from the other unions on TWA property. We had support from all kinds of union groups across the country. If our own pilots supported us, we'd have won hands down.

BILL: Or TWA would have failed.

YVETTE: I don't think it would have failed. I think both groups would have been stronger.

BILL: TWA pilots have a lot to lose. With a career of twenty, twenty-five years, each of us looked at the financial picture. We sent accountants in and they verified what the company was saying. Concessions were needed in order to make the company viable. How much, who knows? Who knows if it would have made or broken the company? I certainly can't tell you that. But the pilots did feel that way. And do.

YVETTE: So the pilots decided to get in bed with management.

BILL: That's a horrible thing to say.

YVETTE: But that's what it comes down to. Anyway, the strike is technically over and I don't have a job. The girls who replaced us are still working there. The girls who were scabs. Via the rumor mill, we hear they're dropping like flies.

BILL: I'm not anti-union.

YVETTE: Just anti my union.

BILL: I'm anti what you did. I have not gloated over the fact that you are out of work at all. That is very distressing to me. I don't think you realize that.

YVETTE: What I've gotten from you is, Well, you've made your bed, you've got to lie in it.

BILL: I feel that way at times. You've been very stubborn. You're working a job that pays you much less with far poorer conditions.

YVETTE: That's true. I work for a cosmetic line at a major department store. It's very hard and I don't enjoy it one bit. But I don't have to hang my head in shame.

BILL: My son's doing about the same thing. I think that about four thousand of the five thousand that went out on strike are probably doing piddly little jobs at three dollars, four dollars an hour.

He regrets the strike. I made a statement to him last week: ''I wish you still worked for TWA because we're gonna take a trip and I wish you could go with us.'' He said, ''You're taking the words out of my mouth. I wish I did, too.''

YVETTE: That doesn't mean he regrets his decision. Are you misinterpreting his words?

BILL: Maybe I am. I know he's sorry.

YVETTE: We're all sorry that it came to pass. I'm sorry, too, that it boiled down to this.

BILL: I was brought up, especially in the navy and at home, with discipline. I observe the union philosophy to be one of ''Don't you tell me what to do, even though you may own the company. My union is gonna tell you what you can tell me to do.'' I think that's a slap in the face of the manager. If I owned a company, that would be an obstacle to my proper running of that company.

The air controllers didn't feel as I do. They said, ''Baloney. They wouldn't dare do that to us.'' They found out you can't flout the law. I think IFFA didn't believe it was gonna happen to them: We are invulnerable. I think it's been a very hard lesson.

YVETTE: I feel as strong as ever about the union

BILL: The union is doomed. Not unions in general, just this one.

YVETTE: I feel unions are doomed at this time. There are far too many unemployed today that don't have any choice. We have people with families to feed. If I put myself in the place of the young flight attendants, the scabs, I wouldn't have wanted anyone to tell me not to work there.

If I were eighteen years old and I'd just gotten out of a little town I'd probably die in, I wouldn't have listened to anyone who said, ''We have a labor strike going on. This is not a good time.'' I wouldn't have wanted anyone to rain on my parade. I would have wanted to go out there and fly and see the world and feel like I had already made it.

Well, those young flight attendants are finding out it's not what they thought it was. After a time, all these people will need unions, just like the people who worked in factories for many long hours. The unions are taking hard knocks now, but the pendulum will swing back the other way, hopefully. I don't think it will be too soon. It doesn't look too good, but I'm glad to have been on the side I was on.

BOOK 2

GOD

Well, I left my home and kindred
And started for the Promised Land,
Now the grace of God upon me
And the Bible in my hand.

Well, in distant land I trod,
Cryin', "Sinners come to God."
I'm on the battlefield for my Lord . . .

—*A spiritual*

ROY LARSON

He had been a Methodist minister for nineteen years. From 1969 to 1985, he was religion editor of the Chicago Sun-Times. *He is currently publisher-editor of the* Chicago Reporter, *a journal that monitors racial issues in the city, and often scoops the mainstream press.*

Unfortunately (laughs), America has got religion in a way that it hasn't had before. When I started the religious beat, mainline churches were out in the forefront. Now they're battered and exhausted, losing numbers, and don't seem to know what they're doing. In a way, they're the religious reflection of liberals generally. Out of focus and out of gas.

Other people are moving in to fill the gap, especially the fundamentalists. There is an upsurge.

Shrewd political people have recognized the potential of grabbing hold of the religious constituency. They sense the possibilities of glomming onto this vast market. Then there's the sheer technocracy of it all. Television is here. These people have mastered it. The mainliners are so scrupulous, they don't know how to use it. The others have no scruples at all, so they use it well.

Their basic appeal is to people who feel left out. Marginalized people, who have an emotional hunger. W. H. Auden has a line about the wild prayers of longing. For ten, fifteen years, we've had these wild prayers of longing. In a world that's in chaos, fundamentalist religion provides you with a very well ordered world, an architectonic world. It helps you get through.

These programs have a lot of appeal to people without a sense of history. You don't have to learn anything before you listen to these television programs. You do not have to have mastered the liturgy. It's fast food. It's just there, it's bland, it's inoffensive, it fills you up for a while. And it helps. Sadly. You're given answers. You're not presented with problems. The idea is not to reflect, because that's disturbing. What the television preachers do not do is challenge you, challenge your existing way of looking at things. They reinforce it. Rilke says when you look at a great piece of art, it tells you, you must change your life. Television preachers say, What you're doing is right. It just reinforces a deadly, stale conventionalism.

Their followers are what you'd call nice people. They're nicely dressed, kind of informal, hearty, rather outgoing. They're very pleasant, always smiling. It's a smile that doesn't seem connected to the rest of the body. It has no connection with feeling or thought. It's almost like watching a television show. It has all the depth of a television commercial or a sitcom. There's no texture, no history. You don't have to know anything. It's a handicap if you do.

With the upsurge in conventionalism, there's a broader interest in religion among young adults. Some are going to church for the first time. What they feel is pretty much a reflection of bourgeois values. Conventionalism, not traditionalism. There's a difference.

There's always been a prophetic strain within religion. It goes against the grain. It's always been a minority viewpoint. But it's the salt. The New Testament warned us about the salt that loses its savor. A religion that loses its prophetic oomph really is salt-free. Bland. Tasteless.

When I was going to college and seminary, we too were an extremely dull, unimaginative lot. I'd say we were as bland as the present generation. Yet my colleagues emerged in the 1960s as people who were willing to take risks.

Many of us were exposed to first-rate theological minds: Reinhold Niebuhr, Paul Tillich, Martin Buber. They kept saying: You cannot identify God with any one strain in a community. God is not middle-class, God is not a Methodist, God is not a Republican or a Democrat. You never get caught up in American jingoism. You don't get caught up in suburban values. You distrust everything to a certain extent. There's always a critical distance. That laid the base for later activism.

I find much of theology today quite unreadable. There are some competent people around, but they remind you of jazz pianists who play for a small coterie, or modern poets who write to be read only by a few peers. It seems so goddamn precious to me. Part of the fundamentalist appeal is their address to the ordinary person.

What the church needs right now is a kind of Pepperidge Farm theology. Theologians can't just write for other theologians. Otherwise, the demagogues will go in there and provide food for people who are desperately hungry. The terrible, light-hearted simplifiers.

This is the time of the simplifiers and technicians. This is what concerns me. Technocrats were the ones who devised the ovens in Germany. Technically competent barbarians. Our schools are turning out technicians who have no sense of history. You can get a master's in journalism without knowing anything of cultural and social history. You can get out of a theological seminary without really possessing your own tradition. You've bought the trappings. It's like buying a Brooks Brothers suit and thinking you're a traditionalist. You can't purchase tradition. You have to earn it and acquire it slowly.

It seems to me something fundamental changed within a twenty-four-hour period in May of 1970 at Kent State University. The mood shifted, as though there were a before and after. There was a kind of universal exhaustion, a feeling that it's too big, we can't fight it. It was just like someone stuck a pin in the balloon.

But the fervor never completely dies. The Sanctuary movement today is attracting that remnant similar in many ways to the people in the sixties. They regard themselves as faithful Americans, who also stand apart from society at large. Who feel their loyalty to God forces them to disobey the law. The salt is still there.

WILLOW CREEK LOBBY

"It is among the largest and fastest-growing congregations in the Chicago area, offering its ever-increasing throng of well-scrubbed and youthful adherents an energetic blend of religious pop music, originally scripted dramas, morality plays, and plain-spoken sermons delivered by Willow Creek's founder and senior pastor, Bill Hybels.

"The church has a profound appeal to upwardly mobile young professionals, who faithfully negotiate their

*turbocharged foreign automobiles through the monumental
congestion in Willow Creek's 1,400-car parking lot on
Sundays for a low-key taste of "biblical principles" before
brunch.*

*"From the start, the church has targeted 'nonchurched
Harry' as its principal prey, conducting door-to-door
marketing research in its early days to determine the best
means of rousing him from his house. . . . "*

—Bruce Buursma, Religion Editor, Chicago
Tribune, *July 21, 1985*

*Off the expressways, past the airport, is a complex of
suburbs—Schaumburg, Hoffman Estates, South
Barrington. In other parts, the Sun Belt, the Northwest,
New England, they have names equally recognizable to
dwellers of those precincts.*

*Following a labyrinthine path, we arrive at the glass,
ultramodern structure. It's the church. There are booths in
the crowded lobby. There are two young women in each,
answering all sorts of inquiries. There is a line of
parishioners eager to buy instant tapes. As soon as Bill
Hybels finishes his sermon, "We'll have the message on tape
in five minutes." It sells at two bucks per copy. They sell
seven hundred that morning.*

*"An awful lot of people give the tapes to neighbors and
friends who can benefit from the message," says a
volunteer. Today's message is: God Loves Me.*

MIKE : I work in data processing. I lived as an agnostic, although
I really don't know why. I realized my need for God in 1975. I know
He wanted a relationship with me. The girl I was going out with
challenged my Christian faith. I said, ''Don't come on to me with
that holier-than-thou attitude,'' but I was defensive. I just said,
''I'll just check out Scriptures.'' I did. And I was sold.

I think there's a spiritual vacuum in this country. There's been so much religion without substance. That's why there's such an exodus from the mainstream churches, if you will. I voted for Reagan, though I disagree with him on so many things.

Mark, Connie and their babe in arms, Jason, appear. Connie's button reads, "Jesus put a song in my heart—it's a melody." Mark is a computer technician and Connie is "a stay-at-home mom."

CONNIE: President Reagan does not represent what I feel. He uses a lot of godly references, but I don't feel he's a Christian in any sense of the word. Jimmy Carter was a Christian, I felt. I saw Reagan on the news, calling people "sons of bitches" and stuff like that. I voted for him, because this is a wordly world, not a Christian world.

Since I became a Christian, I don't worry about the Bomb. It's in God's hand. Before, I was always afraid somebody was gonna push the button or some accident was gonna happen. And we'd all die. Now, I don't have that fear. I wouldn't have had another baby if I were afraid. I think there will be a nuclear war, but the events leading up to it haven't happened yet, so why not have children?

A smiling Dave appears.

DAVE: I wouldn't want to see a nuclear war happen, but if it did and I died or my wife died, if we accepted the Lord as our savior, we'd be in heaven. That's better than being on earth.

Before the sermon really gets under way, Bill Hybels, at the pulpit, speaks of other matters.

HYBELS: Next Sunday morning, we're going to have some cameras set up in just a couple of aisles down here. We'll be taping the service for the purpose of making that available. So you'll want to wear your best Sunday makeup next week, ladies (laughter from the congregation). Be careful who you sit next to because you may be seen with them in the future on tape (laughter). Now don't dress up too much, because we don't want anybody to think this is a traditional church. So wear the bare jerseys and short pants, whatever, when you come in here (laughter).

KAREN BALLARD

"In the last four years, I've had an upside-down change in my life."

She is an executive in a nationwide society, engaged in charitable funding. Her background: rural Midwest.

"My folks never talked about politics at home. My mom and dad would never tell me who they voted for. Or to each other. You go into that little booth and cast your vote. But you don't talk about it, you don't debate, you don't discuss. We wouldn't talk about it at the dinner table.

"When one of my high school friends was killed in Vietnam, we all acknowledged what a shame and what a waste it was. The war came home. But people pretty much forgot about it and went their own ways."

Her husband, Bill, an architect, occasionally joins in the conversation.

I came to Chicago in 1968 and was very much into a self-centered life-style. I was earning enough money, going out to good restaurants, looking down upon the unsophisticated, who really didn't know what was going on in the world. I did.

I came from a simple life of meat and potatoes, eggs and bacon. I was now eating gourmet food, painting my nails, wearing the latest fashions. I was a pre-yuppie yuppie (laughs).

I was sympathetic to the Vietnam War protesters and would go to demonstrations, write letters to Congress. But I myself was not in the front line. I was involved in a safe way. I was not really ready to risk myself.

When I got this job twelve years ago, I thought I could change things within the system. What happened is that I became part of the system. I found it very comfortable. I viewed myself as a career woman. I had my little briefcase. I had a nice apartment. I liked it.

My folks were happy to see me settle into this respectable, normal life-style. They always had this concern about me being a single woman, living in the city. Bill and I were married in '80.

We both had grown up in religious families. I grew up Missouri Synod Lutheran. Mo Syn. It was so conservative, we could not go to the high school baccalaureate, because we should not pray with people of other faiths.

I rebelled against it when I left home and went to college. Little did they know that when I got exposed to some of the social issues, my Sunday school faith went out the window. I see a lot of hypocrisy in organized religion. I don't need it.

Bill's background: United Church of Christ. "In 1964, my family and I were Goldwater supporters. The war affected me because of the draft. It forced me to think about my attitudes. At the time, I felt if you're gonna fight a war, you might as well fight it, win, and get it over with. But at school, it got to seem ridiculous fighting a war, nobody really knew why. And they were gonna ask me to fight . . ." (Laughs.)

Through friends, we casually visited the Wellington Avenue Church. We liked the minister, Dave Chevrier. We liked the people. They were a kind we'd never met. They challenged our ideas a little bit, very gently. It wasn't all of a sudden, but I felt like I had a need to be religious again.

It's a small community with a track record of being involved in social actions. It takes stands. The first year, we were low-key, Sunday members. We resisted because we already had a very tight-knit circle of friends: young couples who were doing very well. Eating out at the latest restaurants was a big part of our life. This church really works on a simple life-style. Here we are with a Cuisinart and all that good stuff. I was feeling some discord between what we were professing and our life. As things progressed I felt more conflict.

One day, I went to a meeting and this woman from a religious task force came over and said she wanted to talk about Sanctuary. I thought: What do you mean, talk to us about Sanctuary? In my mind, sanctuary was a safe place for birds and wildlife. Or a place of worship. We've already got a sanctuary upstairs.

She told us that a church in Tucson declared itself a sanctuary for refugees from Guatemala and El Salvador. She asked us to send a letter of support. I thought: Fine, sounds good, great. We'll help those people coming across the borders and endorse the action that community of faith was taking. It was risk-free.

The other thing she asked us: would we consider doing likewise? Would we, at the Wellington Church, declare itself a public sanctuary? I sat straight up and listened with a different ear. Our Immigration and Naturalization Service was denying these people political asylum.

I was hoping the whole thing would just go away. I was staring at a cash-flow deficit of $5,000 and wondered how we could be responsible for these refugees. I was concerned about the harassment that would come from challenging the government. Surveillance. And what if the insurance company canceled because we were breaking the law? As finance committee head, I'd be the one who'd have to deal with it. I went through a whole list of what-ifs. It was my way of saying we shouldn't do it. Perhaps a more wealthy church with more members should take this on. But we're so small. Why us, dear God, why us? (Laughs.) It didn't go away.

Here I was with a good job, respectable. What would the people I work with think of being involved in an unlawful action? Could my job be on the line? If the government decided to prosecute, the thought of facing possible imprisonment was scary. I was the one in the community really resisting.

What turned me around was a refugee from El Salvador. She came to the church and told her story. She was a beautiful young woman who had worked with Archbishop Oscar Romero among the poor. Literacy, cooperatives: programs I had by now come to consider God's work. She had to flee the country to save her life. As she was talking, I was saying to myself, That's not right, that's not right. At that point, I realized I had to make a choice.

I began to study our government's policy toward refugees. I listened more carefully to Dave Chevrier's Sunday morning sermons. Old and New Testament stories of cities of sanctuary, of welcoming strangers, of feeding the hungry and clothing the naked, about the 1860s and the Underground Railroad, I realized it was just people being gutsy and committed. I couldn't sit on the fence any more.

Our first refugee was Juan, a young man from El Salvador. He was coming in a week. There was a flurry of activity and everybody was coming together. All of us were very moved by his story. He was driving a truck, had seen all sorts of bodies along the road. One day, he got picked up. He was imprisoned, tortured, and let go because of Amnesty International's efforts. He was pursued, lived in the wilderness, eating roots. We were so moved by Juan, we felt the spirit was at work among us. We felt sad when he needed to move on.

The next week, we welcomed the Vargas family of six. It was filmed on television. I was on the welcoming committee.

The next day, a woman at work said, "I saw someone who looked like you on television, giving a loaf of bread to an alien." "It was me." (Laughs.) She said, "Oh, oh, I never thought you'd do something like that." She turned and walked away.

At a staff meeting that day, another of my colleagues said, "She was on TV last night, did everybody see it?" The room got very quiet and without any comment, we moved on to the next agenda item. Nobody says anything to me about it. They just ignore it. None are especially sympathetic. They just don't care to hear about it. It's as though somebody in a family did something embarrassing.

Fortunately, I'm very competent at my job, I'm respected for that. For a while, I felt schizophrenic. I had my work life and I had my other life. All of a sudden, I felt I was more than my job. My work was more than my job. I considered Sanctuary part of my work in this lifetime.

I used my vacation time to go down to El Salvador and to visit Guatemala, to see firsthand. At work, they think it's weird. Why don't I go to the beach and lay under the sun? When they heard I was going, all they said was, Wear your gun belt. When I came back, no one asked how it was, not a word.

I got to know the Vargas family very well. During Christmas, they wanted to call their daughter who was still in El Salvador. We said they could place the call from our house. The whole family came over. Placing a call there is an arduous process. Someone gets on a bicycle, rides to her house, she walks, runs back to the phone office. Our day progressed and progressed. No return call.

It got dark. They were worried, our conversation lost its laughter. All of a sudden, it was time to eat. We had no idea they'd stay for supper. I thought, I don't have any food in the house. What am I going to do? The mother said to me in Spanish, "*Tiene arroz?* (Do you have rice?)" Instead of a turkey and dressing and apple pie and all that for Christmas, I found a few green beans, some onions, carrots—and rice. I will fix dinner, the mother said.

We had a marvelous rice dinner. We sat around the table and

shared our experiences of Christmas. This was three years ago. It broke a whole lot of things open for me. It made me realize the joy in just being alive. Just knowing that people you love are alive.

It got to be eight o'clock and still there was no call back from El Salvador. We wanted the family to have a poinsettia. We got it out and were set to take them back to the church. We opened the door and the phone rang. It was their daughter.

The excitement that ran through the family was just wonderful. She was all right. That was always a constant worry. After we came back, Bill and I both agreed it was the best Christmas we ever had.

My hope is that someday we won't need to be sanctuaries. Many times, I get discouraged. I go up and down. My faith has certainly been stretched. I don't feel like I've got all the answers, but I feel that I'm being faithful. It's been the most satisfying experience of my life.

PASTOR RICHARD JOHN NEUHAUS

He had been the first cochairman of Clergy and Laity Concerned, along with Daniel Berrigan and Abraham Heschel. He has since switched. He is director of the Center on Religion and Society, a division of the Rockford Institute: indubitably conservative.

"Cardinal Newman said that to live is to change. To be perfect is to have changed often. So I'm on my way to perfection (laughs). If people say that Neuhaus has gone from being a radical to being a neoconservative, I don't argue with them. As Norman Podhoretz puts it, I was breaking ranks."

We're a little like a circus clown on a big rubber ball. You're trying to maintain your balance and on the ball are words: liberal, radical, conservative, reactionary, neoconservative, neoliberal. As you try to keep your balance, you are, the clown on top of the ball, maintaining your own point of gravity. Obviously, where you are standing on the ball changes, so people say you've changed. Where I am today and where I was in the sixties has more continuity, much more striking than the discontinuity. There is a dissonance between how I perceive myself and how I am perceived.

I was very much perceived as a man of the left in the sixties, a kind of ethical apologist for a radical position to the left of the liberal Democrat. In 1967, I wrote an article in *Commonweal* critical of the movement in New York to liberalize the abortion law. It was six years before *Roe* vs. *Wade*. It obviously alienated a good many friends from the left. That was my first experience of the illiberality of liberalism. I was breaking ranks, okay?

In 1975, '76, the parting of the ways came over the question of U.S. responsibility after the collapse of Saigon. When the United States was being pushed out of South Vietnam, I had written a number of pieces about our moral responsibility for the people who were our allies in the peace movement during all those antiwar years. The so-called Third Force, the Buddhist monks. We should not cut and run. At the time, we said there will be a bloodbath. Most of the peace movement belittled us. We know now things couldn't be worse than what they are. If we look at the killing fields of Cambodia and Pol Pot and all, you don't even have to ask the question of whose fault it was.

As for the Sanctuary movement, one should not impugn the motives of the people involved. But we do tend to forget that there are Nicaraguan refugees as well as Salvadoran and Guatemalan.

There's a basic confusion at the very core of the Sanctuary movement itself. Is it religiously, morally motivated or is it political? Here are people in a bad situation and it is the obligation of the church to reach out in a caring way. Or is the movement simply using the sufferings of a people to advance a partisan position against the administration's policies in Central America? I think there's an element of truth in both. I'm not looking at it cynically, simply highly critical.

There's nothing wrong with someone saying, I have thought this through and I believe the administration is dead wrong. But for the sake of honesty, you should not confuse your stated moral purpose with your agenda to advance a partisan cause.

Then there's the whole question of immigration laws. Archbishop Malone of Los Angeles says that the United States should receive everybody who wants to come to the United States, period. In effect, it's for the abolition of immigration laws. We know it won't fly politically. We have to ask the moral question, too: Is that our obligation as a nation? Should we receive, without question, into the mainstream of American society and labor force, with all its welfare benefits, fifteen, twenty million people from the rest of the world? I think the answer, morally as well as politically, is no. A nation has to have immigration laws, okay.

The Sanctuary movement would be rendering a much greater service if it elevated the moral discourse of the debate about the ethics of the immigration policy. We're in a state of total confusion about this. We have people on the left as well as on the right who are espousing what is essentially a nativist, anti-immigrant kind of attitude.

There is an argument to be made for a very restrictive immigration policy. This may come from the labor side: competition for jobs. I am for a generous, inclusive immigration policy, but I don't pretend to know how to restructure it. Congress has been cowardly and fuzzy-minded in refusing to wrestle with these questions because they're political hot potatoes. I think the Sanctuary movement could be valuable if it really became much more upfront in addressing these questions.

> *INS* has specifically said that Guatemalans and Salvadorans are not political refugees: they're here for jobs and better things; the immigration laws should be strictly enforced in these instances. The Nicaraguans, on the other hand, are political refugees. They make no bones about this. Isn't there a double standard at work?*

Frequently there are going to be unfair decisions. *If* that is official U.S. policy, it would be grossly unfair, stupid, okay? I think our immigration policy is a shame and a shambles, okay? I don't blame any one specific person for this. It's been that way for a long time and it's getting worse. My own feeling is that this administration, the Carter administration, and whatever the next one will be is going to be incompetent in making this decision.

* Immigration and Naturalization Service.

DAVID FENCL

*"Seven peace demonstrators accused of mob action and
resisting arrest were acquitted Monday by 12 Lake County
jurors who said they gained a new awareness of U.S.
policies in Central America during the trial. The jurors,
who were chosen carefully from more than 80 people
because of their political neutrality, said the 3½ day court
trial had become a dramatic and emotional education for
them."*

—Chicago Tribune, *April 16, 1985*

*He was foreman of the jury. He is twenty-nine, in market
research, and lives with his wife and small daughter in a
middle-class suburb of Chicago.*

*"I lean toward the conservative side—voted for Reagan
—though I don't always buy everything that the
government does." He regularly attends a Lutheran
church. "At school, you're taught evolution. That's
certainly one way to look at it. But there was a time when I
began to say, It can't be just that, it can't just be a fluke.
Jesus Christ Superstar came out at that time. I began to
read the Bible on my own, starting with the New
Testament. A conversion happened . . .*

*"Where I work, there is an uncommonly large number of
young people who have become more religious. Most of 'em
have gone to college: computer programmers, today's blue-
collars."*

In court, you're hearing stuff that
you don't read anywhere else. We
heard from a fellow who actually serves as attorney in the World
Court. We had an ex-CIA agent giving testimony. Can this possibly

be true? We jurors, during those three days, looked at each other's faces without speaking words. Amazement that this kind of thing went on.

You hear allegations from all sorts of people about what the government does, you just shrug it off. Because it doesn't appear as fact anywhere. But when you hear testimony of a man who spent a good part of his life doing this, all of a sudden, a new reality you're confronted with. It's not just stories from some crazy liberal any more. It's facts. Here's a guy who was there. He was in Laos, he was in Vietnam, he was part of the covert action. It's mind-boggling that there's people in the world that think they can go in and desta-bilize some other country's government and talk about the toll in human life as just part of the way to get there. Who do they think they are that they can make other people's lives so insignificant in light of some goals they're after, which may or may not be right in the first place?

When the trial ended and the judge was thanking the jury for its decision, one thing went through my mind: I wanted to reach out and thank these people for forcing me to sit through this whole process and learn something I wouldn't have learned any other way.

The case was a group of protestors who put on a demonstration at the navy base near Waukegan. They saw our involvement in Central America as another Vietnam around the corner. Catholic folks, Quakers, students, just a lot of concerned people. They were picket-ing at one of the entrance gates, sat down in the middle of the road, trying to stop traffic. Trying to get people to think about it.

For me, it was things I hadn't felt for a while. I went through high school and teenage years during the height of the Vietnam War. Listening to all those antiwar songs. Then you get into the work world and forget it. Here I was, forced to put work out of my mind for a week. I began to notice some of the feelings coming back that I hadn't felt for a long time.

They admitted what they did. They willfully committed an act of civil disobedience in order to call attention in hopes of preventing a greater harm. They felt that sitting down in the road for a few minutes was a mild transgression compared to what they were trying to stop.

Just talking amongst ourselves in the jury room, there was a couple of people who said, Well, they did break the law. We just can't let people go around and sit in the middle of the road protest-ing.

We were a cross-section of middle-class suburban people : a couple of homemakers, two bankers, I think, owner of a cleaning establishment, a teacher, a clerical worker, and a fellow who was doing crossword puzzles almost the whole time.

The defense was : a greater necessity. The judge allowed it. People can be found not guilty by reason of necessity. If you're speeding down the road with a bleeding child in your car, and they arrest you, you can plead innocent by reason of necessity.

There was really very little deliberation. The bailiff had said, "Now who wants chicken ?" We all gave our orders and he went out for it. We started to talk and on the first vote it was agreed : not guilty. It was unanimous.

When the verdict was announced, there was cheering in the courtroom. The judge nodded to the jury and said, "I agree with your findings." That made us all feel good.

> *Sister Dorothy Gartland, a defendant, recalls the moment:*
> *"I don't think anyone in that courtroom would have been*
> *able to walk out of it without being moved. We found it all*
> *the way down to the bailiff. He was hushing people at the*
> *beginning. At the end, he was willing to do whatever*
> *possible. Even the prosecutor, toward the end, wasn't even*
> *objecting. He wanted to hear this testimony."*

Last week I was on a call-in radio show in Waukegan. Some of the callers said, "This is just terrible, these people should be ashamed of themselves. They should be glad they can live in a country where they can go out and demonstrate without being shot, like these other countries." Here's a privilege, but don't dare use it.

I don't know if it's affected my actions too much yet, other than just telling people about it, spreading the word that way. I usually bring it up at social gatherings. If there's just a stonewall face, you drop it. Sometimes people get turned off and steer away. Others become very interested and want to talk about it.

Now, whenever I hear just the first couple of words dealing with the nuclear issue or Central America, I tune in and want to hear more about it. As you talk to people, you find more and more who are also interested. You're just more attuned to what our government is really doing, then you start asking yourself, What can I begin to do ?

Just the other night, I was listening to Public Radio and heard a former CIA agent, John Stockwell. I came home and there was a guy in the driveway, picking up his daughter, who was babysitting for us. He's another fella from the church. I told him about this guy Stockwell and about our trial. So from that, the two of us are going to hear him when he comes to Highland Park to talk. Then, I want to get all the books he listed and read them all and share them all. So you find a couple of people who are quiet in their disturbance. These are quiet people generally, but once they're confronted with facts, they're really hard to let go of.

You begin to see how one-sided a lot of the news broadcasts are on the networks, how nearsighted. How we blow up a lot of things that aren't important and never talk about things that are important. We see on the news today something happened. A week later, something else is presented just as important. It's got the same kind of emphasis in the speaker's voice, the same amount of time, the same color pictures. All of a sudden last week is gone, behind us. Certainly a year ago is even further gone . . .

I don't want my daughter to go through her formative years the way I went through mine, when there's a war going on. From fourth grade through high school, I lived with *Life* magazine, *Time,* and all the newscasts telling me body counts, showing me people with their arms blown off. It was a distant place, but it was here in our living room. I would like her to grow up in something a little more peaceful.

NOTE : *The conversation took place before the Iran-Contra scandal broke.*

REVEREND BILL HYBELS

At thirty-four, he is senior pastor of the Willow Creek Community Church. He also acts as chaplain of the Chicago Bears. Several of its star players are among his parishioners.

The congregation is predominantly youthful. It is a

glowing, smiling aggregate of young couples with small children, some in arms. There are singles, of course, eyes bright and wandering. The occasional wrinkled feature stands out like a wart on an otherwise unblemished face.

We're in his expansive office suite on the second floor. It is shortly after the early service, attended by a full house— 3,500. In about an hour, the second service will get under way. Another full house is expected. This is par for the course each Sunday.

Outside, hundreds of cars are snaking their way out of the parking lot. A long line of others, some distance off, is waiting to get in. Ushers, in glow-orange jackets, are, in the manner of seasoned traffic cops, directing the flow.

He casually slips off his jacket, loosens his tie, props his feet on the coffee table, and is ready. He is a laid-back pastor, clean-cut, handsome.

I am someone who grew up frustrated with the conventional church. I went to church all my life and came from a Christian home. I felt that God was real and was reaching out with His love —you heard my sermon this morning. Standing in the way of my responding to the Lord's love was the church. It was a slice of the past. It was predictable, it was boring, it was negative, it was narrow.

In my college years, I began to wonder: what would happen if there were a creative church instead of a boring one? Contemporary, down to earth, free-wheeling. An honest church. I felt the Lord saying, Give it a shot.

When I was in high school in the late sixties, nobody had a clear sense of what the road was. This was in Kalamazoo, Michigan. I saw the fear of my peers, the turmoil, the running off to Canada. If ever Jesus' words applied, they did then: I see sheep without a shepherd (laughs).

I was being groomed to take over the family business. I majored in economics and business administration before I sensed that God wanted me to make a church for a new generation.

At that age, I didn't understand the war in Vietnam. I was just surprised that everybody felt so strongly about it. In conflicting ways (laughs). The people running to Canada felt strongly about it. The people signing up to go over and fight felt strongly about it. The people marching on the campuses felt strongly about it. The people burning draft cards felt strongly about it. I didn't see any clear path emerging.

> *Answering the call, he had formed a church in 1975, at the age of twenty-three. It was in a suburb not unlike his present locale: middle-class, conservative, upwardly mobile. It was in a movie theater, a church "relieved of all the excess baggage." For a subsequent three years, he developed a youth ministry in still another suburb, older, more staid in nature.*

You won't see the youth in conventional churches today. If you were to attend fifty such churches and count gray hairs versus young couples, you'd find very few of the younger generation.

For the last thirty, forty years, you'd find services without variation, without creativity. My generation has grown up with television and videotape, with lasers, rock concerts. The church is still using eighteenth-century robed-choir music and a man standing behind a wood pulpit for forty minutes, lecturing on doctrinal issues that aren't relevant to life.

> *His sermon has been offered behind a transparent glass— or was it plastic?—pulpit. It was hardly visible to the congregation. There was a much more intimate, informal feel to it, a sort of pressing of the flesh.*
>
> *The stage was festooned with colorful banners: GOD LOVES ME. It was the subject of his sermon.*

Denominationalism is dying. I have no need to move onward and upward to a larger parish and maybe someday make it to headquarters. In a church like ours, there's no place for me to go. I'm not vying for anybody else's position. I'm not gonna climb a ladder.

I just finished a series of sermons called "Modern Day Madness." First week was on substance abuse. We are the most chemically dependent society in the history of the world. That's scary. Second week was on pornography. Third week was on homosexuality. Fourth week was on something else—I forget now.

The biggest issue in homosexuality is what causes it. There are major passages in the Bible forbidding the practice. It's not an issue whether I'm for it or against it. I'm totally committed to the word of God, which binds me to Scripture at that point.

I say, All right, I know Scripture forbids the practice of homosexuality. I'm trying to figure out what makes a person homosexual. The issue becomes: How do you restore people to wholeness? Not how badly we'll condemn people who are living in a homosexual style.

We have many homosexuals in our church. They are accepted as they are. Our Sunday morning is open to any and all. However, if a homosexual would apply for membership, we'd say: Now what are you doing about this? Are you a practicing rebellious homosexual in the eyes of God?

If the person said, I have identified that I am a homosexual, I am in a support group right now because I don't want to disobey the Lord, I no longer lead a gay life-style—our membership would be open to him.

We say: If you really are in relationship with the Lord, part of the miracle of God infusing His divine nature into your life, it is for you to desire to be God-like in all your actions and values. God loves thieves. But at some point, if you're in relationship with God, the thievery has got to stop. It's the same with homosexuality.

There's no point for me to spend sermon time on the arms race. I make references to the power of prayer in changing the hearts of people who can solve these problems. When you know Christ, you can have peace, in spite of the uncertainty in our world.

I'm not in a position to bring an end to the arms race. Reagan tried in Iceland, face-to-face with Gorbachev, and he didn't make a whole lot of progress. Why should I inflict this issue on my people? I help them with it as best I can.

I encourage our people all the time: Be as active as God leads you to be. With this pornography thing, I said: If you want to start a letter-writing campaign to Attorney General Meese, go ahead. If you want to march around abortion clinics, march. Go for it. But the church itself can't be reduced to a political action committee.

I read the whole Meese Commission Report. I feel it was accurate and well-balanced. I feel that the American people, especially the liberal element, are tragically naive to the amount of damage done by the almost unlimited flow of pornographic material. It inevitably falls into the hands of children and it destroys marriages. I could go on and on.

We have a yuppie crowd, upper-middle. We say, Once a yuppie has bought his second BMW, then what? They're thirty-four years old, they're an investment banker, they've got their home and two BMWs, and they're empty. They're saying, I'm only thirty-four, what is this all about? I don't need a third BMW. That's when they start looking.

They come here and they perceive me as their peer. They say, "There's another yuppie." I don't have two BMWs, to be sure (laughs). They say, "There's a guy who could qualify, but he has some direction to his life. I think I'll listen to him." He sees other people his own age singing songs about direction. He sees a creative drama about it on stage. There's a band playing that could play at any lounge anywhere. They have to take this seriously.

We say, "All you have to do is listen. If this isn't what you're looking for, go try for the third BMW." It's a little different from the conventional church, which says, "If you don't join us, boom." Heavy-handed threats. We say, "If this is not for you, run out and buy those sports cars. You'll be back, because you're not gonna find what you're lookin' for out there."

We treat Scripture close to the way of the fundamentalists. But we broaden out. We say, You can have any kind of political affiliation, any kind of life-style—it's between you and the Lord.

If you panned the audience of Jerry Falwell's church, everyone's hair is cut the same, everyone dresses the same. They stamp out Christians. Pan the crowd at Willow Creek. We have variety in politics and life-style.

I go to the Bears on Mondays and teach Bible studies to the players. I just tell people don't blame me when they lose and don't credit me then they win (laughs).

There's never been an age more ripe for the message of hope in Christ and love in God than right now. As for the danger of war and the Bomb, I am concerned as a citizen of the planet. Have I lost one wink's sleep over it? No. *I* have peace, in spite of the fact that the world may not have peace. I would love to see it.

DR. RON SABLE

He is an internist at Cook County Hospital, Chicago. He campaigned as an openly gay candidate for alderman in a Near North Side ward. Though he lost, he polled forty-seven percent of the vote.

Since Stonewall,* there's been an explosion of gay political activism. Before 1961, all fifty states had sodomy laws. Twenty-five have since eliminated them. At the moment of our flowering as a community, AIDS appeared.

It has been a terrible blow. Our people are dying. On the other hand, it's been a stimulus for us to look critically on how we live our lives. It has taught gay and lesbian people a sense of community. AIDS does not affect the lesbian community as much as it does gay men. Sexually transmitted diseases among women are virtually non-existent. Yet they haven't abandoned us in this struggle. There has been a pulling together.

AIDS, of course, has further stigmatized the gay community. There has been a sharp upswing in antigay violence: epithets shouted, graffiti scratched on walls, physical attacks. At the same time, there have been as many thoughtful reactions from the mainstream community as there has been hysteria. I think of Arcadia, Florida, where a family was burned out, and Arcadia, Indiana, where a family of hemophilic children was welcomed. Both towns represent the heartland of America. These two events occurred at a time when our national administration has failed miserably in dealing with the threat of AIDS.

Middle-class white men among us feel more vulnerable today than they ever felt before. It has made them more generous and human. They have been contributing money and time. They never

---

* Beginning at Stonewall, a bar in Greenwich Village, gay street people, long harassed by the police, fought it out with them for three nights in June 1969. "It is celebrated every year during Gay Pride Week. It is our Independence Day, our Bastille Day."

did before. The greatest antagonism toward the gay community since AIDS has come upon us is from people who are insecure about their own sexuality. They see a threat in us, dangerous and contagious. The major and most powerful enemy to the humanity of gay people has been the fundamentalist church, white and black. They have labeled us sinful. They believe our homosexuality is a threat and that AIDS is a punishment visited upon us.*

AIDS is a viral illness that is spreading throughout the world. It is transmitted sexually and by blood-to-blood contact in ways we don't understand. There are other diseases, polio, cancer, heart failure. Do we call them wages of sin? We haven't found the magic bullet for AIDS, so we've been thrown back to olden fears and superstitions.

My mother came out of a Southern Baptist tradition. When I came out of the closet, after serving in Vietnam, she thought it was sinful. The Bible told her so. I said to her that the Bible can be interpreted in many ways. When I read the gay novel *The Best Little Boy in the World,* I recognized myself. The perfect kid: Eagle Scout, National Honor Society, the works. When I came out, it was to my mother a blot on my record. I had been afraid to do so most of my young life because I had personally accepted the stigma.

It was probably the most important step of my life. It gave me rich experiences and taught me what love was really like. My mother has come around enormously. My father was always easier about it. His attitude was more laissez-faire. He felt sad that I would miss out on wife and family and children. I told him I have a family. The gay community has always had a feeling of family. We have lifelong relationships neither acknowledged nor sanctioned by the larger community.

There are gays who are self-hating, who blame themselves. I don't blame them. I blame society. I find it remarkable that any gay feels good about himself. We all grew up in heterosexual families. All the messages were: homosexuality is sick, sinful, illegal, and we'll all go to hell. At the very least, we'll get arrested and our lives will be ruined. Some people describe this as child abuse. I feel that every gay person has been an abused child by virtue of being raised in a

---

* Some secular commentators have joined the parade. "One can weep for the children, but it is hard to work up much sympathy for the sodomists and addicts who have brought this on themselves" (James J. Kilpatrick, *Chicago Sun-Times,* November 14, 1987).

heterosexual society. We have never been acknowledged as normal people.

We're a sexually uptight society. There are huge battles in schools concerning sexual education, yet we are bombarded daily with sexual messages in thousands of commercials from toilet-bowl cleaners to autos. The images, blatant and subliminal, overwhelm us. But don't dare mention condoms. We are crippled in our approach to sexuality, so our response is backward. The most powerful country in the world is the most fearful. But we bristle with our military hardware. There's no need for me to get Freudian about it. I don't have to.

There are very few gays who have denounced themselves as sinful. Now and then, you run across one who says, "It's my fault." The much larger response is to the challenge. Friends care for their dying loved ones. In many cases, where their blood families reject victims, our gay community becomes that family. There are gay men taking in children of others stricken by AIDS. Our community has pulled together extraordinarily and has organized far more effectively than most civil rights groups. In this time of adversity, we have become stronger in many ways.

With the current hysteria, gays worry about concentration camps. They think of Nazi Germany. I don't think it's so wild a notion. But I do believe the epidemic has taught people in the gay community to call upon all their inner resources. So it's not all been negative.

I'm proud of what I am. I have nothing to apologize for. It's been a privilege for me to come through the way I did and feel as I do. That's the way it ought to be for everyone. Every black child should feel good about what he, she is. Jewish kids—in the culture of all these people, there are opportunities for this. It's never been there for gays growing up. Now we are providing it for each other. AIDS has been a devastating blow, but we're making lemonade of the lemon we've been handed.

JULI LOESCH

*Despite her crutches, she gets around with what appears to
be remarkable ease. Immediately, her fervor and
enthusiasm come forth: hers is a personal crusade.*

*She is founder of Justlife, an anti-abortion, antiwar,
anti-nuclear-power group. She is opposed to the death
penalty.*

*She is thirty-five years old. "I was born and raised in
Erie, Pennsylvania. We were part of the working poor. My
parents had to sacrifice considerably to send my brother
and me to Catholic schools. My father was a laborer who
loved books. He would go to secondhand bookstores and
bring home boxes full of them. I read everything."*

My aim in life was to work against war and against violence. I left
Antioch College after three months because I wanted to get more
involved in the antiwar movement. I was disillusioned by the so-
called radicals who were more interested in smoking dope and getting laid.

I went to work for the United Farm Workers in California as a
boycott organizer. I learned more about nonviolent social change
from the farm workers than I did at college.

I did a lot of drifting between the ages of eighteen and twenty.
In the lives of the saints, this would be the sins-of-youth period. I
saw a lot of casualties in my generation: casualties of the sexual
revolution, drugs, militant politics. It shook me up. I saw girls my
age getting abortions, getting venereal disease, and messed up personally.

In 1972, I went back home to Erie. I worked as a waitress till I
was fired because I dumped a cup of hot coffee in the lap of a half-
drunk guy who was pinching my butt (laughs).

During that time, I organized organic garden groups in the
neighborhoods of Erie. Heavily blue-collar. No controversy here: no

one's antigarden. Naturally, I began reading environmental things and the dangers threatening the air, the water, the soil, the crops. I became aware of things outside my little garden (laughs).

I began going around giving talks against nuclear power. That was ten years ago. If there's a nuclear war, it's gonna blow up everything. Why should I plant blueberries if the world might not last two years? I mean, I was that depressed.

I started reading about prenatal development because I wanted to be able to tell people, If you care for your own children, you got to stop this stuff. That's when I began to realize that I was asking everyone to be concerned about everyone else's unborn children, while these same children were being torn to pieces by abortion.

Up to that moment, I was a pro-choice ambivalent feminist. I'm still a feminist. I even wrote a pro-choice article that said it's outrageous for a male-dominated legislature to tell us what to do with our bodies. I was even taking a pro-choice stand in the early seventies, even though I thought it was a lousy choice. I didn't think I would ever have an abortion, because I'm a peace woman and peace women don't do violent things.

There's no way to nonviolently get an abortion. If you want a baby dead when it comes out, you have to tear it to pieces. It's not a philosophical question. I know the difference between a live fetus and a dead one. In order to go from alive to dead, you've got to kill something. This is baby talk. Everyone knows this.

One day, as I was talking to a group about nuclear radiation, a woman said, "If you think it's wrong to injure these kids accidentally, don't you think it's wrong to kill them deliberately?" I said, "These are two separate issues. Nuclear radiation is a corporate crime, it's the government, it's global. Abortion is personal, it's private." This other woman kept at it: "You're tryin' to get us to feel responsible for everyone's unborn children all over the world. On the other hand, you're saying each individual pregnant woman has the choice to kill or not to kill, period." This woman was sharp. She was pointing out to me my own glaring inconsistency.

The fetus as human life is undeniable from a biological point of view. It's a living individual of our species. It's your son or your daughter. Planned Parenthood knows this, abortionists know this: they have to kill a living being every time they do an abortion. The question is, Are we going to discriminate against certain forms of human life or not? Are we going to say some humans have rights and some of them don't?

Are there no circumstances in which you'd recognize the need?

It's a real toss-up, if it's a life for a life, a genuine toss-up between the mother's life and the baby's. If it's a tubal pregnancy, that's life-threatening to the mother and the baby can't survive it either. The surgical removal of this tubal pregnancy is morally not the same as an abortion.

If the woman is raped—?

I don't believe in the death penalty for the rapist. Why should I want to kill a rapist's child? It's the woman's child, too. But the child is its own child, too. The child is not the property of one or the other, the mother or the father.

Embryologists have said—forget the theologians—that human life is transmitted to a new generation every time a child is conceived, every time fertilization occurs. You can discern an individual human life, at least, by day 12 after fertilization.

When that woman challenged me at the antinuke meeting, I didn't jump to my feet and say, Oh, you're absolutely right, let's go join the right-to-life movement. Not at all. I didn't want to hear this stuff. The reason why it upset me is that is exactly what I was hearing from the antinuclear movement. From Helen Caldicott, from Rosalie Bertell: human life in its delicate beginnings is very precious.

I wasn't attracted to the right-to-life movement at all. They're usually promilitary, hawkish, inconsistent. This woman was concerned about the arms race. She was not rigid, uncaring, authoritarian. She was open-minded and willing to listen to the other point of view. But she wanted to be heard, too. I owed it to her.

I don't think any decent human society will allow the destruction of our youngest children. It hurts women, too. One of the fastest-growing sectors in the pro-life movement are women who have had abortions and are now anti-abortion. There's a group called WEBA,

Women Exploited by Abortion. They're just like the Vietnam Veterans Against the War. They came back and said, We were there, it was terrible.

In the peace movement, I found other people that were anti-abortion, but they were keeping their mouths shut, because they felt it made them freakish.

After Three Mile Island happened, I was tearing around Erie getting people on a bus to Washington to protest nuclear power. The organizers gave me a packet of literature. In it was this proabortion leaflet: why we should have government-funded abortions. Because women in the Harrisburg area may have gotten contaminated. Why should they suffer the suspense and fear of possibly giving birth to a child with a defect?

I have genetic defects. I have rheumatoid arthritis. This is a disease that can be crippling and deforming, as well as painful and deadly. But I'm alive and I find it worthwhile to be alive even with a defect. We're all vulnerable, unprotected human flesh.

I began to realize that it was bigotry of the worst kind to say that it's better to be dead than to be born retarded or blind or without a limb. It's a value judgment you're making about someone's life, based on their degree of perfection. Are you perfect?

> *What happens to the lives of parents whose child is born a vegetable?*

I guess they're challenged. It challenges you to love or reject. This is what makes us human.

DR. HUGH R. K. BARBER

For twenty-six years, he has been the director of obstetrics and gynecology at Lenox Hill Hospital in New York. He has written hundreds of papers and a score of books. He had been chairman of the department at New York Medical

*College, affiliated with the Roman Catholic Archdiocese,
for nine years, until his resignation in 1987. He has
practiced for thirty-two years. He is a Catholic.*
He, too, was born in Erie, Pennsylvania.

I was always totally against abortion. But at this point in time, I
have a deeper insight into it. I know no matter what the national
government says, if a young woman wants an abortion, she will have
one. In the old days, many of these young girls would die, often
from butcher operations. When I was young, I used to look at those
deaths as a form of retribution. But then I took care of these young
women and talked to them and emerged with a different feeling.

I am a practicing Catholic. I believe strongly in the Catholic
religion. I think it's great. But the Catholic hierarchy in this country, in this century, has been a disaster. If it hadn't been for the
strength of the religion, the whole thing would have gone down.
They've never had a dialogue with their people. They're primarily
businessmen and they forget that the priests and nuns, working out
at the grass roots, are keeping things alive for them.

Ever since I was growing up, it was difficult for me to defend my
church—not my religion. I always found my religion easy to defend. I couldn't tolerate some of the interpretations of the church
in history, from Galileo to Darwin. I remember, much closer to
our doorstep, how they tried to silence John Rock, father of the
Pill.

We know the most awesome force the world has ever known is the
power of reproduction. If we can harness all other things, why can't
we harness this force? How do I know we don't have a moral obligation to do it?

When the abortion bill went through in New York, my friends
poked at me and said, It hasn't done any of these horrible things
you thought it would, except women aren't coming in here and
dying. I started to wonder. I'd taken care of lots of women who had
illegal abortions. They came in here and died. Innocent victims. In
those days, we looked upon them as though they had done something
bad. Of course, they had not.

The big jolt for me came in 1960, when New York passed the

abortion bill. I was named as a prominent practicing Catholic, who was resisting and fighting abortion. The prochoice people picketed my house, they picketed the hospital. They were giving me a hard time. Doctors were calling me up.

My wife said, ''Why are you taking such a beating? There isn't a doctor that's head of a department of gynecology and obstetrics at any of the Catholic hospitals that has spoken out. The Archdiocese of New York has been totally silent.'' I thought, Gee, why *am* I taking such beating? One of my friends, the most devout Catholic I knew in college, said, ''I've thought over all these things, when we were in the fight. There are some mistakes we've made.'' He was right.

As I thought about it, I realized some very devout Catholics had abortions done on members of their family. I realized we had a pluralistic religion as well as a pluralistic society. It's not the religion of a hundred years ago or even of twenty years ago. I began to realize that some of my views were wrong.

I've never done an abortion nor do I ever plan to do one. Whether I were a Catholic or not, I'd have this attitude. You have a feeling that there's life there, even though we haven't really defined life at this point. Surely nobody's defined when a soul is present.

On the other hand, I think I was too rigid in my judgment on those that had abortions. As I talked to them, I began to have doubts. They have to make a decision guided by their background, their conscience, their training. We have to equate having an abortion against the trauma that it would cause families. Do they have a responsibility to the community not to have a baby that has to be attended by the state or society?

You're not going to stop these young kids from being sexually active. The Lord oriented them that way. They're healthier, they have more leisure, they have more money. They aren't fighting for existence as they did fifty years ago. If they had education in sex as well as contraception, we'd obviously have fewer abortions.

Even in those days, when I was rigid in my thoughts and wondered if it was justice or retribution, it was disturbing to me to see somebody die young. I wondered what creativity might have been in that body, in that mind that was dying. This smoldered in me. Finally, it just surfaced.

The anti-abortion people use the phrase ''pro-life'' to describe themselves. Theoretically, when you do an abortion you're depriving a life. On the other hand, if we didn't have the abortion bill, there'd be a trade-off. In some of those butchered cases, you'd lose two lives instead of one—if we ever get an agreement as to when life starts. The concept of pro-life is great. But sometimes it's misdirected. It's pro-life, too, if you're protecting the mother.

Before it was declared legal, we used to have a great number of deaths secondary to abortion. They usually occurred from hemorrhage and infection. They'd become septic and die. Some were so young and innocent, they looked like little dolls. They never had a chance. In those days, I didn't realize I was standing in judgment. Who was I to stand in judgment on this poor person?

As to the question When does life begin?—I've always had a struggle. I think it is the moment of fertilization. Now, is that life as a human being? I can't answer. The other question I'd have trouble with: When is the soul there?

If the United States government became ultraconservative and reversed the abortion law, Americans would pay no attention to it. If we say it's wrong, we're standing in judgment on a fellow citizen. We are the jurors sitting there. Is this woman a criminal? Has she done something bad? I wonder if the right-to-life people, sitting on the jury, equating abortion with murder, would say this woman should be put to death? An eye for an eye and a tooth for a tooth.

I think it is fear we must deal with. Before, we were an immigrant society. We worked hard, had integrity, sent kids off to school. Yet, the fear instilled in most Catholics was the fear of going to hell. With the diminishing of this fear, with education, it's a new world we're living in.

DENNIS MCGRATH

> *He is forty, a radio engineer, married, and has an eight-year-old son. He is active in a fundamentalist church in a lower-middle-class suburb.*
>
> *He was born and raised in Brooklyn, of an Irish Catholic blue-collar family. He attended parochial schools.*

I was afraid that anyone who didn't believe would go to hell. I was trying to be good, but the things I was taught didn't help me get at peace with God. People asked me, What did you do so bad that makes you feel this way? I would go to confession, tell the priest my sins. Confession was supposed to give you grace, to strengthen you to not sin again. But I was repeating the same thing. It seemed like I was out of control. So I stopped going to confession.

I couldn't tell my mother. On Saturday afternoons, I'd go for a long walk. My mother thought I was going to confession. This business of lying to my mother went on for seven years. I struggled: If I'm sorry enough when I die, I won't go to hell. But what if I walk out in the middle of the street and a truck runs me down and I don't have time to be sorry? I'm in trouble.

I finally came to the conclusion that I was going to hell and there was nothing I could do about it. My Catholic friends were in the same boat. We joked about it. I'm goin' to hell, but all my friends are goin' to be there, too. So what?

After high school in '63, I worked for the telephone company. While there, I met a fellow who walked around with his Bible. He wouldn't take part in the dirty jokes, in the carousing, the drinking. It seemed to me he was doing the right thing. I told Peter one day, I'd like to be like him, but I can't.

When I was in school, they talked about the saints. I thought, Boy, it would be great to be a saint. To know that you were going to heaven. But I wasn't good enough and didn't know anybody I could classify as that kind of person. It's just that I knew what to do right and wasn't doin' it.

Peter was the first person I ever met who struck me as being a genuine Christian. That was twenty years ago. At the time, it was considered a sin to go to another church if you were a Catholic. One day, he said, "I'm going to visit a pastor friend of mine. Would you like to come along?" I jumped at the chance.

I went to church with him and saw the people there. They really loved God. You can tell when a person loves someone The way they speak about Him. With real reverence. I could see they knew Jesus, knew the Father.

After the service, at the pastor's house, they said to me, If anyone trusts Christ as savior, He will make them a child of God and give them eternal life. I didn't understand what they were talking about at the time. But they gave me simple answers. They had authority because the Bible is one of the written documents that the Christian church offers as truth.

They were people I could relate to. It excited my desire to know God. That evening blew my resolve to be a saint. I knew I wasn't perfect. If I told you I never sinned, I'd be lying to you. They said it's okay.

I got down at my bedside and I prayed: "Jesus, you died for me. I want you to come into my life. Change me and make me what you want me to be." On that note, I went to bed. The next morning, despite not going to confession, I knew I was forgiven. I knew Jesus was right there with me. I'm talkin' to Him all the way to work. I could see He was enjoying the conversation. The first time in my life, I knew that God was with me.

The first thing I noticed was my change in attitude toward cards. I loved acey-deucey, which we played at work for nickels and dimes. I'd do whatever I could to get somebody to drop out, so I could get in the game. That's how bad I wanted to play.

Now, I was uncomfortable by the nasty comments going back and forth between the guys. I'm not trying to be Joe Religious, but I no longer enjoyed it because they were cuttin' each other down, calling each other names. It bothered the daylights out of me, so I gave up the game. I found the power to say no.

Peter said, "You have accepted Christ." I gave up trying to live good enough myself and gave myself to Him and trusted Him to save me.

I was living a double religious life. Six-thirty Sunday morning, I'm at mass. Then I'd jump into my car and go to Calvary Baptist miles away. There I learned more about the Bible. All of a sudden, it's an open book. Before, I had someone explain it to me. Now I read it myself and it was clear. I stopped going to the Catholic church because I found what I was looking for. I found Christ to give me strength to live the way I should. Never perfect. I'll never be perfect till I'm with Him.

Not long after, I spent two years in the service, '66 and '67, and met a lot of Christians there. I was with the Seabees in Guantánamo Bay, Cuba. I didn't develop any negative feelings about the Vietnam War that a lot of people did. The war became unpopular while I was in service. I was insulated from that. I was just glad I wasn't over there. I requested an extension, so I could spend the whole tour where I was. At the Baptist church, it was understood that if you're called to service, you go.

When I got out, I was undecided what to with my life. The pastor suggested radio work for the Lord. Moody Bible Institute in Chicago had an extremely good radio tech course.

In the past few years, being a Christian has become a pop thing among the young. I have mixed feelings about it. There's a lot of people genuinely becoming Christians, but it used to be so clear. If you said you were born again, people knew what you meant. Nowadays, when somebody tells me that, I'm not sure he knows what he's talking about.

The truth about war is a real problem. I don't see anything in Scripture that says you can't be a soldier. There were Christians in the Roman army. If you are a soldier, be a good one.* Wherever you're put, be the best you can. Nobody likes to kill anybody. I'm glad I never had to. I have a Christian friend, whom I admire greatly. He really has it together. He was in Vietnam and he had to kill people. So he can relate to other Christian soldiers.

I'm not sure about war resisters. I tend to believe we should obey our government. Scriptures say obey our leaders. If they tell me to denounce my religion, I won't do that because I know it's wrong. If they tell me I have to be a soldier, that's war. That's the function of a government.

If the government makes a law 180 degrees opposed to Christian belief, you can't obey it. Daniel in the Old Testament was required to do things against his faith and he refused. The Bible is the only absolute standard. I don't think much about the Bomb. I know God's will will be done. If that includes an atomic war, there really isn't a whole lot I can do about it. If I can vote for somebody against atomic war, I'm gonna do it.

We're seeing an increase in wars and unrest and more natural disasters. People are more aware that they're going to die and it might be right away. If a bomb drops, it's gonna be pretty quick

---

* An armed services television commercial: a young son tells his father he's joined. The father, deeply moved, embraces the boy: "Be a good one."

here in Chicago (laughs). I'm much more secure, now that I know where I'm going when I die. I know I'm going to heaven, for sure. My wife's gonna go to heaven with me. My son's accepted Christ, too. When he was three years old, he was asking questions about the Bible and about sin. He said, I want Jesus as my savior.

Christ covers babies because they don't know any better. But when they're aware, they're sinners. They can decide. If they accept the gift offered by Him who paid the penalty for their sins, in God's sight it's as if they never sinned.

Most problems in public schools come from our throwing out prayer. Where's the authority? It comes from God. Armageddon will come, of course.

Can anything be done to prevent Armageddon?

No, it's part of God's plan. Why stop it? I see no reason to stop it.

JEAN GUMP

A grandmother; mother of twelve, ranging in age from twenty-two to thirty-five. She and her family have lived in a middle-class western suburb of Chicago for thirty-two years.

She has, all her adult life, been active in church and community work: Christian Family Movement; president of the high school PTA; League of Women Voters; executive secretary of the township's Human Relations Council. She was a delegate to the 1972 Democratic Convention. A neighbor recalls: "I'd come into her kitchen, she'd have the phone on one ear, as she'd be mixing a pot of spaghetti and talking to me all at the same time."

For something she did on Good Friday, 1986, she was arrested. Along with her, four other Catholics, young enough to be her children, have been sentenced to different terms in prison. Their group is called Silo Plowshares. This conversation took place shortly after her arrest. It had hardly made the news.

We commemorated the crucifixion of Christ by entering a missile silo near Holden, Missouri. We hung a banner on the outside of the chain-link fence that read: SWORDS INTO PLOWSHARES, AN ACT OF HEALING. Isaiah 2, from Scriptures: We will pound our swords into plowshares and we will study war no more.

It's a Minuteman II silo, a first-strike weapon. There are 150 of these missiles. If one of these missiles were to leave the ground, it would decimate an area of seventy-two miles. And all the children and others. We wanted to make this weapon inoperable. We succeeded.

We carried three hammers, a wire clipper, three baby bottles with our blood, papers with an indictment against the United States and against the Christian church for its complicity. Ken Ripito, who is twenty-three, and Ken Moreland, who is twenty-five, went with me. The other two went to another silo about five miles away.

It is going to be the citizens that will have to eliminate these weapons. They were built by human hands. People are frightened of them, yet view them as our Gods of Metal. It is a chain-link fence with barbed wire on top. We have become so accustomed to these monstrosities that there are no guards. It is nondescript. If you were passing it on the road, you would see this fence. The silo itself is maybe a foot or two out of the earth. It looks like a great concrete patio. It's very innocuous.

To get through the fence, we used a wire clipper. We had practiced in the park the day before. Once we were in, I proceeded to use the blood and I made a cross on top of the silo. Underneath, I wrote the words, in black spray paint: DISARM AND LIVE.

We sat down and waited in prayer. We thanked God, first of all, that we were alive. We expected a helicopter to come over and kill us terrorists. We thanked God for our successful dismantling, more or less, of this weapon. We assumed the responsibility for our actions and we waited to be apprehended.

About forty minutes later, the soldiers arrived in an armored vehicle. There was a machine-gun turret at the top. The commander used a megaphone and said, ''Will all the personnel on top of the silo please leave the premises with your hands raised?'' So all of us personnel (laughs) left the silo. I was concerned because it would be difficult getting out of that little hole in the fence with our hands up. We made it fine.

They put the men up against the fence in a spread-eagle position. They asked the female—myself—to ''take ten steps and stand with your hands raised.'' I did it for a few minutes and my fingers were beginning to tingle. I put my hands down. The soldier said, ''You must put your hands up.'' I said, ''No, I have a little funny circulation.'' He said, ''You must put your hands up.'' I said, ''Shoot me.'' He chose not to, which I thought was good.

I said, ''I'll compromise with you. I will raise my hands for five minutes and I will put them down for five minutes.'' He said, ''You can't put them down.'' I said, ''But I will.'' It was hysterical.

I wanted to turn around to see if my friends were being maltreated. The soldier who had his gun aimed at me said, ''You can't turn around.'' I did. I was watching them try to put handcuffs on the two men. I have been arrested in Chicago. I've seen an efficient police force put handcuffs on people in two seconds. It must have taken these soldiers fifteen minutes. I had to tell them they were doing it wrong. With my suggestions, they finally did it right.

There was a big discussion about what to do with the female suspect. Apparently they weren't allowed to frisk a female suspect. I was kind of wondering what they were going to do with me. They asked me to remove my coat, which I did. He said, ''Throw it ten feet over here.'' I said, ''I'll never make it, but I'll do the best I can.''

They took things out of my pocket and put them on the ground. One of the items was a handkerchief. I said, ''It's getting a little chilly, I think I'm getting a cold and a runny nose. I will have to get my handkerchief.'' It was about three feet away. The soldier said, ''Don't you dare move.'' I said, ''I'm going to get this handkerchief and I'm going to blow my nose.'' I did that and put the handkerchief in my pocket. The soldier said, ''You have to leave your handkerchief over here.'' I said, ''All right. But if my nose should run again, I'll go over there and I will get my handkerchief and I will blow my nose.'' At this point, the poor soldier looked sort of crestfallen. He was about the age of my youngest child.

By this time, the area was filled with about eight automobiles. FBI, local sheriffs, and so on. They took us into this armored vehicle. On its right-hand side was a big sign: PEACEKEEPER. I said, "Young man, have an opportunity to read Orwell's *1984.*" He said, "I'm not allowed to talk to you." I said, "I'll talk to you, then." He said, "If I had my uniform off, we could talk." I said, "Maybe we'll meet and have coffee someday."

At the police station, we were treated rather deferentially. Someone from the sheriff's office asked if we wanted coffee. There had been no charges made. We were very, very tired. We were allowed to make one phone call. We'd been given the name of a young lawyer, who had worked with a previous group, the Silo Pruning Hooks.

One of the jail guards was handing our tray through a slot in the door. She said, "Mrs. Gump, I want to thank you for what you did." I said, "You're welcome." Then when I saw her lined up with all the other guards, she had a wholly different demeanor.

The FBI came to interview us. I find them very funny. They come in like yuppies, all immaculately dressed. Probably six or eight. The five of us are now together. The gentleman behind the desk wanted to read me the Miranda rights. "You have a right to remain silent." I said, "You're right. I do and I am."

At the Federal Building in Kansas City, where we were taken, I was asleep on the bench. A nice young man joined me: "We might be able to negotiate something to get you out on bail." I said, "Young man, there's no way I'd pay a nickel for bail money. You're wasting your time." Darla, my co-cellmate, she's twenty-two, agreed also not to answer.

The judge said he'd like to let us out on a $5,000 bond, with our signature. We'd not commit any crimes between now and the arraignment date. John Volpe said, "I don't really know if I can, because there are a lot of silos out there."

My children knew nothing about this. Mother's doing her thing, is what they always say. As I leave the house, they often say, "Don't get arrested, ma." I'd been arrested five other times for civil disobedience.

I felt peace marching was fine, but what we needed was a freeze group. After campaigning in Morton Grove, we had a referendum. Five thousand voted for the freeze, two thousand against.

When I came back from Kansas City on Easter Sunday morning, the children had learned about it. There were tears between times of much laughter. They were supportive, though it's an imposition on their lives.

My one daughter graduates from the University of California. I will not be there. My other daughter is getting married. I will not be there. I want more than anything in the world to be there. These are my children and I love them. But if they're going to have a world, we have to stop this madness. I think they understand that as much as I want to be with them and with my loving husband— He wasn't with me on this at first, but now he's all the way.

About three weeks ago, I had asked for certain things to be done. I wanted the power of attorney for all our property to be in his hands. As he was going out the door, he said, "Jean, you're planning to die, aren't you?" It startled me because I'd been thinking about that. I thought it was something that could happen. Hearing him say it made it very real. I said, "Yeah, Joe." So we took up our lives again and our love affair has never been nicer.

My mother was a person that believed, I mean really believed, in justice. Maybe it came from her. When the kids were little, I always said, "Don't ever look to the next guy to affect change. Do it yourself."

I remember one day, golly, it was 1967. I was watching television. This was the time when the people came over the bridge with Martin Luther King and with the hoses. My little son turned to me and said, "Mother, what are you going to do about this?" What could I say? I went down to Selma.

I suppose my neighbors out here think I'm kind of a kook. I'm pretty ordinary (laughs). When I'm not doing these things, I'm a good cook and I have swell parties. A sense of humor helps. They don't know yet about what happened in Missouri. There is a suspicion. If somebody has cancer, you don't say, How's your cancer today? If I meet somebody on the street, it's, "Hi, Jean, how are things going?" "Swell, how are things going with you?"

Shortly before she entered the federal prison, she and two other members spoke at her church: St. Martha's. Four people attended. They had come to tell her they disapproved of her actions.

Joe Gump: "At a gathering in our church two weeks after Jean's arrest, not a single person came up to me to ask how she was doing. At another gathering, they seemed shocked that anyone they had known would do something like this."

The Gumps had been regular parishioners of the church for thirty-two years.

"Now and then, there's an encouraging word," says Joe. "I dropped something off at a repair shop and the salesclerk whispered, 'Mr. Gump, God bless your wife.' "

Their son, Joe, Jr., has occasional encounters: "Once in a while, a person who knows about the case comes up to me, holds my hand, and says, 'God bless your mother.' "

There's a ripple effect from what we're doing. That's quite exciting. You never know where it's going to hit. You just know you must do what you must do and let the chips fall where they may.

All I wanted to do when I was young is to be like everybody else. The same thing all nice little Catholic girls want. Periodically, I found I had to separate myself. I tried not to do that, because who wants to be different?

When I started dating my husband, right after World War Two, my aunt said, "Jean is going to marry a Hun." I thought, What the hell is a Hun? My husband's of German descent. We had just gotten through a war and we had to hate Germans. They were bad people. We certainly had to hate the Japanese. They were bad people. Through these years, I found out there's a lot of people that I have to hate.

We have to hate the Iranians, 'cause we have to go over there and kill 'em. I had to hate the Vietnamese people. I have to hate the commies. Everybody has to hate the commies. There is no end to my nation's enemies. But I don't think they're my enemies. I think, God help me, these are people.

What I did on Good Friday in Holden, Missouri, is only the expression of my Christianity. This is God's world, okay? We are stewards of the earth. I think we're rather bad stewards.

You know, I have never been so hopeful. If I can change my way of thinking, anybody can. I don't want to be singled out as anybody special, because I'm not. We have got to have a future for our children and we've got to make some sacrifices for it, okay?

Call it a legacy, if you want to. What else is there? My grand-child, I want to offer him a life, that's all. We all had a crack at it, so I think it's fair that this generation should.

POSTSCRIPT: Jean Gump was sentenced to eight years at a federal penitentiary on the charge of conspiracy and destroying public property. The presiding judge, at Christmastime, reduced her sentence to six.

For the past eleven months, she has been #03789-045 at the Correctional Institution for Women, Alderson, West Virginia.

'68 AND AFTER

Boy, you gonna carry that weight,
Carry that weight a long time . . .

—The Beatles, "Carry That Weight"

LARRY HEINEMANN

His demeanor, at first glance, is a cool customer's. As he recounts the Chicago moment of nineteen years ago, a feverishness sets in.

His family background is blue-collar. He is married and has two small children.

He has written two novels, based upon his experience in Vietnam. His second, Paco's Story, *won the 1987 National Book Award.*

I'm forty-three, close enough to be called a boom baby.

I was in college for the same reason everybody else was: to stay out of the draft. Ran out of money. Got drafted in May of '66. I was twenty-two. My younger brother and I were drafted at the same time. He couldn't adjust. He came back from Germany with a discharge in his hand on the same day I left for San Francisco. We had two hours in the kitchen to sit and talk. He was home and I got a year overseas. Vietnam. I was in combat from March of '67 to March of '68, a couple of months after the Tet offensive began.

I left Vietnam on a Sunday afternoon at four o'clock and was home in my own bedroom Mondy night at two. Half the people in my platoon were either dead or in the hospital. It was disorienting, I must say.

In my household, there was never any political discussion. We were raised to just submit to the draft, stiffly and strict. I went there scared and came back bitter. Everybody knows it was a waste.

I wasn't willing to go to jail. Nobody told me I could go to Canada. Out of four brothers, three of us served in the armed forces. My youngest brother, a two-time marine, was wounded, sent back, and has had a very hard time of it since.

It was clear from the first day that it was a bunch of bullshit. We were there to shoot off a bunch of ammo and kill a bunch of people. We were really indifferent. The whole country was indifferent: Why are we fighting in Vietnam?

When I got back here, I was scared and grateful and ashamed that I had lived, 'cause I started getting letters: So-and-so got hit, So-and-so burned to death. My good friend flipped a truck over an embankment and it hit him in the head. I had been given my life back, I felt a tremendous energy. At the same time, I felt like shit.

Right after I got back, I was in Kentucky where my wife was going to school. Martin Luther King was shot dead—was it April 4, 1968? I was gettin' a haircut for my wedding. These guys in the barber shop were talking, I remember: Somebody finally got that nigger.

Black cities were just going up in flames. And then Bobby Kennedy was shot. It was almost as if I had brought the war home myself. I didn't want any part of it whatever.

I didn't get involved with any antiwar movement. I felt I would be breaking faith with my friends who were still overseas. Now I'm sorry I didn't.

Some guys are bemoaning that they didn't share the rite of passage, fighting in Vietnam. They regret they have no war stories to tell. I would trade them my stories for my grief any time.

The summer of '68, I got a job driving a CTA bus.* It was the worst decision I ever made. I had come from a place where I drove a fifteen-ton armored personnel carrier, and we didn't take shit from anybody. I had a .45 and a shotgun while I drove. We had the road to ourselves. I was living every eighteen-year-old's fantasy about having a big ugly-sounding car and being able to drive anywhere we wanted. The whorehouses were all in a row and it was one car wash after another. I didn't wanna take shit from anybody.

The one thing they teach about bus driving is that you're a public servant, okay? Any asshole with a fare can give you shit and you have to sit there and take it. Anyone gave me an argument, I threw 'em off the bus. This transfer's no good—woooshh!—get out! I was never that way before Vietnam.

Halfway through that Chicago summer in '68, the streets were just crazy. I was driving a bus. The drivers were all tense. There were still reverberations of the King assassination. A week before

---

* Chicago Transit Authority.

the convention, the black drivers called a wildcat strike. Anywhere you went, there was this undercurrent. I was at the end of my rope.

That night, I'm driving down Clark Street, past Lincoln Park. I look out under the trees to see what's happening. You could see the silhouettes of cops, cop cars, and kids. I heard there was tear gas and cops beating up kids. When I was in Vietnam, we used tear gas to flush people out of tunnels.

You know that somebody's in a spider hole and you'll just go *Lah-dee, lah-dee*. I don't know how it's spelled, it means come out. If they didn't, you'd pop tear gas. It would make you extraordinarily sick. It has a very distinctive smell. Like the one this night.

Near Lincoln Park, I could see the cop cars and the kids. As we came closer, I pulled the brake and said, "I'm sorry, we're not goin' anywhere. I'm not gonna get mixed up in this at all." I waited until the whole carbony smell died down.

The passengers hollered go on, go on. I said no, no, no, no. "You don't want to get a snort of that tear gas, it'll make you sick." I stayed at that corner maybe fifteen, twenty minutes. Guys behind me were pissed off, but passed me up. The supervisor argued with me. I fully expected people were gonna get killed.

I think the police riot was the next night. I came to this light, through the south end of the Loop. All four curbs were bumper-to-bumper buses, which held maybe sixty guys. They were just filled with cops and all the lights were off. All I could see was riot gear: helmets and billy clubs. One guy looks through the window as if I'm a hippie who has stolen the bus. It was the look on his face: Who are you? What are you doing here? I just showed him my CTA badge. If I didn't—(laughs).

I knew exactly what was gonna happen. These guys were gonna do the same thing I had done overseas. They were gonna go wherever they were gonna go and they were just gonna smash people. I just turned my bus around, the hell with it.

I was not one of those GIs who came back and didn't say boo about it. I was vocal. Anybody asked me, I told them it was a lot of evil bullshit. We did mean things to people. It made you into a mean person. I stayed away from the other vets. It was self-imposed isolation. I was going through the classic symptoms of what is now called delayed stress. Luckily some people started putting books in my hand.

I knew something was wrong when I saw the Vietnam Veterans' Parade in Chicago. There were an awful lot of K-Mart cammies marching in it. Camouflage fatigues. Overseas everybody wore these jungle fatigues, just plain faded jade green. Now the fashion is these K-Mart cammies, which are like costumes. Nobody in his right mind would have worn them overseas.

When I heard General Westmoreland was going to be the parade marshal, I said, No way. I'm not marchin' in that fuckin' parade. I wouldn't get in line behind him if he was goin' to the shithouse.

I had ambivalent feelings about the parade. There were good things and bad things about it. You weren't allowed to have any banners expressing any political opinion. There was this celebration of the war being a good thing and why didn't we do more? At the same time, we were together for the first time in twenty years as brothers.

Now there's a kind of amnesia. But a tremendous curiosity. There are college courses on it. I'm lecturing at Lindblom* next week in the history class. It is beginning to happen. My daughter who is nine wants to know. The war is in our house.

Vietnam veterans took a lot of shit from World War Two people. They said we lost the war. I was never in a firefight and lost. We killed plenty of people. I mean me, me, me. A soldier is a soldier and the process is the same. We're simply sons of bitches, just as mean as anybody else.

I think the kids today want to do the right thing and get on with their lives. I see a lot of energy used pointlessly. I don't think Americans understand exactly the way the rest of the world sees us. We don't understand what people respect about us and envy or despise us for. They just wish we'd go home. We feel everything has to go our way, no matter what. I think this attitude is gonna get us into big trouble.

I haven't seen my oldest brother since 1970. My next younger brother loves Reagan. He and I never talk politics. My youngest brother, the two-time marine, hasn't talked to me for ten years. He thought we did the right thing. He despised me because I went to our old family lawyer and asked him how I could get my kid brother from going over the second time. He wanted to go. When he left, I couldn't bring myself to write to him. Our friendship ended with a bitter argument. My little brother, I haven't seen him since 1982. I don't know what he's doing.

I don't think the country's learned anything from the war. The

* A Chicago public high school.

guys who organized the Vietnam Veterans' Parade wanted it to be remembered as a nostalgic positive experience. They wanted so hard for it to be all right. It's not. It's going to be an evil thing in our lives and nothing's gonna change it.

RICHARD AND BONNIE D'ANDREA

They live in the suburb Lancashire. Their next-door neighbors are Ray and Sandy Scholl.

He had been a social worker in Dayton, Ohio. "At $12,000 a year, with a growing family, I couldn't afford this profession." He became an insurance underwriter, was transferred to Chicago, and was laid off as the result of a merger. He is now in his last year at law school.

She is a registered nurse, working at a local hospital.

They have three daughters, eleven, ten, and eight.

RICHARD: I was never really comfortable as a businessman. I have very soft values. I have no understanding of money at all and I don't understand people who do (laughs). After I was laid off, I couldn't go back to social work—drug-abuse counseling. It wasn't just the low salary. I was burnt out.

I had wanted to go to law school since I was fifteen. Sometimes life gets in your way. You're in the army, you bounce around, get married, have kids. How can you go to law school?

Because of my social work experience, I'm thinking of a practice involving family. Abused children, domestic violence, divorce mediation. Some sort of public-interest law. I never bought into the traditional American dream: to accumulate as much money as you can, get yourself the nicest house, the biggest car. I don't think the things you have to do to your soul to get that big beautiful house are worth doin'.

By time I got into high school, I had read Sinclair Lewis, *Babbitt*,

Grapes of Wrath, Dickens. They influenced my values. I don't see it in business today. I don't see it in law school.

BONNIE: When he was in insurance, I could see where his unhappiness was comin' from. He has a very strong social concern and I think it's fantastic. On the other hand (laughs), it's a hindrance, because you don't have a lot of money that way. But in the long run, you're better off.

RICHARD: I had toyed with the idea of the priesthood several times. When I got out of the army, I was thinking of joining the Maryknollers. But I think they've gone off the deep end. I wouldn't be a Maryknoller in Latin America. I think they're screwballs today. I can't argue with the nobility of their feelings, but they're comin' up with the wrong answers.

I have the same thoughts about the Sanctuary movement. I don't like it, not in the least. It fosters disrespect for the law. Before you can have any social justice in the world, you have to have an ordered society. In order to have that, you have to have a respect for the law.

I don't think we should have gone to Vietnam the way we did. But since we did, we owed our military personnel the full force of our power: to go over there and win the war. Johnson was a political coward. He didn't apply the power that we had.

In the sixties, I saw passion. I'm a traditional conservative. When my peers were out protesting the war, I turned around and enlisted. I'm the first person in my family to graduate from college, all right? I felt very honored. My parents were blue-collar working-class people, who had come over as Italian immigrants. I felt very strongly my obligation as a citizen.

I'm a Vietnam veteran and I'm proud of it. But at least those people who were protesting were concerned. I believe they were wrong, but they were committed. I don't see that anywhere today.

BONNIE: I see the same thing in the new nurses that are graduating. A real lack of concern. They're just not gonna put up with things the way we used to. In the old days, it was a self-sacrificing type of thing. It's hard, a lot of stress, tough physical work. The other day, a young one said to me, "Hey, I don't intend to do this for the rest of my life."

I was very much against the protesters. I really didn't think the war was right, but we were in it. You can't say no, I won't go. The conscientious objectors were okay, but there were a lot of people took advantage of it.

RICHARD: I graduated from high school a Goldwater Republican, but I have strong progressive views on domestic issues. I would be a socialist if I believed socialism works. I don't believe it does. I believe in capitalism with a human face: a temperance in this demand for profit.

I voted for Nixon in '68. I think he's a genius in foreign affairs. I voted for McGovern in '72, when I got out of the army. Perhaps it was the influence of the war and of my peers. I voted for Reagan, though I think he's a jerk. Do you think I'm schizophrenic? (Laughs.)

There are lots of black people in this community. There's a problem and I feel strongly about this. Three, four years ago, the Chicago Housing Authority shipped large numbers of people from the inner-city ghettoes out to the suburbs. I think it's ridiculous. You don't uproot people, put 'em in a different environment, and call it progress. They were scattered throughout Lancashire. There was no cohesiveness. I felt resentful of that. People feel most comfortable when they're with others of the same value system.

It's not a question of race. If you don't have the financial resources to live here, you shouldn't live here. If I buy this home for $50,000 and I'm payin' $500 a month mortgage payments and somebody moves across the street in the same house, payin' $100 a month, having the Housing Authority susidizing the other $400, I take exception. Especially when the people moving in don't have the same values I do.

I don't think there's been any deterioration in property values, no. The community is fairly stable. But people who are renters don't have the same investment in the property.

I'm not aware of any blacks around here. But I don't meet *any* of my neighbors. They come and go so fast. The kids meet them and play with them and that's fine.

BONNIE: There isn't any camaraderie, no.

RICHARD: The extent of my social circle is a buddy who comes over about twice a month to listen to music with me. This is just a place where I sleep. (Sighs.) Marriage has a way of focusing your perceptions on yourself. You become more involved with your immediate circumstances. Over the past ten years, I've tended to become more concerned about me personally, who I am and why I am and where I want to go. I've become less involved with the world around me. Especially when I left social work seven years ago. I don't know if I've grown.

BONNIE: I think Dick's big change is his responsibility to his family. Otherwise, he would never have gotten out of social work. He's had to compromise a lot of his feelings with his, quote, duty, unquote, to the family. As far as his personal life, I think he's come a long way. He's a lot more docile.

When we first got married, I thought I'd be living the type of life my mother did. Now I don't see it that way. I see myself working continuously until retirement. It doesn't bother me because I enjoy nursing. I happen to have a job right now I'm very happy with.

At a certain time in my life. I wasn't too happy with nursing. I suffered burnout. But it's just a matter of life. There's very few times people can get along with one income.

RICHARD: But it's all so ironic. We're much better off than our parents were.

BONNIE: Do you really think our children will be better off than us?

RICHARD: I don't know.

BONNIE: I don't really think so. We always thought we could go up the ladder, like each generation before us—

RICHARD: My children are better off than I was. Economically, I have no idea. My daughter may end up as a grocery clerk makin' $5,000 a year. A lot depends on what they do with their lives. My daughter is eleven years old and she's been playin' piano for two years. My other children will. There's a love of music that will stay with her for the rest of her life. They've gone to museums, plays, movies. They've got books. As for the world around them, I don't know.

PATT SHAW

She is a waitress at an upscale restaurant in Chicago. It may be the busiest in town. Most of its patrons are young entrepreneurs; others are visiting firemen who have heard this is the place most in vogue.

I recognized her as from another time and place. "These yuppies were little children during the sixties."

You know what sticks in my mind? The Democratic riots of 1968 or something. I was workin' in the store that night. It was a small dress shop I owned, around the corner from Second City. I waited on tables there, part-time. Some of the people I knew then are still stuck in that time warp. They seem to be almost an anachronism.

I was in the store late that night, a special order I was trying to get out. All of a sudden, there was a CTA bus in front of my door. Policemen in gas masks were getting on. I'm thinkin' all there is between me and them is a plate-glass window. What is going on?

What is going on? That's what everybody was asking in those days. I think the idealism of that time has just totally washed away. I don't see anybody these days who really cares the way I thought we cared at that time. I don't understand yuppies, I really don't.

Sometimes I wish I had a pair of scissors in my jacket pocket. If I see another yellow tie—it's this year's yuppie *in* tie, with the little foulard-type prints—if I see another gray BMW, I'm gonna throw up (laughs).

They did an exit survey here one day. They came up with a figure of the average salary. $75,000 a year. That's a lotta bucks. I haven't the vaguest idea where it all comes from.

The only time you hear conversation about politics is when the servers are talking to each other. Everybody's playing it safe. I think Reagan appeals to a lot of people because they don't find him threatening. Because he's no brighter than they are.

I've voted for losers all the way down the line for the past eighteen years. In this last election, one out of twelve people I voted for actually got elected. How off the wall can I get?

I'd like to think some of us have grown up and have become responsible. One of my friends was a rep for several large companies. But she also became involved. She went to Nicaragua last June on her own, because she wanted to see what was going on. I thought it was a little foolhardy. God knows, I chewed my knuckles for a while until she was back. She quit a very good job because she couldn't get a leave of absence. So it was: Okay, you guys, that's the way you think about it? There'll be another job.

Someone once referred to me as a survivor. I'm also a taxpayer, I own a house. There are certain obligations to be taken care of, so I work. It's really nice to see women working in restaurants of this type where you never have seen anything but a waiter before. Some of them are captains.

When she called me a survivor she meant that whatever it took to make it or to get along, that I was—that I would adapt myself in order to do it. (Suddenly) Hey! I don't know if I should consider it a flattering comment or not (laughs).

Yeah, I think I've changed during these twenty years or so. I'm not as aware politically. I don't read the newspaper with any great regularity. I'm buying it mainly for the weekend entertainment section.

I did pay more attention then than I do now. I thought at that time that some kind of change could be brought about. It's been proved down the line that us liberals are really *bleeding* liberals. Every time one of our boys went down for the count, it's disheartening.

I remember the night at Second City that we all wore black armbands over our uniforms because of what happened in Lincoln Park. I don't feel that kind of commitment to anything any more. Except maybe making my mortgage payment. None of the people I know are involved, really, except this one friend who did leave her job to spend time in Nicaragua. No one else I know is remotely interested.

A young waitress here said to me the other day, "Lunch is so much fun, all these businessmen." I said, "Are you serious? Have you seen any one of 'em you'd want to have a drink with?" They look alike, they dress alike, and they have no faces. They're not dead, just vapid.

I'm not sure it has anything to do with getting older. It may be that none of the things we cared about made any real difference. Fighting didn't add up to anything. You just couldn't buck the system.

I don't have any super expectations for anything anyone is doing politically at this point. Maybe that's why I'm removed from it. If you don't get involved, you don't get hurt. It's a very, very different time from those other days.

FRED WINSTON

A Chicago disk jockey. His listeners hear the popular music of the moment: the Top 40. "It could be Gregorian chants or grunting. It depends on what the market is buying."

He is forty. "I saw the cover of Time *magazine. I'm a boom baby."*

He's on the air from 5:30 to 10:00 A.M. It is his sixteenth year at this station.

Ten years ago, I would have said, I'm a disk jockey. Now I'm a communicator. I try to reflect the society around me. I try to stimulate people's thoughts by pointing out the obvious that we all tend to overlook. Slice of life.

The role of a radio personality has changed greatly in the last decade. Back then, we were given a pile of records and a few flip cards to read. Keep the conversation down to a minimum. I once worked for a guy who had a stopwatch. If you talked over eight seconds, you'd get in trouble. Today, people want to hear what the individual has to say. In the old days, we could squeeze in eight, ten records an hour. Now I'm lucky if I get in two.

My listeners, they're mainly females, mid-thirties to late forties. Yuppie males seem to go in for more irreverence: sick humor, cruel humor. How long did it take for the shuttle jokes, the Challenger jokes, to come out? A week.

My listeners seem to follow the pack of propriety. Not that I don't enjoy sick humor, but there are some things still sacred. I do entertainment-type chatter. Well—a gentleman in Manitoba who's curator of a toenail museum. Here's one about a home radiation monitor. That's topical on the heels of the Soviet nuclear disaster. I deal with a lot of show business, a lot of bizarre stuff. Life-style, I guess you could call it.

Nuclear dangers? Oh, absolutely. They're concerned about that. Terrorism too. We had a radio promotion this week: a trip to Paris, ten couples. We had to scrap it because of the Qaddafi thing.

They're very reactionary. They climb on bandwagons. If you go on the air and start bitching about terrorism, they call up and want to bitch too.

Socioeconomically, most of them are blue-collar. You'll find a heavy concentration of Indiana and the 'burbs of Chicago. AM radio is not an urban thing any more. FM fragmentation has killed us. Fifteen years ago, we'd have a 12-to-15 share in the ARB rations. We're now fighting for a 4 share.

Would you believe the program that got the most calls? In chatting with my wife on the air about *Dallas* and *Falcon Crest*—I called them video valium shows—I mentioned, in passing, that Bobby Ewing showed his face. I said, "Gee, I'm not sure how he got there." Bango! The phones started, all ten lines. And they kept ringing. You could ask about a pressing political issue and one call might come dribbling in (sighs). They don't offer much when it comes to politics. That's something I try to stay away from—politics and religion. They're progovernment, pro-Reagan. All the artists are jumping on the patriotism bandwagon. Bob Seger is doing some. Springsteen is the pioneer. "Born in the U.S.A.," my God! It went platinum a couple of times.

There's a great deal of pride now in being a Vietnam veteran. I know how I felt when I was younger. I didn't want to go. I didn't think it was a moral war. I never took part in demonstrations. We were cautioned. A friend of mine was fired from WBZ in Boston for taking part in an antiwar thing. We were too busy hacking, flogging hits. If I were drafted today, I wouldn't feel great about going to war. But I'd certainly have a more patriotic flair today than I would fifteen, twenty years ago. I'm prouder to be an American today than I was then.

I like Reagan. Granted he's put a lot of show-business flair into the White House, but I like that. It gives me the feeling of propriety, of something to hang on to.

I'm very concerned about Nicaragua. It's closer than Libya. Are you familiar with the story of the Texas sheriff? He requested federal aid to buy Uzis for his men. He said they were gonna come through Mexico into Texas and he wanted submachine guns for his patrolmen. In case the Nicaraguans decided to march up through there. I think he's a little reactionary. But at the risk of waving the flag, we should take all chances we have to ensure freedom. And Nicaragua's too close to home.

Many of the listeners like *Rambo*. It's a pro-U.S.A. type of thing. A few parent groups got together and bitched about it—the movie glorifying killing, glorifying weapons. It was their teenagers who loved it. It's the nature of the teenage beast, one of general discontentment, you know.

Back in the sixties and early seventies, music reflected the antiwar effort in the hands of a few key musicians and the media's exploitation. You had people saying the war is no good, the country is no good, what are we fighting for? Buffalo Springfield et al. ad nauseam. Now the single voice is saying it's okay. Born in the U.S.A. I'm proud to be an American.

Fifteen, twenty years ago, it was considered a disgrace to wear an item of clothing made out of the flag. Most of the war protesters were doing that. Now, having a U.S. flag T-shirt is patriotism. The whole thing is inverted. What I find repugnant is young people and their Walkman in their ears. It seems to me they're tuning out society, tuning out their environment. Actually, it's taking our listeners away, because they'll throw a cassette in and listen to that rather than the radio.

Some of my friends and business associates listen to a tape of *Think and Grow Rich*. Napoleon Hill, one of my favorite people.* I believe he was a disciple of Dale Carnegie. His basic premise is to surround yourself with positives. Get a goal, an objective: great wealth. Embrace it, savor it, talk about it, program your mind to

---

* In 1968, W. Clement Stone, the celebrated philanthropist and centimillionaire, presented me with a copy of *Think and Grow Rich*. ''That's the greatest book that came out of the Depression. That book motivated more people to success than any book you can buy by a living author.''

accept it. Deal in positives only. Eventually the goal you'll want to attain will be yours.

Of course the flow of life can't operate alone on positives. You have to have negatives. The yin and yang thing.

CLARENCE PAGE

He is a columnist and member of the editorial board of the Chicago Tribune. *He is thirty-nine.*

I would describe myself as a black baby boomer. I came of age in the sixties, several years after the '54 school desegregation decision.

I was born in Dayton, Ohio. My parents had come up from the South during the black migration. They had met in the kitchen of the house where my mother was working as a domestic servant. My father was working for a catering service. It was during a party.

My father, during the late days of the Depression, shined shoes and swept up at a restaurant. He did a little bit of everything. He always prided himself on never going on relief.

There was always that upward-mobility feeling. They did not have a lot of formal education, but they were definitely imbued with that Protestant work ethic. They were very religious and very family-oriented. They were low-income, they were not lower-class. Those were the values they conveyed to me. All those good old-fashioned values (laughs).

I've often said the first word I learned was not "mama," it was "college." As far back as I can remember, it was understood that I was going to college.

When I was growing up, we had whites and blacks living in the same area. In the school, too. We were all blue-collar families. Everybody in Middletown worked for the steel mill or the paper mill.

My first exposure to race prejudice came when I was six years old. I was watching TV and I saw an advertisement for a amusement park, near Middletown: Le Sourdville Lake. I said to my folks, "Why don't we go there this weekend?" My parents looked at each other, and finally my mother said little colored kids can't go to Le Sourdville Lake. That was the first time I knew there was a difference. I think that's something every little black kid knows in America: there's a difference. That memory stuck with me all through my childhood.

My folks were not political people. Because they were older, they tended to vote Republican. Lincoln's party that freed the slaves, you know (laughs). My father was the oldest of five brothers and the most conservative. His younger brother jumped to the Democratic Party with FDR.

Seeing the Little Rock incident on television affected me greatly. I'll never forget seeing a couple of National Guard troopers marching with bayonets on their rifles behind a couple of girls. I had not yet heard of Martin Luther King.

My mother and father were very quiet about it. I didn't find out until years later that they were very hopeful. At the same time, their feeling was, Don't make waves, don't rock the boat. Just prepare yourself, because someday the doors of opportunity would open. Be ready to step inside. They never stressed that we should try to bring that opportunity about more quickly. That came from me (laughs).

We lived near the Baltimore and Ohio tracks. The train meant a lot. I always wanted to see what was on the other end of the tracks. As a teenager, I remembered the Freedom Riders. A lot of them started right from where we lived: the Western College for Women, at Oxford, Ohio.

I was fascinated by the Freedom Riders. In '63, when the March on Washington occurred, there were black families passing through. We put some of them up in a spare room in our house. My parents were pretty skeptical about these people. That's what's so funny about it (laughs). They put 'em up because they were good Christian people. You always welcome strangers at the back door, take 'em in, and give 'em a warm meal, that kind of thing. My father was a deacon in the Baptist church. My mother bakes sacrament bread every month, on the first Sunday.

My parents and I never talked much in depth about this, but there was a feeling that a better day was going to come. Everybody knew that these forces of history were moving and you don't want to stand in their way. At the same time, you didn't want to stand out in front.

When I was about fifteen, sixteen, I decided I wanted to be a journalist. My mother wanted me to be a doctor, like a good middle-class mom would want (laughs). I liked the sciences a lot. I was crazy about the space program. I grew up with that, too. Sputnik was launched in '57. It affected our whole generation.

There were all these freedom rallies and sit-ins down South. There was the beginning of the antiwar movement, just starting out in Berkeley. Kennedy had just been assassinated. The Beatles were rolling in. A cultural upheaval. I wanted to be part of that.

I was curious about Malcolm X. I thought he was an unlikable guy. 'Cause here was a guy who was so angry at white people that he was as prejudiced as white bigots. When I saw him interviewed late at night on a television talk show, I changed my mind about him. Oh, I'm a child of the TV age, too (laughs).

In the early sixties, the big newspapers had no black reporters, maybe one. Isolated as I was in Middletown, I had no role models.

In '64, the Goldwater campaign got me reading about politics. I started reading the *National Review*. It was a lot easier to buy in Middletown, Ohio, than *The Nation* or *Village Voice*. You just couldn't get them. I said I *read* the *National Review*. I didn't say I *believed* it (laughs).

Prior to that, all I knew was that Eisenhower was good because he was a Republican. But Kennedy's Catholicism went over well in the black community. The Catholic church would never turn away a black person at the door. Whereas, eleven o'clock on Sunday morning was the most segregated hour of the week among Protestant churches. There were white Baptist churches and black Baptist churches, there were white Methodist churches and black Methodist churches, but there was only one Catholic church.

I went to Ohio University. We called it Harvard on the Hocking or Berkeley of the Backwoods. I majored in journalism. I worked in a steel mill because I was turned down for a summer job at the *Middletown Journal*. I was told they weren't hiring any high school kids. I looked around and they did hire a white girl, daughter of the executive editor. That was one of my first lessons in life about who you know versus what you know.

It was with no small amount of justice that years later—after

I came to the *Chicago Tribune*—I heard that the *Middletown Journal*'s editor would really love it if I would come back as city editor.

I felt that things were gonna get better for *me*. Things in general, for that matter. The Voting Rights Act of '65 had passed. On the other hand, Vietnam was heating up. The first combat troops went in in '65, just when I was starting college.

At the time, I was in favor of the war. So was the majority of students on campus. There were only about thirty students out of fifteen thousand that demonstrated. They were spat upon. They were threatened with beatings. Four years later, when I graduated, it was just the opposite. You might have had thirty kids on that whole campus who were in favor of the war.

For me, the change took place in my freshman year. I went to a couple of campus teach-ins and got my mind changed. I was astounded how weak the argument in favor of our involvement was, how easily anybody who stood forth to defend our government's position was trounced.

Remember, we're talking about Middle America. During my freshman year, Eisenhower came to the campus. Everybody liked Ike. I'll never forget his speech: "Kids, just remember to have fun. This is the last time you'll really have a chance to enjoy yourselves and learn something, too." It was so charming, so irrelevant.

When Dean Rusk came, the people really got their dander up. Our newspaper came out with a strong statement against the war. Boy, did we catch it from a lot of students. The conservatives were still in the big majority. Especially the fraternities. The trustees were livid.

Things didn't really change until my junior year, '67, '68. The assassinations, the Tet offensive, LBJ's withdrawal—all within a few months. What happened in Chicago at the '68 convention was inevitable.

I was a summer intern at the *Dayton Journal* newsroom. I watched it on television. We had our own demonstrations at Dayton. I covered one race riot and almost became part of it (laughs). It was one hell of a summer.

My folks were disturbed. The black power movement was also happening. My hair was too long to suit them. They couldn't understand why I seemed so opposed to the many things they had worked so hard to get. Why was I so cynical of their middle-class values? They said they were gonna pray for me and everything would be all right. The late sixties was a great time to be a black journalist. That was how I came to Chicago eighteen years ago.

Something's happened in those years, hasn't it? It's become less of a civil rights struggle and more of a class struggle. It's hard for me to talk about social injustice—I'm better off than most white people are in this country. But what about the great many other blacks?

I wonder if we can any longer use civil rights tactics against economic problems. We can march for justice in Forsyth County, Georgia. We can march against apartheid in South Africa. But what do we do against the grinding problems in the black community— illiteracy, teen pregnancy, homelessness, malnutrition? We've got the poorest children of any industrialized country in the world. Civil rights marching is not going to solve it. It has to be a social justice movement in some big way.

What good does it do if you have the right to do a job, but not the education to get it? What good does it do if you have the right to go to a hotel, but you can't afford it? You have the *right* to sit at a lunch counter or go to a restaurant, but... In some ways, we're worse off as a people today than we were twenty years ago.

There is a rage inside, an anger that certain people have tried to turn these advances around and say whatever advances black people have made have been at the expense of somebody else.

In the new racism, everybody's a victim (laughs). There are no bigots any more. A Southern leader quit the Klan and formed a new group called the National Association for the Advancement of White People. It's predicated on the notion that the whites are an oppressed class now. They borrow the rhetoric of the civil rights movement, but not its essence. Is the ex-Klansman much different from the Reagan administration that puts forth black spokesmen to oppose affirmative action because this oppresses white males?

What concerns me is that I am so alone now. There are so few blacks who have shared in this opportunity. A few of us are allowed in the door and then it's shut. No more. I see a gap within our own community. It reflects to some degree our society at large. When the barriers of segregation fell, there was a massive rush, like a coiled spring finally unleashed. Too many of our brothers and sisters were left behind. That's what we're stuck with today.

It's too large for just the black middle class to solve alone. It has to be a society-wide effort. It's not just the black community. It's the Hispanic and certain parts of the white community, as well.

I think these people are worse off than twenty years ago because they are more isolated. There's less a sense of hope. I was not born rich, but as long as my family had hope, that's all that mattered. But if you don't have any hope and all you look forward to is producing more and more generations of welfare kids, you're definitely worse off. That is the big gap, the Great Divide.

JACKIE KENDALL

She is director of the Midwest Academy, a training school for community organizers. She is married and has four children. "We work with everyday people, trying to change their communities. I never thought I'd be doing what I'm doing. Neither did the others."

Her family was blue-collar Brooklyn Irish. Her father had worked as a flyboy. "He caught newspapers as they came off the press, stacked them, and tossed them onto trucks."

They lived in Bedford-Stuyvesant, which "had already changed from white to black to Puerto Rican. We were one of the three white families left. We couldn't afford to move.

"I grew up very schizophrenic: part of me wanted to be a nun, the other part wanted to get married and have twelve kids." (Laughs.)

"When I decided to go to Brooklyn College, the nuns went crazy. They thought I'd become a communist. The first speaker I ever heard on campus was Malcolm X. There was a big uproar. People were trying to keep him out, others fighting to get him in. I'd lived among enough black people, so I could understand how he felt. I'd probably feel the same way."

She joined the Newman Club at school, "almost a little Catholic ghetto." She met her husband there, a member of Young Americans for Freedom. "His father was a cop. We used to fight constantly."

One time, I had gone back to my old neighborhood. A toothless fat old black woman was coming toward me. Fifty was old, right? She goes, "Jackie!" Throws her arms around me and hugs me. I had no idea who she was. She said, "It's me, Hazel." Hazel Clayton was my age, my friend. She lived three doors away from me. I was eighteen, nineteen, and she looked fifty.

I knew all the people on that block. I don't know where they went. I got out unscathed. Most of the others were dead, dope addicts. I realized that could just as easily have been me. I was lucky. It wasn't just because I was white. I had a cousin downstairs who ended up like Hazel, maybe even worse off.

I was working part-time at Sears and there's no union. They used to give turkeys to all employees at Thanksgiving, except part-timers. This didn't seem fair. I thought we should get half a turkey. In a fit of pique, yelling at some manager, I said, "That's it! I'm forming a union." That just set them off.

There I am in the president's office. They thought I was some kind of union organizer. What is it we wanted? I better quick come up with some demands. We should at least have a turkey dinner. So I made them give us all a turkey dinner before Thanksgiving.

It was amazing how this head of Sears reacted. They kind of panicked. I thought, Wow, they're afraid of us. So anytime they wanted something from us, I would just organize this little group and say, Wait a minute, we don't have to take minimum wage for this.

I always intended to get a degree, never did. Got married, and by that time my husband was in law school. This was still Brooklyn Irish Catholic, so we just hoped that God would keep babies off until he graduated. By the time he graduated, we had two kids (laughs). I was trying to be a mother, scraping by with next to nothing, being married to a law student. I never had that much money, so it wasn't a big deal. We could live very, very frugally. He got a job in Washington with the Federal Power Commission. Hey, we're gonna be rich someday. There's marches on Washington, there's sit-ins. I'm home working with the kids. I still wanted twelve.

By this time, my husband was changing, and while still working for the government was doing local aid for draft resisters. From YAF to this (laughs).

We didn't like living in Washington. He got two offers: one for a fellowship to do legal assistance on an Indian reservation and the other from Baxter Laboratories in Chicago as a corporate lawyer.

He was tormented, trying to make a decision. On the way to O'Hare, he starts talkin' to this black cabdriver. He has this crazy notion that cabdrivers know everything. He says, "Look, I got this problem." (Laughs.) The cabdriver says, "What are you, stupid? Go for the money." So we decided we're gonna go for the money (laughs).

That was the week Bobby Kennedy got shot, the Poor People's March, Resurrection City. They want volunteers to find housing for the people who couldn't stay in the tents. So I ended up on the phone, calling thousands of people, finding housing and loving it. I felt I was part of this thing even though I didn't even know what it was.

We now have a little tract house in Palatine.* This was heaven. Three kids now. Imagine, actually living in a house! I remember growing up and watching *Father Knows Best* and my dream was to be able to say to the kids, "Go upstairs to bed."

It was a growing company and he was one of the two lawyers at the time—they have fifty now—and we're gonna be really rich.

I had to do something, more than just grunt work for the Democrat running against Phil Crane.† I started getting active in consumer stuff. We went to the supermarket every week, fighting with them to put dates on the food instead of codes.

There was an article in the paper, with my picture and my three kids standing outside the supermart, with picket signs. The next day, it appears on my husband's desk with a little note from the vice-president: "I didn't know your wife was a rabble-rouser." He was a little worried, but not enough to make me stop.

National Food was the big supermarket here and Kirkland, Ellis

* A middle-class suburb near Chicago.
† Conservative Republican congressman, regularly re-elected.

was their law firm. I didn't know we were messing with the big guys. We were just housewives, picketing supermarkets. All we wanted were freshness dates on food. You couldn't tell from the codes how old the food was.

My husband gets a call one day from one of their top lawyers: "How would you like to have lunch?" It's one of those clubs where the boys with power belong. The guy says, "The president of this club is the president of your company. And if your wife continues to do what she's doing—" My husband stops him and says, "Don't go any further. If this is a threat, I will have you disbarred. Keep your mouth shut and we'll just consider this a friendly lunch" (laughs). Of course, we knew his days were numbered.

Nobody ever said anything directly. Shortly after, he was taken out for a drink by the company president, the VP, and a couple of other big shots. At the bar, one says to the other, "Why don't you tell Walt about the guy we almost hired." They tell him about this man they almost hired till they found out his wife was a real troublemaker (laughs).

He wanted to go off and take a legal aid job at $7,000 a year. I said, "Wait a minute. We got four kids now." Here's this YAF person and he's about to wear a hairshirt and I'm saying wait a minute. I'm all for helping people who are poor, but I don't want to be poor. I've been there already.

He got a job at John Marshall Law School, teaching. And that's perfect. Since he took a $15,000 pay cut to do this, I started thinking maybe I should go to work. That's how I came to the Midwest Academy.

In the late sixties, when the grape boycott was going on, I saw a woman on the picket line. I had never been on a picket line before, and I wasn't sure I wanted to be on one. This woman was carrying one child and was pushing another in a carriage. It was a dreary, miserable day and I thought, Oh my gosh, if she can be out there with these two kids, by God I should be on that line, too. So I got on the line.

Years later, when I wanted to study at this school for organizers, I went to see the director, Heather Booth. She was the woman on the picket line. It was like light bulbs going off. It was everything that I had thought over for twenty years suddenly falling into place. I was in my mid-thirties and finally found out what I wanted to be.

I see things changing now. I travel around the country and *listen* to all kinds of people. There's a gnawing away at people who feel things aren't right. My brother, a year younger than me, is making a lot of money and living in a fancy house.

He says, "It's getting harder because every day I have to walk through Penn Station and see those people who live there. It's not just one or two bums who are hanging out with a bottle. I don't know what I have to do, but I have to do something, right?" I said, "Yeah." (Laughs.)

I think he represents a lot of people, who have made it but something's eating at them. It's not idealism. It's realism. Think back to 1980. How many people were sleeping in Penn Station then? Nowhere near as many as there are now. That didn't just happen accidentally. It happened because Ronald Reagan changed things. The only way to have less people sleepin' there is have somebody change it back. I don't think that's idealism at all. I think that's wakin' up.

THIS TRAIN

This train don't carry no liars,
No pocket pickers and no bar flyers,
This train is bound for glory,
This train.
This train don't carry nothin' but the righteous and the
  holy, this train.

—An old spiritual

TIMUEL BLACK

*The March on Washington, led by Martin Luther King,
took place on August 28, 1963. Hundreds of thousands
gathered together in the nation's capital, far more than had
been anticipated. They came by bus, car, plane, and train.*

*From Chicago, a train (it had to be split into two
sections; there were more than 1,600 passengers) was
chartered. The captain of our train was Timuel Black, a
Chicago City College teacher. He was accompanied by his
ten-year-old son, Timmy, and by his sixteen-year-old
daughter, Emitra.*

*On the return journey, the passengers, though weary,
were exuberant. It seems that everybody aboard, between
catnaps, had something to say, including the train's
captain:*

*"I've been in only one other such event in my life. I was
in Paris one day after its liberation. The Resistance was
driving the Germans out of the city. The exhilaration and
discipline of the crowd was as encouraging as the courage
of the people. I was a member of the First Army in the
quartermaster corps. This march reminded me so much of
that moment.*

*"We heard there would be incidents of violence. As we
entered the march, we realized all the anxiety created by
the news and media were unfounded. A lack of confidence
in the people."* *

---

* "Today is the day to breathe a prayer for peace in Washington. This is the day of the
march for civil rights in the nation's capital and the dread specter of possible violence
hangs over the proceedings. . . . Never have we felt less like saying 'We told you so.' We

Muses) Twenty-four years ago. Hard to believe. The Monument, the reflecting pool, all those people, black, white, King's speech, so pure, so touching. We thought America would be moved by this event. This is going to do it. Such a feeling of joy and relief. But reality hit us very quickly, didn't it?

When we were coming back, a bunch of papers were tossed on the train. I think it was in Cleveland. It was the *Sun-Times*. In essence, it said, You've been to Washington, so what?

> *It was in South Bend, Indiana. Bundles of papers were offered gratis to the passengers. The editorial was headlined: Now That the March Is Over. "America breathes easier today because the march on Washington was accomplished without untoward incident.... The question now arises, was it worth the effort? Now that it has gone off without a hitch, can it be said that it advanced the cause? ... There is a good deal of knowledgeability in Dirksen's remark [Senator Everett M. Dirksen of Illinois, sonorously eloquent, the sweet singer from Pekin]: 'I don't think any legislator worth his salt would let mere noise and fireworks change his convictions.'" There followed an ad hominem attack on Bayard Rustin, one of the organizers of the march. It ended with a plea for "substantial citizens of the Negro community" to take over the cause.*

It was such an insult. We felt it was so unnecessary. Some of our young people walked off the train straight to the *Sun-Times* to demand an apology. I realized we had a lot more work to do.

In less than twenty-four hours, I experienced the dream and the reality. The dream: to keep hope alive. The reality: America was not going to be changed very much by a march.

It would not be honest to say progress has not been made. Con-

---

hope it won't be necessary to say that tomorrow" (Editorial, *Chicago Sun-Times,* August 28, 1963).

sciousness has been raised by people like Dr. King and events like the march. Women have come to say to white men, We'll not be treated like niggers, we don't like it. But the hopes and dreams of that moment have not been realized in too many other ways.

A permanent underclass has come into being. A disproportionate number of black youth is part of it. Numerically, this underclass is more white than black, but our leadership imposes the idea that it is really a black, useless, lazy underclass.

After twenty-four years, I find among black students, though I have some whites in my classes, a deep cynicism, a feeling of being trapped and hopeless. I'm talking of college kids. There is ambivalence and confusion. A self-centeredness that is frightening. They will say, I can't make it without college, but I know that my friends who went to college aren't doing so well. So a lack of trust has come into being, not just at older people but among themselves.

Their chances during these twenty-four years have, if anything, been reduced. They're sweet kids, both the blacks and the few whites I teach. They're looking desperately for some answers. They're very much interested in American history, the course I teach. My classes are always full.

There's been an increase in fundamentalist churchgoing among these students. I am amazed. The churches are full. They find no answers they can depend on in the secular world. To get rid of their anxieties and tensions, they seek out the apostolic, evangelical, fundamentalist church. There are ready answers there. It frightens me.

There is one church I attend. It is old-line middle-class black. Many of the young now go to it. This pastor engages in evangelism but he speaks out on issues : apartheid, Nicaragua.

In the lower-class black church, which many of the blue-collar young attend, the problems are more personal and immediate.

As my young black friends, professional, highly trained, Harvard, Stanford alumni, have moved up into the corporate world, they have found their mobility limited. As his white counterpart moves along, he sits there, frustrated, beginning to doubt himself. Has he been passed over because he's not qualified or because he's black ? He's confused.

Some of them just withdraw and return to less well paying jobs somewhere else. In the black community, if possible. Some just break down. It's more than they can handle.

It's frightening and growing : the class gap in the black community itself. It's going to be very difficult to close.

There is a growing feeling among whites that the blacks have finally become equal, as result of the benevolence of whites (laughs). We gave it to you, you have it now, you ought to be satisfied. It's someone else's turn now. The less well trained white, who is now threatened by the less well trained black—or the well-trained black—is resentful. Affirmative action is, of course, the natural target.

They figure they've sacrificed enough for these blacks, they've given up enough. They're not ready to give up any more at all. They see their own well-being challenged. They don't see, as in the early sixties, the need for more unity on the jobs issue. Full employment is hardly talked about any more. The black male has growing competition from women, black and white. A black woman, well trained, has a tremendous advantage over a black man in the field. As I ride public transportation, I hear fewer black male voices giving directions. More women and more Hispanics. I begin to wonder whether the black male has become an endangered species?

The ratio of black female to male in college is three to one. The kids come out of homes where the female is already dominant and the male is reduced. The girls see leadership immediately. The boys see no leadership, because there are very few black males around who are successful.

Unless there are substantial changes, political, economic, and I don't see that happening, the future looks gloomy. For the few blacks who have made it, it's very, very good. Emotionally, it's not that good. There's a feeling of isolation.

Since that march of '63, there were moves in a positive way and changes for the better have occurred. With Nixon, it was slowed down. With Reagan, it has been reversed. When Reagan came into office, there were more than a million and a quarter black students in colleges. That number's down to around 700,000 today. The reduction in student aid and the emphasis on the military has decreased the number of blacks in college and increased their number in the service. The army has become their only way out. Along with poor Southern whites, they've become the hardest and toughest soldiers. Is that the answer?

T. KERRIGAN BLACK

*Timuel Black's son. He was Timmy, the ten-year-old boy,
on that train to Washington, August 28 and 29, 1963. He
was especially excited on the return journey.*

*"I liked all the landmarks. The Lincoln Memorial, the
Washington Monument. The White House. The Capitol.
I've always seen them in the pictures. One of my favorite
subjects is history. This is history to me."*

*He is thirty-two, a composer and musician, living in
Berkeley, California.*

I remember the excitement of everyone on that train, the togetherness. I think I understood why we were going, the cause. I had no idea of the scale of the march in which we were participating. It was incredible. I'd never seen that many people before (laughs).

I've been doing a lot of thinking lately about race and racism. I live in an area that prides itself on being very liberal. It's not really as open-minded as it likes to think it is.

Considering that my father was a political activist, from as early as I can remember, I grew up fairly naive as to the way the world works. It's been a revelation to me how very strong the prejudices still are.

I've been fortunate to go to three of the best schools in the country. By all reasonable criteria, I'm generally well qualified in the things I try to do. But I still find a lot of barriers. I've been successful because I'm tenacious and have a fairly good reputation.

When my wife's friends start complaining about overt racism, I've generally found the white people will try to smooth things over rather than confront those close to them, who may be racists. I've heard a lot more complaints recently, especially around Martin Luther King's birthday. Nasty jokes...

The tone of the country has been, Okay, we did what we could in the sixties and it didn't work. Opportunities dried up and we're all fighting for the same little apple. We're gonna keep ours, we're gonna keep as much as possible, and they're just gonna have to fend for themselves. I'm not sure if the Reagan administration has led in this or has just been symptomatic of the times.

I think that Reagan has set the tone for the eighties and is probably the most racist president we've had since Woodrow Wilson. Yet he is typical of the times. You would never hear a racist word from him. But the actions he condones—the kind of things in the Justice Department—are what would have been done early in the century.

A friend of mine, a black woman, was with a group of white friends. Her boyfriend, who is white, was talking about basketball. he was talking about a pick-up game he was in, and the players being pretty aggressive. So the other guy says, "Oh, you mean spearchucker basketball." I had never heard that term until she told me. Spearchucker. It makes me furious even to recount it.

He wouldn't have said nigger in a group of people, but that's exactly what that means. She was absolutely shocked. She didn't know how to react or what to say. It's like you're walking down the street and someone walks up and slaps you. You don't necessarily react. She was furious later and started crying.

These are all Berkeley people. This guy was her boyfriend's best friend. No one said anything. No one said, How can you say anything like that? That's horrible thing to say. Not a word was said to him.

I went to Phillips Academy in Andover, Massachusetts. This would have been in 1969. George Bush's son was in my class (laughs). We had a larger percentage of black students than Stanford, where I went to college. One day I was in the dormitory with a couple of white students. I had just bought these big boots for mountain climbing. I liked them and had them on. This student who was friendly to me looked down at them and said, "Oh, you got your nigger-kickers on." Then he looked at me . . .

It was the measure of his acceptance that he hadn't really thought of me as black when he made that statement. He immediately realized what he'd said. The other white student just howled with laughter because the guy was so embarrassed. I mean, he turned about fifteen shades of scarlet. I just looked at him. That was the first time I had heard that expression.

It was obviously such a common term that it just rolled off his tongue and he'd use it with anyone he felt comfortable with. And he felt comfortable with me at that point. Without realizing that I was the nigger to be kicked (laughs).

Early 1984, February or something, I was playing a gig in Death Valley, California. It was down in the desert. This was a very expensive hotel. Very up. This group came into the lounge. I was singer-pianist. They listened to a set and seemed to enjoy it. They asked me to come and sit down with them.

They bought me a drink and we talked of various things. The party was going skiing the next day. This one gentleman insisted I go skiing with them. He kept insisting. Then he addressed the rest of the table: "Well, there'll be one way to get rid of the niggers. You know, in the snow."

There were several conversations going on at the same time. There were about six of us at the table. I'm not the type of person who reacts very quickly to insults. Manners are very important to me. When someone shows poor manners, it's such a surprise to me that I just don't react immediately. I react later and get very angry.

The guy next to me, who was in his party, was furious and started calling him all sorts of names. "How would you like it if somebody called you a honky?" Blah, blah, blah. At this point, the other conversations stopped. Everybody was trying to calm down my defender. I just looked at the guy who made the crack and he passed it off as a joke. I left the table. They left immediately afterwards. They all seemed quite embarrassed.

As a child in Chicago, I spent most of my time on the South Side and downtown. There was an elderly white woman, a concert artist, who felt I had some musical talent and she offered me free piano lessons. I was so excited. Then we found out she lived on the Far North Side. I must've been ten or eleven at the time. My mother and I never discussed it, but we never took up that offer. I knew the reason, of course (laughs). As a young black boy, I couldn't go up to where she lived.

In my lifetime, I know there have been some truly revolutionary changes. *Brown versus Board of Education,* of course. And twenty years ago, no one would have predicted that the number one television show in the country would be about a black middle-class family.

That's progress of a sort. But it doesn't necessarily affect millions of black people in their everyday lives. It's like the best of times and the worst of times. There are some opportunities we've never had before. On the other hand, the overall mass of black people are not that much better off than they were twenty years ago. Probably worse off.

If I feel angry and frustrated at some of the limitations placed on me, how must an ordinary black guy on the street, without my privileges, feel—who can't make a living, who can't find a job? And then bear the insults of people pretending he can't find a job because he doesn't want to work. To be called names like spearchucker. To bear insults from Nakasone of Japan, whose cars we buy, saying the United States would be further ahead if it weren't for the blacks and Chicanos.

I have a feeling that the nineties is going to be a very turbulent decade, in the way that the sixties was. There's going to be an eruption of anger among people who have played the game and feel that they are still shut out. It's going to be a world thing.

What's so frustrating is that it's so difficult to get people to acknowledge that racism exists. It's, I made it, why can't they make it? They won't acknowledge there are so many barriers. The big one is education. It's the difference between where I have gotten and someone who may be just as talented as me. This is a very wasteful country. It wastes its natural resources, but it wastes its natural talents even more.

NEIGHBORS

They had no homes on the streets where they were born.
Their lack of communication with the world had left them
unconnected to themselves. Since they did not know the
name of the world, they did not know their own names.
This was the beginning of that strange change in America
from the first person to the third.

—*Nelson Algren,* Who Lost an American?, *1960*

MARIA ELENA RODRIGUEZ-MONTES

"I was born with an excessive amount of energy. My daily schedule is very busy. People ask me, How do you do it? I don't know. God gave me something."

To say she is active in her community and city is to say Babe Ruth was a baseball player. She serves on a dozen or so committees, among them: Board of Trustees of the City Colleges of Chicago; chairman, UNO,* Southeast Branch; director of Illinois Fiesta Advocativa...

She is petite, delicate-featured, offering the impression of a china doll. She is twenty-nine, a mother of three children, twelve, eight, and six. "I was seventeen when I got married, a senior in high school. I don't have a formal education. I think of going back to school. My parents were migrant workers. There were seven of us. I'm the pickle in the middle.

"I'm a person who was born and raised on the Southeast Side of Chicago, two blocks from where I now live."

Five years ago, August 1982, an organizer from UNO knocked on my door. He was knocking on a lot of doors, trying to get people to fight the proposed landfill for the neighborhood—289 acres, for toxic waste. Waste Management, the company, is the largest in the world.

Two hundred and eighty-nine acres, in comparison to sixteen acres in Love Canal. Two, three blocks away from the school our kids go to. It scared me.

Would you be willing to host a small meeting at your house? Sure.

---

* United Neighborhood Organization, a citywide community action group.

Four people showed. We called others. A couple of weeks later, there were thirty, meeting in the basement. We had expected twenty at most. There was an interest. People who had just bought homes in the area were afraid the property values would go down. Senior citizens were scared. The smell was bad already, and it was going to get worse with this.

We identified IEPA* as responsible. At the first meeting with them, they said talk to the alderman, talk to the mayor, talk to USEPA.† Passing the buck. It was somebody's else's problem, not ours.

About thirty of us went to the governor's office downtown. How can we get these guys to respond? Our strategy was: We'll take our kids down, with taffy apples. The kids were grabbing things, getting all the furniture sticky. The secretaries and staff were getting real upset—(laughs)—how else would we get their attention, unless we disrupted formal office procedure?

This was our first action.‡ It was kinda scary. I had never been so assertive before. I was the spokesperson. I said to this guy, the state director of EPA, we're not leaving. Of course, our kids are running around with their sticky taffy apples.

He got the governor on the telephone and wanted me to go in the next room to talk to him. I said, ''I'll talk to him over the phone with these people present.'' So every time the governor said something to me over the phone, I would turn to my people and ask them, ''What do you think?'' The governor agreed to come to our meeting. It was our first victory, our first sense of power.

He didn't show, but sent the IEPA director. There were about two hundred people. We demanded a study of contamination in our soil, water, air. And no permit issued to Waste Management until the results were in. They agreed. Again, we felt it was a tremendous victory. People by this time were feeling good.

It wasn't a great study. Yes, we have cancers higher than in other parts of the city. Yes, we have a lot of lead around. Yes, we have a lot of toxins in the air. ''But you're not really at that much of a risk.''

Congressman Washington was running for mayor and needed the

---

* Illinois Environmental Protection Agency.

† United States EPA.

‡ A phrase coined by Saul Alinsky in *Reveille for Radicals*, an early guide to community organizing.

Hispanic vote. When he was elected, we had a big meeting at St. Kevin's Church. Six hundred people showed up. I was chairing the meeting. It was my debut as a community leader.

The mayor came out with the kind of speech you expect from a politician, okay? It was many, many words. He talked wonderfully and the people applauded. They thought he had said something, but I knew he hadn't. He was shaking people's hands as he was walking away.

> *As she recreates the moment, she walks around the room, ignoring the microphone, hilariously simulating the mayor's departure. Often, during the conversation, she demonstrated, tape recorder be damned.*

I remember feeling angry. Did he really think he was fooling us? I called out, "Mayor, will you please come back here? We're not done with you yet, buddy." (Laughs.) I said, "You spoke a long time, but you haven't answered any of my questions. I'm going through them, one by one, and I want an answer to each one." You don't normally speak to a mayor like that, but I wanted somebody to be accountable. Why not the mayor?

"Will you look at that zoning permit, and if possible revoke it? Yes or no?" He'd look at me: "Yes, Mrs. Montes." (Laughs.) "Will you, as soon as you get back to City Hall, look at those contracts?" We went through them all. "Final question—let me make this clear —will you keep this company out of our neighborhood? Yes or no?" He said yes.

I remember I grabbed him, hugged him, and kissed him on the cheek. The whole crowd was standing and applauding. It was the best thing ever happened to us. It was great. We got a real commitment that day. The mayor did put a moratorium in effect.

It does not allow any new landfills in the city of Chicago. Waste Management is still out. Waste Management is still thinking of coming in the neighborhood. I personally will not allow it.

We took two hundred people and jammed the annual stockholders' meeting of Waste Management. Sisters of Mercy, who own some stock, gave us their proxies. They stopped us at the door, but we created such a ruckus that their stock went down three, four points the next day.

We knew we had to aggravate them. So we formed a human chain that didn't allow the garbage trucks into the landfill. We had a big sign: THE MUCK STOPS HERE. We're talking about the Dan Ryan Expressway, okay? Trucks were backed up for miles. A week later, we brought double amount of people and our kids, too. Again, we backed the trucks up for miles.

They brought in the paddy wagons. It was scary because none of us had ever been arrested before, okay? We had people there who weren't willing to be arrested and certain ones who were willing to go all the way. The police got very confused and arrested the wrong people. They arrested one little girl of four or five. I was the last one they took away.

We were singing all the time: "All we're asking is give South Deering a chance." I remember saying, 'If we don't get to see the president, we'll be back. I don't care if we have to go to his house, his church, or the school where his kids go." These things made us all the tighter.

I may have got some of this energy from my mother. She was active in bringing in bilingual education. She was PTA president. She worked hard forming youth groups in the community. She was in everything.

Two years ago, when my daughter was ten, she organized an action. My children go to a magnet school, so they're bused. The driver was drinking. He'd stop, go to a bar, and leave all the children in the bus. My daughter and another leader decided they weren't going to allow this to continue. They organized thirty, forty kids on the bus and decided to go see the principal. The person at the top. They all marched into the principal's office and requested a meeting then and there. She came out, they explained the situation and made demands. The principal was impressed. They made a difference: the driver was fired.

Maybe I'm not always at home, not as much as I should be, as much as some parents are, but I'm giving them a vision. I'm an example to them that as individuals, we can make a difference in life.

There's a young lady that I just recently met. She reminds me of myself when I was younger. Her mother said, "I want you to be her mentor." I want this young lady to feel the way I feel now, okay?

ED NOVAK

He is twenty-eight, a member of the Ku Klux Klan.

"I come from a Lithuanian and Slovak background. I was raised a Catholic and belonged to the parish Providence of God."

His father, a dock hand, and his mother, a factory worker, died when he was in his adolescence. He subsequently lived with relatives in the Marquette Park area of Chicago.* He lives alone these days.

"My goal in life was law enforcement. Because of my politics and run-ins with the law, my career is neither here nor there."

When I was seventeen, I got my first introduction to white supremist views through the National Socialist Party. I attended rallies, absorbed every piece of literature I could get my hands on concerning Aryan man and his future. I just couldn't get enough to read.

The Nazis gave me a White Power T-shirt. I wouldn't wear it at work because it was owned by Jewish people. I don't think that would go over too well (laughs). I don't have any animosity toward Jews, just Zionism. I felt the Nazi approach on the American continent is not feasible, so I got involved with the Ku Klux Klan.

I was born and raised in Pilsen, a fast-changing neighborhood. It was predominantly Slovak and I had seen block after block go nonwhite. Specifically, Mexican. I seen good people, who were there for generations, get run out of the neighborhood with the intimidation and fears from the street gangs, the blackmail, the robberies. Crime just shot up so high. If there wasn't a week there wasn't a shooting, it was an awful quiet week.

---

* An ethnic neighborhood of two-flats and bungalows on Chicago's Southwest Side. It is adjacent to an expanding black community. It had been the scene of racial confrontations, notably the march led by Martin Luther King in 1966.

I started to consider the future. Why did it have to be this way? This influx of nonwhites into our beautiful, well-knit community? Was there something in my lifetime that I could do to change that around?

The blacks, they didn't come into Pilsen. If you'd seen 'em, they just went through the neighborhood. If they tried to settle in, they were burned out. Local people just could not stomach the black thing. They tried it, but they were burned out by whites.

They had just been through the riots of the sixties. When the black families tried to move in, a gentleman, a little older than myself, led the locals to the streets at night. They'd firebomb the apartments, so they moved out.

They probably came from another black neighborhood and wanted to get away from the crime. What's the old saying? If you let one in, they're all gonna come in.

I remember bits and parts of Martin Luther King's speeches and seein' his face on television. As I got into the white racialist movement, I found out a lot more about King than meets the average person's eye on the street. Martin Luther King, from my knowledge, was a member of sixty-two different communist organizations. Robert Kennedy was the attorney general, he had wiretaps on King completely sealed for fifty years. We ask, why? Why does this man have a national holiday in his honor, but we aren't able to listen to these tapes? There's something not quite right here.

The information I have was mostly compiled by different white racialist groups. We tried the Freedom of Information Act, but we were stopped cold. The National States' Rights Party of Mr. J. B. Stoner did some real good research. We have done a piece ourself. We got a lot of our information from the Un-American Activities Commission.

I remember in Pilsen, nice kids in the block disappearing and being replaced with people that didn't even speak English. I remember a four-story building with a nice yard and very nice flowers, roses. Mexicans bought the building and within five years, it was totally destroyed.

White kids would go to school and study and were disciplined. Mexican kids lacked manners. There was no discipline, just let 'em on the street, wild. That's how they got involved in gangs.

I saw a firebombing once when the blacks moved in. A black family moved into a building across from the local tavern. The guys walked across the street (laughs lightly) and took something out of the trunk of a car, it looked like a bottle, and they threw it through the window and it exploded. They just went across the street and watched the place burn. I think I was about fourteen years old.

Remember your feelings when you saw that?

I felt that the blacks didn't belong there. The people in the neighborhood feared if one family moved in, there'd be another and sooner or later, they'd take over the community.

They were in there, tryin' to put out the fire. It wasn't much, just the front room. The fire department got there and put it out. I remember the next day seein' them packing their station wagon and moving. It was a husband, wife, and a daughter, about seventeen. They were warned. Somebody attached a note to their door and asked them politely to leave.

I wondered if there was anybody in there. Then we heard voices. When the curtains went up in flames, you could see them standing. It's kind of a frightening experience, you don't want to see anybody get hurt. But in the back of your head is the idea—they don't belong here.

The crowd outside just kinda looked and turned around and walked away. A couple a cheers here and there. Of course, everybody would leave before the police got there, because nobody wanted to be a witness.

I don't believe all black people are bad and I don't believe all Mexican people are bad. But the large majority of 'em are totally for the preservation of their culture. I, as a white man, want to have pride in my race, my culture. But the status quo today is if you have that opinion as a white man, you're a racist, you're a bigot, you're a hate-monger. The Farrakhans, the Jesse Jacksons are fine and dandy.

> *"My dad's racial views were pretty close to mine. He set a good example. He's from the old school, that a man is king of the castle. He thought it was an abomination for a white to mix with a black."*

I remember seein' cars overturned with the black occupants in Marquette Park. They'd be drivin' by slowly, 'cause of the crowds of white people on the street corners. They'd bomb their car with bricks and bottles and the blacks would try to flee the area. If they got caught, they get beat right on the spot. They'd flip their cars over and try to set them on fire. I was there spectating. I saw some females out there, cheerin' them on. I thought it was great. Fight fire with fire.

With the Nazi Party, our target market was young people of voting age. We had older people comin' up all the time that would donate money. People from the old country. It was impressive to see a foreign-speaking individual, who had survived World War Two, come out in our support.

Our target market was these young people, before they went to these so-called colleges, where their minds are polluted with what we call One-Worldness.

One-Worldism is that everybody's equal, everybody is happy. We call certain individuals who expouse this Joe Six-Pack. He sits at home, watches blacks play ball on television, and drinks his beer and he pays his bills. He's concerned about his mortgage, his car payment, what time he'll get to work, and that's it. He's not concerned about what really goes on around him, as long as it doesn't affect Joe Six-Pack. We wanna reach his kids.

Our Klan works with different white survivalist groups. Aryan Nations is the overall umbrella. We had an annual congress and I participated. It was very uplifting of the spirits.

The Klan gets a lot more acceptance in Chicago than the Nazi Party. To most people, that's a foreign ideology and you have World War Two as an obstacle. The Klan is American as mom and apple pie. It's family-oriented. I saw *Birth of a Nation* and I loved it.

We're not anti-black, just pro-white. Slowly, the white people of this country are starting to wake up. We see the federal government setting up civil rights bills that say you have to hire X amount of nonwhites. So now we have discrimination against one set of people —and that's us. Ronald Reagan tries to run a conservative administration, but it's Congress. We refer to the federal government as ZOG, the Zionist Occupation Government. There isn't one politician in this country willing to stand up for white people. There have been a few attempts in the Justice Department to change some of these civil rights bills. Reagan's a sell-out. He was endorsed by the Ku Klux Klan and he turns it down.

We're headed for a race war, there's no doubt in my mind. There's a lot of hostility out there and white people just aren't aware how bad it is.

I like Louis Farrakhan. I understand him. He and I both believe in one hundred percent separation of races. I know he and I could agree to work this out, nonviolently. That's beautiful. Why slaughter each other, if we could one day sit down and cut out part of the country for blacks and another for whites?

Mr. Farrakhan puts his cards on the table. He shoots from the hip when he has to. I have respect for that type of caliber of black man. He is honest, sincere, and brings it all out in the open. He recognizes the Zionist operation in La Cesspool Grande, D.C.

We hope to avoid a race war. If we can have five northwestern states and Minister Farrakhan can have their piece of America, we can live a separate but equal peace.

SYLVESTER MONROE

He is a correspondent for Newsweek.

He had written a cover story for the magazine: the twenty-fifth anniversary of the Robert Taylor Homes, Chicago's largest public housing project. He himself as a child and adolescent had lived there with his family.

A reunion had been arranged with his boyhood friends, who had also been residents.

When the Robert Taylor Homes opened in the spring of 1962, most of the guys moved in immediately. My family came in '64. It was the best place my mother'd ever lived. We'd sort of flopped around from one tenement to another. Here was a place that was warm, with hot water, there were no roaches, no rats, the grounds were kept. For the first time, I had a bedroom with a door on it. We were ecstatic.

The people who lived in here never saw it as a permanent residence. It was a way station on the road to something better. I'm not sure that was the intention when they were built. I think they were built where they are to contain the black ghetto.

My mother is a registered pharmacist. She just graduated from high school last summer. Something she always wanted to do. She got her GED a long time ago. She always saw education as a way for her children to do better than she did.

When we moved in, the gangs had not yet taken hold. The major Chicago street gangs were on the West Side. We formed a gang to protect ourselves. We didn't see ourselves as a gang.

All of us had one kind of dream or another. We broke these guys down into three groups. The strivers were the guys who got out and had some degree of success in the business world. The scufflers were in the middle: working hard, just keeping even. The others referred to themselves as the outlaws.

Hunk described himself as the baddest dude on Trey-Nine.* His dream was making money. When he was a kid of seven, his role models, the guys he saw with money and prestige, were the players, pimps on the street. He didn't see there was an option, another way.

Billy Harris, from the time he was eleven years old, had the dream of being a professional basketball player. He realized it, but the dream was dashed when the All-American Basketball Association failed and folded. Billy had been recruited from all over the country.

Poor black people don't put too much stock in dreams. You know they're gonna be dashed. I remember from the time I was knee-high to a duck listening to the men in my family, Mississippi Delta sharecroppers. They came up on the Illinois Central in the forties and I could hear them sayin' black people can't do this, can't do that. Aspirations were circumscribed by race.

Guys like Hunk didn't have what I had: my mother's voice telling me for a black man to make it, he's got to be twice as good as anybody else and work twice as hard. The way to do it is through education.

I grew up in a classic mother-headed family. What sometimes happens in a black community is that you get a surrogate father. That's what Leroy Lovelace was to me. He was freshman English teacher at Wendell Phillips High.

He arranged for me to go to a prep school in Rhode Island, St. George's. An extremely upper-class Episcopal boarding school

---

* It was the name they called the group. The first of the Robert Taylor Homes was at 3919 South Federal Street. He and some of the others lived there; hence, the name.

(laughs). I really didn't want to go there. I was happy at Wendell Phillips. I was on the track team, making good grades. I could go home every night to the people I knew. Somehow I knew St. George's would change my life, but I didn't really see how.

It was culture shock. I grew up as part of a street gang, and in those times we dressed a certain way. I always loved dark glasses, leather coats, and wing-tipped shoes. When I arrived, it was as big a shock for my adviser as it was for me. I had just turned fifteen.

I used to tell them stories about where I came from and what it was like at Robert Taylor Homes. I got the feeling they really didn't believe what I was telling them. You're talking about people gettin' shot, gettin' killed, gang fights.

In a way, they were almost as strange to me. The Taylor Homes is a world unto itself. Even a trip to downtown Chicago was a big deal.

My fear was I wouldn't be able to do the work. I'm makin' straight A's at an all-black high school, but in the back of my mind I ask, Am I good enough to compete with these guys? The first marking period comes out, and lo and behold, I'm fifth or sixth in the class. From that moment on, I never worried about whether I could do the work. What I did worry about was getting used to that world. I wrote many letters to the guys from Trey-Nine, back and forth.

I got accepted at Harvard. What bothered me here was what bothered me at St. George's. They were uncomfortable with my being black. At St. George's, a teacher said to me, We're color blind. We don't see black students, we don't see white students. We just see students. I didn't want him not to see what I was. I didn't want to be separated from those guys at Robert Taylor.

When black students started to go off to predominantly white schools, they continued to hang out with each other. White kids took it as an antiwhite statement. But it really wasn't. We were just sort of circlin' the wagons. Nobody wanted to deal with the fact that you were black. Or hear anything of blackness. It's just that this was the way to help get through culture shock.

The mid-sixties, early seventies, was a period of great hope and opportunity for young black people. The doors swung open for people like me and a couple of others of Trey-Nine, who went to college. I think that door has closed. There's a change in climate. Reagan merely reflects it. I think there's far less of a chance for the black kids of Robert Taylor Homes today than it was for us in 1966.

Things are much tougher now, certainly for the masses of black people.

I find Americans a very faddish people. Things are one day in, next day out. It applies to people as well. Black people have had their day in the sixties. The feeling is any black person who hadn't made it by now was 'cause he didn't wanna make it. And that he wasn't giving up one iota for a black person.

There's a finite pie and everybody wants his piece. Everybody is afraid of losing his piece of the pie. That's what the fight against affirmative action is all about. People feel threatened. As for blacks, they're passé. They're not in any more. Nobody wants to talk about race. We've solved that problem.

It's not that race has become a less important factor. It's that class, the division between the haves and have-nots, has become more critical. It cuts across race lines. The poorest people in this country are women and children. If you're black, it's all the more worse.

At the reunion, I was one of them. I was not into their stuff, yet my success was their success. They knew that the lives of us eleven guys were interchangeable. With a couple of little things going one way or the other Hunk could've been me.

Robert Taylor Homes is no longer a way station. People who live there are the people who can't live anywhere else. They're not headed anywhere, most of 'em. It's just a warehouse for poor people. When I went back, the thing that struck me was how desperate a place it had become.

When we were there, people had hope. What gives you hope is people like my mother pushing and Leroy Lovelace. People who take you as a child step by step. The children in these projects today never get even the first step. They're beaten before they start.

The fathers aren't there. The mothers are younger than our mothers were, and less in control. Robert Taylor Homes is now run by teenage boys who terrorize the place. Many of them were born in the projects.

Tough as we were supposed to be in those street gangs, we had respect for adults. The mothers kept the kids on a close rein. If I was out and my mother wasn't around, Billy's mother saw me, Roy's mother saw me. It was the same as my mother. That doesn't happen now. The respect is gone.

Vernon Jarrett, a Chicago journalist, reflects: "The other day a black mailman was describing a ghetto scene. The father was giving his son a lecture about staying away from a vicious street gang, to get him to stop threatening and robbing storekeepers. The kid said, 'Who the fuck do you think you are? You ain't shit. How in the hell are you gonna tell me what to do?' The man has no prestige with his own child.

"A few weeks ago, we were sitting there, watching TV. We had our windows open. There was a walkway alongside. I heard what appeared to be an explosion. I had one of these Mattel guns. Have you seen these toy guns? They're very realistic. This gun looked like a high-powered rifle. Someone had given it to my sons for Christmas. It gives you an indication of the kind of toys they're selling (laughs). I grabbed this gun because I didn't know if somebody was trying to break in.

"Here was an unarmed black kid sauntering in the gangway. He had evidently leaped up, hit a light bulb, and made it explode. I thought when he saw me coming down with a gun drawn—it looked like the real thing—he would have held up his hands and said, 'Don't shoot, mister, I was just playing.' He didn't do a thing but look at me out of the side of his head and say, 'What are you excited about, motherfucker? Go ahead and shoot.' He didn't give a damn. This kid went away into anonymity.

"I remember men in the South who were yard boys, never called mister, who were considered Uncle Toms. But their children looked up to them. At home, they represented somebody trying. The janitor in the school where my father was principal was chairman of the board of trustees of the church my dad attended. This will never happen again in our lifetime." *

I don't blame Ronald Reagan for the change in the tone of our country today. But he allows it to resonate. When he tries to gut the

---

* *American Dreams: Lost and Found* (New York: Pantheon Books, 1980).

Civil Rights Commission, when he tries to give tax tuition credits to segregated schools, when he tries to squash the Voting Rights Act, he gives the signal.

The American dream may have been deferred, but just because you live in a housing project doesn't mean it's dead. I don't think it leads inevitably to disaster, but it's much tougher, much harder than when I was there.

JOHN DUFFY

I grew up in the South Bronx. It's a unique experience growin' up in a neighborhood, black and Puerto Rican, bein' a minority in a minority.

My mother and father were both born in Ireland. She was a maid, a household servant, when she first came here. My father worked in a factory. He contracted a disease when he was in the Philippines as a GI and died of walkin' pneumonia. My mother lived off VA benefits and social security.

I dropped out of school when I was fifteen. I went back at twenty-five, got my college degree, and am now working on a master's.

The neighborhood was Jewish and Irish when I was real young. By the time I was eight, nine, Puerto Ricans and blacks had moved in from Harlem. The only whites who stayed were too poor to move. I didn't notice the change much, it just happened. You just make friends with everybody. Fort Apache was the name given it by the police. The name caught on through the movie. People in the neighborhood didn't call it that.

Just bein' a kid, it was easier to change. I just took on some cultural things. I like black music, my speech patterns tended to be street black. I hung out with Puerto Ricans, I learned some Spanish. I like Spanish food. Whites saw me as a a nigger lover. At the age of thirteen, fourteen, I started to identify more with bein' black than white. It was a weird process, a sort of reverse clash.

My mother got along real good with her new neighbors. She was very religious and had a heart of gold. Everybody loved her, because she'd bring the kids into my house, give them food, black kids, Puerto Rican kids. She really didn't understand the race thing. She didn't understand it as any politics or nothin'. They're human beings and you're good to human beings and they're good to you. She gave more than she had.

It's a high crime area, but my family was never robbed. Lookin' back at it, I didn't find it all that tough. You lived and you played ball and you went to parties and you did like everybody else. After my brother and me moved away, my mother stayed in the neighborhood by herself. The kids looked out for her, even those strung out on drugs. They watched out and made sure nothin' happened to her. She was never mugged, never ripped off. If they didn't know her, it might have been different.

I was workin' since the age of twelve in a grocery store, deliverin' orders, packin' groceries. I became the cashier, workin' about sixty hours a week. Playin' basketball. And I read.

My brother, four years older, was hangin' around in the Village and started bringin' home radical papers. Everything from *The Seed,* in Chicago, to *Muhammad Speaks.* He got into the hippie movement, long hair and all that. I got into mystical stuff and eventually more and more into politics.

I joined a group called White Lightnin', because a lot of my friends were strung out on heroin and dyin' from it. We were a radical antidrug group. We worked for better housing and were anti-Vietnam. My mother thought me and my brother had gotten a little crazy. She understood the ideas but just we went off on the deep end. She was afraid for us.

My mother was dyin' at the time, so that pulled me back. I had to take care of her. After ten years, my brother and me were still too poor to pay for her burial. That bothered me. I was spending so much time doin' everything that I wasn't able to do a little bit for my own family. It shook me.

I went through a time of just layin' low and tryin' to figure out where my life had been and where I was goin'. I ended up gettin' a job as a youth organizer for a Bronx community and clergy coalition. It came out of the Catholic church and does a lot of organizing on housing issues. I felt it was more grass-roots, more down to earth. Less linked to dogmatic theories, but out there helpin' people who needed help and tryin' to empower 'em in some fashion. But I had to get more money. It didn't pay enough (laughs).

I got other jobs. One was with People's Fire House. A Polish group in Brooklyn took over a firehouse that was closed down. I worked for them a year and a half, community organizin' and arson prevention.

Some of my street friends have survived in a fashion. They're doin' good, with regular jobs. Some are still out there, usin' drugs. Another, a white guy, who was in radical politics with me, kicked drugs and became a counselor. Now he's a Latin musician, even though he's Ukrainian (laughs).

The people I stay in touch with haven't become conservative, just older. They have family concerns, the kids, bills, all that stuff. They just aren't active as they once were. Maybe it's just a stage we're goin' through.

I've followed people who've become Puerto Rican musicians, Young Lords who are now TV newscasters. I think we can get a lot of people who can really do somethin' for the South Bronx. Reagan came here and Carter came here and neither one really did anything. South Bronx wasn't changed for better behind two presidents.

I think the people who grew up there could do more than the two presidents did. It would make a statement of a sort. They came from there and they can help themselves. People need to do that. That's another of my dreams, I guess.

MARY FRANCES SHEEHAN

A mother of thirteen—"the oldest is twenty-two, the baby is four." She was born and raised on Chicago's Southwest Side. Her husband is a firefighter, as her father was.

The neighborhood is going through some change. Hispanics and blacks have moved in. There's a lot of fear. They really can't afford to move, but they're feeling pressured and forced.

I've been through neighborhood change three times. The last time it happened, we firmly believed it could integrate. I believe neighborhoods can, if real estates will leave them alone. I know there's decent real estate people, but when a neighborhood starts to change, the vultures move in. It's amazing how they do it. Block by block by block (she walks her fingers across the table), they make hundreds of thousands of dollars.

I had a real estate agent call me and offer me a $3,000 cash bonus. Two of my little girls were beaten the day before on their way to school. This guy found out just by talk in the neighborhood. He said, "Don't you want your children to be safe?"

On one block where a family moved in a year ago, there's already thirteen black families. I have a black family across the street and I'm not afraid of them. My kids play with their kids. They have the same moral values I do. Middle-class. But real estate doesn't care who it sells to. The last time this happened to me, the kids were kept in the house eleven months. I couldn't let them out. When the racial numbers changed, they were being harassed. That's what I'm afraid of mostly.

There's a great number of senior citizens living alone. Unscrupulous realtors think nothing of calling them and telling them if they don't get out, they'll lose the value of their homes.

Our federation is proposing a home equity program to the city. It's like an insurance policy. If your home is appraised at, say, $50,000 and you stay five years and you get only $45,000, they'll give you the other $5,000. It's a hopeful plan, not only for white families. The people in Chatham* are very excited about it. For middle-class people like us, the home is the only thing they own. They don't have other properties, yachts or things like that. If they knew they weren't going to lose any value on the home, they would risk staying and finding out what integration really is about.

I don't have much interaction with black families, so I don't know all their problems. The first family that moved in was sold an American dream they couldn't afford. I understand from people who live next door to them, there are people sleeping on mattresses in the basement. They were supposed to be middle-class, a family tryin' to drag themselves out of the ghetto. That's what *I* was told. Now they got all kinds of people hangin' out there, five or six people sleepin' in the basement. It's like a flea-bit hotel, people coming in and out all hours of the night. It's not how we were raised.

The people next door saw this. Now all this is hearsay. I don't

* A black middle-class community.

know these people. They kinda showed on the TV last summer. This family had just moved in and things looked in quite a disarray from what you could see. But I wouldn't want to jump to conclusions.

The Hispanic people from Pilsen have moved here, God love them, to get away from *their* gangs. I don't see them as having a big problem here. I know a number of Hispanic families have told *me* that *they're* concerned about total racial change. Some white kid tried to firebomb their home. It wasn't any great shake. That kid didn't even live here. He's in jail as far as I know. You don't take one teenager's deed and blow it out of proportion. The real estate agent who sold them the house told them they were moving into an integrated community.

People are just scared. Almost to a person, they said, ''We can't afford to wait around till my house isn't worth anything.'' As soon as the family moved in, there was a lot of talk: ''How could this happen?'' ''Are you gonna sell?'' Immediately the houses on either side of them were up for sale.

I know of a real estate agent who wouldn't sell to a white family that was interested in living in an integrated community. He was deliberately selling it to a lower-income minority family. To create more problems for the people on the block. It sounds incredible, but it's *true*. No white families have been showed any of the homes on that block. It's racial steering. It's real hard to prove. Who's gonna testify? Not the people movin' out. They don't care. They just want out.

We care about the way our children are raised, I certainly wouldn't want my kids with people sleeping on mattresses in the basement. That's the thing people are afraid of. It isn't so much the color of people's skin. It's whether they can take care of their property, their moral values. I'm real hung up on manners and decent language. I don't want my fifteen-year-old boy telling someone to f—— (laughs), you know the four-letter word. If he's going to do it with the guys, that's one thing, but not to some old woman sitting on the porch, minding her own business.

I believe in moral values like taking care of your property. I certainly don't live in a palace, I have thirteen kids and we do what we can to keep it clean. We don't have grass, God knows, but we've got about thirty kids playing out there every day and it's neat, clean. That's important to people around me. We don't want to live in dirt and filth. Most of the time, when lower-income people move in, they don't have these same cares, values.

I don't *ever* want to live through what I lived through in West Englewood.* I don't ever want to have that same fear again. I have to take a stand *somewhere*. This is my city, too. I'm sick of being pushed around by real estate people out to make a killing. It's not fair to the people who already *own* property there and it's not fair to the black families they *sell* it to. Because there's no way they can make it and they're made to believe they can.

I didn't know black people when I was little. Now I know several. I mean it's like the old adage: we have black friends. That sounds so bigoted. Everyone assumes you are a bigot because you're trying to fight all this neighborhood change. I'm only fighting unscrupulous turnover, block by block. I'm not fighting black families moving in. It's a nice place. That's why *I* moved here. But I'm afraid of *total* turnover.

My husband works in the firehouse with them. They depend on each other's lives. They come over to the house and we have barbecues. I'm not telling my kids, Don't go near them. But when a whole community starts changing . . .

I was probably more bigoted when I was younger. I'm certainly more liberal now than when I lived in West Englewood. I don't honestly think I ever *hated any*body. I never hated anyone just 'cause he was black. I'm very Christian, not overly Christian (laughs). There's only a couple of people I really dislike and they are definitely white! (Laughs.) I don't know any black people well enough to hate 'em. (General laughter.) Those I know, I like.

I would love to see my baby, Kevin, graduate from St. Clare's and walk safely all the way to St. Rita High School and graduate as all his brothers before him. I guess that's not a lot to ask for, but it seems monumental right now.

Our home is not a palace in Winnetka, but I *hate* to give up, you know! We love Chicago. We don't *want* to move. I really think the neighborhood can work, if we get these real estate vultures out of our hair. I think it can be an integrated community as long as it's racially balanced. I can live with that. I think a *lot* of people can live with that. We can *make* it.

---

* A community that in the past decade or so has become wholly black.

IRENE JOHNSON

LeClaire Courts is one of Chicago's oldest public housing projects. It was built in 1950. It runs five square blocks (96 acres); 615 families live here—3,500 people.

What distinguishes this enclave from the city's more "celebrated" projects, such as Robert Taylor Homes and Cabrini-Green, is its lack of height. These are all row houses.

As you approach, you are astonished by its resemblance to the small-town community you've read about in chamber of commerce booklets. Lawns well-kept; small arbors of trees, all sorts of greenery; children gliding by on bicycles; an occasional schoolgirl with her book opened, relaxed against a tree-trunk. It is a pleasant June afternoon.

We're in the office of the LeClaire Courts Advisory Council. "That's the liaison group between the tenants and the Chicago Housing Authority staff," she says. She is vice-president of the council and works as clerk-typist in the office. It is a busy place. The phone rings often. She goes about her work easily, good-naturedly; she seems to have everything under control. Residents come in and out, with an inquiry or an announcement of a meeting. It is casual, informal. There are bulletin boards and posters on all the walls. LUNGS AT WORK: NO SMOKING. FREE JOB TRAINING. PARTY TONIGHT. A calendar of events. FREE LEGAL AID. GOD LOVES YOU. An announcement of a discussion: WOMEN IN PUBLIC HOUSING, STRENGTH, UNCLAIMED POWER. A hand-lettered poster: I KNOW I'M SOMEBODY, 'CAUSE GOD DON'T MAKE NO JUNK.

Her family has lived here for twenty years. Her husband and she came to Chicago twenty-six years ago from Mississippi. He has been unemployed ever since the plant shut down. He was a forklift operator. Two of their three sons are college graduates. The youngest just graduated from high school.

You teach the children that this is home. You can beautify it the way you want. You can have a little flowerbed or grow your own hedge or have a rosebush. You have to maintain it like you would if you was in a house.

We feel this is our property, our community. Just last year we formed the LeClaire Resident Management Corporation. It consists of all the tenants. Each family has a vote. We have a thirteen-member board chosen by the residents.

I'm sure there are families in Robert Taylor that have the love and concern for one another that we have. But we have so much open space, yet and still we're so close. It's easier to show that concern. Here, it reminds me of a small town. We're in a suburban settin' and yet we're city dwellers. Most of us have backgrounds from comin' from the South. You're concerned about your neighbor and your neighbor help raise your children. Through the years, I can name five or six ladies that really assisted me in raisin' my sons. I know the majority of people out here.

I don't know if I could say the feelin's different here from other projects. I think each mother love her children in her own way. But here, you don't have the fear of elevators goin' up and down. Our reports from the high-rises is they fear they have to get the children in the house before certain hours because there's no lights on the stairways and elevators not workin'.

We're able to do night activities with our kids, with the neighbors, even if it's just takin' a walk or eatin' a sandwich together or sittin' on the steps when it's hot and cool off. Whereas in the high-rise, you have to get in before dark. Here, you just go visit, or go to the neighborhood park. We do that a lot late at night. We'll do barbeque together, call each other over. All you have to do is call a neighbor and say, I'm goin' out of the neighborhood and I want you to keep an eye on my kids.

Oh yes, there are signs of gangs. Graffiti on the walls. We know some of our young people that is involved. The young people had a community meetin' last night. They talked about kids tryin' to get into gangs. We told them we're disturbed. They explained to us that they were concerned about just alleviating any kind of idea of the gang.

We have a Neighborhood Watch program. Each neighbor watch for each other. You put a sign in your window: Warning, we will call the police if we see a crime happening. We exchange telephone numbers. We call each other. Say someone's breakin' in at 4910, we get on the telephone, everybody call 911, jam it. We had not much police service before. But when we got organized, the commander came down to see us, to consult with us.

In the council, you talk about your concerns with the Housing Authority, how the property is kept, social issues, whatever. When tenants put in a work order to the Housing Authority and they do not respond in so many days, they will call our office. We would call management to see why they didn't take care of that order. Say your commode breaks. You put in an emergency call: the water is runnin' over. If the Housing Authority doesn't respond, we do a follow-up right away. In many instances, where we make the call, they take care of it in less than that eight-hour workday.

You raise your children this is home: don't write on walls. This is home: you make the place comfortable and livable. This is a way of life with us, 'cause this is what we love.

What makes life difficult for the people in high-rise public housin' is not just the structures. I personally feel the program itself is designed to downplay a people livin' in public housing. Somehow I think the people that make the rules forget that people of low income still have capabilities and a high level of intelligence. They got the same feelin's we have.

We are settin' standards. Your lease requires that you are responsible for the inside and the outside of your unit. We get addresses of unsightly places. We turn it in to the management with the recommendation that they call that family in. We had families responded: they would take the debris away from their back doors, and garbage. They have made an attempt to plant some grass. Presently, we are participating with the manager in screening new tenants.

We are still in training, we're not managin' the property yet. We're just advisin'. Our plan is, when we take charge, we'll do everything democratically and we will have rules to go by. Every family will be given a chance to change or improve before the rules are implemented. But we have no intentions of havin' this place like a Gestapo compound. No way. Within a year, we'll have full control. We lookin' forward to it.

Private managers? Of public housing? Oh yeah, I've heard talk of it. Won't solve the problem. Who are these private managers anyway? With resident management, you have the people themselves. What's a private manager gonna do? You won't change the heart of the people. Resident management is an avenue where we ourselves become part of the constructional society. Takin' responsibility is the whole name of the game.

The dream of the tenants is to restore LeClaire to a facsimile of how it was back in the early days. Where families could dwell together in a beautiful setting. Where neighbor respected neighbor. We just want to be a functional community where we can be part of the overall society.

LAWRY PRICE

It is the archetypal neighborhood tavern in a large American city: a ma-and-pa place. His parents opened it the year he was born, 1938. The family lived "upstairs," of course. He now lives two blocks away with his wife and three children.

"We still serve food three nights a week. Some of the regulars are fourth-generation people that have been coming in here. Less than in the old days." During the past ten years, the neighborhood has become gentrified.

My children, myself, have lived in this neighborhood all our lives. We all went to the same parochial school up the street. It was a working-class neighborhood. It isn't that way now.

There used to be a bar on every corner, ma and pa. They all lived here. Now most of these places are owned by two or three guys who are lawyers or stockbrokers. They have managers there. They don't use it as their livelihood like I do. They tell their friends, "Come down to my bar.'' It's more of a bragging right and a tax write-off. Same thing with the buildings around here. They pay exorbitant prices for them. They used to be two-flats. They lived downstairs in one and rented the second floor to help pay the mortgage.

They were the regulars here. Pa worked, ma stayed home with the kids. He'd go to the bar until dinner was ready. There were maybe twenty, thirty guys and they all knew ma had dinner on the table and they had to be there at a certain time. They'd stay home with the kids until maybe eight, nine o'clock. They they'd all come back. Business kept going just like that. They played a lot of cribbage and gin and could roll the dice for a drink. In the old days, people didn't get around like they do today.

The neighborhood sort of gradually changed. A young priest over at St. Sebastian's got it in his head that Hispanics ought to be taken care of. He brought them all over here, got them housing, and the neighborhood turned toward the down side. Later on, he gave up the ministry and became a director of the ACLU.

The Hispanics were just floundering around. There were a lot of them. The neighborhood really took a change when the people with money decided to buy out all the housing units and chased all the Hispanics out. I have no idea where they went.

These new people were called yuppies in those days. Upwardly mobile. Now they're called dinks: double income, no kids. Next thing you know, everything turned condo. These upward mobiles started buying up some of these old houses, remodeling, going to cathedral ceilings. All this time, you could see the old families moving out. The price of the property went sky-high. The old-timers decided it was time to bail out. They never heard of sixty, eighty thousand dollars for a house. They were paying four, five thousand when they bought it.

They said, Hey, I'm old, bingo, I'm going to Florida, Arizona, retiring. A few of their kids stayed on, remodeling and becoming financially well-off. A good number moved back from the suburbs, because this area gives them quick rapid transit to the Loop. They don't have to spend all that time going to work. They're all trying to get back in the city now. Everybody's buying up every empty lot they can find and building townhouses. They all look the same, all hooked together.

My business has changed because the neighborhood has changed. The dinks don't come out as regularly as the old-timers. Back in those days, pa had, say, fifteen dollars to spend. If he spent it in one night, you didn't see him the rest of the week. If he spent three dollars a night, you see him five days of the week. We always got the fifteen. You look at the books, there was no peaks and valleys like there are now.

See, there's nobody here now. (It is six-thirty Tuesday evening.) The dinks come out on Monday night because it's football. Sunday is slow. It used to be a good day. Now, they're running around, on their sailboats, out there on their skis. A new crowd. The wave of the future.

In the old days, the grown kids would come home on Sunday to see pa. Pa and the son would go out and have a few beers. The women used to stay home and the men were out. Now women are out here buying guys drinks. They use the same language that some of the road gang did.

Years ago, if some guy said fuck in front of a woman, you'd say, Excuse me, sir, that language isn't appropriate. Now you sit there and the word fuck comes out of the woman's mouth. You can't go to the woman and say, Excuse me, this man becomes offended by that use of language. These women are doing everything guys are. They're out riding motorcycles and parachuting and everything. That's the way things have changed. I'm from the old school, I'm a family man.

I'd prefer to have it the old way because it was steady every day. You knew what was gonna happen. Now you don't know. When they had America's cup from New Zealand? Yacht racing. Years ago, if they put the America's Cup on television, nobody'd be here. Maybe two, three people. Now there's fifty of them come in here to watch it. This is eleven in the morning.

You can't seem to warm up to these new ones. Their values are different. I think these kids have never wanted for anything. If they wanted something, they got it. When their fathers came home from the war, '45, '46, they'd say, Here, kid, here's a buck, go to the show. Your mother and I want to be alone together. The kids got the idea: you keep asking, you keep getting. They're passing it on to their kids.

I notice an old-time sign on the wall: CHILDREN MUST BE SEATED AT ALL TIMES.

It's a new sign. These new children don't seem to have the discipline. The parents think you ought to baby-sit for 'em. The kids walk around and do anything. You have to go over and reprimand them: Would you kindly keep your child at the table? These are the upwardly mobile who have kids.

Years ago, when parents brought their children in, it was a learning experience. They'd teach them how to act in restaurants, show them what knives and forks to use. Now all they want to do is have conversation with their friends. Oh, is Junior in your way? You're walking with a couple of plates or dishes, and Junior is running around.

I hate to say it, but I think some of them feel the kids are a mistake. They wish they didn't have them, but it was the thing to do. Here's that dollar, go leave us alone. They're just not concerned.

One of these days, if the market ever goes down some more, all these people that live on credit—boy!* They don't know what it's like to be without, not to get what they want. They just go use the plastic and get it. But if there's a crash, boy. I think some of these yuppie restaurants are starting to feel it now.

I have to like Ronald Reagan because I'm one of those who feel you should live within your means. The credit card is something you only use in a bind. I don't see how the country can survive unless they can get that deficit down. I voted for him, but then I voted for Kennedy, too. I voted for Reagan because I felt spending should be cut down. You just can't be giving and giving and giving. I don't know what they're going to do with Social Security when all these people become eligible for it. There's gonna be more people eligible than there are people making money. The government's in debt up to its eyeballs as it is.

Maybe it's just that I like people who are hard-liners. They're disciplined. They have a set of principles that they live by. Ditka, Halas, guys that are disciplinarians.† I thought Kennedy was, and I think Reagan is a guy that sets his line and stays there. He doesn't deviate, he's honest. If he was younger and a third term was allowed, I'd vote for him again.

Party lines don't mean that much to me. If I think a guy's qualified, I'd vote for him. I voted for Hart the first time he ran.

---

* The conversation took place shortly after the stock market crash of October 19, 1987.
† Mike Ditka, coach of the Chicago Bears. George Halas was their founder, owner, and coach for many years.

Did the Contragate scandal bother you?

Watergate? Oh, Oliver North. I followed most of it. I think Reagan probably knew about it, but they did a nice job of covering everything up. I'm not too sure I know as much about the Central American issue as I suppose I should. The big thing is everybody is worried about trying to get the deficit down. If they can cut down on the weaponry, it'd be great. But you still can't give everything away. I think the Russian people and the American people, there's no difference between them. It's only the difference between the heads of state and their ideologies.

Being in this business, my biggest worry is the criminal element, that somebody's gonna walk through the door and try to get what you got. I don't mind them taking what I have, but I mind if they shoot me. The older people don't seem to come out late at night. Ten o'clock and they're through.

Years ago, you could plan on people coming in here at twelve, twelve-thirty, because they had different shifts at work. We used to open up at seven o'clock in the morning. Now we don't open till eleven. Pa always used to come in for his eye-opener. They still have it in some ethnic neighborhoods, but not around here any more. Now, all they want to do is get up in the morning, work out on their exercise bike, and drink their fruit juice.

You never know what to expect any more. I'm not looking for any high-falutin' ideas. I'd just like everything to be moving along steadily and not to have any big surprises. I like to have control of most situations. Now, I just don't know.

LISA ROMANO

She's going on twenty-six. She lives with John, who comes from the same neighborhood. They have a three-year-old child. "My folks are pretty open-minded. They'd like it better if we were married, but they don't make a big stink out of it."

All her life, she's lived in this blue-collar suburb fifteen miles west of Chicago.

I don't like where I grew up. It's just the attitude of the town. It's one thing to be ignorant about things, but it's another one to be proud of your ignorance. I don't want to sound so negative about my town, but there's nothing much good I can say about it.

It's just all these sleazy little bars that stay open late. There are these sleazy-type characters that make fun of people who want to do something different with their life. They laugh at someone who has a different view from theirs. They're real closed-minded.

I always felt I had to get out of there. I looked forward to graduating from high school so I could go to college and just get free.

Ever since I was little I liked to read. You realize there's a whole world out there. My parents never talked much about the world. Now and then, they'd talk about some piece of news, like the O'Hare plane crash or the John Gacey case.* Not Vietnam.

I remember bits and pieces. I was five years old when my neighbor Eddie was killed. That was one year after the war started. It was kind of a momentous day. One of those things that burst in your head. Something changed, you know what I mean? I remember my brother born in 1966 and my mother was already nervous. She was thinking if this war drags on, her son might be fighting in it.

Vietnam is still so confusing. I don't think I know enough, I don't have the authority to say what's right and what's wrong. I've always wondered what I would do if I were a student back then. I'd like to think I would have been protesting, but who knows?

We were not very religious. We were raised Catholic, but I don't consider myself one. You don't have to be in a church to speak to God. My dad alway proclaimed himself an atheist. That got us, because we always had to go to church as children.

He and my mom have been divorced five years, and the woman he goes with is a real strong Christian. So he believes now. He got baptized at the church last Christmas. It's a real big church. I've been there for my dad's baptism and another time. It's nice.

People are always telling others about this church, spreads by

---

* John Wayne Gacey was convicted of a mass murder of boys.

word of mouth. It's amazingly big. People are directing traffic in the parking lots. Thousands belong to it. It looks like a huge convention center. Willow Creek, ever hear of it?

I like it so much. The minister speaks like he's speaking to me. It's not threatening at all. It plays uplifting type of music. It's real laid-back.

I'd never been to a church like that before. The Catholic Church is just so heavily ritual. The incense burning, the purple robes. This is completely different. In his sermon—Hybels, that's his name, right—he said some people want a fun fix instead of pure inner joy. He contrasted the two. He's into sports cars, and he talks about seeing an ad for a big fancy sports car but what he should be buying is a relationship with God. He was even joking about Jim and Tammy, making light of it. I was glad to see that, laughing at people who were a disgrace. He mentioned something about Nicaragua, but I can't remember.

I saw some documentaries on Nicaragua by people who had been down there and I remember walking out so angry at Reagan. But then I read the papers and the syndicated columnists and I've learned to take it with a grain of salt. I still believe more the way of the documentaries, but you have to watch your emotions. Not to get carried away. Because who is telling the truth?

Now, I'm back in my old neighborhood. I'm not as close to the ones I went to high school with. They're just willing to go with the flow, not much interested in anything. John plays softball, so after the game we all go to the bar, talk about the game, their jobs. The same things their parents talked about. I think there should be an outreach to the world outside their neighborhood.

John's a real Reaganite. After a few drinks, we get into big arguments about it. I've just given up arguing. He thinks that anyone who doesn't agree with Reagan is not as informed as he is. He really gets to me. They like to boast about their views as the right views and that people who get involved are dumb.

I want to get out and do something, but they think people are just a bunch of bleeding-heart liberals if they go and protest. Greenpeace or people against nuclear arms. I get mad at him when he says that, because I think that's the only way to make changes in the world. They think you're overreacting if you get passionate about it.

When you're laughed at—it's bad because I've been keeping my mouth shut for quite a while. They're not really friends any more. They're from the same neighborhood, but I'm different. I've been going on this way for three years. I've kind of been buried with a whole bunch of ashes over me. It's like this hunger inside me. I feel I'm on the verge of a change.

ANNDRENA BELCHER

She appears considerably younger than her thirty-six years. You see the small perky child even now: an air of wonder, yet a sense of knowing. Her long, dangly Indian earrings do not seem at all incongruous. She is a storyteller.

I am a child of the Appalachian mountains.

I was born in eastern Kentucky and brought up to Chicago when I was seven. My family moved up here because they needed work. Coal fields were going bust because the mines brought in a lot of machinery. That put thousands of people out of work.

I was in second grade when mother and daddy came to Chicago and got jobs. Daddy on the railroad and mother in a factory. Life started changing.

We lived in Chicago, but I'm not sure where we were at. We always said down home. When we first moved up here, we would go home once a month. Daddy would load up the car after work, we'd get a roll of baloney and a loaf of rye bread and travel all night long. Spend the weekend with our grandmas and our cousins and then come back, go to work.

My daddy says it took twelve hours, but that was driving seventy miles an hour on a good road. Just to spend the weekend, get to see your cousins, eat some biscuits and gravy, and visit. We were never settled in to being home in Chicago.

We did go back home once and stayed a year, but work was still bad. You either work for the coal industry or you don't work. My father has always been pretty rebellious politically. Would say, I don't want to kiss somebody's rear end to get a job and keep kissing it to keep it, just couldn't stand it.

My Grandpa Belcher worked in the mines since he was thirteen, when they still used ponies to haul the coal out. My Granddaddy Mullin was a coal miner, too. My dad didn't like the mines. When he said he's going to Chicago, his pa said, Get gone.

We're three girls, I'm the oldest. I was always the whine bag. Kind of melancholy and a little bit more dissatisfied. I still had a yearning for the mountains, a sense that there was where I belonged. I got it from my mother and father, I got it from my grandparents. My dad was very verbal, so he talked a lot about old times, about growing up in the coal camps, he talked a lot about poor people getting messed over, he talked a lot about social change. The pictures were real clear to me.

They worked in factories and we didn't eat together much any more, but on Sunday afternoon we'd be around the house and he'd get goin'. My dad's a great storyteller, a great joketeller, and a good cusser, too. He'd get to talking and I wanted to know those people.

For one thing, I heard lots of others say bad things about mountain people: dumb hillbilly, lazy hillbillies. I read things in the paper, so it really made me question: Who am I? Am I dumb? Am I lazy because I'm a mountain person?

There were things written in newspapers about mountain people, most of it negative: people were sitting on the stoops, people would leave work to go home in the springtime. The same thing they said about black people, the same thing they said about Native American people, the same thing they said about anybody who wasn't white, middle-class mainstream American.

Every time I'd hear somebody say something bad about mountain people, I'd think about my grandparents and I'd think, They're not stupid. They're some of the most intelligent people I know, even though they don't have a ton of formal education. They're poets and philosophers, and I like their stories.

When I got into high school, it was really hard. Very few mountain kids made it to the front door. My sister Sherry quit school when she was sixteen, because the history teacher called her a dumb hillbilly in front of the whole class. She left school the next day.

I began to see that I had to talk up about these things that are wrong. It wasn't right to just let it go by. A lot of time in class, I couldn't say what I wanted to say—to explain things about mountain people and how things got to be the way they were.

We were studying American history, we were studying the time when the big corporations were buying out the little businesses. The teacher was talking about how good it was. We were talkin' about the Pinkertons breaking up the mine strikes down in the mountains. The teacher was talkin' about it like it was a good thing. So I'm sittin' there, thinkin' about my grandfather and all the people who worked before. I felt trapped because I was too embarrassed to talk and I didn't have the words. I sat there, I turned red in the face, my stomach tightened up, and I didn't know how to deal with it.

So that made me read more on mountain history. I won a scholarship to Berea College. I wanted to go back home.

The next year, I got a scholarship in an experimental program in Uptown. I rode to school with this Native American woman and she said, "I always heard that hillbillies were drunks and the men beat their wives." I said I heard the same thing about Indians. So we began to break down the stereotypes. Same old stuff about blacks, too.

If we keep being taught the same things about each other, does it not keep us apart? As long as we're split up all over the place, scratching each other's eyes out, nobody has to worry about us over in this little neighborhood, 'cause we'll just wipe ourselves out.

My people worked real hard, made lots of money for the coal companies, and had nothing. But in that little house, my grandma Molly sat down and taught my grandfather Glen how to read and write. He started in those mines when he was thirteen. She said, "if you're gonna work in the coal mines, I want you to be able to get a better job, maybe get your bossin' papers." So he could be a supervisor or somethin'. He eventually got to be a mine inspector, so it was a little bit better.

My grandma Molly went to eighth grade, which was pretty unusual for a woman. She came from a family of fourteen kids, they played music. She played the organ, the concertina, the harmonica. She sung the old songs, mostly hymns, she was old regular Baptist. They didn't believe in the frolicky stuff, but she would sing a love song now and then. She recited poetry.

My granny Belcher had a much more tragic story. She was orphaned at five. Sort of like Cinderella, she was kicked from pillar to post. She had to do washings and ironings for people, but she yearned for learning. She'd say: Take care of your teeth, take care of your health, take care of your education.

I always had in mind to go back. It came when I was twelve. We went home one summer and I was sittin' on the front porch of my uncle's house. I was lookin' up at the mountains. It was a real pretty evening. I said, "I'm comin' back when I get through school." He says, "You're gonna move back here and stay by yourself?" Each year, see, my father would say, Come next spring, we'll go home. He meant that. But each spring would come and there wasn't any work at home. I knew that they weren't going to be able to go back. So my fantasy was that I would go back first and then maybe I could make a way for them to come back.

I finished my master's, so I could go back to the mountains and find out just what was happening. The job paid $250 a month. I had to travel five states in Appalachia, recruiting students, helping them design programs for their communities.

I felt very bitter about the coal industry. I don't think the jobs are worth the price people have to pay for their health, for the way the land has been ravaged. I don't like driving down the road and having coal trucks drive over in the middle and me feel like a powerless little thing over on my side. My daddy says he expected me to get shot for saying something against strip mining. It's a hard place to live.

When I left my parents back in Chicago, my daddy, for a graduate present, bought me an old Plymouth, paid $1,300 for it. I had $200, got on the Outer Drive and headed south. Cried, all the way to Cincinnati, till my eyes got so red and so puffy I couldn't cry any more. Then I made my way to Lexington and back home.

It was hard to leave. It's hard for me to talk about it now. I was leaving part of me here. I was leaving my mommy and my daddy and my sisters. The same thing had happened to them, only I was doing it in reverse. My grandma cried, we all cried, when we left the mountains. Here I am saying good-bye again, going back, trying to get hold of something I'd left back there, but leaving part of myself here too.

I have found a lot of what I'm looking for. I'm still lookin'. I still have the fantasy of having my family be together. But my folks have been in the big city for over twenty years now. This is their home a lot.

It's interesting to come back here and see how the city's changed, how Uptown as a neighborhood has changed. When I try to get in touch with the Appalachian community, people have been urban-removed, they're gone.

As far as this country, what hits me in my gut is that we've just gotten more removed from human feelings. We've taken a big step backwards.

I go into schools around home even and young people are talking about computers. They want to get into computers and engineering because that's where the bucks are. We're not so interested in helping other people any more. During the sixties, we were trying to make a difference. When I tell stories in the schools down here, I tell the kids to dress up like their favorite storybook character. I get them to talk about that during my performance.

One day, a bunch of these little boys came in with all this camouflage stuff. I asked them what book they had read. They said, Oh, I didn't read a book, I saw a movie. They start tellin' me about Rambo, about motorcycle gangs and killing people. We've gotten away from reading. We've gotten away from our imaginations.

We did sit around the fire, my grandma and grandpa did that. I'm right on the borderline of the generation that quit doing that. When we moved to the cities, we had people working in factories, in different shifts, so you didn't have as much time to sit around, you didn't have time on the porch to whittle and sing. You had to just get out and bust your butt.

In the mountains, we're still closer to the old ways, but it's changing here, too. With the consolidation of schools, with having to leave their farm and work in the factories, the life-style changes. You're working for somebody else to get money to buy stuff, so you're not out there being resourceful and imaginative.

There's a real race to be like everybody else. For a long time, mountain people have been told they're backwards and behind. Now it's important that we buy things and put clothes on our bodies, so that we look like anybody else in these magazines.

I notice there are more people beginning to say maybe this is going a little bit too far. They are beginning to look back. People say, I haven't told my kids about the old days. My kids come and ask me for the old photographs. I sense right now the beginning of a new swing a little bit more back . . .

There are industries beginnin' to locate in the mountains because they think they won't have to worry about people unionizing. There's been a big push away from unions, that's one change I've seen. We're the third poorest county in Virginia, people dying for jobs, so they get 'em, without unions, without benefits, to work in the sewing factories and paper mills around here.

The Vietnam War was fought by blacks and hillbillies. Good hunters, good people in the woods. People who didn't have anywhere else to go.

Around home, there just aren't the options any more. They can't come to Chicago any more, there's not the work here there once was. They can't go to Detroit, the car industry isn't what it was. Some people went to Houston, and you know they came back. And now the only option for some women is the army.

Mountain people have always been pretty patriotic. That's because they felt like they really owned the place and cared for it, and wanted to fight for that reason. But now we have this new patriotism. It's a different definition than the one I would have.

My daddy used to say this system has to burn itself out before people will say the earth is important. I have to have some clean food and some clean air. I have to have some silence. I have to be able to get out and go to the lake or see the stars or hear the wind blow.

There's a hunger for stories. There's a hunger for people to be real. We voted for Reagan because we're movie-star-struck. The reason we're image-struck is because we don't like who we are. We don't like saying we're okay as regular people.

AFTER SCHOOL

FORD SZYMANSKI

If you were to choose the archetypal young middle-class
American male, he, in appearance, would be a good bet.
He'd certainly qualify as a model in a men's fashion
magazine. He is not cool; his enthusiasm overwhelms.

He is a certified public accountant at one of the
country's largest consulting firms. He had just turned
twenty-five.

I swear to God I'd love to be president of the United States. Last
week was my birthday. I always on this day look at myself retrospectively. Have I screwed up? Have I got my shit together? I don't
know quite what else I could expect from myself, being twenty-five.
I have incredible goals for the future.

At high school in Indianapolis, they picked me as someone who
had leadership potential. I joined a fraternity. I won a Lions Club
scholarship, studied in West Germany for the summer, I graduated
from Indiana University and got a job with this company.

During my annual review at the company, one of the partners
asked what I want to do with my life. I go, "Sir, I swear to God I
want to be president of the United States." During the last election
year, Ronald Reagan was in town. I wanted to get tickets because
before, when I was younger, I shook hands with Harold Wilson of
Great Britain, and I once met Gerald Ford. I spent two hours one
morning at work trying to get tickets to hear the president. I called
Washington, the Republican National Committee, the White House.
I figured there's got to be a partner of the company who belongs to
the club where Ronald Reagan will speak. He said I could use his
tickets as long as I paid for them. I was so lucky.

The next morning I went to this thing, and here I was in the
president's presence. I think if you were the most liberal, commu-

nist, whatever person in the entire world, just to see someone who represents our nation to the world—you can hate this guy, but your heart, it just has to skip a beat.

This woman with a beautiful voice says, ''Ladies and gentlemen, the President of the United States.'' Everyone stands up and starts clapping. It's such a rush to the head. I was just excited. I mean, the man is our whole nation.

I used to like Ronald Reagan a lot, but I don't understand what he's thinking. You have to be an intelligent person to be president, to be more than a figurehead. He's got so many people working for him, but I don't think he knows what's going on. I have four staff people working for me, but if they tell me something, I've got to understand what they're saying.

I don't think Ronald Reagan's even a servant to the people any more. Everything's so crystal-clear to him. ''He's a communist, bad; he's not a communist, good.'' The Sandinistas and the contras, one's right and one's wrong. Things aren't that clear. I used to be caught up in that whole role, all the romantic aspects of it. I don't like him now, even though I used to. Oh, man, I wouldn't vote for him again.

If I were president, I'd pay more attention to the educational system. We need to have teachers who are the most respected people in the world, who educate students in the theoretical as well as the practical sides of the mind. I'd throw out a lot of the defense stuff.

I used to be really scared of Russia. A couple of months ago, something happened that really bothered me. I was in an airport and there was a woman standing in front of me. She was portly and had a round face. I thought she was from an Eastern bloc country.

She put her passport on the table, and it was a Soviet diplomatic passport. She could tell I was looking at her and she just smiled. I wanted so much to ask this woman if I could buy her a cup of coffee, just to talk to her. But I was scared. I mean she's just a person, she's not gonna stab me.

I was scared because I just saw *The Falcon and the Snowman*. The movie where these kids get involved in espionage and all that. I never wanted anything I did to be misconstrued, because I love the United States so much. But I just wanted to prove to myself that this woman is a great, great person. She might support this other government, but someone loves her and she loves someone else. She may stand for a different government, but she's loved. I wanted to be friends with her because I don't know anything about her, and that goes back to education. Why was I scared to talk to her? What could happen to me?

I was in Europe right after Chernobyl. I was there after the attack on Libya. I was down in Greece. I was in front of that McDonald's in Rome where that guy was with the machine gun. And was never scared.

I was scared of this woman. I was thinkin', All of a sudden they have my name. And they might contact me in the future and try to get me to do this . . .

Who's they?

The KGB. What bothered me is that I'm an intelligent person and I was thinking like that.

I just want to know about everything. I grew up in a very white neighborhood and went to a very white school. There's no minorities at all. The guy I was working with was black. I asked him some stupid questions, about like being black. I know his life is different and I just wanted to know. I thought he'd get mad. He laughed. He said, ''Ford, sometimes I get so sick of being around white people all the time.'' He didn't mean, I don't like you. But I had all these questions. I mean, he's just a normal guy, has the same thoughts and feelings I have, but I just don't know enough about him.

When I was a senior in high school, I had a teacher who told me there's natural differences between black and white people. He said, ''They aren't your equal.'' This was in an American public school! Indianapolis. I mean, he honestly believed it. I was seventeen and I didn't know what to believe.

My parents never, ever discussed things like this or politics. I don't think my dad even reads the paper. He was an air controller. When they had that strike, there was no way he'd ever do that. He crossed the picket line, I'm sure. He had an obligation, he had signed a contract. You have to hold true to your word, and my dad had made a promise. He also made a promise to his family that he would support those he loved. This obligation came before his work.

I have a feeling that in these last three years, I'm becoming—I don't know exactly what. I'm leaving this cloistered world I grew up in. If I didn't grow, I'd hate myself. For a long time, I never cared about growing. I would be exactly that kind of person described as a yuppie. Unfortunately. You have a professional job, you earn okay money, enough to go on vacations, buy clothes, go out to eat, have lots of friends, and no commitments.

I love taking totally opposite positions sometimes, 'cause that's the way I can learn. I would say I'm a conservative liberal (laughs). I started out as a straight conservative. It's your upbringing. A lot of times you just go from where you were born and that's what you are your whole life. I know I'm changing.

I would never do anything directly against the government. I don't think about Nicaragua too much, but if there was a war, I'd fight. I have a responsibility to my mom and my sister and the girls I go out with. I have to protect the people I love.

I can question but I don't have all the knowledge and I realize maybe I'm screwed up. There are people wiser than me.

It was sad that those Libyan children died. But we come first. If some kid's gonna die—I'd rather have the little kid next door to me living rather than the little kid in Libya a lot further away. I can live more with the death of a child there than the death of a child here.

If I was president and knew that a hundred nuclear warheads were coming directly at the United States, I wouldn't push the button, even though our whole nation would be destroyed. I'd never do it. Because then the whole world would be destroyed. If we were going to die, why, to make ourselves happy in our death, would we destroy everyone else? The world is going to evolve back again—it may take a million years, but I don't need to just go off and kill everyone. There's no reason to destroy everything.

NANCY MILES

She's twenty-three. She's an engineer working for a nonprofit group: Center for Neighborhood Technology.

She graduated from Cornell in 1985. "For a long time I wanted to be an engineer. I always wanted to work with trains, right?" (Laughs.)

"The attrition rate is enormous, people leaving engineering, especially women. There's a lot against us.

*There are engineering fraternities, all your professors are
men. There was only one woman teacher and she was on
leave while I was there.''*

She is diffident in manner and speaks softly.

Ｗe work with people in the neighborhoods to figure out how their
economy works, to develop jobs in their own community rather than
chains like McDonald's: in controlling their economic future.

When I graduated, all sorts of offers came, because companies
were looking for women engineers. I was on the dean's list most of
the time, top ten percent or something. I got offers from AT&T,
Pacific Gas and Electric—to start at $27,000. A lot of money. Much
more than I get paid now (laughs). I didn't think I'd be happy. I
think it's real hard to spend eight hours a day working on something
you don't believe in. If I went into management, I probably would
have wound up making six figures. But it wouldn't have been any
challenge.

Many of the jobs, especially large engineering firms, have contracts with the Defense Department to build rockets or communications systems, a real waste of money, so . . .

My dad is really afraid of political activity. His father had to
appear before a grand jury during the McCarthy era. Lost his job,
lost all their money, lost everything. He's very afraid.

When I got politically active, he said, ''Nancy, I know you're
doing what you believe in, but you're on somebody's list. You're
gonna find out later in life that you've been on somebody's list and
you're gonna lose your job or something's gonna happen to you.''
He thinks it's fine for me to have my beliefs, but he's real concerned
about my acting on 'em.

My mother's much more willing to encourage me. She encourages
us to do whatever we want. She was a graduate student at Northwestern when all the Vietnam protests were going on. She's not
politically active now. She's spending all her time on her career.

In engineering school, we get this constant barrage of companies
coming to hire us and telling us how much money is spent on defense
in this country. Many of them are real clear about the politics they
use to get that kind of money from the Pentagon. It's an old boys'
network. Seeing how it worked disgusted me.

I became the political conscience of the class. There were three women in our class. I was the one who would get upset when they made sexist jokes. I developed a reputation.

The men were all in fraternities. Some would agree with me at times, but then they'd say, I have to worry about myself. I have to get a good job. I have to pay back enormous debts that I've accrued. I thought, well, sure, I have to worry about myself, but what am I gonna get out of working for AT&T or McDonnell Douglas? Besides money, which I'm not gonna have time to spend, I didn't think I'd get very much. So it was a conscious decision not to work in any of these places.

During the interviews, the company would ask if you could get security clearance. Wow, I'm gonna be working at a place where the government has to know about me, know what I do, know my politics. How much of myself am I willing to give up to work in Silicon Valley?

At the time of these interviews, the South African protest had become big. In '85, there had hardly been any political activity. We helped protest against the companies when they would come and recruit. We had a small discussion group and most of my activity was outside the engineering school. We were trying to get the school to divest.

In the spring of my senior year, everything exploded. Campuses all over the country were doing it. We held daily protests of two thousand people. People were getting arrested. A lot of them were real concerned: What is this going to mean to my security clearance? They decided to do it anyway, which made me hopeful. I said, How are you gonna feel working for these companies with big investments in South Africa, now that you've registered your complaint? Most of 'em were thinking of this protest as a one-time shot.

Political involvement is real scary for some people. The first time you do it, you realize maybe it's not so scary and you wonder what holds people back. But it's uncomfortable. How are other people gonna react to them after they do it?

Summer of '86, I went to Nicaragua to work with Técnica: it's a technical assistance program for their schools, hospitals, water projects.* I worked with the Central Bank, helping to set up a system to track loans to small farmers. There were seven of us from Chicago.

---

* Ben Linder of Portland, Oregon, who was killed by the contras, was engaged in similar work.

When I got back, I needed a job. I had heard about this center. I had been looking for a place like this and hadn't found it, 'cause they don't come to campuses to recruit. I got hired in twenty minutes (laughs).

Our program is targeted at lower-income neighborhoods. Daycare centers, shelters, schools. In some of the projects, I oversee the work: assess building conditions, write specifications, recommend. I like the work because it's challenging. When I'm working at something until eight o'clock at night, it's for a reason. Right now, I'm working with Latino Youth Services in Pilsen. They're rehabbing a building and I'm designing the heating system. Teenagers, along with contractors, are doing some of the work and they're really good, learning fast.

If I were working at Grumman Aerospace until eight o'clock at night, I'd get a headache. I'd wonder what I was doing. To design a rocket?

My parents want me to go to graduate school. I think my dad gets a kick out of it, but he figures I'll get tired of it. They're worried about what's going to happen ten years from now. What kind of security do I have? And they're right. In the meantime, I support myself and actually save money (laughs).

Just last week, the FBI visited twelve people who had been with Técnica in Nicaragua. It was a coordinated effort at their workplaces. It was somewhat threatening. For the other six from Chicago, it could jeopardize their jobs.

When I got back to the office, our executive director told me about it. Half an hour later, I got a call from one of the agents. In Chicago, they used fourteen agents to talk to seven of us all at the same time. With me they used a man-woman team. She did the talking (laughs).

She told me it was an issue of national security and she couldn't discuss it on the phone. It was urgent that she speak to me. I told her I wasn't interested. She asked if she could come tomorrow. I said no. I had a lawyer call up and say if she had any questions, she could go through him.

I was certainly shocked. I was a little bit scared and then real angry. I'm lucky I chose to work at the center, because they don't care. It's nice to know I don't have to hide my politics. Some of the others are real concerned about their jobs. I'm not. I'm planning to go back to Nicaragua in a few weeks. I haven't told my father yet (laughs). I'm worried about what will happen when he sees the story about the press conference. It'll be in the *Trib* next week. It'll scare him. I need to prepare him for it.

My brother disagrees with me. My sister has become very supportive. She wants to get active again. She played a role in getting me interested in these things when I was younger. Now I've influenced her (laughs). I don't see people my age changing their views a lot. With the Iran-Contragate scandal, maybe they don't trust the federal government as much as they used to, but aside from that, no.

BOB TILLMAN

Like his father and two older brothers, he is a cement mason. He is twenty-two. His sister is a schoolteacher. He lives in a small town on the outskirts of Chicago: blue-collar.

We're in a downtown restaurant-bar frequented by young middle-management types on the rise. He and other construction workers and maintenance people are patrons as well. Their youth and singleness are the ties that bind.

Those two yuppies over there, they're startin' their own business. They're talkin' about how much money they're makin' and how they're gonna do great. See, those two guys and a girl?

They got it good. I kinda envy 'em. If they can figure out a way to make really good money without having to work hard, they deserve to make it. If they're gonna take the time and take the money to go to college, they deserve to make it easier than we do, blue-collars.

There's one word for what I do—backbreaking. Pourin' concrete, boy! So I sit around, drink two beers, go to parties. Go out on weekends. I'm kinda aware of what's goin' on. To a point.

I could've been that (he indicates the three at the bar), but I chose not to. I could still be that if I wanted to. I could go to college real easy. Probably do better than bustin' my back. But it's a fun life. Get to meet a lotta people. Go out, hit the bars. During work hours sometimes. So it isn't too bad. The money's pretty good.

I don't feel bad. I wanted to make my father proud of me, so I did what he did. He raised four kids during hard times, give us everything we ever wanted. So if it's good enough for my father, it's good enough for me.

I went to high school in Elgin, Illinois. It was an all-right school. The education was a little too easy. It was kinda bad in that sense. A lotta racial problems. Black people didn't like white people. There was a lotta Laotians there and they didn't like the black people. The Mexicans didn't like the Laotians. The white people didn't care about anything. Wanted to rule.

I work with blacks all the time. As a rule of thumb, the black people are better to me than the white people are. They're hard workers and they're really down-to-earth people and they treat me like I'm one of the guys. I'm the youngest on the job. The average guy is between thirty and forty. They all got families. Most people I work with are blacks. There's not many white people on this job, so they think they're a minority an' actin' like rulers.

A lotta my white friends are more bigatory than me. They were growin' up in families where they thought black people were not as good.

I got friends who went to Vietnam. From what I understand, it was somethin' they had to do, but none of 'em wanted to do it. If it's your country, you do what you have to do, I would say. I wouldn't protest. I wouldn't do nothin' to hurt the country that feeds me. I would probably try to get away.

I haven't found out the real reason for the war. They say it was to protect democracy, to stop communism. I can understand that. I have faith in my country.

We mostly drink and talk. We talk mainly about old times. If you're in a crowd that's really drinkin', the talk gets louder and louder and more fun. Sports always comes up. The Chicago Bears, that's always a big thing.

Most of 'em don't even vote. They're all still sowin' their wild oats. I always vote. It's my right. I voted for Reagan, all the way. He's doin' good by us. He's maybe got a short fuse, but he keeps everybody from pushin' us around. I assume, from what I hear. You never really know everything. The media don't give the whole story.

So just what I hear is what I go by. I like what he did with our problems in Iran.* And he won't let the Russians push us around.

There's one thing I don't like about Reagan. He's tryin' to get rid of the unions. That's the cause of all the strikes we been havin'. He's the cause. When he broke the air controllers, my father didn't like it. But there wasn't much Reagan could do. That other person would probably do the same thing.

If I was drafted to go to Nicaragua, I would go. I don't know if I'd like it. But I would go because it's my duty. I'd probably question why when I got over there. But I was a born fighter, that's what everybody tells me.

These kids (fifteen and under) are totally different from my generation. They dress different from the way we dressed. They got new fashions, new hairstyle. They let loose a lot more than we did. You look at a girl, she may be thirteen years old, she looks like she's twenty and dresses like she's twenty. You can't even hardly tell the difference nowadays.

I see kids ten, eleven years old swearin' worse than I ever sweared in my whole life. Talkin' to their parents like they were dogs. I know me and my peers never do that, 'cause they'd get slapped right across the face.

I'm thinkin' of a family as soon as I find the right lady. One that'll take me for me and not take anybody else when she's with me. A couple of kids, at least.

My dad said the way I could pay him back for raisin' me is for me to raise a couple of kids. That's what I'm gonna do. Payin' him back. He would have loved it if I went to college. He wanted me to. I coulda went. He woulda paid for it. But when I was in school, I didn't like it that much. I'm more of a physical person. I wanted to get out and do things and get it right away.

Everybody said I was smarter than my sister and I shoulda went to college. But that was my decision. I kinda wish I went to school. It woulda been an easier life. After I come home from work and I'm barely able to walk, I kinda wish I went to college.

---

* The conversation took place before the Iran-contra scandal broke.

KAPHY LONG

At the time of this conversation, she along with the other flight attendants of Trans World Airlines had been on strike for six months.

I'm a very quiet person, on the shy side. But I'm stubborn. I come from a conservative German background where honesty and hard work were the top priorities.

I had wanted to travel from the first time we had geography lessons in school. I even wanted to be a foreign exchange student, but my grades weren't good enough. The idea of being a flight attendant was very attractive to me. One day I saw an ad in the Albuquerque paper. I didn't think I'd get the job because I was nineteen. I was hired.

You have a certain amount of respect as a flight attendant. Wearing a uniform, being in charge. The travel was a plus. I had never been out of Albuquerque before.

I'd never worn makeup. We had to stand in front of the class and let your fellow trainees critique your physical appearance. It was the most humiliating experience I'd ever gone through.

They have a lot of silly rules and regulations to see if you're a dependable type. We even had an oven check one day in training. They would check to see if the ovens in your living center have been cleaned properly. I stayed up until midnight scrubbing the oven. They fired five people out of my group because their ovens did not meet specifications.

One day our instructor said, "I want you to wait out front while I call for taxicabs to drive out to the airport." It was a long wait. We got tired, so we sat on a curb around the corner. She chewed us out and told us she was thinking of firing us, because she had instructed us to *stand in front of the building.*

It's like military training. We all went through grooming checks, where everybody's hair was cut the same way. We all had the bubble hairstyle. Had to wear the same color basic nail polish. We all got

DuBarry makeup. We were even regimented on what jewelry to wear. I had to get approval to wear my class ring on the airplane.

At that time, you had to wear a girdle. I'd never worn a girdle in my life. At nineteen I didn't need one. They used to come around and pinch your fanny to see if you had a girdle on. It's a little more lenient now.

I was brought up to where if your boss said this is what you did, that's what you did. You didn't question authority, that's the way I was brought up. TWA liked that kind of person.

I came to Chicago in 1968. I roomed with the lady I'd gone through training with. The pay was so low that we qualified for food stamps. She absolutely hated the job. I loved it.

The first night we landed in Columbus or Dayton. I'd been on the plane for maybe twelve, fourteen hours. The captain said, "You don't have to report tomorrow until eleven." I'm sitting in the hotel room thinking, They're paying me to sit here and watch television. How lucky can you get?

After the first five years, the novelty wore off. We call it flight-attendant syndrome. All of a sudden you feel in a rut: you find yourself apologizing for a lot of things you aren't responsible for. You're overwhelmed by passenger complaints. And it's not exciting to go to that little pizza place with the captain any more.

We were always a union shop. I went to the meetings because I was forced to pay union dues. I wanted to know what I was getting for my dues. I wasn't a real pro-union person. My feelings about unions were a vision of the teamster, the truckdriver, the longshore-man loading the boat, musclebound. Youse guys better give me what I want in my contract or we'll break some heads around here.

As time went on, I noticed our officials weren't that good. I remember in the early seventies, during a contract negotiation, our union leader stood up: "This is it. I'm tired of negotiating for you girls—you *girls* had better take this package, because it's the best we're gonna do for you." Lump it, you know.

I sign on the dotted line, and before I could get to the mailbox, I see in the company newsletter a picture of our union official shaking hands with the president of the TWA. A deal had been struck. That threw me completely off. I felt the union was in cahoots with the company.

About this time, five or six flight attendants got together and formed our own union—Independent Federation of Flight Attendants. IFFA. We joined. Who can understand better our work force than flight attendants themselves? They get the same salaries we get. For the first time, I started feeling good about the union.

During the late seventies, I started to hear the repeated lies the company would come out with. Before any contract, they'd have a letter-writing campaign sayin' times are bad, we aren't making any money. You *girls* have got to give us some money back. We can give a little raise to the pilots or mechanics, but you *girls* have to do your part. So we'd give. And a couple of weeks later, somebody in the company would get a big golden parachute.

My husband was a union steward when I met him. He'd worked on the ramp as a baggage loader. A ramp rat. He was with the Machinists, IAM. Now he's a reservation agent, so he can't belong.

Since the agents don't have a union, on his own, he handled a lot of grievances for agents who had lost their jobs. He was their rep all over the United States. He helped forty-two people get their jobs back. He eventually got fired for these activities. He's back with the company. He was off work for nine months. We had to go to court, get a lawyer. It cost us $30,000 to get him his job back. A year's salary. That was an eye-opener.

When he'd tell me this agent got fired for this, this, this, I'd always say, ''He must have done something.'' I always felt you had to be guilty of something: the company would treat you fairly if you did follow the rules. It must have been something wrong they did to bring themselves to management attention.

I've changed a hundred percent. My attitude toward unions has risen. In the old days, if management told me to stand on my head, that's what Kaphy Long does. I was nominated for Flight Attendant of the Year. I have had a perfect attendance fifteen years out of the eighteen I've been flying. I did everything by the book. When I was nominated, they had a dinner for me. The supervisor said: You have a lot of positive passenger letters, you have excellent attendance, but you're never gonna win the award. You aren't social enough with the high muckety-mucks, you don't come into the office and chit-chat with us. I felt my job was to chit-chat with the passengers, not to brown-nose management.

My whole attitude toward the job has changed. The next time I go back, I will no longer run up and down the aisles and work as hard as I can to get a service finished because I feel sorry for the passenger in the front row. I will do it as leisurely and politely as I can, because TWA doesn't care if them in the front row gets served or not.

Before, I would give up my own meal. If someone ordered some dietary special and I didn't have it in coach, I would go to first class and make something up. I would take bits of food from the captain's tray and put together a dinner. I was thinking about this passenger who saved up maybe all year to go on his vacation. I won't do those things any more. I won't give that extra that made me perhaps a little better than the average flight attendant. Oh, I've changed.

Millie has gotten in trouble with management for years. She's a flamboyant type who abhors rules and regulations. She'd come on the airplane with a bandanna on her head and pretend she was Butterfly McQueen. She washed her hair once under the faucet in the galley to show that it could curl in minutes. She was always doing off-beat things. I felt she should have been disciplined.

At a union get-together, I saw her use all that energy she had on the plane, in defying silly rules, toward getting our jobs back. My attitude toward her has done a 180-degree turn. I have so much admiration for that same energy I scoffed at before.

I felt that Jill was too forceful, too pushy. So I found out in being with her in the last strike, you have to outspoken, aggressive, to stand up for what you believe.

I feel I'm becoming more like Jill and Millie. I am determined you have to speak out, you have to stand up for yourself. All of a sudden here in Chicago, I'm one of the five or six people who has turned into a leader. That's a real shock to me, who was always the quiet one who went along. All of a sudden, I'm having people call me up and say, "Kaphy, what do you think we should do about this?" It's flooring me.

Any mailings my husband gets from the company, I go through with a fine-tooth comb.

I would try to talk to the new kids. A lot of them were promised that the old kids, us, would be gone. Usually, when you start up at an airline, you're at the bottom of the seniority list. Anytime there's a layoff, you're the one that's gone. These new people coming to TWA realized they were working to lock us out and they'd be senior employees. They *are* different from what we were, I'm afraid. They aren't as sympathetic to their fellow workers. It's even more than that.

Some we'd hire, just before the strike. I'm thirty-seven, they'd be nineteen. We'd be working a service. I'd look up and they're taking a nap in first class. I'd say, "Hey, we've still got people to serve." I don't have to tell you they have no allegiance to unions.

Right now, they're breaking my union and crossing my picket line.

You know who have been doing the most fighting and sticking together in our union? Black women. Here in Chicago, black flight attendants have been our strongest core. They have been able to handle the negatives of being out on strike for six months a lot better than their white counterparts. We've had all kinds of suicides and attempts, all Caucasian. Maybe their background gave them the inner strength to handle it.

People have lost their homes. It's broken up marriages. So when someone says the company is nice—"You don't know how good we really are"—you bet I question it.

I'm more aware of the political scene than I was before. I've started reading the paper a lot more closely, checking up on other strikes in other industries. We were out marching with the steelworkers. I would never thought of doing that six months ago. When I heard of the PATCO* strike I was appalled, I assumed Reagan was right. I'm just ashamed that I didn't get out there and walk with them.

I'd say I've changed in the last six months more than I have in the last ten years. My folks are just amazed. My mother keeps writing and saying, "This doesn't sound like you." It's not that they're against it. It's just that they're amazed I'm so different.

My husband is so proud of me, he's just bursting at the seams. "You finally understand what I meant all these years, don't you?" He would sit up late in the night, typing letters. I'd say, "Oh, come on, it's not gonna do any good." Now, I'm the one sitting down at the typewriter at two o'clock in the morning: We've got to get this done, we'll stick together.

Know what he said the other day? "You have become me. We've had a switch here." (Laughs.) "I've toned down through fifteen years of marriage and suddenly you're the rabble-rouser."

> POSTSCRIPT: *Flight attendants won a major legal*
> *victory in their battle against Trans World Airlines on*
> *May 26, 1987, when the U.S. Court of Appeals for the*
> *Eighth Circuit ordered the reinstatement of up to 1,500*
> *former strikers from the ranks of the Independent*

* Professional Air Traffic Controllers Organization.

Federation of Flight Attendants. Still pending is an IFFA suit against TWA charging the company with bad-faith bargaining and sex and age discrimination. If the union wins that case, all the IFFA strikers could ultimately be reinstated.

TERRI HEMMERT

She's thirty-eight, a disk jockey in Chicago "because I love rock music, political talk, sometimes funny, sometimes serious."

She's from Piqua, Ohio, "just a little town near Dayton. Rock was my one link to the outside: R&B stuff, Elvis . . . I was in fifth grade.

"What really kicked it off was the Beatles in '64. People were depressed, Kennedy's assassination, all of a sudden these four guys from England came over. They were good, high-energy, safe, not quite as filthy as some parents thought.

"The civil rights movement is what got me interested in politics. I was an R&B fan. I loved black music and grew up with it. Gospel music. When I got old enough to realize blacks couldn't do things I was allowed to do, I got mad. Plus I wasn't allowed to do things my brother could do. I was athletic and wasn't allowed to play sports.

"I was hooked on radio. I heard a station down in Nashville that would broadcast R&B. I was the typical kid that had the radio glued to the ear. The thing parents feared most: the kid whose brain was gonna turn to mush. But it was the link to something outside this small town.

"Rock was something universal, something you understood. If you went to California to visit relatives, the

*kids in California knew the same songs. Your parents
didn't. Maybe it was something tribal—but it was real
exciting stuff."*

*Her listeners comprise "the upper end of the baby boom,
twenty-five to thirty-four ..." She's on the air from 6:00 to
10:00 A.M.*

If I were thirty-eight in 1964, trying to talk to eighteen-year-olds,
it wouldn't work. My parents' music was big bands and the Mills
Brothers. You go to a Rolling Stones concert today, you don't see
parents dropping kids off. They're going, too, 'cause they were Rolling Stones fans in 1964. Rock is the generational link.

This is the generation that was in the Vietnam War protests when
we were in college. Of course some people have moved away from
that, consider it naive, part of their past. But there are still a lot in
that age group really concerned. That's why the movie *The Big
Chill* turned me off.

Some people hear "Born in the U.S.A." and think it's red, white,
and blue Sylvester Stallone stuff. You'll notice these people never
go past the first line. That song is about Vietnam vets and the
turmoil they go through here. The polls indicate that an overwhelming majority of the young admire Reagan and back him on anything. Yeah, I know that's out there. But I deal a lot with college
and high school students. They might be the minority but they're
very active. You never hear about them. You always hear about the
kid who wants to get the degree, go into business, and get rich.

I don't even know if it was in the majority in the sixties. That
other stuff was goin' on in the sixties, too. There were people who
didn't care about the war. They just wanted to make some bucks.
They just didn't want to get their rear ends sent over to Vietnam
(laughs). And it was hip. We get a lot of college listeners. They tend
not to be so much the jock fraternity, sorority type. There are some
people listen to me that like Reagan. So they might say, Shut up
and play the records. I'm not sayin' everybody agrees with me.

I see a lot of similarities between now and the sixties. But the
perception is real different. When I was in school in the sixties, it
was on the news every night—unrest on the campus. There's not
that confrontation. The stuff they're doin' now isn't news. People

338

assume that means nothing's going on. Talk of apathy on the campus makes me sick. I think if you say it enough, people are gonna believe it (laughs). People are gonna get apathetic.

People are attracted to different styles. Some people like my show because I do talk about the stuff. Some people hate my guts because I talk about the stuff. Rock fans don't always agree on politics. I'm not trying to paint a picture of some kind of unity or somethin'. But there's more interest and activity out there than people see.

Sometimes I get a little nervous when someone gets too preachy and moves away from music. It's like reading a pamphlet. But I think Bruce and John Mellencamp move people. Music has the ability to more than inform people.

A phenomenon I've seen with college students is a sort of nostalgia about the sixties. They look up to the sixties as being really Nirvana. Some kind of happening time when things really mattered more than they matter now. Whereas, things really *do* matter now.

College students back then, they thought Nixon was cool and they liked LBJ, so they were no different than the kids that like Reagan now. When things got hairy, when people got drafted, when they were losing boyfriends and brothers, they became involved. Do I see a possible parallel? I sure do.

I don't think everybody listened to the lyrics in the sixties either. I think sometimes we get too sentimental about the sixties. And we short-sell the eighties.

I don't think lookin' back too much is healthy. Sort of like they lost touch with that part of them that cared about somethin' other than their career. You become jaded and say, Yeah, when I was twenty, I felt that way, but not any more. Now I'm more realistic and blah-blah-blah. There's that emptiness, that hollowness.

There's also a sense of powerlessness when you're not active. There's a sense of—I can't help the way things are, I have no control of the world around me. I think more active people feel less helpless.

I don't think anybody's born an activist. Certain things happen to us and influence us. Some very personal things and some media-type things. If Ronald Reagan sat down and listened to a U2 album, I don't think he would change. But some kid, who's maybe nineteen, twenty years old, just starting to feel out things, they hear this song and—''I want to do something about it.''

Something happened to me—this is the late sixties—when Kent State occurred. I was going to Elmhurst College, out here in Republican Du Page County. Kent State shocked everybody. Every college student felt it could have been them. I knew Kent State was not Berkeley. For that to happen at Kent State was a real shock. I remember somebody asking a bunch of us if we'd go speak to this high school youth group. We were thinking there was solidarity between high school and college students, 'cause they're only a couple of years apart. We're not talking about a huge generation gap. I went out that night, we thought people were gonna say, "Oh, that's awful!" We heard these kids sayin', "They shoulda gotten more than four. They shouldn't have been there in the first place. They got what they deserved." First it was a yelling match, and finally I said, "Time out! Let's talk about why this happened." By the end of the night—I'm not saying we worked miracles—these kids who came in with this attitude left saying, Let's get together again. What should we read? Give us a list.

I think there's always that potential there. I think there's always that mistake of writing them off. My college friends, they were writing them off, saying, Aw, these bunch of conservative kids, they're livin' with their parents in Elmhurst, da-ta-ta. I was thinkin' we weren't too far from that a few years ago either.

There's that fear. Sometimes it paralyzes people, sometimes it gets their juices flowing. That's where rock music comes in as a force. It can't change people but it can make them active, speak out and do things. I like people to figure out where they fit in. They might not agree with me one hundred percent, but I like to fire them up a little bit, goose them, encourage them. If I was just talking politics, I wouldn't be where I am now. It's because I'm playin' rock records.

POSTGRADUATE

MAGGIE KUHN

"I'll be eighty-two this coming Monday."

She is grand convener of the Gray Panthers, a national organization militantly concerned with the rights of the elderly. Its campaigns have cut across generations.

"I wish that people would not always put themselves down, fearing their own lack of power. The empowerment of the powerless is a beautiful thing.

"With the best of intentions, there are some who are doing things they say are 'for our own good.' Employers know what is best for employees. The doctor makes a decision for the nurses and for his staff and for the patient. He is not all-wise, but he becomes all-powerful. It is a gross misuse of power."

Though she appears frail, her manner, her voice, are vibrant. Her energy is astonishing; as is her schedule. "I am going to Hopkinsville, Kentucky, this afternoon. Then I'm flying to Toledo to try to raise some money. Then I fly to San Francisco to do an all-day program at the University of California..."

I was going to be sixty-five in August of 1970. I was working for the United Presbyterian Church. In the spring, my boss said, ''I understand that you have a birthday coming up. You know the rule: people retire at sixty-five. We'll ease things for you. Why don't you take it easy now?''

He was gracious about it, but I was really upset. I was doing a lot of social-action work. I wanted to help in the struggle. I remember I went into my office, closed the door, and cried. I couldn't stop.

One of the men couldn't understand: "You'll get your salary till the end of the year. We appreciate what you've done."

Then came anger. I became more mad than sad. If that's the way it is, I'm just gonna work on my own agenda on company time. I wrote a memo to five of my friends in the same fix: What are we going to do about it? We decided we would not abandon each other. We sent out working papers to all the retired people we could think of. We got an immediate response.

We quickly assembled about a hundred, ready to march and kick up our heels (laughs). Some of us got ourselves arrested for demonstrating at draft boards. We had put our warm old bodies on the line to help the young resist the draft. The Gray Panthers was formed, a coalition of old and young.

An ironic touch has been added during these past ten years. Our life-cycle has lengthened in every decade, yet we are seeing early retirement more and more frequently. At fifty, fifty-five. That's the *au courant* phrase these days: early retirement. In some cases, it's a euphemism for being fired.

It may be a case of wanting a younger person. Or they may just do away with the job. The job is robotized or faded out. They occur more frequently these days with plant mergers and closures. The job is eliminated. Of course, for people this age it is difficult to find work again.*

They declare the thousands they retire every year as waste folk. They go through the motions of a retirement club, a Fifty-plus or Twenty-five-plus Club. They give them a great dinner every year at company expense. There are favors and fancy programs and somebody sings and dances. The conversation makes you heartsick. Who's alive? Who's sick? Do you remember when? Old Charlie greets you. Mary and Della get together and talk about the old days. They're not talking about the present. It's kind of a banquet of ghosts.

People who have had power, when they become powerless, are really tragic, particularly the men. We just allow ourselves to be conditioned by a society so we become as important as we're supposed to be. It becomes a self-fulfilling prophecy.

---

* "They made me an offer I couldn't refuse," said my neighbor, a middle manager at a leading accounting firm. He didn't crack a smile. He was "offered" early retirement. "They needed younger blood." He is fifty-four. His optimism undiminished, he spoke of vast possibilities as a "consultant." As he reached for the drink, his hand trembled slightly.

When I was forced to retire, I was still technically on the payroll. The xerox machine was down the hall. That's terribly important. You don't build a movement without a mimeograph machine. I had access to all these things and a WATS line. I've told many people since then, when you're forced to retire, before they really shaft you, organize. Nobody can fire us, make us slow down. We can really raise Cain about the war, social injustice, anything.

Reaching sixty-five, for my five friends and me, became a crossroads. We said, We have nothing to lose, so we can raise hell. Nobody can stop us. It was a transcendence. That's the whole idea of the Gray Panthers. You couldn't care less about Golden Buckeye discounts. Old people get fifteen or twenty percent off. I call that novocaine. They give that to old Americans instead of a guaranteed annual wage or a decent pension system. They numb us with a few little goodies.

I had an American Express card all the time I was working. I had airline travel cards. After I retired, it took me six months to get a card. The old and the young are not good credit risks. We both have trouble getting jobs. I'm not talking about the kiddie tycoons, the yuppies, who seem to be the only ones we hear about. There's that flaccid middle that's still in control. They have the power. The big challenge is to bring the generations together.

In the last five years, there's been a contrived conflict between the old and the young. AGE, Americans for Generational Equity, has been set up to affirm the rights of the young people who are being shafted by the old people. We're told the old have never had it so good and the young are being victimized. The charge is that the old are getting too many benefits; the young have to pay out of their earnings a very large proportion out of their salaries. Of course it's a challenge to the Social Security System. What we're saying is that the generations have much in common and need each other. The antagonism between the two is contrived.

I sense a new public awareness of the class divisions in our society, too. Ronnie is the perfect example. He's rich and he's old, but he doesn't identify with people who are old. Old people who are rich are not deemed old.

With all these attacks on the old, people have had to get on the stick and fight. There is more organizing than ever these days, even among doctors. Reagan is going to put on his old boots and ride off into the sunset and off the set.

A friend of mine describes our American society as rampant

ennui. Twenty-five years ago, gerontologists said the way to success-fully age was to disengage. Many people in old age did just that. Most are not gonna rock the boat, even though they have nothing to lose by rocking the boat.

Society tells you that after you've worked hard, it's time to play. You deserve it. It's novocaine, to keep you out of any position of influence and power. By the year 2020, the year of perfect vision, the old will outnumber the young. People over sixty-five will out-number people under twenty-five. If the majority of people are disengaged, who's gonna do the work? If most of us will live in age-segregated communities, like Sun City, living in a leisure world of kiddieland, how will our society survive?

I'm not despairing and I'm not cynical. This is a revolutionary time. I've traveled hundreds of thousands of miles in the past few years, crisscrossing the country. I see all kinds of people getting together. I see a gradual—in some cases sudden—recognition of our potential.

THE PUBLIC EYE

CHIEF ANTHONY BOUZA

Since 1980, he has been chief of police in Minneapolis.

Mention of his name in the corridors of City Hall brings forth a curious smile, not at all unfriendly; much as word of the Picasso sculpture might evoke in Chicago: something different.

In the anteroom of his office, his secretary offers coffee. There's a five-minute-or-so wait while his business with another visitor (I was about to say guest) is concluded.

"It's completely open-door. The previous chiefs had a buzzer on the door. He removed it. He'll see anyone who comes—even you. He doesn't differentiate between quote, important people and unimportant people. If a council member comes into the office, he sees him. If a person from the streets comes in—a bag lady—he'll see her. You don't have to have an appointment. All the saints and angels in heaven must have been with me when I got this job. It's been an education all the way through. I love 'im."

I believe in the populist idea: total accessibility. I think this business of screening calls is absolute nonsense. Self-important, pompous bullshit. Anybody comes to the door gets to see me. My number's in the phone book. Citizens call me at home at all hours of the day and night. A public servant is a public servant. Why should that be a radical idea?

"I was born in Spain. I came to this country as an impoverished immigrant at the age of nine. My father shoveled coal into the bellies of ships. I was fifteen when he

died. My mother was a seamstress. We experienced
tremendous poverty. This country educated me, nurtured
me, cared for me, made me rich. I wanted to become an
altruist when my belly was full. I'm not giving it all back.
I'm giving some of it back. I was a feckless youngster,
stumbling around in a series of dead-end jobs in the
garment center, sweeping, packing, heading nowhere. I had
very low self-esteem. I'm driven more by fear of failure
than by any promises of success. My mother said, 'Your
sister married a cop and if Henry can be a cop, you can be
a cop.' So I studied hard and became a New York cop on
January 1, 1953, after three years in the army.

"I had failed at every single thing I had ever tried. So it
was a revelation. I thought, I'm never gonna get by on
charm and good looks, so I studied hard and worked. I was
going to school, learning about the law, the Constitution,
how to listen, how to speak, how to write.

"I went from patrolman to detective. I worked all over,
black Harlem, Spanish Harlem, I could speak Spanish.
They used me all over the place. I worked on up from the
ranks. Sometimes a headquarters brat, a Svengali, a speech
writer, somtimes in command situations. I commanded a
division in East Harlem. I became chief of police of the
Bronx for four years."

A police job gives you a ringside seat on the greatest show on earth. You're looking at the human animal in disarray: drunk, in tears, assaulted, murdered, raped, all the awful dishabille that attends the human condition. You're looking at the underbelly of the beast: a fractious beast that needs to be controlled at all times. You become sympathetic to the victims. You become very unsympathetic to the criminals. You're always looking at the darker side of human nature; the dark side always exposed. The rest of the citizens don't. It makes you cynical and suspicious.

It also makes you very insular. The police world is hermetically sealed. We repeat each other's myths. We only talk to each other. The cops are not communicating with the outside world and never have. We learn our own things. You discover you can't talk to civilians.

When I was a young cop, I used to love to sit around with my friends and talk about police work. The cops all said, You're crazy —those people don't know what you're talking about. Well, the cops were right (laughs). In no time, you discover you can't talk about what you see. But I think all this self-importance, self-protectedness, is bullshit.

> "I spent twenty-four years in the New York City Police Department. I left following a tremendous controversy over my handling of the Yankee Stadium incident. A bunch of black and Hispanic kids acted up and bothered a lot of important people going into the stadium that night. There was a terrific ruckus. The press made a big scandal out of it. I was criticized. I fought back, got involved in a public wrangle with the police commissioner, and was exonerated.
>
> "I left in disgust to become number two in the subway police. I served there three years until my boss ran afoul of Mayor Ed Koch. Then, it was a question of making me the chief or firing me. Koch in his whimsical fashion fired me.
>
> "I should have looked elsewhere long ago. I was too safe, warm, and comfortable. I was a coward. I was so glad Koch forced me to do what I should have done in the first place, that is, take control of my life. So I applied to Dade County, Florida, Santa Barbara, Minneapolis, other cities.
>
> "In Minneapolis, 1969, a couple of blacks acted up—a couple of stores, a little looting. It really spooked the Scandinavian community. The president of the police union came forward, said, I can save you. They elected him mayor. He was re-elected. A tremendous spoils system, big raises, bloated staff. The public recoiled and booted him out. His successor served, much like the other. They went back and forth from 1970 to 1980.
>
> "The department was unbelievably screwed up. One supervisor for every employee. No women, no minorities, no efficiency, no cops hired from '76 to '80. Out of control.

When Donald Fraser became mayor, he undertook a search for a new police chief. I responded to an ad. It was as simple as that.

"Minneapolis is a self-contained community. It is not a crossroads. There is no tremendous number of arrivals and departures. It's Protestant, agrarian, very conservative, yet very decent. Liberal in political tradition, conservative fiscally."

The same problems exist here as in every city. In 1968, we had a record number of crimes. White flight. So the city is now becoming the repository of problems: teenage blacks and Native American males, homeless, migrants from other cities, seeking jobs, winding up on welfare, winding up in jail. Here I am, the forty-eighth chief of police. The first outsider. The traditional cops hate me. Just read the latest edition of their paper: Eastern leftist, liberal, no police experience, crazy.

I am a very, very strict law-and-order advocate. Last year we made a record number of arrests for street crime: 7,900. When I arrived they were giving out 13,000 citations. Now, it's 40,000. I'm always pushing them to make arrests. I'm one of the toughest law-and-order advocates in the country. It has to be done *within the law.*

A black man committed this awful crime. He's a monster. Terrific. Attack the monster. I have no problem with attacking a monster. This guy ordered a young white girl killed. I said, He's a monster. Let's destroy him. Let's also ask, Where did he come from? How did we help shape that monster? What is our complicity? Are we like the German people and the Nazis? He's the Nazi but we are the German people.

Let's string him up, no problem. How was he shaped? How are we responsible for his creation? We consign blacks to this life of criminality and violence and abuse and alcoholism and unemployment and illiteracy—and when they respond predictably, we say Gee.

I've arrested my wife five times. She's been to jail. If she breaks the law, she gets arrested, just like anybody else. We are servants of the law, not its masters. The law applies to everyone rigorously.

We had six women on the force. Now we have seventy-six. We have more than doubled the blacks and Native Americans in the department. I have repeatedly moved for the dismissal of charges against people I thought were unjustly arrested. That gets me into lots of trouble. I have upset the normal progression. One of my deputy chiefs was a sergeant. I tapped him as number two. That offends their sense of order.

A police chief makes one important decision when he takes over. Is he gonna serve the people or is he gonna serve his colleagues? You can't do both. If you serve your colleagues, you give them wage increases, promotions, you make their lives comfortable and convenient. You don't work them Friday, Saturday nights. You see that they get all kinds of protection in their contract.

We've grown up believing the force exists for the comfort and convenience of its members. I say it exists to serve the people. So I constantly inconvenience them, chide them, discipline them, and hold them accountable to serve the people better. I'm popular with the people but extremely unpopular with the cops. Both of them are right.

I meet with the cops fairly often. The climate continues to be hostile. Our roll call yesterday wound up in a shouting match. Yes, it was really awful.

Cops are tremendous physical heroes. They have great physical courage. They'll go into burning buildings, face a withering hail of bullets. But they have no moral courage to speak of. You take a room full of cops: they're all saying the job sucks, the jigs are psycho, we're all goin' to hell in a handbasket, it's all fucked up, nobody knows what they're doing. You think any of them would say, Wait a minute, the country is at peace, my family is well fed, I'm being well cared for? No. They'd rather a hundred times go into a blazing building . . .

As for the country, I honestly believe we are observing a decline of the republic. There's a major shift in American values, between the haves and the have-nots, the rich and the poor. We now speak of an underclass. We are screwing the poor people. The family is disintegrating. The divorce rate has tripled. The drug culture among the young is growing. Television is fucking up the country completely, making us more violent and more druggy. The Sistine Chapel ceiling of American creativity is the thirty-second television commercial. That's where America's genius is concentrated. What are they telling us to do? Consume, look after number one, pamper yourself. Your wife isn't pneumatic enough, get yourself a pneumatic wife, trade her in.

We see our children rushing around for structure, for discipline. They join cults. They're looking for direction in their lives.

The police chiefs of major cities asked me to give a speech last June in Salt Lake City. On any subject I wanted. I spoke on the coming holocaust.

I predicted that we would have rioting, pillaging, looting, killing, and burning in the streets of our cities before the end of the century. Simply because of the condition we have visited upon the black citizens and the poor. Nobody talks about the Catholic bishops' pastoral letter on social justice. It's become one of the great irrelevancies of our age.

They agreed with me. Nobody disputed it.

When I first started out, I was at odds with most of the other chiefs. Now I'm much more in tune with them. I think I know why. As whites abandon cities, they're being taken over by blacks. Look at the large cities in the United States. A good number have black mayors, whose white police chiefs, of conservative instincts, have to tailor their jobs to suit the mayor. So the chiefs have become more liberal while the cops are extremely conservative.

The Miranda decision served to professionalize the police. The police world when I entered it was corrupt and brutal. Under the weight of the William O. Douglas decisions, the police have become more efficient and much more professional. And much more educated. In Minneapolis, we require two years of university training and a licensing exam. Our standards are very high.

Yet the peer pressure is unbelievable. Young cops want to be accepted by their colleagues. It's easy to sacrifice Bouza. Fuck him, he's a screwball, yes, I agree with you.

I have told the mayor this is my last term. I have twenty-two months to go, and I intend to look for another job. You can't stay too long. There's a thin line between stability and stagnation. I have brought stability to this agency. I'm now in danger of bringing stagnation to it. It needs another person.

And what our country needs is an agonized national debate. That's how America solves its problems, not with demagogues giving you the answer. Why are we having so much crime? Why so much violence? What about the underclass? What about the division of wealth? Is capitalism the best system ever invented for the fueling of wealth? Indisputably, yes. Is it the most equitable method of distributing wealth? Indisputably, no.

We've got to think the unthinkable. This is a country that doesn't like to think the unthinkable. Is Fidel Castro better for the Cuban people than Fulgencio Batista? I think, yes, he's better for the mass of the people. Is he better for America? No. Batista allowed us to go there and have a good time and he made a playground for us. I think the American candidate has to be Batista. But the Cuban candidate has got to be Fidel Castro. These are things we don't want to think or talk about. The obvious answer is to launch a profound national debate as we did in the civil rights struggle, the Vietnam War, the feminist movement, the environmental battle. Out of this will come a distillation—something original, perhaps.

I would like to be chief of police. I'll probably apply for jobs. If nothing happens, I'll go to Cape Cod, build a house, and look at the waves. I see myself as a slug on the planet, going from rock to rock, another soldier in the battle. A grunt in the trenches.

ERICA BOUZA

She is Chief Bouza's wife.

They have been married thirty years and have two sons, twenty-six and twenty-three. She designs jewelry: "It's my craft."

She was born and educated in England and has been in the United States more than thirty years. "It's a wonderful country for people like myself. For the poor, there is absolutely no chance. It's time we did something about it. I totally support the Catholic bishops' pastoral letter where they call poverty in this country a social scandal."

I've been arrested five times. I'm considered somewhat of a freak because I'm the police chief's wife. I would march with my placard, hoping that the police wouldn't see me. If I saw a policeman, I would hide behind my sign. But they always saw me and they said,

Aha, there she goes, the crazy wife of the police chief. The police all hate my husband, so they think I'm exactly what he deserves. I'm his millstone (laughs).

I went to my first demonstration in October of '83 at Honeywell. The demonstrations are always early in the morning, at six o'clock. It's wonderful, because I'm not doing anything at six anyway, so why not demonstrate?

The first one I went to, we sat in front of the doors at Honeywell and didn't let people in. I was so nervous. It was as though it were happening to someone else, it wasn't happening to me. I did it because I feel that we're going to have a nuclear war if we don't do something about it, and it will be the end of us all.

There's a group called the Honeywell Project, which has been in existence around eighteen years. They planned the demonstrations. Honeywell is making part of the nuclear warhead. It's also making cluster bombs. We'd like to see Honeywell stop making merchandise of war and start making merchandise of peace. We don't want to see anybody lose their job. We'd like to see a conversion. I truly believe it's possible. They would lead you to believe that they're forced to take these contracts. In actual fact, they lobby for them.

I didn't know any of the police. It was all very new to me. It was strange, it was lonely, and it was terrifying. The man who arrested me subsequently became my husband's aide. I've never had the nerve to ask him if it was a promotion or not.

In the first demonstration I was in, we sat right in front of the doors of Honeywell and didn't let people in to work. It was a very difficult thing to do. As they came through, we were sitting on the ground. They looked terrified. I was shocked that we should have been so intimidating.

There were maybe seven hundred, eight hundred pickets. There were about 133 arrests. They're white middle-class people. I think it's only the white middle class who have the luxury to be involved in the peace movement. The poor people are too involved in their own problems.

"I was brought up to believe that I had to marry by a certain age, reproduce by a certain age, and keep the house clean. It took me years to realize that I didn't have to wear white gloves when I went to the city. Or wear black shoes

and a black pocketbook. It takes a while to get over these things.

"I'd been talking about peace for years, but not doing anything. I was ready because we'd moved to a new city. My children were more or less out of the house. So I had the freedom, I had the time."

Tony knew I had been thinking about it. I don't think he thought I'd actually go through it. I think he thought I wouldn't have the nerve. He feels it's an act of conscience. I'm not selling drugs to children. I'm not murdering anybody. But he would never say don't do it. I wouldn't marry a man who—or I wouldn't stay with him.

I was terrified the second time, because I had been to court. I pleaded guilty. A lot of peace people plead not guilty, because they see it differently. I pleaded guilty because I broke the law. I trespassed. They pleaded not guilty because they spoke of a higher law, necessity. They wanted a jury trial. If you have a jury trial, you can make a statement in court. A lot of them are very religious, I'm not. There are priests and nuns, who've become my very good friends.

It was within six months of my first demonstration. I was really uncertain what to do. I was on probation. This judge wanted to fine us, and we refused to pay our fine. It was twenty-five dollars. We wanted to do community work. The judge said no, and put us on probation. If within the next year, we were arrested, in all probability we would get a jail term. I couldn't imagine going to jail. I've led the life of an ordinary middle-class housewife. None of my friends have ever been to jail. I couldn't imagine what it would be like to go to prison, to jail, and to meet inmates.

I always take my handbag to demonstrations, because I like to have my things. When I was arrested and handcuffed, the policeman had to carry my handbag. I spent the day in Hennepin County jail. I wasn't crazy about it. There's not too much to like about jail (laughs).

There were 577 arrests that day. It was one of the biggest mass arrests in the country. Some people sat, some had to be carried. I would not do that. The police are not the enemy. I'm not going to give them a hernia.

I finally wound up in a cell with an authentic criminal (laughs). She was incredibly depressed. I tried to talk to her, but it was absolutely impossible. The others all got out early, and there I was. I thought, It's a plot, they're trying to teach me a lesson. I was there all day. I was paranoid: they're telling me the chief's wife should know better than to go around getting herself arrested. It was nothing of the sort.

That arrest, when I went to jail, went worldwide. It was on television in Tokyo, Mexico, England, France, Italy, everywhere. I never, never dreamt it would make national news, let alone worldwide.

I went to court, pleaded guilty, and was given ten days in the workhouse. It's nothing. There's no work in the workhouse (laughs).

What I've learned in our society, if you're going to commit a crime, make it a worthwhile one. They you can get a year and a day. If you get a year and a day here, you can go to Stillwater. You may work, you have recreation, you may have a television set in your cell. You can make coffee. You can exercise, earn a little money. But if you commit a lesser crime . . .

I was outraged how they treated the women in the jail. You do nothing. You just sit there. You smoke, you watch sitcoms.

They had me in solitary confinement most of the time I was there. I was in jail about a day and a half. I was playing cards with the inmates. They were teaching me poker. I'm not competitive, I don't care if I win or lose. I played the wrong card and one of the women got very irritated. Just then, I was called to the front office.

They showed me a formal-type note: We have received an anonymous call that someone in jail is going to kill you. Kill me. Then they sent me back to the card game. Well, now, not only did I not care if I won or lost, I couldn't concentrate. Kill me.

They received another note, they said, that someone within jail was going to poison me. So they put me in a cell and locked the door. It was not a punishment. It's called administrative separation. However, had I done anything wrong, the rules would have been exactly the same (laughs). I felt perfectly safe in that jail.

In retrospect, I'm glad they put me into solitary. I could see what they were doing to the other women in that jail. They're what I call the casualties of society. They've been sexually abused, physically abused. In that particular jail, they would put them in solitary confinement if they gave each other a cigarette or exchanged an item of clothing or were sick. I tried to change that.

The time after that, I hadn't the slightest intention of getting arrested. I had just got back from England and bought myself a wonderful big hat that I was wearing to the demonstration. Honey-well had put up this big fence. The demonstrators built a ladder, which meant you had to go up ten feet in the air over the ladder and down the other side. I didn't like the idea of heights. But then I saw these young people getting arrested, seventeen, eighteen years old, still in school. I thought, how can I leave all the dirty work to them? I can't.

Tony was across the street, being interviewed by the press. He always likes to be there, to see that everything goes smoothly. To see that there's no violence on the part of the police or the picketers.

Suddenly, he looks up and sees me across the street on top of that ladder. He recognized my big hat. And he said, "Son of a bitch, there goes my wife over the fence!" (Laughs.)

I climbed over and I was arrested. I pleaded guilty. This time I got to do community work. It depends on the judge. Some judges are sympathetic and some aren't. The judge that gave me ten days —Tony met him at a dinner. In fact, the judge had to introduce Tony. This is the day before I was sentenced. Tony said to him, "I hope you're not one of those woolly-headed liberals that are going to give her a tap on the wrist. I hope you'll give her at least two years." (Laughs.) He gave me ten days. (Laughs.)

I worked at a shelter with the street people. I do not consider that a punishment. None of the peace people consider community work a punishment. We think it's something we should do, and we're happy to do it. Actually, it's ridiculous for the taxpayer to pay for us to go to jail, because it's not going to rehabilitate us. It's perfectly fair that we go to jail, but it's not going to change us.

The next time, I was arrested on the steps of the federal building. I was protesting aid to the contras. I don't like getting arrested. I hate making a spectacle of myself. I hate the fact that I get into the papers and my family has to read about it. But I feel so strongly about some things that I just can't leave it up to somebody else. Just because I'm fortunate enough to have a comfortable life and to make speeches, it's totally unfair of me to let others go to jail and for me not to take chances.

Yes, I've broken the law and I should pay the penalty. Otherwise, we'd have total anarchy. But I do believe in this type of demonstra-tion. When you've written to your president, to your congressman, to your senator and nothing, nothing has come of it, you take to the streets.

I don't believe women would have gotten the vote when they did if they hadn't broken the law. I don't believe the blacks in the South would have integrated—and God knows it took long enough—if there hadn't been the Freedom Riders. And if the people hadn't taken to the streets, the Vietnam War would have gone on much, much longer.

When I went to jail, I got around four hundred letters. Ninety-five percent of them were from middle-aged middle-class women like myself. They were wonderful. Five percent were pretty awful.

The press has been accurate and fair. I have absolutely no complaints. Our oldest son, who's a lawyer, thought I was going to destroy my husband's life and my own. Our younger son has always been supportive, right from the beginning.

When people ask if my sons signed up for the draft—which they did—I'm not happy about it. It's their lives and they have to decide. I tell people the only impact I've had on my children is that they're both punctual and they eat with their mouths closed.

It's much easier for me now to get arrested. It's only happened in my husband's town. I haven't done it anywhere else. I imagine I will one of these days.

One of the reasons I do it is because I'm very grateful to the United States. I've had a wonderful life here. You get to a certain point in your life and you have to pay back. You have to do something in return. Because I'm a citizen and I have freedom of speech, I have to utilize these things. If I'm critical of my country, I do it in the same way that I'm critical of my children. I want to make it better and stronger. Where I'm not happy with what is happening, I have to speak up. I don't think being a citizen is just standing up and singing the national anthem or saying the pledge of allegiance. It's being informed and speaking out. I believe each human being can change the world a little bit. If you do nothing, nothing will change.

I'd say I'm far more interesting to live with now than I was before. In the past I would just talk. Whatever came into my mind would just bubble out of my mouth. After I was arrested, I was asked to speak. One day somebody asked me something and I realized they were listening. Since then I've become far more aware. I read as much as I can, I learn as much as I can. I think I've become a more interesting companion for my husband.

To the average person, it's kind of shocking that I would go out and get arrested and maybe take a chance of destroying my husband's life. When I led an ordinary middle-class housewife's life, I couldn't imagine it. But I think it's been good to get rid of your fears. I used to suffer from claustrophobia. I didn't like sitting in the center of the row in a theater. Since I've been in jail, in solitary confinement, that doesn't bother me any more. I had all kinds of fears that don't bother me any more. If I can deal with that, obviously I can deal with many other things.

SUGAR RAUTBORD

She is a member of Chicago's young social set. It is difficult to point to any one magazine or tabloid where her face and story have not appeared.

Though a novel on which she collaborated has been less than critically acclaimed, "it's been on the Tribune *best-seller list for ten weeks and is in its fourth printing. And a miniseries in the works. Not bad for a first novel. It is a fun book, good trash."*

Her horizons have extended to Washington, where she tossed a dinner for President and Mrs. Reagan.

I think of myself as an upper-class working girl. The handle the press has given me is "socialite." A rather peculiar word, I think, 'cause I don't know what it means. A socialite in today's world is a well-dressed fund raiser. I can't imagine the kind of women that sat lying on their backs, looking at the ceiling, eating bonbons and rummaging through jewelry catalogues.

Socialite women meet socialite men and mate and breed socialite children so that we can fund small opera companies and ballet troupes because there is no government subsidy. And charities, of course.

The party I gave in Washington was for Nicaraguan refugee children. It wasn't for the contras, although I'm sure that would be fun. I did meet an awful lot of contras, all sorts of interesting people.

I had a briefing at the White House given by a very interesting gentleman, a marine lieutenant colonel named Oliver North. And then I had another briefing with a very interesting gentleman named Robert McFarlane. Then there was a knock on the door and it was a gentleman by the name of Adolfo Calero, who came to see me. Patrick Buchanan was another one I spoke to. I learned a lot about political science, just by osmosis.

The dinner was not for the contras?

No, it was for Nicaraguan refugee children. The dinner itself— God knows where the funds went. It was a visible success. I had a feeling that a lot of the funds went to these ten or twelve public relations groups or other Central American groups that were involved in espousing their causes. I'd love to know where some of those funds went. I asked for some accounting figures.

They all were sincere and extremely patriotic. I often have dinner in Washington and have sat next to a gentleman on my left who might be on an investigation committee, while on my right was someone being investigated. Whereas they might not be talking to one another, they would both be talking to me. I was the lady in the middle. See how exciting the life of a socialite could be? It beats defrosting the roast in the freezer.

In the political world, people are out there trying to make a difference. Adolfo Calero, for one. He was charming. He took me to a hearty breakfast one morning—bacon, eggs, toast, orange juice— all-American boy. So many of those from the Somoza regime are so Americanized.

I hope the president and Mrs. Reagan remember me. I've been to dinner once or twice at the White House. I worked on the Blair restoration this year, which I thought was nice.

You must remember fund raising is my work. Sometimes you have to be a little dramatic if you're trying to solicit. It's hard to separate people from their money. As I was riding around New York in a limousine during a hotel strike and there was no place to go, I said, ''Now I know what it feels like to be a bag lady.'' Of course, it was an absurd remark. I got a lot of attention with that and people did start to think.

I have seen people in New York on their way to the opera walk over somebody lying on the street. You don't know what to do. You can't pick up every homeless person and bring them home. Something isn't right here. But if you can help by saying something entertaining, you bring a light into their eyes. Maybe that's what the word socialite means.

You don't want to depress somebody by saying please give me this money, it is so sad, people are on the street dying, starving. People are funny. They don't want to hear ugliness twenty-four hours a day. If you tell them an anecdote about not having a place to stay and imagine what those bag ladies feel like, sometimes you can get a little money. There are a lot of social issues that need attention, so if you can be this sort of light that can turn it around in a small way, it's not such a small thing to be doing.

Of course, I run a business. I have my own investment company. I'm the president of an art consulting firm. I've worked in the art business. I've published art criticism. We do scholarship for a couple of snappy collectors and find some paintings.

You're sort of like . . . ?

The Sherlock Holmes. Which is the fun part. I have a network of people across the world, many of whom were my professors at Sarah Lawrence College.

What the president and Mrs. Reagan have done is extraordinary at a time in our history when there was a depressed mood in this country. They came and made it positive. How can you put a value on that? After we had gone through the morass and self-hatred and all that of Vietnam, it is psychologically important that we have, A, a couple who adore each other, B, are supportive of each other, and, C, a man who is a great communicator and can make things happen. If we have all these negative feelings, I don't think we can function well as an individual or as a family or as a nation. Didn't it make you feel better? That the nation itself was having a better feeling about itself?

It's not what he does; it's what he is. He's a survivor. He's a man who with one fell swoop can stop a speeding bullet. He's a superman. With one fell swoop—he almost looked like the original Superman —he could spread his cape and stop a strike. The fact that a man in his seventies could take a bullet in his lung and show no bitterness is as important as passing twenty-eight pieces of legislation. It just does something for everyone.

About the Iran-contra scandal, I don't think we've had a president unscathed in the last twelve years or something like that. I admire people who give public service. You lose your privacy. You can be denigrated by the press.

When I was briefed by the White House, they said to me it was off the record (laughs). I got to see slides of Grenada. I got to see those weapons that had been confiscated during an attack. They had Bulgarian registration, were used by the Viet Cong, were made in America, and were now being used in Grenada.

Grenada? We beat Grenada. We won the war there.

Well, whatever. We live in a democracy, so everyone has a right to an opinion. If they're intelligent, they should act on it. People who were marching in the sixties were my friends. I did some marching in the sixties. That's what Sarah Lawrence was about. I think it was very important. I was seventeen, eighteen years old. I marched against the Vietnam War. What I learned out of that experience was it was sometimes easier to make a difference on the other side, too.

I don't think there's any change. It is still a matter of being a social activist, if you will. I believe that children shall not be allowed to die in Central America because of a war situation. And they shouldn't be allowed to die of polio, mumps, or chickenpox when they can so easily be vaccinated. Isn't that the same as marching down the street to saying people should not be allowed to die over there?

Hopefully, the people that marched in the sixties will be activists from a different pulpit in the eighties and nineties. And they'll take that same fervor to their children, who don't seem so interested in effecting change the way we did.

That dinner in Washington served a purpose if it only called attention to the fact that not only is there a political contest going on, there are children not being allowed to go to school, that are being raised like feral beasts.

Like what?

Feral beasts. In Central America.

The dinner was supposed to have been, from my understanding, for refugee children. There were so many hands involved that one wonders where everything actually went.

I'm going to Andy Warhol's funeral on Monday. It's in keeping with Andy's tongue-in-cheek approach to everything. The memorial service is at St. Patrick's in New York on April Fool's Day.

I did graduate work at the University of Chicago in art history. Some of the press will say socialite So-and-So is doing this or that. Just realize without what we're doing, maybe that ballet company isn't opening that night. So if you have to make something entertaining and fun and funds come in, that's okay.

Every once in a while, you get involved with something like the Nicaragua thing, which I must say is fascinating. If you're sitting there doing a dinner and you've got Ollie North briefing you and Bud McFarlane and Adolfo Calero taking you to breakfast, you don't think that's interesting? I mean, that's more fun than just going out for a beer with the boys every night.

My friends whom I marched with in the sixties would understand this is a maturation process. You get more things done by making more friends in this world than you do by walking around with a hostile chip on your shoulder.

It may be naive, but I still think we can soothe savages with Beethoven. I still think it makes a difference when we send over Wyeth pictures to the Soviet Union. If we can learn to laugh at the same comedy, to cry at the same tragedy, to be moved by the same arts, we've moved closer to an understanding. If you don't understand people, then you bring out the bullets.

Someone's got to raise money for it. Sometimes corporations do it. Sometimes the government does it. Sometimes it is left to us ladies running around. With our Tiffany cups out.

Tiffany what?

Cups out. Panhandling, you know.

BOB ECKHARDT

He had served as congressman from the Eighth District
(Houston) of Texas for seven terms, 1967 through 1980. He
was defeated in his run for an eighth term.

He now practices law in Washington, D.C. As we are
seated in the patio, sipping bourbon and puffing at stogies,
he, in flowing bow tie and courtly manner, evokes the
portrait of a congressman of a long-gone time.

I did everything wrong from the standpoint of present-day politics. I was opposing the most powerful interest in my district: oil. I had thought at the time that there were more people that bought gasoline than got dividends from Humble Oil. It had really worked for twenty-two years in politics. But as politics became more polarized and people began to take it for granted that you ought to represent the biggest power interest in your district, I got defeated. Frankly, my concept of politics was wrong.

What troubles me a great deal today is the single-interest type of approach to politics. It's a very narrow special concern. Blacks have known where they stand on the broad and important issues. It's not something like gun control, whether you're permitted or not to carry a pistol. Or a tax policy looked at very narrowly. The new wave of congressmen is much more cautious. There is no broad concern. The old members of the House were just as reactionary, but they stood on a kind of principle. I wrote a poem about three of them one time:

It's good enough for Mr. Bowe
Just to preserve the status quo.
But Dr. Hall will gladly tell them
His status quo is ante-bellum.
"What bellum then?" cried Mr. Gross.

"The Civil War is much too close.
I'd fain retreat with right good speed
To England prior to Runnymede."

One time I wanted to delay action on the House floor. I knew it was gonna lose if it came to a vote. I went over to Dr. Hall. He was the last of the three still in the House. I said, "I know that you and Mr. Gross had a regular technique to bog down the House." He was kind enough to give me this long mimeographed sheet, where you made a point of order and got them to read the *Journal*. It really worked pretty well. I wonder how they'd feel about what is happening today. They had dreams of a golden age that appears to be crumbling.

I always thought of liberal and conservative as adjectives, not as nouns. About ten years ago, Congress began to change when politics became more mechanized. It used to be of interest to members to discuss matters of the day on the floor. We spoke more casually. When we debated, it was an exchange of ideas. There was more personality to the matter. They were not merely little Univac machines. At no time was there an immediate demand that you join a particular ideological group. The real test was whether or not your decisions withstood the test of time. Today, everything is an instant reaction to an instant poll. Members don't act like persons, they act like machines.

I had a rather broad program, a lot of it to do with environmental protection, consumer protection, industrial safety. Real issues, I thought, rather than issues brought up by professional advisers, by ideological organizations that stamp you liberal or conservative. What defeated me in last election was not the fact that I voted against the oil companies, who put up the money. I was beaten by the accusation that I was for gun control, and that I had voted against curtailment of the right of the court to insist on the abolition of segregation. They liked to call it busing.

My stand was that busing ought to be required where it was necessary in order to do away with the vestiges of segregation. Most of these were cases where the court ordered that. It would not have defeated me in the old regime. It would not have overwhelmed other things on my record, as it did in a concentrated blitz, within three months before the election. There was something like $850,000 spent against me. To about $350. A record of twenty-two years in an elective office in essentially the same district can be overwhelmed in three months.

The third issue was prayer in schools. If there were a real debate on the issue, I would have won out. I was favor of the Supreme Court decision that prevented religious intrusion into the schools. My opponent challenged me to a debate, and when I accepted, he withdrew. It was presented in twenty-second television spots, in overwhelming abundance. I'd have been able, with time or in debate, to show it was a single, more or less meaningless exercise that had absolutely nothing to do with anybody's true beliefs, aside from being against the law of the land. You can't do that in twenty seconds.

Television could be a very great thing for politics. It could create a revival of the stump. Instead, it actually destroys analysis, debate, reason, and substitutes advertising. One-liners. Two-liners take up too much time.

There's a TV picture of a politician. He comes from Texas and he's got a bunch of Brahman cattle behind him and his family is romping through the woods. It has nothing to do with politics. You've got an unlimited amount of time for this kind of programming, if you've got the money. I'd limit the appearance to the person himself, speaking in his own voice, without any background. Most politicians that haven't got much to say would soon exhaust the public's interest in them.

The scandals, open or secret, are happening so regularly, it's as if one is constantly irritated by a blow on the shins to a point where he's no longer sensitive. What the Reagan administration has discovered is that that which becomes commonplace is no longer a scandal. The violations have been unprecedented in their repetitiousness. People have lost their sense of outrage.

Know why? People are really not interested in politics. They've got too many other interests. You find people know so much about football. If they knew the same amount about the stock market, they'd be millionaires. Trivialities have overwhelmed us.

The press and political advisers have learned that if they use generalities and get them fixed in people's minds, they'll win: Get the government off our backs; deregulation is desirable. People are naturally conservative. They don't want to see much changed.

If you can present a matter as a specific issue—Teapot Dome or Hooker Chemical's pollution at Love Canal—people are liberal.

Reagan succeeded because of general propositions: He's a nice fella; he's gettin' the government off our backs; he doesn't want any new taxes. People remember Big Government and forget big crooks.

I think Americans have lost a sense of healthy skepticism. I always remember those old conversations with my family. My father was a doctor, who was not particularly political, always talking to his daddy's brother or to his sisters. They questioned the president. They questioned Congress. The issues were specific. It wasn't just an attitude: Oh, they're just a bunch of scoundrels in Washington. It had to do with just not quite believing everything that came their way. I think we've lost that.

CONGRESSMAN PHILIP M. CRANE

He is serving his tenth term, and is running for his eleventh, as Republican congressman from "the state's fast-growing" district, a complex of suburbs bordering Chicago on the northwest and extending to the Wisconsin border.

Before reapportionment, "my old district, along the lake, was more affluent than the one I represent today. It's like the eastern seaboard of the United States. You bet they lock their doors. My folks today are from the old neighborhood. They don't lock their doors.

"Notwithstanding all their wealth, many of the folks in the eastern part were liberals. They could afford to indulge themselves in compassion, in creating a lot of government programs. But the ones who picked up the tab were the folks of the western part."

I'm not worried about Democrats moving out here. Your typical city Democrat is a God-fearing person, who believes in family and traditional values, who's not trying to put his hands in your pocket, who wants to work. And when the country goes to war, he's pushing you out of line to get in front. I was brought up with these self-same values. We all pushed those big carts with the high wheels to deliver our *Chicago Daily News* for ten dollars a month. Some life-long Democrats are among my staunchest supporters.

> *He has a Ph.D. in American history and had been*
> *headmaster of a Christian nondenominational school until*
> *his entrance into politics.*

I was brought up not to pass laws to redistribute income. I was raised as a tither. I've always given ten percent of what I make to charitable causes. I got it from my dad and his mother.* I have difficulty with the idea of legislating charity. I'm not opposed to caring for people who can't provide for themselves. We have an obligation. But we've stretched this to intolerable limits, considering the magnitude of our deficit today.

Unless there's a national emergency such as war, we're better letting local communities retain the money and address the problems. Case in point: food stamps. They are unsupervised today and not distributed faithfully.

Once I stopped off at a grocery store in a little Wisconsin town. A well-groomed, attractive woman was in line ahead of me. She had a gallon of ice cream and two candy bars, paid for it with a twenty-dollar food stamp, and got change. You're not supposed to get change from food stamps. How's that money going to be spent? Maybe she gambles with it or goes out to buy booze or cigarettes. If you're gonna enforce the program, you've got to have a cop at every checkout line. It's impossible. Some of these food stamps are used in poker games by the fathers of indigent kids.

In earlier days, you had a township commissioner who knew the families in need. If the father was irresponsible, the kids were taken care of. It was a personal concern. My people are willing to help those less fortunate, but don't need the heavy hand of national government involved in our lives and affairs.

When you see street people on the grates, wrapping themselves in newspapers, it's heart-wrenching. This is uncivilized. To be sure,

---

* His father, Dr. George Crane, had been for many years a widely syndicated advice columnist.

many of them are mentally troubled, psychologically disturbed. When cops try to get them into warmth and shelter, some of them are positively belligerent.

There is a depersonalization of help today, from the assumption of an all-provident father in Washington shoveling out billions of dollars to address these problems. So it's become Washington's problem and no longer ours. It is a community obligation. Let's get the responsible people together, with all the churches, have a community drive, and raise the money.

There is indeed a great deal of unemployment today. Yet I've got eight kids and seven of them are working. They're not making a whale of a lot of money.

When we had double-digit unemployment, a lot of people said, "This job is demeaning, I won't take it." I was brought up to believe any work is dignified. I don't care if you're digging ditches, if you don't have a job, take it until you see a better opportunity. One of my youngsters had held down a half-a-dozen different jobs, hired to this one, went on to another.

I say take any job until you find a better one. The government can't create jobs. When the government creates make-work jobs, capital is lost that can be used in the private sector to create a productive job. The government is denying potential for growth, when it takes out tax monies to create make-work.

My constituency is really Middle America, middle-income, Middle West. God's country. We are the hub that holds the extremities from going into orbit. They resent Congress not having the discipline to do something about budget deficits. They're paying an arm and a leg and not getting what they're paying for. They resent government regulation and red tape, all of which hurts their competitive capabilities.

Pentagon expenditures? Look, there are excesses in every department. It's endemic to every agency in government. If you put an auditor at the General Accounting Office to work a year at Health, Education, and Welfare's one-year budget, it would take twenty years. To blame defense on government's excess spending is misleading.

I'm for contra aid, of course. Nicaragua with all the Soviet armaments will be able to control every other Central American country. Central America has some shining examples. Costa Rica first comes to mind. It's more literate than the United States of America and has no military.

Arias, the president of Costa Rica, is for negotiations rather than a military solution—

Our president doesn't like the Arias plan and I don't either. Ortega's ultimate objective is direct confrontation with the U.S. Marines. I don't want our American boys down there. If you have people, the contras, willing to fight for freedom, support them.

What exercises me most is the failure of the American voter to understand who does what to whom. They don't understand the role of the president.

In the contra-Iran hearings, we've seen that our administration is more laid-back than I'd be comfortable with. Our president has a macromanagement style. It's preferable to Jimmy Carter's micromanagement style. He tried to master every issue and couldn't see the forest for the trees.

Sure, I would have wanted to know more about the excess payments to the Ayatollah's government, the Swiss bank account, the routing of contra aid. I would have made the decision myself: Go ahead, do it. I don't see any constitutional impropriety in that.

It's not a burning issue in my district. After Ollie North appeared before the committee, we got hundreds of phone calls supportive as could be. I think it's because Ollie cuts a fine figure, is a patriotic gentleman, and thought he was doing the right thing. I don't see any basis for indicting him. Ollie is still very popular in my district. Frankly, the whole thing is ho-hum to them. There are far more burning issues affecting their daily lives: irresponsible government spending.

My dad taught psychology to salesmen. Across your chest, he told them, are the words: HERE, NOW. If you forget those words, you lose a customer. People are saying: ME, HERE, NOW. They don't even know where Iran is. It's an abstraction. Vietnam was an abstraction, until it started to affect enough families.

My awareness of what Washington was doing to us came from my father, who was a rock-ribbed Republican. His adrenaline got really charged, all the time, just thinking about FDR.

By 1960, I was really turned off politics. It was Tweedledum versus Tweedledee or hold your nose and vote. I got actively involved in helping Goldwater, because he was articulating things. He got back to basics: This God-fearing country is the greatest and we shouldn't be bullied or pushed around or take a back seat to anybody. We should be proud of this country and its work ethic and the free enterprise that built it. Let's go out and do it, instead of whining. Why don't we roll up our sleeves and go to work? What made America great is when the going gets tough, the tough get going.

I really got turned on by THE speech of that '64 campaign delivered by Ronald Reagan. It was that half-hour television speech in support of Goldwater. I was a surrogate speaker for him in Illinois. Whenever our dobbers got low, we'd just replay the Reagan speech and we'd get charged up again.

What did he say?

It was a general speech. It was supportive of the principles. Let's face it, Reagan at his best is doggone good. I was trying to get him the nomination in '68 because I didn't trust Nixon.

Can you remember what he said in THE speech?

He talked about patriotism, pride in ourselves as a country. There's no country that can compare with what we've done. You know, give us your poor and huddled masses and we'll turn them into independent, self-supporting people, who'll enjoy the material blessings that no society has ever seen before, 'cause we're the freeest society on the face of the earth. (He pauses.) It wasn't just the speech so much. It charged our batteries.

Ronald Reagan's enduring contribution will be the consequences of his rhetoric. Think about it. We know Jimmy Carter was a very pious man, yet he was afraid to invoke God's name in a public forum. There was some confusion about separation of church and state. Reagan never signs off a State of the Union address without saying God bless you. He invokes God's name comfortably, and Americans relate to that. It's a good value and one we should keep in mind. He has restored patriotism. Americans feel good about themselves again.

TOM GRISSOM

*In 1985, he resigned from his job as nuclear physicist at
Sandia National Laboratories in Albuquerque, New Mexico.
He had been there fifteen years and was regarded as among
the most respected and promising. "I was promoted more
quickly than usual, made head of a department and getting
more money all the time."*

*Sandia is the largest of three national laboratories
devoted to nuclear weaponry, the others being at Los
Alamos and Livermore, California. Its annual budget is one
billion dollars. "One out of every thousand tax dollars goes
directly to our lab.*

*"It is wholly owned by the Department of Energy and
managed by Western Electric. This helps confuse people.
It's not listed in the military budget, so the Defense
Department gets the warheads for free. Since the money is
appropriated in strange bills like in Inland Waterways
Act, it hardly gets any scrutiny from Congress. It's part of
the secrecy of how much we invest in nuclear weapons."*

*He grew up in Mississippi, "not far from Senator
Eastland's plantation in Sunflower County." Among the
teachers he encountered at the University of Mississippi
was James Silver, author of* Mississippi : The Closed
Society. *"He had to leave during the time of the civil rights
unrest because his unpopular stance had become one of
personal danger. He was a voice in the wilderness, but he
made a lasting impression on me. When I began to reassess
my life, I thought of him."*

The seductiveness of technologi-
cally challenging work is some-
thing that consumes people entirely. We form a small society of
people interested in the same challenge, competition, and success. I

was consumed with living up to the goals I had set for myself and conforming to society's picture of what success is.

I agonized a *little* bit, but I decided that after many years in school, in training myself in physics and research, I owed it to myself, my family, and society to do what was expected : good work, good science.

I always treated it as a basic research program, never really associating it with weapons. I could write and publish papers on it. It was exciting. There was a feeling of camaraderie among us here, talented people, all enthusiastic about their work. We were literate, well-trained, patriotic, tax-paying citizens, community, church leaders. Interested in the arts, opera, Little League baseball, Boy Scout troops . . .

What was frightening about all this is that I never encountered anyone among the eight thousand who worked here who raised the question of the end result of our work : nuclear weapons. Among all these bright, articulate people, I never ran into *anyone* who raised *the* subject. Openly.

Gordon McClure, who hired me, one of the best physicists I had ever worked with, was bothered. We hadn't ever talked about it, but I discovered one day that he was agonizing privately as I was. As he was about to retire, he confessed to me that he was terribly bothered by the mission of our laboratory and the direction of our national policy. This came up ten years after he and I had worked together.

I began to talk to other people with whom I felt comfortable. The concern was still nonexistent. It was reassuring to find one person who *did* feel as I do, but that was small comfort.

Western Electric has tried to play down its management role. The laboratory was afraid of drawing attention to its mission. In the sixties and early seventies, during the Vietnam War, there was quite a bit of concern about the protests.

We're on an air force base, Kirtland, so it's easy to deny access to protest groups. In the mid-seventies, a few lone protesters appeared outside the gates. One in particular, Chuck Hosking, a Quaker, began to show up every day. He would carry a sign, DON'T HUG YOUR CHILDREN WITH NUCLEAR ARMS. People would stop and talk with him. He'd share his views about Gandhi and nonviolence. We passed him every day.

He was always talked about as someone naive, whose view was of no consequence. A minority of one, sort of laughed at. But those who had stopped and talked with him came to realize that for him it was no laughing matter. There was a curiosity: why would he do this?

I was keeping my doubts to myself, really *afraid* to talk to anyone about it, even my family. I started to do a lot of reading, delving into things I had once been interested in. I had put them on the back burner in the interest of my career. Literature, history, poetry.* I was looking for truths that were different than technical truths.

It was right at the time they were moving me up into the supervisory ranks. I was on the threshold of another promotion when these questions began to really torment me. I subverted these concerns, took the promotion, and once again became totally absorbed with my job.

I was now responsible for the actual devices that went in weapons. It had nothing to do any more with basic science. My specific job had to do with the trigger of the weapons. It was one of the most exciting technologies in the whole laboratory. I couldn't escape.

It was the gradual realization that you can't escape the consequences of your personal responsibility. It got to the point where I just didn't want to have a damn thing to do with it. I decided that if these weapons are ever used, the survivors would be totally justified in gathering up all the people like myself and trying us for crimes against humanity. It would be the same thing that happened at Nuremberg. Our crime would be staggering in proportion.

I began to see myself, not as one little cog out of eight thousand who wouldn't be singled out, but as someone *personally* responsible for all this.

Never once, in my entire fifteen years here, at any management meeting, has anyone questioned the appropriateness of what the labs were doing. When every new weapon was proposed, no one ever stood up and said, Is this right?

Suddenly, Chuck Hosking, whom I'd pass every day, became not a symbol of foolishness and futility but a symbol of great courage. And I didn't have the courage to do what I felt really deep down inside me I should be doing.

I was suddenly not interested in material things any more. This produced great tension in my marriage. I was trying to tell my wife of the values I'd come to believe in. She and all the others felt it was something caused not by introspection but by emotional stress. Perhaps I had mental problems, coming unglued. I began to wonder if

---

* He has published three collections of his own poetry.

375

there was something wrong with me.* In 1985, I decided I had to be true to what I felt. I had to act on it. As I was walking from the parking lot to my office, I composed a letter of resignation in my head. I was going to tell them how I felt about the laboratory, nuclear weapons, and personal responsibility. When I got to my office, I wrote it down pretty much the way I had composed it. I set it aside for a while. Perhaps I was a bit intemperate. A week later, I read it and decided I wouldn't change a word of it. It was exactly how I felt.

I called my entire department together, about seventy people. I knew them all and liked them all really well. I suspect they liked me. I told them I didn't want to be associated with nuclear weapons and was quitting. I had no other job. I had no idea what I was going to do. I made it clear to them it was a studied, reflective response. I handed them all copies of the letter.

Generally, the reaction was friendly. Some told me they disagreed, but there was no acrimony. There was one, an engineer, who happens to be my best friend at the lab. Privately, he told me he agreed, wished he could do the same thing, but couldn't bring himself to it.

There's a feeling at the laboratories that things can't continue as they are forever. It's an amazingly stable insitution, one of unbroken growth, always supported by Congress, by the country. Inwardly, they may feel uncomfortable, but they view each day, each year, pragmatically. Is the budget going to be as big next year? Will I get promoted? There is no long view. It's a matter of individual welfare in the short term. Most people who get into technology and engineering think that way.

The management started circulating copies of the letter. The director in charge of national security got it in his head that I was a security risk: overwrought, emotionally disturbed. It was required reading for all the directors. Yet, of all the managers I talked to, not one ever mentioned he had seen the letter. Or that it even existed. It was the policy to draw no attention to it at all or to give anyone a forum to talk about it.

My resignation was treated by my colleagues as one thing and my personal relationship as something else. I was a person with two separate compartments. One, they would not acknowledge; the other, the personal, was something else.

* Eventually there was a divorce. He has since remarried.

My last act at the lab was a debriefing interview with my boss, one of the directors. His secretary asked me for a copy of the letter. She was crying. I was affected. I had no idea others may have felt that way.

I gave a copy to Chuck Hosking, of course. And to Gordon McClure. There are more people in our society who are concerned about this issue than I was ever aware of when I was in the laboratory. We're in a closed society not much different than James Silver's description of Mississippi. I was reminded of Silver. He was right then as I was right now.

I wanted to get back into teaching, not just physics and math, but the other, bigger issues. I'm now beginning my third year at Evergreen State College in Olympia, Washington. It's a liberal arts college, experimenting in education. I earn very little compared to my former salary, but I haven't been as contented in years.

I don't think my action and that of a few other individuals is going to have any great impact. I think it's going to take a more widespread change in basic values. I did what I did simply because it became terribly important to *me*. If I can influence somebody else, that's a plus.

GOD II

PASTOR DOUGLAS ROTH

He is the first pastor in the history of the Lutheran Church of America to have been defrocked. Subsequently, a colleague, Pastor Daniel Solberg, was similarly punished.

En route from the Pittsburgh airport to the steel-mill town Clairton, where he had his parish and where he still lives, we pass other such communities: Munhall, Duquesne (with its award-winning blast furnace, endearingly named Dorothy); Homestead, of bloody labor history and lore; McKeesport, Hazelwood ...

It is impossible to distinguish one from the other: the same rows of smokeless chimneys, vestigial remainders of what were once furiously engaged steel mills; the same gray landscape, superimposed on the obstinate green of the trees; the same frame houses, long in need of repair; the same silence.

His house, in this hilly terrain, is closely surrounded by other such homes, company-built, as though all were on stilts.

We're seated at the kitchen table. His wife, Nadine, occasionally joins in the conversation. Two of their four small children are around and about; the other two are at school. They range in age: eleven, nine, seven, and two.

They are both from farm families: he, from Nebraska; she, from Kansas. They had met at a junior college affiliated with the Lutheran Church—Missouri Synod.

It began as an ordinary mill-town ministry. Our first call. In '78, the mills were working pretty good. Our plan was to stay three years and head back to the Midwest. Then prophetic things began to happen (laughs).

It's a calling. God places things on us all. Throughout Scriptures, you read about how all the prophets were fighting it: Moses and Isaiah, Ezekiel. Don't make me do this (laughs). Get anybody else. 'Cause you know it's gonna be unpopular, it's gonna be dangerous.

Well, the time came to stand up for your people. The suicide rate is phenomenal here. Unemployment is just so devastating. Fifty-five percent of the heads of households in these towns are unemployed. They lose their house, they lose their car, their marriage, they're snappin' at each other, they turn to drink, abuse of children, run out of food, abandon their families, they lose hope.

What does that trigger inside you? You have a friend who walks out the door because he can't look at the wife and kids any more because he can't support 'em. Every marriage that goes through two, three years of unemployment is damaged. I look at the kids that don't get proper medical care, don't get fed properly, their teeth, their values getting twisted around sideways—we're gonna be paying the price for this for years to come.

> Nadine interjects: "Three of my close friends have husbands unemployed for a long time. I knew something had to be done when one told me she's contemplating suicide."

We're having two suicides a day. At Christmastime, we had one weekend of fourteen suicides. Fishin' 'em out of the river here. I had a guy that was fifty-seven years old and had worked in the mills since he was sixteen. Had forty years at the mill and got laid off. It just worked on him. He got some odd jobs. Finally the stress and strain was too much. He had a heart attack and died. I buried him. I ask myself, Would he have had the heart attack anyway? I don't know. A twenty-three-year-old guy drowns in the river after drinking heavily. He's been laid off. This same river, the Monongahela.

Where should he have been on a Tuesday morning? He should have been at work. Here's an unemployment-related death that doesn't make the statistics. The names, the faces, you fish 'em out of the river.

The bishop doesn't live here. Where does he have his lunch? Who does he spend time with? Not with these people. To live here and to experience it day after day, to know the names and faces, can you go into their homes and tell them, Well, that's the way things are? Global competition, you know. Go tell it to *them*.

Sure, we approach it in traditional ways, we hand out food, we hand out clothes, sometimes, shelter.* We finally said, We've got to address the root causes. What's doin' this? We allied with the labor people and did research. We, the Denominational Ministry Strategy.

> *The Denominational Ministry Strategy (DMS) was suggested by the bishop and the Synod to "revitalize the church in these old and dying communities." How do you get a decent youth group really going? What about the old folks in town? How do we keep it from losing all those values we pass on from one generation to the next?*
>
> *The Synod hired Charles Honeywell as organizer. He had been trained by Saul Alinsky of the Industrial Areas Foundation. Since the conflict that led to the defrocking of Pastors Roth and Solberg, Honeywell had been fired. He still works with the DMS, the beleaguered pastors, and their twenty-three colleagues. He was the son of a Baptist minister.*
>
> *Honeywell's missionary fervor is undiminished: "The early Christians who were persecuted had to form unions. Groupings of communities to protect themselves. They were called churches. Today we're finding you can't separate the church from the corporate world. They have the same leaders.*

---

* At a church in the adjacent parish of his colleague, Pastor John Gropp, I attended a food and fellowship night. Once a week, a full meal is served; food contributed by local merchants and friends. The cooking is done by the women of the parish. In another room are heaps of used clothes. Hundreds, it seemed, men, women, children, were at the welcome tables. On this night the gourmet meal consisted of meatballs, mashed potatoes, peas, and macaroni. It was filling.

"Even many of the unions have gone corrupt, but at least they have kept corporate heads off their boards. The church hasn't. The church still has these same guys."

Pastor Richard John Neuhaus is bemused. "Charles Honeywell is from the fever swamps. He's just beyond the pale of the Alinsky tradition. Needless to say, if you talk to Lutheran officials, they are uncomplimentary (laughs). Roth, Solberg, and the others have been sucked into Honeywell's orbit and control. I know Solberg's parents very well. They're wonderful, devout, caring people."

The catalytic event was when the city of Clairton here went bankrupt. They had no money for police or firemen or any other city workers. We decided to call for disaster aid. This is just as violent as a tornado or flood. We researched the law and it said anything that affects the safety, health, and welfare of a commonwealth is a disaster. The mayor called on the governor, who said no. In our research, we discovered the chief cause behind everything was a massive disinvestment. The money was leaving this valley at a fantastic rate, going overseas, to the Third World and cheap labor.

The number one culprit is the Mellon Bank. They run Pittsburgh: every institution from the churches, to the schools, to the various corporations across the board. All roads lead to the Mellon Bank.

The church is real good about writing up all kinds of statements on economic justice, wonderful words. We said we have to go beyond that. So we devised a whole series of actions.

We began by doing something very mild. We asked the people to put their money into a bank that would pledge to keep the money here, to reinvest in the valley to put people back to work.

We put out a whole series of flyers. The most famous dealt with the closing of Mesta Machine Company. It makes the equipment that goes in a steel mill. It's one of the oldest, most respected companies around. They foreclosed on them for 13 million dollars. At the same time, they were loaning millions to Sumatoma in Japan. It's a huge conglomerate that makes the same product.

That got a huge reaction of the people around here. The Mellon Bank holds a lot of pension money for these men and are using their money against 'em. They put their life savings into this institution, they built it. And now they turn around . . . We had a pledge D-Day, June 6, 1983. It was disinvestment day, and we organized massive withdrawals from the Mellon Bank.

In October came our next step, something more active. It was the penny action with about a hundred union workers. They went into the bank with ten dollars each and said, "I want ten dollars worth of penⁿes. I wanna count them out, make sure they're here . . . four, five" . . . drop half on the floor, crawling around. There was general confusion and chaos. They finally get back in line, drop some more, pick 'em up. Oh, I got these pennies, I want nickels. So they tied up all the tellers.

There were many police, many security guards. Meanwhile, the pastors were outside and we had signs: MELLON IS THE FELON.

The bank did no meaningful business that day. Tension kept going up and up and up. Finally, a security guard snapped. He took a billy club out and beat our guy over the head, blood streaming.

We did another penny action. This time we added fish. It was Friday. Our guys were taking out safety deposit boxes: we want to do business with you. The workers would then bring in a frozen block of fish and deposit it in their safety boxes. Fishes and loaves. Before this we'd had hours of meeting with the executives of the Mellon bank. They just kept telling us how they had this fiduciary responsibility to their stockholders. They were just bankers and had no real power. That's when we decided to take the fishes and loaves, give them to the Mellon Bank, and see if they could feed the multitudes.*

By Monday, they were beginning to raise their own odor. Boy, it was really something! They had to drill out the boxes. They didn't know who was who and what was what. They drilled into one lady's jewels and somebody else's heroin. That got the Mafia all excited. Of course, if you're gonna attack corporate evil, they just don't sit there and take it. It counterattacks. Mellon has a very strong network into the parishes. Every corporate leader is a church member. The same people that run the corporations also run the churches.

My own little church, Trinity, is working-class. An overwhelming number work in the mills, more than half retired. We had some foremen and their wives, so I always had this current of dissent.

---

* Pastor Gropp: "Christ was able to do it. Well, Mellon's the God of Pittsburgh. We provided him the fishes and the God of Pittsburgh couldn't do it. All it did was raise a real stink."

NADINE: *"If you look at any little church on the corner, the majority of the people don't like to be challenged by what the Bible may say. Their agenda is to have a quiet, warm, take-care-of-ourselves little group. One of the main people against Doug said, 'We're close-knit, we take care of our own.'"*

Our church, I'd say, is typical. A small number may understand what ministry's about. About the same number are in active opposition. In the middle is the huge majority: they'll vote against any tension in their lives. They just don't want to get involved.

The bishop comes to me and says, "Doug, you're hurting the money and the image of the church." August 4, 1984. I remember because it was the date of the investigative hearing.

At that time, we'd already had some people falling back, 'cause the church was beginning to come after us. I had my council behind me. They agreed with me: you've got to get into people's lives and when they hurt, we hurt. Otherwise the church is just an empty shell.

At the hearing, there was talk of reconciliation. We accepted: God says when people offer reconciliation, you accept it. Their minds were made up: we were too much trouble. The bishop declared my pulpit vacant, no theological charges, no biblical hearing, no appeal. The way they phrased it, it was a matter of expediency based on the principles of Christian love.

Well, that's right out of the Bible: when Caiaphas says it's expedient that one man should die, so we don't bring down this terrible wrath of the Roman Empire on us. We don't bring down the wrath of the Mellon empire, the corporate empire, on the church.

They declared the pulpit vacant and I said no. They said, We have a charge. You are disobedient to the Constitution. The Lutheran Church had its own firm of lawyers for years. All of a sudden, Mellon's law firm jumped in and volunteered their services. Know their history? They're the ones who hired Pinkertons in the Homestead Strike of 1892. They got an injunction to have me removed from the property.

I told the judge I have to obey God. I've been called to ministry and I'm going to stand by my people until God tells me to quit. So I moved into the church and stayed there.

The siege was on. We locked up the church. The sheriff was not very anxious to come and arrest me. It's political poison to arrest a pastor. I held services for whoever would come. I was in the church from Sunday to Wednesday, when I was arrested. The sheriff sent in two deputies, women, like I was gonna fight or something. The judge said, ''You are in contempt of court. Ninety days and a $1,200 fine.'' I went to jail.

The bishop still did not have control of the church, because the council was still there. They said, He's still our pastor. You can send all the guys you want, we're gonna continue to have our services. They had selected other pastors from our group to cover for me.

Meanwhile, I was writing sermons from prison and sending them out. That drove 'em wild. The judge added sixty more days to my ninety, for those sermons. They didn't have control over this, and control is what it's all about. So the executive board of the Synod declared the church defunct.

They now began the disciplinary process. Since I was in jail— how to do it? They held it in jail. Even the worst criminal, a murderer, has his day in open court. They took me in handcuffs into the warden's area. They sent five pastors. My lawyer could not be part of it because he's a Presbyterian. They said, We only let Lutherans in here. They wouldn't let Nadine in.

Meanwhile, eight people, four of 'em council members, remained in the church, even though the Synod declared it defunct: We're not leaving.

> NADINE: *"First, they took us to court for an injunction, before the same judge who sentenced Doug. He ruled we had to give up the property to the Synod. We said, Absolutely not, because we have been declared defunct illegally.*
>
> *"We went into the church on the twenty-seventh of December. On the fourth of January, the police came in, forty-five fully armed riot-clad police. They surrounded the church, axed down the back door, and took the eight of us off to jail. That's when I wound up in jail.*
>
> *"I grew up in a very neat conservative community. I don't think I ever knew anybody who went to jail. We were in for sixty days. Doug was in the county jail in Pittsburgh, but they wouldn't put the rest of us with him. So they transported us a three-hour drive from here.*
>
> *"I learned a lot about myself. I learned a lot about my relationship with God, with my family. We're trying to pass*

on some values here. If we say one thing and do another, the children read that just so quick.

"Growing up in my middle-class mindset, I had great fears about coming back to my community. How would I be accepted? What would my next-door neighbor say? It was unbelievable. Everybody said, We may not totally go along with what you're doing, but we admire you terribly for standing up for what you believe in."

It's never gonna be a mass movement. When we talk about something prophetic, it's never gonna be popular to act that strongly. But there's always gonna be the dissenting voice that says we need justice. When you consider that labor unions were born in blood and have a violent history—we cannot be violent, but can make use of new tactics.

One week after I got out of jail in March of '85, we had the final disciplinary hearing in Pittsburgh, at the bishop's church. There were many police cars to guarantee they'd be safe and secure. Again, I was not allowed to take my lawyer. Nadine went whether they liked it or not. She said, "You're gonna have to put me in jail, 'cause I'm going with my husband." I took Wayne Cochran as my counsel.* They said, Oh, you've got a tape recorder. You can't have that. There will be no record of these proceedings. I was defrocked. It had never happened before in America in the Lutheran Church.

Some of the local union leaders support us. Not the top-level international ones. They're the guys in three-piece suits goin' to lunch at the Duquesne Club with the corporate guys.

I would have preferred not to go to jail. Nobody wants to have this kind of experience. I would have liked to have my life-style remain the same. But you can't regret ministry. Sometimes you wish you had more allies. The media is not our friend. They make us sound bizarre. They have to cover us because we do things out of the ordinary, creative, but they like to paint us as some sort of kooks.

Yet you can't walk the streets of Pittsburgh without people coming up to shake your hand. Every time. I cannot go in downtown Pittsburgh without that happening. Yeah, we're behind you, they say. Often way behind (laughs). They can't bring themselves to take

---

* A retired Clairton bus driver, chairman of Trinity Church's council. He was one of the eight who locked themselves in the church and subsequently spent sixty days in jail. He was seventy.

a public stand. They don't want the waves in their personal lives. It makes them vulnerable. Will they get laid off, get attacked?

There's fear, a lot. Even the police. My wife went to church here a couple weeks ago and was turned away. She said, "What about my children? Can they go?" Know what they said? "It wouldn't be fair to let the children and not you." She said, "Will you escort us so we can quietly worship?" They said, "We don't want to get involved."

I see the country heading for almost a police state. We're gonna have more and more rules to keep down any dissent. The violation of constitutional rights, with the approval of the masses. Of course, we want to keep law and order, we don't want waves. Teaching us to be, oh, so polite. For one thing, it's not scriptural (laughs). I see our country headed for dark times.

Dietrich Bonhoeffer said it about the Nazis: They've become so stupid you couldn't even fight 'em. Banality? Yes, that's about it.

But we'll still be around for a while. We've cost the Mellon Bank millions of dollars to restructure their ad campaign. They had a famous one: A Neighbor You Can Count On. We did that one in. By their own admission, it cost them a quarter of a million dollars to put us in jail. So, we'll stick around.

The last two weeks I was at Trinity, I received fifty new members. We were the fastest-growing church in the Synod. This is the one they declared defunct because it was wasting away. These new members were saying, This is my kind of church, my kind of pastor. He's taking a stand for me and I want to be part of it. But they weren't "our kind of people." That's a quote from one of the corporate people in the parish: the ones who wanted me out.

Know who these new people were? The unemployed black working class. Clairton happens to be forty percent black. We had never had these people in our church before.

We'd been holding services in my house. This coming Sunday morning, we're going to be in a church for the first time in quite a while. We'll be sharing service in the building of the Free Holiness Church of the Deliverance—a black church.

We still have a remnant of the Trinity congregation, about forty. Plus the fifty new members. Many have to come from quite a distance, so on a typical Sunday we'll have only about thirty, forty.

My income is about a third of what it used to be. The remnant congregation supports me. You're dealing with unemployed people who don't have the resources.

Do you ever have second thoughts . . . ?

We have 'em daily.

> NADINE: *"Every day (laughs). We're struggling to make our mortgage payment real hard this month and it's always in the back of your mind—why would you do that?"*

Read about Jeremiah and he says, Gosh, I wanna quit. Lord, get off my back and let me alone. And the Lord says, I'll give you the strength again, come on. We just take it one step at a time.

> NADINE: *"Doug always told me: Being a pastor doesn't pay all that well, but it's great job security." (Laughs.)*

And a lifetime call (laughs).

PASTOR RICHARD JOHN NEUHAUS

The use of Scripture in DMS is a species of fundamentalism. What's happening today is a revival of varieties of fundamentalism. There is also a peculiar fundamentalism of the left. DMS is a case of it. It fails just as Jerry Falwell fails. They tend to self-righteously posture over against the judgment of anybody else. I mean, they have the truth. If you don't agree, you're on the side of the devil.

One could make a case that they were doing what many of us were doing through civil disobedience in the civil rights and antiwar movements. They are certainly right when they say that the Lutheran Church or, for that matter, churches in general today are not ruled by theological conviction. They are ruled by bureaucratic imperatives.

I am sympathetic to the DMS when they say Scriptures ought to be normative in what we do. But I object to the use of Scriptures as a species of fundamentalism. You find it in the Jerry Falwells and

Pat Robertsons, of course. But you find it among these well-meaning young pastors of DMS, as well. They leap from a Bible passage and take the most literal, simplistic reading. Some of the other churches are inclined to do it, too. They immediately leap from Scripture to, say, nuclear weapons.

I say you have to move from Scripture, through the exercise of reason, to prudential judgment. Ethical responsibility is always a question of prudential judgment.

A church ought to be throughly grounded in its belief system as far as Christians are concerned: the revelation of God in history and in the person, death, and resurrection of Jesus Christ. If it isn't that, it's simply another human institution floating and flopping about in a pitiful manner.

That sharply relativizes everything else. The most important thing is not the arms race, is not world hunger, is not the denial of human rights. It's not unemployment in Pennsylvania. Only by relativizing the idolatrous assertion that political questions are finally the most important, by challenging and debunking it, do we get our priorities straight. The ultimately important thing is God's saving grace and Jesus Christ.

Then we ask, What ought we to do in the political arena? We move into this arena as fallible human beings. We ought to have the great courage to say, I don't know, I don't have the answer. We have to act always in the courage of our uncertainties. Right and left in American religion must be criticized because they are constantly claiming a Thus Saith the Lord kind of certainty. We must act as fallible participants in a community of fallible participants.

We should give it our best shot carefully, thoughtfully, responsibly, and when necessary be radical in pressing what needs to be done. My vocation, as I see it, is not to urge the church to support this policy rather than that policy, to be for or against the contras, to be for or against MX missiles. My job is to call the Christian community, the religious community, across the board, to greater reflectiveness about the alternatives that face us.

I have positions on numerous things, but that's not the most important thing. What's more important is how we contend for these positions in a way that respects the priority of religious belief and the pluralism of the civil society.

It's not a cop-out, because the disease with which we're all afflicted is the notion that the only significant decision one makes is political. If I spend whatever credibility I have on taking positions on everything I feel strongly about, what I'm saying is not going to be heard. I'm simply going to be one more partisan actor in the political arena who happens to wear a clerical collar. God knows there are quite enough already. It's a much more difficult course I'm charting.

It would be easier for me to make up my little list of what is, quote, the moral position on policies from A to Z. Whether it's DMS or the World Council of Churches or Jerry Falwell, they all have their little lists, okay? That simply debases the role of religion as well as of political discourse. It ends up with each one playing more righteous than thou. That's no way for a liberal democracy to conduct its public business.

Moral relativist? I'm anything but that. I subscribe to the classic creed of the church. I believe there is an absolute good, but our apprehension of it is always partial and imperfect. This is not moral relativism, it's simply an awareness of our limitations.

I hope I'm doing what God intends for me to do with my life. I could be much more energetic in the political arena, as I once was. I could be a parish pastor in Bedford-Stuyvesant, as I once was.* There are many things I could do. I certainly encourage other people who believe that is their vocation. I don't care about their position as long as they act in a spiritually, rationally careful way. I haven't told you where Richard John Neuhaus stands on these matters, have I?

DARRELL BECKER

He was one of the eight parishioners who had locked themselves inside Trinity Lutheran Church. He, too, was jailed for defying a court injunction.

He is local president of the Industrial Union of Marine and Shipbuilding Workers of America. "My shipyard eventually shut down and about two thousand guys lost their jobs. I work sixty to eighty hours a week as union

* He had been a pastor in a black ghetto church for seventeen years.

president, and I get paid $56 a week." He and his wife, Dee Dee, have a daughter, eleven, and a son, eight.

His mother, Helen, who lives nearby, is visiting.

I'm the black sheep of the family. All the others are in management. I was drawn into the union by the guys I work with. They elected me steward and I represented four hundred guys. When we discovered the union had become corrupt, sweethearts with the company, I got drafted to run for president of the local. At the national convention, they didn't wanna hear nothin' I had to say.

HELEN: *"Do you remember when you left, with high ideals, great expectations? You were really gung-ho. When you came back, there was a totally different feeling. Your bubble of ideals was broken, wasn't it?"*

They let me out to dry. They struck my name from the ballot, so I couldn't run. I ran on stickers. I got guys to lick the stickers and put 'em on the ballot in protest. I beat the other guy 3 to 1. It took seven months to be rightfully installed as president and it's been a battle ever since.

This whole struggle has been kind of a rude awakening. First it was the union, then the church. Both institutions have reacted exactly the same. Removing the pastor from his pulpit is what they did to me.

When Roth and the others took on Mellon, I went along. It's natural to fall right into this battle. It was drawn along class lines. The people who had the money, the corporate heads and the pillars of the community, are the same people who sit on church boards. These are the same people who removed the minister.

I started going to Pastor Roth's church. When they put him in jail, I'm still going to his church. That's when the values started pullin' at me. Where do I belong? I got two thousand guys who lost their jobs, and the same power structure that's put them on the street is movin' to remove the council that's locked itself in the church. There was no way I could stay out of that church. I mean, I couldn't live with myself.

The church had become a symbol of the defiant posture that had to be taken. I had to defend that symbol. Someone has to stand up and say no. I don't care if you've got 38 billion dollars. No. I don't care if you own the courts. No. I don't care if you can buy the judge. No. You're wrong. So I went in the church. We barricaded ourselves inside.

On a Friday morning about quarter to seven, I was asleep on the table. I was sick as a dog, bronchitis, pleurisy. I heard all this racket and noise. Somebody said, "They're comin'! They're comin'!" I rolled off this table, went to the front of the church, and saw nothin' but policemen everywhere. I couldn't believe it. There were about ninety of them. They were dressed in full riot gear. They had shotguns with the shells out of the case wrapped in gum bands, so they could pull the shells out one at a time, I mean quickly. They were ready. They had a helicopter overhead. I mean, it's totally unbelievable. Because we refused to leave the church. Everybody's startin' to get dressed, and they're startin' to axe down the back door. We weren't scared, but we said, My God, they're really doin' it!

We had plywood up against the windows so that if they shot tear gas—I mean, it was like a fortress. We quickly ran to the front, ripped the plywood off, because we wanted the news media to be able to see. 'Cause, man, they had clubs about eight feet long. They were ready to swat some heads.

We were all huddled in front of the church. We had our Bible in our hands. When they finally broke the door down, they rushed in and they stood there. It seemed like an eternity. They were afraid to move. *They* were afraid of *me*!

We were huddled up like a little wagon train right by the front door. They didn't know what to do. They just stood there and looked —with clubs, guns, full riot gear. We looked at them. I'll never forget the feeling. I felt sorry for them. You could see they didn't wanna do what they were doin'. They didn't know what was gonna come next.

They were told we were going to resist and they were ready for a fight, I guess. There we were, standin' peacefully, waitin' to be arrested. I guess they were waitin' for someone to tell 'em what to do. We wouldn't move.

They formed a circle around the church and pushed the news media far enough back so they couldn't see what was goin' on. The thing I was afraid of is that they were gonna start indiscriminately beating on people, which woulda led me to be right in front of the pack. I wasn't gonna let 'em violate Pastor Roth's wife or Becky.

We stood there and we locked arms. They yanked us outa there and whisked us out the back door, into the paddy wagon. Nobody even knew we were out of the church, and away we went.

In jail, I'm torn with this value of what am I doing to my children and my family? At the same time, I'm being told by the judge that I had the keys to my cell. All I had to do is recant and say, "I'll never go to that church again." They'll let me go free.

It was a difficult time, those jail days. But it was one I wouldn't change for all the tea in China. I actually had a chance to sit there and read Scripture uninterrupted. When you read the Epistles in jail, it has a strange meaning, because the people who wrote it were in jail when they wrote it.

The people in jail related to us extremely well. It was like we were a symbol also. Yeah, we been readin' about you guys. I think we brought a sense of dignity to the inmates. We started to organize —that's when they had to get us out of there.

It was hard to see my wife and kids lookin' through the glass. I'll never forget my second youngest brother. He sat across the window and couldn't talk. He just cried. He said, "You don't belong in there." I think that's when he began to understand what this meant. He just couldn't put his finger on it. He'd seen his brother drawn and quartered in the newspapers and on TV. It's funny, when people get to know you, after you spend some time with somebody, you know what kind of values they have. Even your brother.

> HELEN: *"I'm being drawn and pulled in a million different directions. Darrell's father is a manager of a country club, where you have a political base of Republicans who come from money. He's feeling very embarrassed when they say, Now what's your son doing? Constantly, constantly. He was feeling the threat was there.*
>
> *"I couldn't go to court one day, my job and certain things I was responsible for. I said, 'One of his parents needs to be there.' So he went to court feeling Darrell was wrong: putting jobs of the family in jeopardy. He went, and that was a rude awakening for Darrell's father.*
>
> *"He came back from court and couldn't believe it. He was totally changed. He couldn't believe how that judge was sitting on the bench. He was shaken from his world of everything being nice and okay and honest. He couldn't believe*

that respectable people with money and education would do
these kinds of things. He's now totally with Darrell."

You want to talk about painful re-evaluation. It breaks down stereotypes. People believe when it's on TV, it's gotta be the truth. People believe it when they read it in the newspaper. I believed that, too. I was an avid reader of the newspaper. I figured the guy that wrote it was the guy that knew the facts. So there was no other side.

Where does this leave me? I wouldn't trade it for anything in the world because it's broadened my horizons. It's made me see we live in a corrupt world. There's a lot of genuinely decent human beings of deep moral values, but the whole system's pretty damn corrupt. People that are on the top are the ones controlling it. Power breeds corruption. It's scary.

I look at my two children and I wonder what kind of world am I gonna leave them? If I had the ability to change this world, even turn that thumbscrew just a hair, to make it right, and don't do it 'cause it's easier to just go get a job somewhere, forget about this, and let somebody else worry about it—well, you can't, once you're drawn into it and you know what's wrong . . .

It all boils down to the fact that you learn in struggle.

> POSTSCRIPT: *Dee Dee, Darrell's wife, says, "Our*
> *neighbors are still our neighbors. They haven't disowned us.*
> *They've talked to us about the case on quite a few occasions.*
>
> *"My neighbor across the street was having problems with*
> *her car. Her daughter said to her, 'See that? If you were as*
> *strong and bullheaded as Darrell, we would have had this*
> *problem figured out a long time ago.'"* (Laughs.)

COLLEEN GROPP

She is the wife of Pastor John Gropp, a member of
Denominational Ministry Strategy (DMS). Though he was
not defrocked as were Pastors Roth and Solberg, he shared

their ordeal. Though he retained his parish, he, like his colleagues, is under fire.

She was raised in Mount Lebanon, Pittsburgh's most posh suburb. Her family was upper-middle-class, conservative in politics and religion; her father, a utilities executive.

She met John Gropp at Slippery Rock College, seventy miles north of Pittsburgh. "The football scores of Slippery Rock are the second most requested in the nation, next to Notre Dame."

Their lively, chatty little daughter is five. The boy is at school.

When the bishop called John to Duquesne, I kept saying, Oh Lord, please don't let Duquesne be where you want me, but if it is, I'm willing to go. And things happened that led us to know this is where we had to be.

Mount Lebanon and Duquesne are in the same city, yet they are different worlds. Duquesne, at this point, is very poor. The majority of people had jobs that were in the mill. They called the mill thirteenth grade. After you graduated high school, you went down the hill to the mill. Even now, they will say, If you had a job at the mill, you were set for life. All those people are now unemployed.

When I grew up, I just felt that the whole world lived like we did. Kids drove their own cars to school. My father was sensible enough that we didn't have those kinds of things. Now, on my own, I see the way other people live. I realize how much we had.

I look back on it now, at different times, I see people driving around in their Cadillacs and their Oldsmobile 98's, big cars, I think —Boy, if I had married a Mount Lebanon boy, that probably would have been me. I can't be hard on them, because I could very easily see myself fitting in that kind of pattern. You've never really been challenged to think otherwise, it's the way you've been brought up, it's the way you've always been. You've never seen the other side. So it's not really fair to totally condemn 'em, 'cause they don't know what the rest of world's living like.

When John got involved with DMS, I had a very hard time dealing with it. I churned and churned, it just went through my mind, day and night. You have to realize that the people they are challenging are my parents' friends. They are also the people who I grew up with.

The father of my very best friend—and we're still very good friends—is chairman of the board of the largest company in Pittsburgh. He's also on the Allegheny Conference: thirty-six corporate heads of Pittsburgh. They decide what's going on in the city. And here my husband is challenging them. Mr. M. used to take Jean and me on flights to Florida.

When we first got into this, I couldn't believe any of my friends' parents were involved. It was always other people making the decisions. But the more you get into it, the more you realize that *these* are the people making the decisions.

My father's a wonderful Christian man. He would never do anything to hurt people. But I think he wouldn't look at the corporation as bad, because they've got to do what they've got to do. It's not the corporation's fault. They're in it to make money. He's a corporate man and he's got to look at it that way.

See, I'm living with the people who are hurting. I can see what's happening to them. I see the devastation that goes on in families. Yet I kept thinking, No, these guys can't be involved in hurting other people's lives. In the back of my head, I blot that out. They don't realize because they live among all their wealthy friends, and they can't actually see with their own eyes what's going on. I'm sure they can also justify it by saying it's all for the good. It's to make the town more beautiful. I have no problem with that, but to devastate a whole valley of people to do it is wrong.

Every day is a new revelation. Considering what they're supposed to be—quote, the respectables—what's probably happened is I've lost my respect for them. They may have made it to the top, but only by sacrificing those they consider beneath them. I can't say I admire what they've done to get there.

I was concerned about what are people thinking, people I've grown up with, my parents' friends. That used to bother me. I understood their goals and what you have to do to get those goals. I also understood what the people are feeling in the valley. Totally hopeless and lost. They're going through a time when they can't speak for themselves. If they can't, somebody's got to do it for them. So it's got to be us.

I really believed what people wrote. If you were arrested, you did something wrong. You were really a bad guy. You were deserving of being arrested. You did something absolutely wrong.

I realized at this point how bought-off everything is. Policemen are not acting on their own. They're acting for who's controlling them. Whether it be Mob, whether it be corporate heads. They're acting out what they've been told to do. I believed they were doing it because they had good values, because they knew right from wrong. Now I've switched. Getting arrested is the hardest decision I ever had to make.

Doug Roth was in jail. This is a very dangerous thing when they start putting pastors in jail for standing up for what they believe in. It does remind me of Nazi Germany when the pastors were not free to stand up and say what they believed was right. I think it parallels what's going on up here.

Okay, Doug was in jail. They closed his church and the bishop said to Nadine Roth, "You don't have to go there, you can go to any other Lutheran church." So Nadine said, "Okay, I'm going to the bishop's church." It could have been my husband sitting in jail. Then I could be saying, "Well, I'm going to the bishop's church to worship." Nadine said, "I don't really want to go alone. Would you go with me?" She asked several other pastors' wives. When John asked me if I would go, I said, "Oh, John, not me."

It took me a few days to decide. It was not something in minutes. Nadine was here, her husband was in jail, and she said, "I'm going, whether anyone goes with me or I go alone. Are you willing to go with me?" I knew in the back of my mind there was a good possibility I'd be arrested. I said, "Okay, Nadine, I'll go with you."

This was after several days of thinking about it day and night. A conservative person who's wondering. I just thought, Why me? Why do *I* have to do this? Then again, it could be my husband and I wouldn't want to go by myself.

Probably the hardest part for me was I did not have the support of my parents, which all my life I'd had. The only way my parents really knew what was going on is by hearing it from friends and reading. Hearsay.

One time, John had mentioned something to my dad, and he said very bluntly, "I don't want to hear about it, I don't live in Pittsburgh any more." I think he realized he might have to be confronted himself. My dad comes from a military background. He was a lieutenant colonel in the marines. When you're in the Marine Corps, you don't ask questions, you just do what you're told. We were raised very much like that. You didn't question. If you were told to do it, you did it. He really feels that if this is the way society is, you go by it. Because this is the best country in the world to live in.

My mother said that to me at different times. I said, "Mother, I know it's the best country to live in. I wouldn't want to live anywhere else. But when you see something is wrong, why is it not worth fighting to change?"

I think they feel, What can a small group of people do except to make the news, make headlines, and look bad? You definitely do not want to look bad. Unless all the publicity is in your favor and you look good, why would you want to be involved?

I knew what I had to do and why I was doing it. But I never had such a hard time sleeping. I can sleep through anything. I knew it was right. I also knew how it was going to turn out.

I was scared to death. I can remember almost everything that happened. I was sick, I couldn't eat, I couldn't sleep. As we drove up there, I kept thinking, Oh Lord, I wish this was over. This is gonna sound dumb, like I'm paralleling myself with Jesus, and I'm not. But going through what I went through really helped me realize what Christ went through when He went to the cross.

It's easy to say Christ died for our sins and just talk about it and not really realize what He went through. And all I had to do was walk to a church! He had all the pain and suffering to go through.

After they arrested us, it was a relief. That was the most emotional thing I've had to go through in my life. I think the charge was trespassing on private property or disrupting a meeting, which we hadn't even gotten to. We were asked to leave and we didn't.

They took us to the police station. The officers were very nice to us. All they were doing was their job. They were doing what they were told to do. I think the charge was disorderly conduct. We appealed and we finally got off.

In the back of my mind, I never would have believed it was me. Before this happened, I believed it was enough just to do nice things. Even in Mount Lebanon, I remember as a kid, we went over to the housing projects three days a week and helped poor people. That's what my parents would believe. Charity. Now I look at it and say, Let's get to the root of it and find out what's causing the problem. Corporate greed.

Mellon Bank is the key. If you start doing a chart of who's connected to who and what's connected to what, you'll find out why the Mellon Bank is involved in everything in Pittsburgh. You look at who's on the boards even of community groups, women's, men's, you'll see who controls everything.

Oh yes, I've run into old friends. They'll say things like, Oh, I saw you on TV. I saw your husband on TV. They usually don't say too much. I find it interesting how people that have known us as personal friends will say, I don't know what's going on there, but somebody's covering up something because I know John Gropp and he wouldn't be involved in something wrong. That is, people who've known us personally. Others, I don't know how they feel.

I think we have a new outlook that we can present to our children: that people who stand up for what they believe in are not always bad for being arrested, that not everybody who's arrested is necessarily bad.

YOUNGLINGS

CHARLIE WATERS

"I'm fifteen, short, blond hair, slightly bizarre."
He bears an obvious resemblance to Michael J. Fox.
Everyone tells him that. There's a touch of Holden
Caulfield as well. Though formal in manner, he's pretty
much at home anywhere, it seems.

My attitudes are off the beaten path. I've noticed the majority of people at school are just kinda apathetic about all the political stuff. It's the biggest mix I've ever seen in a school. Blacks, whites, Hispanics, rich, poor, everything. It takes people from all over the city.

It's a pretty integrated neighborhood. In most cases, blacks hang around with blacks and whites hang around with whites. There's a little hostility. I mean there's always gang violence, but not that much, though.

I've always attended public schools and have lived in the same house for fifteen years.

I think I'm more liberal than most people I know. Whenever there's some petition out to stop the arms race or stop the bombing in Central America and things like that, I always sign. There are some people who are more active than I am, but—I don't know—not too many.

I got into a big argument in my class about whether or not to aid the contras. I was vehemently against it. A couple of the kids were really for it. Most of 'em really didn't know what to feel. I felt a challenge to try to sway them.

The future? (Sighs.) That's one of life's great mysteries. I look at my friends and I tend to think that we're gonna be a more idealistic generation, more like the sixties. Then I talk to some other people and that makes me think maybe we'll be just as materialistic as the yuppies.

When I think sixties, I think the Vietnam War, hippies, antiwar demonstrations, ideals and visions, people standing up against the looming establishment.

What's your source of information?

Hearsay and stereotypes. My parents talked about what the sixties were like. You can't always take their word as gospel. Sometimes I see a documentary or two. Sometimes I think it would have been nice to live in the sixties, where a majority of the people had the same sort of views that I did. But then sometimes I think I might have been drafted, which I definitely wouldn't have liked.

That was a period of striving for peace and idealism, but also of extreme violence. That's one aspect I wouldn't have liked: to have to fear violence of not only the establishment but of extremists expressing your views.

There's always the usual fifteen-year-old worries about school and friends and social life, etcetera. Also worries about the world, what we're doing to other countries. The usual worries are more self-centered—if I'm going to be happy or not. But the deep-seated ones are more worldly.

The nuclear bomb is mentioned occasionally, sometimes in a cynical context. Like—who cares? We're all gonna be gone in fifteen years anyway. It's amazing, considering how innocent and unjaundiced kids are portrayed to be, how cynical and hardened they can get by age fifteen. What use is it all anyway? We have no control over our own destinies. Some other times, you feel, well, I can do something about it. Sometimes you really get a surge of idealism and want to go out and participate in a demonstration or petition something.

I think it's a minority that ever goes out and marches or stands on a street corner petitioning people. You compare the magnitude of, say, the peace marches in the 1980s to the ones in the 1960s, and they are tiny. Most people will just sit back and say, Nothing really happening to me now, so why should I go out and demonstrate? In the sixties, there was an actual, immediate crisis. It was a tangible evil they could strike out against.

You can read about nuclear weapons and how the world can destroy the world twenty-six times over. That breeds the cynicism: there's nothing I can do about it, so why should I try? You see it in schools, in drug addiction, teen pregnancy, and things.

I just lately saw a grade-school friend of mine. We drifted apart. I hadn't seen him, like a month and a half. I found out he's in drug rehab. It hits so close, and the weird thing is I wasn't even shocked. It's just, oh, that's too bad. My eye is jaundiced and my feelings are hardened by the evils in society I've already experienced.

I may feel more cynical than I used to, but I really don't think so. I hope I won't ever get to the point where I say to myself there's nothing I can do, so why try? I always wanna go out there and give a try to control what's gonna happen to me.

At this point last year, I was settling in with a group of people who all had the same views. We'd seen the advertisement about the demonstration, it had been hyped for a long time: No Business As Usual Day. It was antinuclear. We all managed to get down there. Unfortunately, it was a disillusioning experience.

In the beginning of the day, it was good. There were about three hundred of us. I was surprised to see how many young people there were. I had a slightly bad feeling about it from the start. The slogan was They Won't Listen to Reason. This kind of implies a revolutionary tinge, which might involve violence. It was just in the back of my mind.

Everything went well until the end of the day. There was a thing, a panic run. The demonstration was to simulate what would happen when a bomb was dropped: to try to show people that business wouldn't be as usual.

There'd be a countdown and then simulate the panic of a crowd after hearing a bomb had been dropped. The demonstration suddenly spread in different directions. We'd been briefed in the morning. One of the leaders at an opportune moment shouts ''Panic run!'' Then do a countdown and everyone would panic and run. Everybody would suddenly scream and act as if a bomb were being dropped, and run in different directions. To attract the attention of downtown merchants. On State Street. We were to shout things like ''A bomb! A bomb! Panic! Run!'' Things like that. But by the end of the day, the whole attitude of the demonstrators was really hostile. There were people using the panic run as excuses for running into people and to vent hostilities. A couple of times, people tried to loot stores. There were a whole lot of arrests, though the police were not acting too great themselves.

There was another thing called a die-in. There's a countdown and people just lay down and play dead wherever they were. We happened to do it like in the middle of Randolph, and the police got pretty mad. Cars stopped. They didn't want to run over three hundred people. The police started hauling off and bashing people. That was pretty disturbing, too. I was lying down. But after I saw the cops hauling off people, roughing them up, I kind of stood up ... (laughs).

It was a school day, and for the people who couldn't be down at the demonstration, they staged die-ins in classes. In one class, at eleven o'clock, the whole class just counted down and died. The teacher was threatening to fail them. Luckily, you can't fail the whole class. There were about thirty.

They lay down and died, you say?

They kinda slumped on their desks.

Actually, there was really very little media coverage. It was a hush-up. They didn't want the public to know this was happening. A lot of the newspapers and networks didn't really feel it was newsworthy. The general public just didn't really care.

I was fourteen. I'd say the youngest was about ten. The leaders were kind of rebels out of the yuppie generation, in their thirties and late twenties. The majority were about sixteen, seventeen. My friend was arrested. He was badgered by the cops. After the first batch was arrested, we marched down to police headquarters at Eleventh and State. A lot of people were getting pretty hostile toward the cops, myself included.

The intentions of most people were good. The organization was not advocating violence, but not condemning it either. They support revolution. I've even got a pamphlet for the next demonstration. (Reads) ''They won't listen to reason. They won't be bound by votes. The government must be stopped from launching World War Three, no matter what it takes.'' The slogan itself sounds violent. Which I can't abide.

What sort of demonstration would you like to see?

I'd try to get more people, just to attract attention by the sheer turnout and magnitude. To get a lot of people just marching, not doing panic runs and things. Not yelling and whipping people into hysteria. Just showing people what they feel. I think a lot of people at that demonstration got disillusioned.

Will you attend the next one?

I don't think so. If there's one I saw promising, I might go. If it were sponsored, say, by Amnesty International, something I have particular feelings about. Not just: Oh, it's a demonstration, what the heck, I'll go. No more of that.

As I get older and I see all my friends get older, there's a lot more cynicism and indifference. People seem to be caring a little less . . .

PETER SZATMARY

He's eighteen, a bartender at Ariadne. It is a young people's juice bar: razzleberry, cider, spice; orange, cranberry nectar; New York Seltzer, with orange, vanilla, blueberry. Perrier and Evian, too, my God!

It is a seedy, barely lighted, two-story walk-up. You can hardly make out the shadows, the few at this early hour: Saturday, 6:00 P.M. It is not yet open for business; the silhouetted ones may or may not be working here, as they appear and as suddenly disappear.

Neighbors have complained of too much noise and loud music at hours when "these crazy kids shoulda been home long ago."

I encounter a young guy in a leather jacket. As I address a few words to him, a voice is heard behind me: "'At's a statue. It's made from tin. T'ought it was real, huh?"

As I turn away from Leather Jacket, I hear music. Where's it coming from? Is it the Phantom of the Opera at the organ?

He is rail-skinny; his coiffure, not quite skinhead, not quite crew-cut. His manner is soft, gentle, friendly, slightly bewildered. He's the oldest of three children. His pa does electrical maintenance; his ma, housecleaning. He attends high school in Antioch, a blue-collar suburb of Chicago: "a booneyville kind of place."

"We were Catholics and turned Jehovah's Witness. So I had a real strict childhood. I was always gettin' in trouble because I was the outgoing of all of them. I made my stand: I told them I didn't wanna go to church any more. 'Cause the Jehovah's Witness believes that you're supposed to get along, but they never got along. My parents were always fighting.

"I'm like an outcast of the family. They really don't talk to me a lot. My mom bothers me all the time and I get mad and yell back at her. She hit me for no reason a couple times and I would hit her back.

"I just moved back with my parents."

When I first came here, I was just a regular person. I was more like a wimp when I was at grammar school. I started going to teen dance bars. I had my Marshall Field clothes. Jerbods. Pretty expensive baggy pants. Then came the stages with hair stickin' up, the combats. I had my Mohawk.

I felt like a wimp because of my parents. I stayed home all the time. They tried to isolate me from the world. Boys would always pick on me: I'm weak, I'm stupid, 'cause I'm a Jehovah's Witness. I couldn't do certain things. Like I couldn't celebrate with them for the holidays. I couldn't go to dances, 'cause it's worldly association. They had me stay out with the people in church.

Well, I changed my hygiene. I started buyin' my own clothes and to become more independent. I started workin' out. I got to a point where I'm pretty glad where I am. I'm pretty glad I can bench two hundred pounds. No, it's not really macho. It's more of a manly kind of thing. Qualities that just regular people want to have, regular guys.

I just wanna protect myself from people that think they're so bad. Because of this New Wave stuff, they think they're new and bad and try to start shit. They'll beat up people for their haircuts sometimes. Some of those are Nazi skins. And there's the regular Bomber Boy skins.

> *A shadow appears at the bar. He adds his two cents: "The Bomber Boys, they fight against the Nazis. They're pro-American. They're very working-class kids. The Nazis hang out with Klansmen. They put up literature everywhere. They don't come in here. We don't let 'em in. I know who they are. I'm security here."*

If security needs help, I'll help. I'm here just Saturdays nights.

I have full classes at school. I'm an A student. I take anything that's industrial: welding, cabinetmaking. Sewing, too. I've got my U.S. history and things like that, math. After high school, I'm thinkin maybe goin' into the army. The benefits involved. They give me training in whatever trade I want to pick. Also I get some fun out of it. I get to jump out of planes.

I saw these TV commercials. Mostly I think the movies. *Top Gun* was a real good movie about the air force. They kinda like showed all the good things that they do there. It's very go-go navy, go-go air force. You can picture yourself in that person's place.

Rambo is more like a game kind of thing. It's kinda stupid. Someone just comin' in there by themselves, beating up everybody and not getting—not dying or whatever. In war, everybody dies in a war. A lotta guys like *Rambo* 'cause it was action. That's what people want these days. Action and sex.

Reagan's got some good ideas. I like the way he does things. I really don't try to get into the world. I try to stay out of it. But he's tryin' hard to keep up with the Soviets. He figures if he can get this Star Wars thing, he can finally have some agreement that Soviets and them will stop fighting over each other.

I don't know that much about the Soviets. They've got their way of life and many people don't seem happy there. 'Cause my parents came from Hungary, so they escaped. Some people like it, some who are upper. They're like the doctors, the politicians. And they're always ahead. From what my parents told me, they always get what they want.

A poster, perceived in the semidark: an American flag; faintly superimposed, a swastika crossed out, a hammer and sickle crossed out; a figure nailed to the cross, not quite Christlike, is in braces, combat boots, jeans, and shaved head.

Shadow explains: "Those are Doc Martens, good English boots, really comfortable. He's a skinhead, crucified, because of what America does to people like that. Tries to shut 'em out and make 'em think skinheads are bad. It's a radical group, man. A lotta them are into white power.

"I'm in a minority of skinheads because I'm not a racist to the point that I hate all colors. America is a potpourri of everything, right?

"I stand for myself, my friends, for our country. I'll pretty much do anything for the country, okay? As for the politicians, the people who run, I'm not gonna follow them blindly, you know?

"Reagan is very good for our country. I'm glad he's got a lotta people into the pro-American thing. It's dangerous in a way, but I think it's necessary. We haven't had this much Americanism since World War Two.

"To be pro-American is to fight for our rights. The contras are fighting for their freedom wherever they are in Central America. Nicaragua is tryin' to turn communist. I think the people there are in real bad shape.

"I follow the media. That's another thing, I have a real hard time trustin' the media. I watch the educational channel a lot. I read the papers. I read editorials. I'm like a TV freak (laughs). I watch GI Joe cartoons and things like that. I'm kinda favorites of those cartoons.

"I wanna be my own boss. The way I'm goin' about is through real estate. I wanna get my act together, buy some houses. You gotta start small, you gotta start small. With my case, I started out with nothin'. But I've saved up and I recently just bought a house. I wanna go through real

estate, that's the best way. I think it's solid, something they
can't take away from you."

I like to be a loner. I like to be by myself. That's why I like it
here. A lotta people here dance by themselves and don't touch, because they're scared to be askin' other people. Even when you're
dancin' *with* somebody, it doesn't seem like you are. It's not like a
waltz where you're always holding someone's hand. You can be like
three feet away and to somebody else you can be dancing by yourself.

I guess I'm a loner, 'cause I wanna be my own person. Maybe
own my own business one day. I feel that's what America is. Getting
your own business and prospering from that will make it easy when
you get older. You can just sit back and rest. My life was good and
I think I did good and I benefitted. The army'll help on that road.

> *POSTSCRIPT: Vampira appears at the business end of the*
> *bar. Where did she come from? Is Charles Addams on the*
> *premises? Pale, ghostly white face; purple eyeshadow,*
> *eyeliner, mascara; black lipstick. "You look mysterious," I*
> *say. "I'm nineteen," she replies. "And my lipstick is*
> *wearing off." Her hair is non-Vampiresque: spiky.*
>
> *I slowly, ever so slowly, carefully, descend the staircase;*
> *it is neck-breakable. Who put out the lights?*
>
> *Outside, under the L tracks, a woman who has seen me*
> *leave the club mutters, "Them kids."*

BARBARA KELLER

> *She was born in 1968. She is a late child, her parents in*
> *their early sixties and her two brothers in their thirties.*
> *Her father is a carpenter; her mother, a housewife.*
>
> *She is a freshman in the College of Du Page. Thirty*

miles west of Chicago, the county is regarded as the most
conservative in Illinois.

I kind of grew up by myself.

There's not much going on for average young persons like me out here. I'm starting to resent that.

Both my parents tend to go along with things as they are. Money has always been—I shouldn't say tight, but I don't go on shopping sprees for girls or have a fancy bike.

A lot of things my family believes in, I don't see as really adaptable to the way society is changing. They've always told me to be happy and make enough money to accomplish that. They've always said college education is not really important. I hate to say it, but I'm going to tell my kids to go to college. If they don't, it's their decision. My folks have always left my decisions up to me, but they're always there to say ''I told you so'' if you do something that gets you in trouble.

No speaker has come to our college in the last few years to talk of issues, like race. I went around asking students and teachers. They said no. Three years back, Governor Thompson had come to speak, but it wasn't political.

I heard of a class at night, off-campus, in sixties and seventies politics. Me, being nineteen, I didn't go through any of these things. I must have been the baby of the class. We had a sixty-five-year-old woman there. I thought maybe I'd get different views from people of different ages.

The topic of Vietnam stirred up a lot of emotions in our class. A lot of people were angry we ever got involved in it. That class taught me an awful lot. People my age don't know anything about it. I would come out of class and I would ask somebody, Who is Ho Chi Minh? I'm also taking an international relations class to get my wheels working even more.

My parents never talked about it. They told me that they withdrew from politics around the time of Vietnam. Maybe it's bad, but I just don't want to have anything to do with it. Maybe they were ashamed their country would go and do something like that. And on top of it, boast how progress was being made, and lose everything.

411

I had to write a class paper, so I read one of the books the teacher assigned. It was *Fire in the Lake* by Frances FitzGerald. I learned an awful lot from it because it didn't only give the American side of it. It also gave the Vietnamese side. It was very, very interesting to find out the discrepancies between what our government told us and what the Vietnamese would come and tell you.

I told my parents about this. They were pleased. They said, Oh, you have such an open mind, you read, you pick things apart, and get to the bottom of it. I said, Well, it's only common sense. I don't know why people think that people my age don't have any common sense. I don't want that happening to my kids.

Why did I take this class? I myself would like to be a journalist. I felt I owe it to the people who will read me someday to inform myself on the issues. I kept all my books because I want to refer back to these things when my memory goes (laughs).

It's really scary to go back and talk to my parents and they say, I don't know if I'm gonna live through your generation. They mean the bomb. That's scary because if they don't, you don't. You're all gonna go. It's kind of frustrating to people my age.

It's good that somebody's speaking up about it. A lot of times, protest people in the streets come right up to us with pamphlets. They're so willing to give you information, it's amazing. I saw some people read it and say, Oh, my gosh. About ten of us went to see a protest one time. We were from this class. I was impressed by the protest people. They took time out from their own jobs. It made me feel good about myself, just from the fact that I was informing myself.

My parents were kind of worried: Why did you do that? Parents are always worried about violence and all that. They say, As long as you don't get hurt, then it's okay.

My father and I don't really talk much. He enters the conversation when I'm talking to my mother about something. He'll kinda come around the corner and listen to me. When I talked about Vietnam, my mother smiled. I said, "What are you smiling about?" She said, "It's just interesting that you're taking an interest. I thought it was a dead issue with kids your age."

Both my brothers dropped out of college and became carpenters like my father. I think my mother smiles at me because she thinks I have potential. She wants to see me living up to it and educating myself. I felt since I was born in a time when a lot of things were happening, I should know.

What did you hear about the year 1968? The very year you were born ...

Well, '68 was the big—think, Barb, think, Barb—that was the big year for Nixon, if I'm not right. The Democratic Convention in Chicago? Was there violence? That's what I heard. A lot of student protest and that. Police brutality, if I'm not correct? I had to wait until that night class to find out.

I did not even know that much about Martin Luther King. All they do in high school is tell you when his birthday is. I wish he had been around to see what is happening now. Because in some ways it's really advanced. You see yuppies that are black. I think most blacks feel that there is more equality now than there was when he was living. He was a good person to have as an idol. He protested with his nonviolence.

I worry about us. Meddling in so many affairs. Good things can come out of meddling sometimes. But a lot of bad things, too. I worry about our government getting involved in something we have no control over.

The time we saw those demonstrators, a lot of the kids were impressed more than anything that people really care that much. They're doing something.

TODD MATTINGLY

Calling long-distance.

In the voice of the nineteen-year-old: exuberance, light-heartedness, a way with the world; a certainty that he'll make it pretty big. The other party on the phone is equally certain.

He is attending a prestigious prep school out East. "It's got a large waterfront program. A lot of students come here to sail. I'm not on the boat any more. But at eighteen, I got my 100-ton inland operator's license." He's there on a

*scholarship. "I'm known as a bit of a nut just because I
wear outrageous outfits to school sometimes."*

*He lives with his mother, "a sales rep and she works for
different companies and goes around and sells stuff."*

"When you called, I thought it was Dialing for Dollars.
*It's a TV show where they have a movie and in the break,
they'll call people up and ask them the amount of money.
Right when he was calling somebody, the phone rang. I
thought you were* Dialing for Dollars *(laughs). I would say
$786, one from the top. And then I'd win $786."*

I just got accepted to the University of Massachusetts liberal arts
program. And then I'll fine-tune my field. I'd like to pursue business
finance, but I also think it's good to get a broad base in literature.
You can relate to situations more readily. Someone tries to hold a
conversation with you, you're more open to understand other people's viewpoints. Oh, it helps in a lot of things. It may give you a
better understanding of what they want.

One of my favorite authors is F. Scott Fitzgerald. I like Jay
Gatsby (laughs). I liked his bankbook, actually (laughs). But I'm
not a money-grubbing, power-seeking swine, so don't worry
(laughs).

If I had a goal, what would it be? Um ... to be independently
wealthy by the time I'm twenty-seven. I'll be young enough to still
enjoy my life, be able to do adventurous things: raft down the
Amazon or whatever. But I'll be old enough to be responsible about
it, too. Right now, if I was given the money, I'd spend it here. Going
to a prep school like this, I've developed expensive tastes.

I'm working with a realtor on the Cape. He's starting a time-
sharing program. Say, you buy a condominium on the Cape, all
right? Now, there's someone who buys a condominium in Acapulco.
All right, say they want to spend a week on the Cape: they'll trade
your condominium for their condominium in Acapulco. There's a
lot of commission in this. By the way, are you interested in a condominium on Cape Cod? (Laughs.)

Right now, I have two jobs. In the summertime, I work for a boat
line. I get to meet a lot of people on those boats. You get a better

understanding. I know how those stewardesses on the planes feel, when people are rude to them. A lot of people on the boat can be very rude. That's why when I go into a restaurant and see waiters being hassled, I feel sorry for them. I know what it's like to be on the other end. I overtip, because I feel they deserve it.

I'm a deck hand. I go around and make sure passengers are comfortable. Check the engine room, make sure nothing's going to explode and kill everybody (laughs). Now that I have my captain's license, I'll be a mate on the boat, which means I get to do nothing but yell orders.

I started my own business and made it work. Costume jewelry. Nothing real, no precious metals or gems. Basically, fun jewelry. I sell it to tourists on Cape Cod. Just your average, everyday person. I'll go up to them and say, "You look like you need a treat today. Treat yourself to some nice jewelry." They just respond in a pleasurable manner. My real specialty are bus tours. I sell jewelry to them. When you're just walking down the dock, you can always pick out a bus-tour person. All the women have blue hair and all the men are wearing their polyester jackets. They'll buy anything.

I'll just set up my little pail and they'll come by. The first order of business is to be very polite and friendly and don't try to force anything on them. They'll usually come right up to you. Once you get them in there buying, you say, Okay, I'll give you this special deal. I'm still making a big profit, but they *are* getting a good deal.

"My mother actually started me out on this. She's involved in the jewelry business. She suggested, 'Why don't you sell some jewelry at school?' I took it one step further. Why don't I do this all the time?

"When I was four years old, my father left, pretty much left my mother bankrupt. She kept me in private school, like with no money at all, being a hostess at a restaurant. The first couple years as a sales rep, she was losing money. But she stuck with it.

"Now she sells everything from gourmet foods to microwave ovens. Candies, clothes, VCRs—gifts. She also has another business, where she wholesales to the military on bases, but that's a totally different company.

"She recently just built a gorgeous home, and she's

wearing fur coats now, and she did it by herself. I've seen my mother work extremely hard. She's always tried to give me the best. The opportunities I have wouldn't have been possible without my mother."

I buy jewelry from a wholesale dealer out of Bedford, Mass. Shell jewelry, most made in the Philippines and Taiwan. I call it summer jewelry. It's very light and airy. He usually gives me a pretty good deal. I'll buy by the dozen and I'll usually get maybe two dozen of these brass collars. They're a hot item. These little crescent-shaped collars, they sit around your neck. They're adjustable, so even fat women can wear them (laughs). And shell earrings and stuff.

I pay probably about 75 cents for each and sell 'em for about $5 (laughs). I'll ask for five and if they want to pay, that's fine. But if they say, I'll give you three for it, I'll say sure. People on buses like to see ambitious young people tryin' to do somethin' positive.

During the summer I make about $3,000 out of an investment of $300.

How old were you when you were first aware of the entrepreneurial life?

I was seven years old. I even remember what I did. I bought these little ray guns, battery-operated, and I sold them in my school. Originally, I was gonna sell 'em for what I paid. But wait a minute, I thought: I can make some money off of this. The profit margin wasn't high (laughs).

Now I've a profit of about $6,000 during the past two summers. I've always been fascinated by the stock market, but I don't want to try too much too early. My grandfather was a stockbroker.

Maybe I'd like to get into foreign policy. Because I feel I'm a good-natured person and I get along with a lot of people that a lot of people don't get along with. I have a fairly long fuse. I mean, I get along with my grandfather and even my grandmother doesn't like my grandfather (laughs).

Hey, if you're ever on Cape Cod, I would definitely like to take you out to lunch. And I'll sell you a condominium (laughs).

DANIEL ROUSCH

He lives in a town thirty-eight miles outside Chicago. His most distinguishing feature is a ponytail, and a wild head of hair.

I'll be twenty in three weeks. People say, You're stuck in the sixties with the long hair. I think I'm holding an attitude for the present and the future.

I've heard about the sixties from my mom's collection of folk music: Joan Baez; Peter, Paul, and Mary. I started advancing with the Beatles and Rolling Stones. The turmoil of the civil rights movement and the Vietnam War fascinated me.

This is a boring little town (laughs). The high point of excitement here is going to the Jewel* and watching people (laughs). I guess it was a fine place to grow up in, but I want to move on to bigger and better things.

People here don't take to change too easily. It's very middle-class and conservative. I think there's been one black family in Lake Zurich all the years I've lived there, and I've lived there fifteen years now. They wanna remain a *peaceful* community on the outskirts of Chicago.

If I had to generalize about my fellow townsmen, I'd have to say their feelings for Martin Luther King would be low.† We've had a lot of talk about low-income housing. The people don't want it. They think the crime rates will go up. I've got a grandfather who lives with us, and I'd call him a bigot, out and out. He doesn't make any more comments because he sees me get upset. But any time Dr. King's name comes up, he mutters under his breath.

When my dad left, we really struggled for a while. Divorce. I was raised a Catholic, but I don't adhere to a lot of its principles. I tend

---

* A chain of supermarkets.
† The conversation took place on Martin Luther King's birthday.

417

to take all religions and put 'em in my mind. I use my mind like a sieve. All the information goes in there and comes out here. Whatever remains, I mold and form, and that is my religion.

My mother does phone sales. She's not very happy with it, but it's the only thing she has. It's tough. I'm almost twenty and child support was cut off at eighteen. My brother Tim, who is nineteen, is in jail. He forged one of my ma's checks for sixty-five dollars. He continued doin' it and my ma flew off the handle and said, No more. He just drove her up the wall and she turned him in.

My brother Jim, he's seventeen, lives with my dad in California. I live with my grandfather now. My mother lives somewhere else. We're very scattered ever since my dad left. We're a conservative town, but I'd say seventy-five percent of my friends come from divorced families.

My family was really fallin' apart and my ma was just goin' crazy. I'm surprised she didn't have a stroke or somethin'. Both my brothers have been involved in crime. Petty larceny. I was the only one that never got in trouble with the law. I had the appearance of somebody who would terrorize the school, 'cause of my hair. I got a lot of respect at school, but I still had problems at home.

In my senior year, everything seemed to go downhill. Two teachers, one in consumer economics and the other the gym teacher, really ganged up on me. I came about two minutes late to a class, the gym teacher says, ''Get an unexcused absence.'' It wasn't even his class. When I questioned him he said, ''You're a real loser.'' He and the other guy were the football coaches. Kinda just makes you wonder, doesn't it?

My psychology teacher said, ''Dan, I think you're a lot smarter than some of the teachers here.'' I felt good, because I was my own person. I didn't care what others thought about long hair and appearance. I was reading stuff that was outside the general interest of most of the students. A lotta times the class would just sit there and put their hands on their heads and let me gab away with the teachers. A lotta times the teacher and I would be the only ones talkin' in class for a good half-hour.

A lotta people would look at my long hair and think I'm a burnout and dumb-ass. I'd just blow 'em away (laughs). Some of 'em I helped with their term papers. I was the only one in school with long hair, and the jocks—I wish I had a better word—hated me. One of 'em had three of his friends hold me down and broke my jaw.

Funny thing is, I'm very moral. I believe stealing is absolutely wrong. That's why I feel so bad about my brother. He did it because he does an incredible amount of drugs. Pot, cocaine, acid. I've done some of the stuff myself, but I've never let it control me. It's prevalent everywhere I go. I'm talking about a white middle-class area. They call themselves weekend hippies.

I think a lot of drug use is out of feeling hopeless. A lotta people see themselves as going nowhere. My brother Tim, especially, feels really hopeless.

I see a lot of my friends get more conservative as they age. Looking to settle down and have a family. Their main concern is money: to earn good cash, cheer for the red, white, and blue, and wave the flag. I don't feel like settlin' down.

My parents were pretty liberal. At the dinner table, as a kid, talks would always revolve around politics. When I was five, I was hearin' Reagan's an ass (laughs). Mom's records influenced me incredibly. I always heard Pete Seeger. Fact, I saw him once (laughs). She didn't go marchin' with the blacks, but she believed in their cause one hundred percent. What's strange about her is she turned a lot more conservative. She's forty-six.

As a little kid, I saw a war happenin' on TV. I'd ask my mother, "Is that World War Two?" She'd say, "No, that's Vietnam." At that time, she was definitely against the war. My mother's opinion at the moment is that we were justified in bein' down there. She talks of the Vietnam vets and their emotional scars. I tried to explain that you can't justify a war just through the pain some people experience. My dad's gone a bit more conservative, but not as much as my mom.

I was always distant from my family. I spent more time with myself, the one walking on his own ledge. There was so much screamin' and yellin' at home, the house goin' to hell, I just couldn't stand it. I'd lock myself in my room or go out to the library and just read. The same stuff happened at school with those two teachers, the football coaches. I only needed two-and-a-half credits to graduate and I didn't. I couldn't take it any more. My mother threw a fit. I got my GED and I'm in college now.

I just love politics and philosophy. And I can't exclude music either. I'm a DJ on the college radio station. I play rock music, from 1965 to 1977. My favorite group is still the Beatles. I get a rush when I hear somethin' that's great lyrically and musically. "Baby, You're a Rich Man" is about searching for a key. You have the answer in yourself—nobody else has the key. I'd like to get into politics, although I don't know if I could lower myself to meet special interests, to lie. All politicians have to lie.

I'd love to change society. There's no excuse for anybody being hungry or homeless in this country. I believe our government has a responsibility to see that each and every citizen has the dignity to live at a certain level. I'm makin' a speech, huh? (Laughs.) I'd probably negotiate with the Soviet Union. I'd say, Listen here, let's lock ourselves in a room and neither one of us is leavin' until we come to an agreement. Let's end all the crap. It's really not that hard.

I got one real good friend and told him to read the *Communist Manifesto* before forming an opinion of it. He went off on that because his parents were from Eastern bloc countries. He went around callin' me a communist. It was almost like I had a scarlet letter with a C on my chest. My mother really flies off the wall when I start off on that stuff. She once questioned. She's a follower now.

I haven't registered for selective service. They absolutely have no right to force me to sign a piece of paper and commit myself to something that I may in the future be against. Nicaragua—it's a real insane situation. We've supported every right-wing dictator down there and here we want to overthrow people who overthrew a dictator. It's absolutely crazy.

Think the world's gonna blow up someday?

If we continue at the pace we're going, there's gonna be no choice. The bomb cannot be disinvented. Every new weapon that was supposed to be a deterrent has been used eventually. That's a given. What is ridiculous is the amount of money being poured into the military on both sides. And so many starving people in the world. I really don't understand it at all.

If you become committed to an idea that there's nothing you can do, then your worst fear is gonna happen. You gotta keep an optimistic pose about this, no matter what the situation is. I have a word for myself: I call myself an optimistic cynic (laughs).

You're wearing a peace symbol around your neck.

That's what I stand for. My friends know me as a mediary. Always a person that will talk people out of fighting.

MARK BECKER

He is seventeen, a senior at a private school in New York.
He is captain and clean-up hitter of the school's baseball
team; he heads the hockey—"it's really rough, I love it"—
and math teams as well. In the citywide math competition,
"we won first place this year."

I run this mutual fund for the students in the school. My father runs his own Wall Street firm and I guess that's where I learned. He's an arbitrager, it's the hottest thing on Wall Street these days. Those are the guys who are getting caught for insider trading. I'm sure my dad's not one of 'em.

I always went to my dad's office. It was fascinating. I always asked a lot of questions at the dinner table. Gradually over seventeen years, I've really picked it up, understood what it is.

At the dinner table, we'd talk about stocks: what happened that day, what stocks he has, what's goin' on. I'd ask, Why does this happen, why does that happen? He'd tell me. After dinner, he'd go watch the news and I'd watch it with him.

When I was a freshman at school, this fund was started. We formed a business club; just a group of people getting together, they were gonna invest in the stock market. Put their money together. I was the youngest. I was thirteen.

Next year, I'm gonna go to Wharton.* They only take about three hundred kids. Oh, I think it's very important to get a background in liberal arts as well as business. I don't want to come out of college and be a business, business, business person. I also want to be someone a person can talk to, to enjoy other things besides business.

I didn't learn for real until I was made chairman of this club, when I was fourteen. It's called BIC, Business Investment Club. It's like a company. What you have here is the annual report. (He

* Wharton School of Finance and Commerce, University of Pennsylvania.

indicates a neat booklet: charts, financial plans, investment summary.) We have 135 investors. We make a lot of money.

The money we started with we pooled together from our own pockets. We made a share system. Each person owned shares. When I was made chairman, I said we should go out and have people invest with us, so we could have more capital to make money with. We got other kids in school to invest their money with us. We have to report to them. We started with $1,600 and we now have $8,000.

A lot of their fathers are in the market. But everything we do is strictly our decisions. We don't ask them for advice.

At first, the school was against having a group of kids have a company run out of school. But when they saw how successful it was and how educational, they began to support it. At our school, there are no courses in business or economics, so this is really a substitute. Now they're very supportive.

When the club started, the value of each share was $1.00. The first year we were learning, it went down to $.82. The next year, when I was made chairman, we really started to take off. We've doubled it from there. Now, we're at $1.75. (He points to a chart in the booklet.) Here's Maxicare, an HMO. We thought that of all the HMOs, its advertising campaign was the most ambitious. We bought the stock at 17⅛ and it went straight up on us. We sold it at 24⅜. There's no technique when to sell. You just have to know.

Union Carbide was on my advice. It was rebounding after the Bhopal incident. Also, the GAF Corporation was trying to take it over. And Union Carbide had done some pretty tough stuff to fight the takeover. It was at a pretty low price after all the things happened to it. So we bought a little at 19⅝. In about three weeks, it was up to 24⅛. We sold it then. We made pretty good money.

There's always a time to sell. You can't be too greedy when you're investing in stocks. At that point, we'd made five points and it was time. You have to know when. After we sold it, it went down. Timing is very important.

About Union Carbide—you know, the stories about
carelessness—you have any thoughts . . . ?

About their ethics? If it is true that they ignored public safety, it's not good. I think it's an example of what's been happening in the business world. People are ignoring public safety or getting greedy. Like the insider trading people. Just to make money. I think we should not forget public safety and fair market ethics and things like that. We were aware of Union Carbide and public opinion. It was just recovering then. The takeover attempt had just ended and Union Carbide had done some restructuring. Taking that into consideration, we thought it was a good buy.

MEI Corporation was also my suggestion. It was a spin-off company. Candy. The original company was so successful, the same management was starting another. I figured this management has got it. A good buy. We really took a chance on this one. You bought two hundred shares and it doubled in two weeks. Then we sold it.

I read the paper every day. The sports section and the business section, that's it (laughs). I look at the funny page, too. I read a little column about companies, three-sentence stories about what's happening. You just can't read about it and buy it. I get the Standard and Poor's sheet. I know what to look for a little bit. That's why I'm goin' to business school, 'cause I'm still only a high school kid.

You hear about the Depression of the thirties?

I took one year of American history. From what I understand, the stock market crash was because of too much buying on margin and then started selling short and it just went all the way.

We study ethics at school and stuff like that. So I'm sure I won't have any problem. I hope not. I don't want to grow up and be greedy. I'm chairman of this, but I don't want it to be the only thing. I want to make sure to be on sports teams and do other things.

My parents voted for Reagan. I get to vote this year, first time. I'm pretty conservative, so . . .

I watch the news on TV, but the only show I really watch is *Dallas* every Friday. It fascinates me, 'cause I like J. R. Ewing. He's very entertaining, to watch him walk around with the confidence he has. He does everything he wants. I love him—he kicks butts. I like to do it in sports. That's why I play hockey. I'm very physical. I'm known as an intimidator.

What I'd really like to be is a professional golfer. I love golf. But, realistically, I'll probably be in business somewhere. I'd like to start my own company, be an entrepreneur.

My grandfather was in textiles. Now he comes to the office and trades stocks. He has four children, three sons and a daughter, and they're all in the market.

A lot of business people wake up at four in the morning, go to work, and don't come home until midnight. I don't think that's good. Even people I met at Wharton. That was a conference of young high school entrepreneurs. They were my age. They walked around with attaché cases and business cards. They were really fooling themselves. They really thought they were real businessmen. These kids had no social life. They really became creeps because all they cared about was business and making money. They really didn't even do that well.

I really learned big lessons from meeting these people. You have to know your place. Maybe financially I'm not seventeen, but emotionally and maturely I'm seventeen. I'm not twenty-five, I'm not in the business world. Just getting a taste of it.

Hockey's a pretty big part of my life right now. Anything that's a challenge attracts me. Competitive sports, math, business—it's all a challenge. I'm a good loser and a good winner. I don't care about the money. None of us really needs the money we're making right now. We're all from well-off families.

The biggest thing that I accomplished from this fund is not that I made that money, but that I was able to lead 135 people and organize it. The challenge.

CHRIS DANIELS

I lived in this neighborhood, in Uptown, all my life. Since I was born, I ain't moved nowhere. This is where I hang out, this is where all my friends live. I got five brothers and one little sister. I live with my ma. Ma and dad are divorced. We're on public aid.

> *At eighteen, he has the appearance of a scruffy, teenage Clint Eastwood. Though he's a city boy, there's a palpable country touch here—something Appalachian. Not accidentally, his mother is a Tennessee emigré.*

Uptown itself is Chicago's most polycultural, polyglot community. As Chris puts it: "If you're gonna be a racist, then you're livin' in the wrong neighborhood. 'Cause there's too many different kinds of nationalities."

The common denominator is poverty, though gentrification is manifestly on the prowl: upscale young couples are busy rehabbing and condo developers are having a field day. Where to, what next, for the emigrés?

I'm a student that was not into goin' to school until I got into Prologue.* Then I started likin' school, 'cause the teachers, you get to talk to 'em as a family and you're all together. I'd say I'm a C average student now, as to before when I was an F student.

I went to public grammar schools, I never had to do nothin'. All I had to do is show up and they would pass me every year. At the end of the year, they give the kids an Iowa test. I always scored above average on these, so I never had to do nothin'. My takin' it was no problem for me. I'm a bright kid, I'm smart. It's just when I was in classes, they never gave me a chance to let 'em know what I know. Some teachers couldn't understand it if I put it into my own words.

I decided to hang out on the streets with my buddies. I got in a lot of trouble with the law. I've been arrested, convicted of crimes. That's when I found out about Prologue. Couple of my friends went there, my older brother went there.

It's for dropouts is what it's for, students who can't make it in a public high school. Not students that are dumb, don't have the brains to make it. It's just somethin' happened with the family or there's gang problems. And they just can't handle a public high school.

The first time I started in Prologue, I was a shy kid. I never talked to anybody. Then the teacher started gettin' me to open up and discuss things with people. Before, I knew answers to questions but I wouldn't answer 'em. I figured somebody'd look at me funny and I might get in a fight with 'em.

I been arrested for different things. Burglary, aggravated assault, disorderlies, stuff like that. For a while I was just out of

* An alternative high school in Uptown.

control and didn't care what anybody thought. First time I was arrested I was thirteen. That was for burglary. Then I was arrested again when I was fourteen. The same year, I was arrested again for aggravated assault. I went to a juvenile detention center. I was in there five times.

> *"So I was gettin' high a lot on pills, drinkin'. I was high and my friend an' me was in the hallway of this building. I had a radio an' plugged it in the wall to see if it worked. The guy come out and told us to leave. I said, Okay. He started pushin' us out the door. I jumped back an' pulled the switchblade out of my pocket an' I told him, Man, just get away from me, we're leavin'. He kept edgin' me on constantly an' I kept backin' up. His wife came out, gave him a baseball bat. Okay, if he's gonna come at me with a bat, I'm gonna cut him. I had the switchblade in my pocket and we ran but the police caught us. I was fourteen, it happened."*

What'd you get in those burglaries?

Caught (laughs). I got caught most of the time, that's why I stopped. It was either that or go to jail for a long time. Two of the guys who was with me are in the penitentiary right now.

I seen where it was leadin' to. I had police officers, if they seen me in the wrong spot in the wrong time, they was gonna shoot me down. The way they talked to me. Cops always wanted to whup on me. My mom was always at the police station. When she'd leave, they'd slap me up. They just disrespected me, they'd talk crazy to me. Like, "I hope we catch you climbin' out a window, bam, bam."

I was on my way to bein' dead or bein' in prison and I was always puttin' a lot of strain and stress on my family. I was sixteen, goin' on seventeen. That's when I got into Prologue.

It's been a year and a half that I been goin' to Prologue every day. I got contemporary history, English, I got writing, literature, and a math class. I'm graduating this year.

> *" 'Bout a month ago, we was on like monarchs and lords and the merchants. If a war started, like a merchant would*

be in the middle. He would try to turn this guy against this guy, so he can sell him weapons and then go over to this guy an' sell him weapons, too. So they sit there and fight and the merchant would be in the middle makin' all the money.

"Like, wow, they're supplyin' Iraq with weapons, already now they're sendin' some to Iran. They send 'em to Israel an' then Israel sells 'em to Iran, so it's like Israel's doin' it. But it's our weapons. We're givin' 'em to 'em, and they're just sellin' 'em for us.

"I watch the news. I like to know these things. The same thing goin' on again. I mean, over an' over it's happened.

"Before I really got into school, people would talk about stuff like that, I'd be like—Man, I don't care about that, it's got nothin' to do with me. Now I realize it's got a lot to do with me.

"It's got a lot to do with me, 'cause I'm eighteen. If they decided to start a draft again, me an' half my family could be drafted. An' we're gonna have to fight a war like Vietnam. To me we shouldn'ta went there. I don't wanna do somethin' like fight for this country and come back and people call me baby-killer and spit on me like they did with some of the Vietnam vets. That's pretty scandalous. I couldn't handle that.

"From the way I understand it, France got us started in it in the first place. They asked us to come over there. We sent advisers and they got killed. Then we sent troops. And then France decided to cut out on us. They said, Hey, this ain't got nothin' to do with us, we're leavin'. They left us there holdin' the ball.

"What really get me is the rich people, their kids, as long as they could afford to go to college, they didn't have to go. Now come on, what kinda stuff is that? You don't have to go 'cause you can afford it? And because your

family don't have money, you gotta go get killed? That's
crazy.

"I'm just hearin' a lotta things, listenin' to people,
watchin' the news. I was talkin' with my ma the other day
about the Vietnam War, 'cause I seen this show on kids like
my age—dead. Kid draggin' him through rice fields. Did
they used to show this on the news during the war? She
said, 'Yeah, every day. It was like a TV show.'"

In my writing class, I'm just learnin' how to punctuate and cap-
italize. I'm writtin' short stories about things that happened in my
life. I just got done doin' a story about the best teacher I ever had.
And then what I think would make a good teacher.

Her name was Tina, I forget her last name. Here in Prologue.
She helped me open up, how to better express myself and talk to
people. To speak my mind an' not do it violently. If I made a
mistake, she would help me out, instead of just tellin' me, You're
wrong, you're wrong.

The type of teacher I would be is instead of forcin' a kid to learn,
sit down an' explain it to him. If he can't understand it, don't say,
You're just too dumb. Sit down and say, Do it this way or that way.
Tell what you do understand and don't understand. Help me learn,
not force me to learn.

If he didn't learn, I wouldn't say, Hey, no problem, I'm gettin'
paid anyway. You wanna be a teacher who really cares. All the
Prologue teachers, they're into the neighborhood, everybody knows
'em.

If it wasn't for Prologue, I wouldn't be expressin' myself like
this right now. I'd probably be in jail or dead. I was really headed
downhill fast.

I've always wanted to be a police officer, so I could see how it
feels and help people out. I might like to be a youth officer that they
bring in when a kid gets arrested. I'd talk to him.

I wouldn't be the kinda police officer that treats a person like
dirt. People do crimes, but they still got rights. You don't have to
treat 'em like you own 'em. You don't have to slap 'em up an'
talkin' about your momma and take 'em to the lake. I don't wanna
be somebody lets the badge go to his head. Because he's wearin' that
little silver star on his chest, he thinks he's king. He's got that pistol
by his waist . . .

If I picked somebody up, I'd take 'im in, read 'im his rights, write 'im up, an' that would be it. I wouldn't try to threaten 'im. Some police, they get wild, start whuppin' up on somebody or they kick somebody's door in. Then they lose cases like that. People get away with maybe a serious crime, 'cause they messed up. I'd be by the book, everything by the book. I'd treat everybody to whatever they got comin'. I don't care if you're black, if you're white, if you're green.

See, it ain't really no problem for me or my family, with race. Long as you give me my respect. I'm gonna give you yours. You disrespect me, I'm gonna give you what you got comin'. It ain't gonna be because you're black or Puerto Rican. You leave me alone, I'll leave you alone. You be cool with me, I be cool with you.

POSTSCRIPT: "I read a news story about this lady, Jean Gump. Ever heard of her?"

She's in this book.

"Yeah? Oh, wow! We watched on TV where she went to this Minuteman silo and beat on the thing. There ain't a lotta people willin' to get up there an' do that. What turned me on to it, she's a grandmother, has grandkids, and she risked her future for a cause, her freedom. It was like—wow!—she did this all to get people thinkin' about what's happenin'. I was like—wow!—that's pretty strange."

WILL THE CIRCLE BE UNBROKEN

There are lots of things in the world which are not allowed to be done. The main thing is that everybody should try to do what he is not allowed to do so that it can be done.

       —*Jaroslav Hašek,* The Good Soldier Schweik

JOE GUMP, JEAN GUMP'S HUSBAND

*It is August 18, 1987. It is thirteen days after his arrest.
His voice, long-distance, sounds high-spirited, buoyant. "It
is now my turn to do a little hammering," he had written in
a letter received after his arrest.*

*He, together with a young Catholic pacifist, Jerry
Ebner, is at the Wyandotte County Jail, Kansas City,
Kansas. "The charge against us is destruction of
government property. Helen Woodson was, in spirit, part
of this action. She's doing twelve years up in Shakopee,
Minnesota, at the state prison."*

*In the letter, Joe said: "There is no group more suited to
work toward the total elimination of these weapons than
my generation. We went to school, spent time in military
service, married, had families, and worked toward
achieving the American dream. We were either silent or
cheered when the Bomb was dropped, paid taxes to develop
more and better bombs. . . . I am not prepared to leave this
legacy to my children or yours. With Jean, I am saying
NO, no longer in my name.*

*"Please forgive me for not sharing my plans with you,
dear friends. My silence in this regard was essential for
your protection. . . . It also saved us from saying good-bye
in a less casual way when we were last together."*

On August 5, 1987, at approximately 5:15 P.M., Jerry and I entered the silo. They call them missile launch facilities. It's near Butler, Missouri, about fifty miles south of Kansas City. The time corresponds to 8:15, August 6, in Hiroshima, when the bomb exploded.

August 6 also happens to celebrate the Feast of Transfiguration. Christ and His apostles Peter, James, and John went to the mountain to pray. He became transfigured and His divinity was revealed. So we took the name Transfiguration Plowshares.

Jean chose silo M-10. About a year and a half later, I chose silo K-9. We had a lot of choices (laughs). There are eleven groups of silos, and 150 warheads in this field. We carried our tools and banners in socks. This was recovered property that Jean and her friends had used on Good Friday. We were recycling (laughs).

We added a banner that had pictures of our two grandsons, who were born since Jean's action. It said: DISARMAMENT INSURES A FUTURE FOR THE CHILDREN. We hung them on the cyclone fence that surrounded the silo. Very ordinary. When you drive past these places, they're hardly noticeable.

We had all sorts of hammers: sledge, ball peen, pick. We chiseled a cross. On top of the cover, I poured three baby bottles of blood, Jerry's and mine, and made a cross out of it. We had brought our Bibles along, and after we had finished what we planned to do we sat on top of the silo, prayed, and sang songs. We drank a lot of ice water. It was about 100 degrees out there.

About forty-two minutes later, an air force station wagon came up the road. We were covered by three guys with automatic rifles. They had us raise our hands. We called out to them that we were unarmed and nonviolent and walked to the gate.

We lay face down on the ground, spread-eagled. They didn't even attempt to frisk us. They were real young kids and seemed rather nervous. They weren't quite sure they knew what they were doing, and a guy on the hill was giving them instructions. We were turned over to the county sheriff and handcuffed. By the time we left, there were about eight cars around.

So we were in a cell. About one-thirty in the morning, a guy from the air force special investigations came in. We refused to answer any of his questions. He was the one from whom we recovered the banners used in the previous Plowshare actions.

The grand jury reconvened yesterday. The charge, destruction of government property, carries a ten years' jail sentence, maximum, and a fine of $250,000. They'll most likely add a conspiracy charge. And possibly, sabotage.

Dan Stewart, the assistant to the U.S. Attorney, who handled

Jean's case, will probably do the major trial work. We keep running into familiar faces. It's unlikely Jean's judge, Elmo Hunter, will handle this one. He recently made some statements in the paper that Jean's sentence wasn't severe enough, because it apparently didn't deter me.

We're going *pro se*. We will be our own attorneys. We will have a lawyer advising us, but he won't represent us in court.

Our defense is that we haven't committed a crime; that the crime really is the existence of these weapons of indiscriminate destruction that are violations of the Nuremburg principles, United Nations principles—that the crime would be for us to sit idly by. It's the necessity defense: the imminent danger posed by these weapons justifies what the law considers an illegal act.

I'm a chemical engineer, with an M.B.A. degree from the University of Chicago. For the past few years, I've worked as a salesman of food process equipment. You become a questionable commodity in the market at my age. The company I worked for had gone out of business, so I took up a new career: a resister to the military build-up. It's a real career change (laughs).

The first thing I did was to go to Alderson and visit Jean for five days. It will be the last time that we will be able to see each other for quite some time now. Actually, Jean will probably visit me in prison the next time.

I didn't tell the kids what I had in mind. They all suspected something, because they observed the way I was behaving over the past year or so. This is not something you just decide to do.

I feel great. This is a happy time right now. It was something I felt increasingly strongly about since Jean was in jail. We've made our statement and I feel good.

I'm sure her example had a lot to do with getting me interested. It's a time of real adjustment: reorientation of things you considered to be important from your earliest days. I guess you'd call it resetting your priorities.

Because our family was raised, I had no strong obligations that prevented me from doing something that would separate me from normal society for a number of years. We're at the point now where we can enjoy some of the free time, enjoy our grandchildren. But it's at this time that we have the freedom to make a statement like this. Ultimately it's going to benefit our grandchildren far more than anything we could do in a more normal course of events. If we're silent, there may be no planet for them to enjoy.

I'm not saying that people should go out and bang on a silo. There are so many other ways to resist. Once you cut through the obfuscation they throw at you, you realize our fate is being determined by pseudo-experts.

I'm going to be someone who questions. I will satisfy my own sense of understanding before I believe anything that is told to me. If I hear something said by the government that is blatantly false, I will speak out against it, I will resist it and I will suffer the consequences.

This feeling of happiness is something that has been acquired. It gives you such delight to be able to just feel this way, it's hard to describe.

> *Postscript: On December 11, 1987, Joe Gump and Jerry Ebner were sentenced to prison terms of thirty and forty months, respectively, and were ordered to make restitution for damages they caused August 5 (*Chicago Sun-Times, *December 12, 1987).*

#03789-045, a.k.a. JEAN GUMP

> *August 15, 1987. It is a long-distance call from the Correctional Institution for Women, Alderson, West Virginia.*
>
> *She is chuckling: "They don't do much correcting here. Heaven knows, they try, but it doesn't seem to be effective." She appears amused during much of the conversation.*

Our conversation is being taped.

Yes, I've got the machine working—

I mean, by others. It's good. I've always believed in education. Of course all my letters are read. I like that. I usually put something in there that I would like the staff to see. If some of the staff are lazy and choose not to read the mail, I usually write on the envelope "Legal Mail." This way it will surely be read. It's important that we educate everybody as we go along.

It's exactly eleven months to this day that I've been here. I think this is the place for me at this time in my life. The feds probably think it's a good place for me for the rest of my life.

There are things here called contraband. Eighty percent of the inmates are here on drug-related charges. Drugs are of course contraband. But another real no-no is a brown paper bag. I'm not sure why. It might be a fire hazard, you think? A real awful thing is bubble gum. A person can go in the hole for that—solitary confinement. It's a funny thing, I haven't been there yet. I'm a kind of law-and-order freak. I follow rules extremely well.

I enjoy the compound and especially enjoy my sister inmates. As for the staff, the system is geared for them to do things they probably wouldn't do on the outside. Most of us would find reading other people's mail detestable. But that's part of the job. Lying is part of the job, too.

I have to think of my guards as individuals. We have to have strip searches. I find it so vulgar, so demeaning, so intrusive, it makes me cringe. But that guard is trying to feed her family—we have male guards here, too. Maybe if there were no other jobs, I'd be doing that, too.

As inmates, we're property. We belong to Mr. Meese, we belong to the Bureau of Prisons. A month ago, a young woman had come here from another federal institution. She had been locked up for fourteen months without seeing the light of day. On arriving here, she was so happy to be out in the sunlight, she lay down and got herself a sunburn. They wrote a shot—that's an incident report. The shot read: Destruction of government property. Her skin, okay?

What did she destroy?

Her skin. She got a sunburn.

You're putting me on.

I wouldn't tease you about a thing like that. That is a fact, okay? Her sunburn deterred her from working. Her skin, her being, is the property of the United States government.

How do the other inmates feel about me? I feel I'm respected, though they may think I'm kind of a ding-a-ling. But nice. I like them, too, though our backgrounds are very different. After eight and a half months, I'm finally in a double room. I'm on the bottom bunk. Unfortunately, my roommate was just put in the hole.

I wake up quite early in the morning and I meditate and read Scripture for an hour. I have to be at work at 7:45. I work in the greenhouse and it's delightful. We're with living plants and we have National Public Radio on all day long. We listen to symphony music and the news. It's a peaceful place.

I get home about 3:45.

Home?

This is home, kid. Every inmate has to be in her room at 4:00. We have a count. They don't like to lose people. By 4:30, they've been able to count the 62 women in this cottage. There's something like 15 cottages, housing from 62 to 70 each. The facility was built to accommodate 300.

So many women here have experienced long separation from families. It hasn't been so with me. I think we're closer now, although I'm not present. When my son, Joey, graduated from law school, they had a big party at the house. They sent me a videotape. It was wonderful.

I'd like to have been there. I said to the warden, "Hey, listen, my son is gonna graduate. I think it would be nice if you gave me a furlough, so I could be there." He said I have to be eligible for release in two years and in community custody. That means the government trusts you enough to go home and say hello. I have what they call out-custody.

Let's say there was a death in the family. I would have to go home with federal marshals. They would take me to the wake in handcuffs to view the body. Then they'd put me in jail for overnight. They'd by staying at a hotel, which I would pay for. I'd pay for their meals as well. The next morning, they'd pick me up for the funeral, which I would attend in handcuffs. They play hard ball here, kid.

In addition to her six-year sentence, there is a five-year
probation period, following release.

I owe the government $424.28 for the repair of the damage done to the nuclear missile. Plus $100 assessment. I chose not to pay this. I don't think nuclear weapons should be repaired. They should be abolished. The government will have to pay it itself, I'm sorry.

I've wondered what would happen, if after I've served my six years and I'm on probation, will I still owe the government the five hundred bucks? The fact of the matter is, I will.* I've written to my judge and told him I won't pay the money. If after I go back for five more years and have served eleven years, will I still owe them the $524.28? I think I will.

You could be in forever.†

I suggested an alternative in a letter to the U.S. Probation Office. I'm always interested in saving money for American taxpayers. It costs taxpayers $28,000 per year per inmate. If my arithmetic is correct, my confinement for eleven years will cost around $308,000. If the government should pay the $524.28, it will save the taxpayers $307,457.52. Not a bad deal, eh?

Did Joe surprise you doing what he did?

Oh, no. I don't know how to explain it. All the things we had most of our lives thought important were no longer that important. He asked me one time, "What would you think if I sat on a missile?" I said, "Joe, I wouldn't advise you on something like that. It's so very personal. It's your entire life we're talking about." I don't think anyone can make that kind of a decision for anyone else.

Each individual brings a certain difference to it. None of us is the same. There was a funny reaction here. I had called my sister at the time of Joe's arrest. I'd been fasting. With the news, it was a

---

* In an exchange of letters with the supervising probation officer, it was determined that her refusal of restitution would constitute violation of parole and she would be subject to further imprisonment.

† A remembrance of a Willie and Eugene Howard sketch is evoked. They were two celebrated vaudeville comics whose most memorable routine dealt with a two-dollar fine and a refusal to pay and years and years in prison.

time of celebration. My sister inmates couldn't understand why one should celebrate a husband's imprisonment.

We were celebrating because someone whom I love very much had decided to take this stand. Oh, it's a hard spot to be in, but it's not an impossible one. It is saying to the people of the world that we have to give up a little of our comfort now, in a critical time, to point up the horrendous errors of a government. I always thought Joe and I had a lovely love affair when we were young. It's only gotten better. We're not going to see each other for a while—that's hard.

My health? Funny you should ask that. I had a little problem with blood pressure prior to coming here. The other day I had it taken and it was 110 over 80. This is what a stressless life will bring you. I'm very much at peace here.

I never viewed myself as a troublemaker. I like things nice and easy, I really do. But I don't want the goodies that the government has to offer at the expense of my grandchildren's future here. Oh, God, I have a tremendous hope. I figure if somebody like me can put aside her selfish interests and do something, anybody in the United States can. When Eisenhower was leaving office, he said, Someday people are going to want peace so bad, the government had better step aside and let them have it. I think that's coming to pass.

(Suddenly) Can you remember your number?

Certainly. It's like my toothbrush. (Rattles it off) 03789-045 (laughs).

ABOUT THE AUTHOR

Born in 1912, Studs Terkel grew up in Chicago. He graduated from the University of Chicago in 1932 and from the Chicago Law School in 1934. He has acted in radio soap operas, has been a disk jockey, sports commentator, and TV emcee, and appears in *Eight Men Out,* a John Sayles feature film about the Black Sox scandal of 1919. For the past thirty-five years, Terkel has hosted an exceedingly popular talk show on WFMT radio; it can now be heard daily throughout the country.

His previous books include *Division Street: America, Hard Times, Working, Talking to Myself, American Dreams: Lost and Found, Chicago,* and the best-selling *"The Good War,"* for which he won a Pulitzer Prize.